Volume 2

International Conference...

Developments in Educational Testing

Edited by Karlheinz Ingenkamp

GORDON AND BREACH
SCIENCE PUBLISHERS
NEW YORK

Library of Congress Catalog Card No. 77-94553

Originally published 1968 as *Möglichkeiten und Grenzen der Testanwendung in der Schule*
Copyright © 1968 Verlag Julius Beltz, Weinheim, Berlin, Basel
English edition. Copyright © 1969 University of London Press Ltd
All rights reserved. No part of this publication may be reproduced or transmitted in any form or by any means, electronic or mechanical, including photocopy, recording, or any information storage and retrieval system, without permission in writing from the publisher.

American edition, published, 1969,
by Gordon and Breach,
Science Publishers, Inc.,
150 Fifth Avenue, New York,
N.Y. 10011

Printed in Great Britain by
Billing and Sons Ltd, Guildford

CONTENTS

Foreword

TESTS FOR SCHOOLS AND UNIVERSITY

Tests for the primary school

School readiness in Austria: problems, attempts at solution and results
Helmut Seyfried — 19

German tests of school readiness: comparison of tests and results of recent research
Rudolf Meis — 29

Testing from six to eight years
Scarvia B. Anderson — 45

The predictive value of tests given at school entry and the use of test results in teaching in reading clinics
Eve Malmquist — 52

Pre-school tests of concept development for children from deprived environments
L. H. E. Reid — 66

Tests for the secondary school

The factorial structure and comparative validity of school marks and attainment tests
F. Bacher — 76

The place of tests in secondary education (entrance, attainment and terminal) and their use in selecting for higher education
H. G. Macintosh — 91

Situation and problems of educational and vocational
guidance in Belgium
J. Stinissen   118

Some experiences with an educational testing
programme at the end of the sixth grade
G. J. Mellenbergh and A. D. de Groot   130

Validity studies on high school level and the
interpretation of inconsistencies in results
Z. Sardi   137

A four-year follow-up of secondary school selection
procedures in central Africa
S. H. Irvine   145

Selection tests for secondary schools in Mali
Y. Kane   152

Selection tests for secondary schools in Kenya
H. J. Kanina   163

Development of Scholastic Aptitude Tests for selection
and guidance in secondary schools
Sabir Ali Alvi   170

Developing descriptions of objectives and test items
J. Douglas Ayers   185

Tests for the university

A critical appraisal of one national testing programme
John M. Duggan   205

A scholastic aptitude test and educational change
C. Tittle   215

Methods of screening by higher educational institutions
Kazuhiko Nakayama   232

The Ontario Tests for Admission to College and
University: What background? What future?
Vincent d'Oyley   243

University selection procedures in Chile
E. Grassau   252

Testing foreign students for admission to universities
Roy Adam   272

Contents 7

Problems involved in selection and placement of
university students in developing countries
Iraj Ayman 278

Testing at the interface between modern and ancient
cultures: verbal and non-verbal tests in Ethiopia
Charles R. Langmuir 285

Economical and objective procedures for the conduct
of intermediate examinations at universities
Erich Hylla 300

THE INFLUENCE OF TESTS ON THE LEARNING PROCESS

Motivation to study for essay and multiple-choice tests
John W. French 309

Influence on a student's learning of the type of test
to be administered
E. Paul Torrance 315

Changes of attitude towards statistics after objective
testing
Nuria Cortada de Kohan 326

TEACHERS AND TESTING TECHNIQUES

Essay or objective test?
Eric F. Gardner 335

Teachers' perceptions of their tests and measurements
needs
Benjamin Rosner 347

Teachers and testing techniques
Scarvia B. Anderson 364

PRESENTATION OF TEST RESULTS TO TEACHERS AND THEIR
INTERPRETATION BY TEACHERS

Helping teachers to make better use of test results
S. S. Dunn 375

The application of test results by teachers to improve
instruction
M. J. Wantman 384

Presentation of test results to teachers in England, and their interpretation with special reference to ranking and grading problems in that country
Daisy M. Penfold — 397

THE USE OF TESTS FOR THE ASSESSMENT AND IMPROVEMENT OF NEW TEACHING METHODS, PARTICULARLY IN THE FIELD OF PROGRAMMED LEARNING

Testing, evaluation and instructional research
C. Tittle — 409

Using tests to improve instruction
Robert L. Ebel — 426

The nature and format of criterion tests in the context of programmed learning
S. S. Kulkarni — 431

PROBLEMS IN ESTABLISHING TEST VALIDITY AND IN THE USE OF PREDICTION TABLES. ADVANTAGES AND DISADVANTAGES OF VARIOUS TYPES OF NORMS

Validity studies and norms as aids in score interpretation
W. B. Schrader — 445

An empirical investigation of the problem of homoscedasticity
Rudolf Groner — 459

THE IMPORTANCE OF EDUCATIONAL TESTING FOR CURRICULUM RESEARCH AND FOR THE EVALUATION OF EDUCATIONAL OBJECTIVES

The place of testing in curriculum development and curriculum evaluation
S. S. Dunn — 475

The relation of tests to educational objectives
Robert L. Ebel — 483

Educational testing for evaluation and improvement: some problems of a society in transition
R. Wong — 493

THE CONTRIBUTORS

Roy Adam, M.A., M.Ed., Ph.D.
Senior Lecturer in Education, University of Western Australia, Nedlands, Western Australia

Sabir Ali Alvi, Ph.D.
Lecturer, Ontario Institute for Studies in Education, 102 Bloor Street West, Toronto 5, Canada

Scarvia B. Anderson, Ph.D.
Director of Curriculum Studies, Educational Testing Service, Princeton, N.J. 08540, USA

J. Douglas Ayers, B.A., B.Ed., Ph.D.
Director, Research and Development Department, California Test Bureau, Del Monte Research Park, Monterey, California 93940, USA

Iraj Ayman, Ph.D.
Professor of Psychology and Director of the Institute for Educational Research and Studies, National Teachers College, P.O. Box 741, Tehran, Iran

F. Bacher, Licence de Psychologie
Chef du Service de Recherche, Institut National D'Etude du Travail et d'Orientation Professionnelle, 41 Rue Gay-Lussac, Paris 5eme, France

John M. Duggan, A.B., M.A., Ph.D.
Vice President, College Entrance Examination Board, 475 Riverside Drive, New York, N.Y. 10027, USA

S. S. Dunn, B.A., B.Ed.
Professor of Education, Monash University, Faculty of Education, Box 92, Clayton, Victoria, Australia

Robert L. Ebel, B.A., M.A., Ph.D.
Professor of Education and Psychology, Michigan State University, East Lansing, Michigan 48823, USA

John W. French, Ph.D.
Professor, New College, Sarasota, Florida 33578, USA

Eric F. Gardner, A.B., Ed.M., Ed.D.
Professor and Chairman, Psychology Department, Syracuse University, 150 Marshall Street, Syracuse, New York 13210, USA

E. Grassau, Dr phil.
Professor, Universidad de Chile, Institut de Investigaciones Estadísticas, J.P. Alessandri 685, Santiago, Chile

Rudolf Groner, Dip.Psych., Dr phil.
Oberassistent-Lektor, Psychologisches Institut, Universität Bern, Sennweg 2, Bern, Switzerland

A. D. de Groot, Dr phil.
Professor, Psychological Laboratory, University of Amsterdam, Schipperstraat 20, Netherlands

Erich Hylla
Professor I.R., Deutsches Institut für Internationale Pädagogische Forschung, 6 Frankfurt/Main, Schloßstr. 29/31, Germany

Karlheinz Ingenkamp, Dip.Psych., Dr phil.
Direktor der Abteilung pädagogische Psychologie, Pädagogisches Zentrum, 1000 Berlin 31, Berliner Str. 40/41, Germany

S. H. Irvine, M.A., M.Ed., Ph.D.
Lecturer in Education, University of Bristol, Institute of Education, 35 Berkeley Square, Bristol 8, England

Y. Kane
Chef de la Section BUS-OSP, Ministre de l'Education Nationale, Bamako, Republic Mali, West Africa

H. J. Kanina, M.Sc., Dip. Ed.
Senior Education Officer, Ministry of Education Nairobi, P.O. Box 30426, Nairobi, Kenya

Nuria Cortada de Kohan, M.A.
Professor of Statistics in Psychology and Sociology, Universidad, Buenos Aires, Azcuenaga 280, Piso 5, Buenos Aires, Argentina

S. S. Kulkarni, Ph.D.
Department of Psychological Foundations, National Council of Educational Research and Training, Meharulli Road, New Delhi 16, India

The contributors

Charles R. Langmuir, Ph.D., Ed.M.
Professor, Heile Sellassie University, P.O. Box 1176, Addis Ababa, Ethiopia

H. G. Macintosh, M.A.
Deputy Secretary, Associated Examining Board for the General Certificate of Education, Wellington House, Station Road, Aldershot, Hampshire, England

Eve Malmquist, Dr phil.
Director of Research, National School for Educational Research, Linköping, Sweden

Rudolf Meis, Dr phil., Dipl.-Psych.
Professor, PH Ruhr, Abt. Kettwig, 4307 Kettwig, Brederbachstr. 11/12, Germany

G. J. Mellenbergh, Doctorandus
Scientific Co-worker (Psychologist), Psychological Laboratory, University of Amsterdam, Schipperstraat 20, Netherlands

Kazuhiko Nakayama, M.A.
Assistant Professor, Graduate School of Education, International Christian University, 1500, Osawa, Mitaka, Tokyo, Japan

Vincent d'Oyley, B.A., M.Ed., Ed.D.
Professor and Chairman, Ontario Institute for Studies in Education, University of Toronto, 102 Bloor Street West, Toronto 5, Ontario, Canada

Daisy M. Penfold, M.Sc., M.A.
Senior Lecturer in Statistics, University of London Institute of Education, Malet Street, London WC1, England

L. H. E. Reid, B.Sc., M.A., Ph.D.
Senior Lecturer, Department of Education, University of the West Indies, Kingston 7, Jamaica

Benjamin Rosner, B.A., M.A., Ed.D.
Board of Higher Education, 535 E 80th Street, New York 10021, USA

Z. Sardi, B.A., M.A.
Director, Hadassah Vocational Guidance Institute, P.O. Box 1406, Jerusalem, Israel

W. B. Schrader, A.B., A.M., Ph.D.
Director, Statistical Analysis Division, Educational Testing Service, Princeton, N.J. 08540, USA

Helmut Seyfried, Dr phil.
Professor, Leiter des schulpsychologischen Dienstes, Bregenz, Montforstr. 12, Voralberg, Österreich

J. Stinissen, Dr phil.
Professor, Psychological Institute of the University of Leuven, Tiensestraat 104, Leuven, Belgium

C. Tittle, B.A., M.A., Ph.D.
Assistant Director, Research Unit, University of London, School Examinations Department, 16 Chenies Street, London WC1, England

E. Paul Torrance, B.A., M.A., Ph.D.
Professor and Chairman, Educational Psychology, University of Georgia, Athens, Georgia 30601, USA

M. J. Wantman, B.A.
Professor of Psychology, City University of New York, Graduate Center, 33 West 42 Street, New York 10036, USA

R. Wong, Ed.D.
Professor and Dean, Faculty of Education, University of Malaya, Kuala Lumpur, Malaya

ACKNOWLEDGMENTS

The editor and the publishers of the English edition would like to thank Miss Elisabeth Henderson, Mrs W. Napthine, Dr and Mrs D. G. Lewis, Dr R. Goldschmidt, Mr M. J. Hutchings and Mr B. L. Phillips for their help in translating the papers given in French and German.

EDITOR'S PREFACE

Objective testing is becoming increasingly important in many countries of the world. The aim to educate more pupils longer and better involves new demands on the teacher's judgment and new calls for his advice. This means that many systems of education, which have clung to the traditional types of examinations, are now beginning to use objective tests more and more. The problems confronting us are similar in many countries; but psychologists, educationists and experts in measurement know too little about the problems found in other countries, and about how they are approached and solved. Besides this they can all learn from one another.

An international conference of experts on educational testing seemed an ideal way of disseminating information and of promoting mutual cooperation. The plan for such a conference was the result of talks between Dr James B. Conant and myself. The Pädagogisches Zentrum in Berlin undertook the whole organization of the conference, and the Educational Testing Service—especially Professor M. J. Wantman, the former director of the advisory and instructional programmes—gave us invaluable help. By its financial support the Ford Foundation made it possible for many non-European experts to join us.

I should like to express my gratitude to everyone who made the conference possible. Special thanks are due to my assistant, Frau Theresia Marsolek, who prepared the numerous details both before and during the conference to the full satisfaction of those who took part. Last, but not least, I should like to thank all the contributors for having put their papers at our disposal for this report.

The first international conference on educational measurement created an opportunity for exchanging experience by means of the papers and the discussions and by informal meetings. It is our wish that the report of the conference, too, may contribute to a better understanding of the varied work going on throughout the world and to the improvement of educational testing.

Karlheinz Ingenkamp

TESTS FOR SCHOOLS AND UNIVERSITY

SCHOOL READINESS IN AUSTRIA: PROBLEMS, ATTEMPTS AT SOLUTION AND RESULTS

HELMUT SEYFRIED

Over forty years ago Penning (1926)* presented a detailed historical survey on the subject of school readiness and the age of school entry. Here it is sufficient to point out that besides noted educationists such as Rousseau, Campe and Fichte who recommended late school entry (some as late as the tenth year), there were also those who favoured the earliest possible start. Thus, for instance, Erasmus, Locke and Basedow, among others, suggested that formal schooling or something akin to it should start as early as the third or fourth year. Comenius, Pestalozzi and several others represented an intermediate position. While the level of development reached by each child must be taken into account, they regarded the age of six or seven as generally suitable for school entry.

In Austria, according to the new education law of 1962, children are deemed to be of school age if they have reached the age of six by 31 August of the current year. In all Austrian provinces school begins in the first half of September. Thus, at the beginning of the school year the youngest children of compulsory school age have barely attained their sixth birthday. The oldest children starting school are already seven. Besides this, in our country it is also possible for children who have their sixth birthday before 31 December to start school early, provided that no doubt exists about their physical and mental readiness. On the other hand, there is also a provision in the education law allowing school entry to be deferred for a year for those children of compulsory school age who do not appear to be ready. So it can happen that at the beginning of the school year the youngest children entering the first class may be as young as five years and eight months, while the oldest, those whose entry has been deferred, may already be eight. It is not possible to defer entry more than once.

School readiness manifests itself as a problem especially in areas where the school authorities provide only one date of entry each calendar year, as is still the case in most European countries at present, or where certain standards must be attained in a number of subjects at each class level before promotion to the next level is possible. In fact, the problem occurs in countries where, as in Austria, the decision to promote a child to the next class must be made at the end of each school year, where children are predominantly taught in chronological

Editor's note: References (if any) are usually listed at the end of each paper, but if there are less than three in one paper, they are given in footnotes.

age groups and where streaming by ability is almost unknown.

The high number of 'repeating' children, as reported in several Austrian studies (Heinzle 1964, Karas 1961, Niederer 1963, Seyfried 1965), is probably comparable with the situation in Germany. The percentage of 'repeaters' shows slight fluctuations, but numbers remain relatively constant. Shortly after the Second World War the figure was approximately 7 per cent. From 1956 until 1966 it varied between 4·0 per cent and 5·8 per cent. This fact was one of the major reasons why the long-standing problem of school entry and school readiness came to the fore in Austria as it had done in Germany. It should be mentioned that as early as 1930 Charlotte and Karl Bühler, working at the Institute of Psychology at the University of Vienna, were investigating the development of six-year-old children and the reasons for failure in the lower classes of the elementary school (Danzinger. 1933, Hetzer 1954, Reininger 1929). During this period the first test of school readiness to be constructed in Austria, Danzinger's School Readiness Test, was produced. Contrary to the opinion of Kern (1954), who held that a marked increase in the number of children starting school late would lead to a considerable reduction in the number of 'repeaters', and whose view was probably somewhat biased, the 'Vienna school' constantly emphasized the many different causes of failure (e.g. lack of perseverance and concentration, extreme slowness, low intelligence, lack of aptitude, negative environmental influences, passivity, physical weakness and special defects).

However, only after the establishment of educational guidance centres in all Austrian provinces did school readiness cease to be treated as a practical problem alone; linking up with the earlier work it could now be studied scientifically in its wider aspects.

In the opinion of educationists the attainment of children who enter school early is often lower than might have been expected on the basis of general impression or estimated intelligence. Teachers tend to seek the cause of poor attainment by these children chiefly in a lack of social and emotional maturity, which is by no means always the case. In order to avoid erroneous administrative decisions and to take special educational measures as early as possible, Austria too is making use of tests of school readiness more frequently. Since it is neither feasible nor necessary to make a complete developmental and intellectual assessment of each child before he enters school, only group tests were considered for the initial selection procedure. Group tests of school readiness have been used in Austria since 1950; at first new tests were specially developed and later other tests were also used. The following tests have been or are being used in Austria:

Flensburg Test of School Readiness
Frankfurt School Readiness Test
Göppingen School Readiness Test
Basic Attainment Test
Munich School Readiness Test
St Gallen School Readiness Test
Styria School Readiness Test
Weilburg Test Problems
Vienna School Readiness Test

For individual testing the developmental tests of Hetzer and Schenk-Danzinger (1953) as well as Klimpfinger's (1949) developmental test for the seventh year are used Strebel's (1957) School Readiness Test is also employed for individual assessments. As regards intelligence tests, those most frequently used are the Binet-Simon-Kramer test, the HAWIK test (Wechsler 1956) and the Stanford test. At present the group test most frequently used in Austria is the Vienna School Readiness Test by Karas and Seyfried (1962).

If by school readiness we understand that stage of a child's intellectual, emotional, social and physical development when he is able to take part successfully in class instruction within our school system without overtaxing himself, then it is these factors which a group test of school readiness should measure. The selection of items for the Vienna School Readiness Test was therefore made from the point of view of their relevance to development, particular stress being placed on those factors which at a specific age are important for the acquisition of social techniques and for the active participation in school activities. The seven parts of the group test and the four parts of the individual test measure the ability to organize ideas, to differentiate and to deduce, to understand and reproduce shapes, drawing ability, the ability to memorize, number perception, concentration and comprehension, as well as willingness to work and perseverance.

Results obtained from all groups tested so far show an approximately normal distribution. About 8 per cent of school-age children taking this test are probably not ready to enter school at the normal time.

The objectivity of the marking system is satisfactory. Test-retest reliability coefficients obtained for various groups lie between $r = 0.84$ and $r = 0.94$ and are statistically satisfactory. The very extensive longitudinal studies yielded validity coefficients of $r_{tc} = 0.54$ to 0.83, the mean value being $r_{tc} = 0.69$. Values of 0.49 to 0.60 were found in isolated classes or schools, but in almost all cases where this occurred marking had been extremely lenient. The validity of individual items is good to satisfactory; only in the case of the assessment of physical readiness is the validity unduly low.

Various studies have shown the following significant differences between the test performance of different groups:
a) Younger children obtain lower scores in school readiness tests than older children.
b) Children who have attended nursery school obtain higher scores than children who have not attended nursery school.
c) Children living in communities with a population greater than 10,000 achieve better test results than children living in smaller communities.
d) Children whose parents are professionally skilled and well qualified obtain higher scores than children whose parents are less well qualified.
e) In individual sub-tests significant differences exist in the performance of boys and girls, but these differences are balanced almost completely in the total score.

Table 1. Test performance and educational level of father (or mother)

Educational level	Test results +	Test results ±	Test results −	N
1	26·3%	66·3%	7·4%	95
2	11·8%	77·3%	10·9%	119
3	7·6%	78·1%	14·3%	105

$CC_{corr} = 0.27$
highly significant

1 = at least higher school leaving examination (Abitur)
2 = professional or vocational training with Abitur
3 = skilled and unskilled workers, shop and office employees

The children of group 1 fathers achieve good results about four times as often as poor ones. In group 2 good and poor results are approximately equal in number. However, children of group 3 fathers have twice as many poor as good results. Our findings are in agreement with those of other experts. We know that the educational level of the father (or mother) is only one of a number of environmental factors, and undoubtedly this masks a number of other less obvious variables. The selection of this factor is only intended to serve as an illustration of the strong influence of the environment on the development of children.

The environmental factor can be shown to be of decisive importance not only on the results of this test, but also on the very great effect it has on the child's later school performance. This becomes obvious from the results shown in table 2.

Table 2. School performance and educational level of father (or mother)

Educational level	School performance		
	+	±	−
1	69%	28·5%	2·5%
2	41%	51%	8%
3	19%	60%	21%

N = 279 $CC_{corr} = 0.45$ (highly significant)

Only very few children of group 1 fathers have serious difficulties during their first two years at school. In group 2 difficulties occur four times as often as in group 1, while in group 3 poor school performance is found nine times as often as in group 1.

Some teachers still attempt, in the short time available when parents bring their children to school for registration, to assess, on the strength of their own experience, the school readiness of a child. Can this practice be defended? It must be stressed that assessments made in this way have negligible value and do not accord with the justifiable desire for the maximum degree of certainty! A comparison of teachers' estimates of apparent school readiness with later school performance (made after observation periods lasting one to two weeks), showed that while in extreme cases such estimates can be correct, generally their validity is not high ($r = 0.44$). An investigation carried out during a 'play-week' in Berlin showed, after the first day, only a modest correlation between this initial estimate and later school performance ($r = 0.39$), and it was only after a whole week that estimates approached the degree of validity achieved by a group test lasting 90 to 100 minutes.

The teacher makes his complete assessment of school readiness partly from the child's age. It can be shown that there is, with increasing age, a decrease in the number of children not considered ready to enter school; in other words, the proportion of children ready for school increases with age. However, while special consideration must be given to children not ready for school, it is no less important to consider the younger children who are ready. It has been found that as many as 20 per cent of the children in the age group 6 years 0 months to 6 years 2 months are ready to start school. Even making allowance for the fact that many teachers mark very leniently in the lowest classes, it can be assumed that even among children below school age there are some who are quite ready to start. Our findings suggest that in the age group 5 years 9 months to 5 years 11 months at least 7 to 10 per cent of the children are ready to start school, and would certainly suffer no harm from starting school before reaching the official school age. Nevertheless, it is advisable that the physical readiness of these children be assessed carefully by the school physician. We know, however, that only in extreme cases is physical development relevant to later school achievement, for in almost all investigations every single item of a school readiness test (e.g. each of the eleven items in our test), was a better predictor than the criteria of somatic growth and development. This finding has been emphasized by the well-known paediatrician Wurst (*et al.* 1961).

Besides giving a general indication of the various validity coefficients as obtained in numerous investigations using the Vienna School Readiness Test, table 3 shows the relation between test scores and school performance.

Table 3. School Readiness Grades and later school performance

School performance

School Readiness Grades	Very good	Good	Fair	Poor	N
1, 1-2 2, 2-3	48%	47·5%	4·5%	0%	137
3	25%	57%	15%	3%	142
3-4	6%	47%	33%	14%	36
4	0%	28%	44%	28%	25
4-5, 5	0%	14%	0%	86%	7

No failures occurred during the first two years at school among children obtaining above-average grades in the School Readiness Test. The large middle group (grade 3) shows the greatest dispersion. Here factors such as diligence or lack of effort, endurance or a tendency to tire easily, accuracy or superficiality, help and co-operation by parents or its lack, may easily influence both actual performance and the capacity to work. Many teachers do take these factors into account, consciously or unconsciously, when making their assessment of school performance. In this connection I would like to point out that our results showed that children graded 'average' or 'satisfactory' show a particularly marked degree of dispersion in their preliminary marks. At present the procedure whereby school entry may in certain cases be deferred is carried out too mechanically, and should in future be treated from an educational standpoint. Unless special educational assistance is made available at the same time, deferred school entry may be of no advantage to the child. Attendance at a school kindergarten of a pre-school nursery class (or in some cases entry into the upper age group of a nursery school) is necessary so that through carefully directed activity the child is helped to make up lost ground in education and development. We prefer the pre-school nursery class attached to an elementary school to the kindergarten, regardless of whether it is staffed by specially trained teachers or by nursery school teachers (who, incidentally, have done a great deal of valuable work in school kindergarten classes).

If, on the other hand, a child is socially, emotionally and physically ready for school, lacking only intellectual readiness, then delaying the date of school entry is seldom effective. This is because, except when a child has previously been living in exceptionally unsuitable conditions, insufficient intellectual development takes place even when circumstances are favourable. Such a child may not be ready to enter elementary school, but may be quite ready to attend a special school (such as a school for educationally backward children or a school for educationally subnormal children). If in a particular locality no opportunity exists for attending a special school, school kindergartens and pre-school nursery classes are usually not available either. In such a case the only solution may be for the child to enter elementary school (despite his lack of readiness) with the aim of transferring him to a suitable special school as soon as possible. The elementary school is seldom the right place for children whose age at the time of school entry is six and a half years or more, and whose scores in the School Readiness Test show that they are not ready. Group tests of school readiness can, and should, assist in the early recognition of children in need of special education. Immediate entry to special schools appears to occur more frequently in Austria than in Germany; this is most certainly due to the increased use made of group tests of school readiness. The percentage of Austrian children whose school entry is deferred seldom exceeds 10 per cent per year. Naturally there are some regions, particularly in isolated mountain areas, where children attain school readiness rather later than elsewhere. These children are frequently not ready until they reach the age of six and a half or seven and a half, and sometimes their physical development is also retarded. Children living on isolated mountain farms receive fewer of the stimuli conducive to general development than children in low-lying regions. In small mountain villages the number of children entering school for the first time each year is always low, and consequently the high percentage of children entering late (50 or more per cent) has little effect on new entrants as a whole.

A lack of kindergartens puts increased demands on the teachers in such areas. Those children whose school entry has been deferred are given an hour's coaching twice a week, from March until July, to prepare them for school. Baar's method for the development of school readiness is used, among others. It is thanks to this social, intellectual and motivational training, together with the intensive efforts made by the teachers, that in the last few years the number of children in these areas who have had to repeat a class has been reduced by half.

Deferred school entry can fail to have the desired effect, especially when such cases are numerous, for, in the absence of the children who are not ready for school, some teachers make increased demands on their classes and present too much new material too quickly. Eventually even children of normal ability may then be overtaxed. Figures relating to deferred school entry as reported by Schüttler-Janikulla (1965) from Berlin must be regarded as unusually high, and may possibly be connected with the conditions referred to above.

Summary

1. When school readiness becomes a problem, this, like the need to repeat a class, may partly be due to the school system.
2. Group tests of school readiness permit a relatively accurate diagnosis of school readiness. Provided that their construction corresponds to that of the individual tests, their prognostic value is almost as high. However, testers must beware of making their evaluations on a purely quantitative basis. It is essential that a qualitative judgment is also made, and that observations of a child's behaviour during the test be taken into account when the final prognosis is made.
3. As a result of comprehensive studies using Karas and Seyfried's Vienna School Readiness Test norms were established for the following groups: (a) older and younger children, (b) children who

had attended nursery school and those who had not, (c) children living in communities with a population greater than 10,000 and those living in smaller communities.
4. Even school readiness tests of proved effectiveness should be kept under regular control in order to eliminate possible sources of error.
5. School readiness tests are suitable for the selection of children who should start school before reaching school age because they are ready to do so.
6. Postponement of school entry is usually advisable only in cases where there is a reasonable expectation of more rapid development during the following year. Children whose entry has been deferred require specialized help in pre-school nursery class or a school kindergarten (or possibly in the upper age group of a nursery school), or from the teacher in the elementary school if there is no other opportunity to be found locally of furthering the development of these children.
7. Postponement of school entry based on lack of intellectual readiness alone cannot generally be justified. After individual testing and examination has been carried out, it is advisable for such children to enter a special school at once rather than wait until failure has occurred in a normal school.

School readiness tests are psychological tools suitable for assessing the developmental level of children reaching school age, and they can make a contribution to giving children a favourable start in their school careers. The ability to cope successfully with the demands made on children at school does not depend solely on their developmental level, but also on a number of important psychological, sociological and, not least, educational-methodological factors.

References

Baar, E. and Tschinkel, I. (1965) *Schulreife-Entwicklungshilfe* (3rd edition). Vienna.
Danzinger, L. (1933) 'Der Schulreifetest.' *Weiner Arbeiten zur pädagogischen Psychologie*, 9.
Heinzle, R. (1964) 'Die Sitzenbleiber im Bezirk Feldkirch.' Unpublished report.
Hetzer, H. (1936) *Die seelischen Veränderungen bei dem ersten Gestaltwandel des Kindes.* Leipzig.
Hetzer, H. (1954) *Entwicklungstestverfahren* (2nd edition). Lindau.
Karas, E. (1961) *Die Sitzenbleiberfrage.* Salzburg.
Karas, E. and Seyfried, H. (1962) *Der Schulreifetest.* Vienna.

Kern, A. (1954) *Sitzenbleiberelend und Schulreife* (2nd edition). Freiburg/Br.
Klimpfinger, S. (1949) 'Eine Entwicklungstestreihe für das siebente Lebensjahr.' *Zeitschrift für Psychologie und Pädagogik*, 2, no. 4.
Kramer, J. (1959) *Intelligenztest* (2nd edition). Solothurn.
Lückert, H. R. (1957) *Stanford-Intelligenz-Test* (German version). Göttingen.
Niederer, E. (1963) 'Die Sitzenbleiber im Bezirk Bregenz.' Unpublished report.
Penning, K. (1926) *Das Problem der Schulreife*. Leipzig.
Reininger, K. (1929) 'Das soziale Verhalten von Schulneulingen.' *Zeitschrift Wiener Arbeiten zur pädagogischen Psychologie*, 7.
Schenk-Danzinger, L. (1953) 'Entwicklungstests für das Schulalter' (I. Teil: Altersstufen 5-11 Jahre). Vienna.
Schüttler-Janikulla, K. (1965) 'Zur Frage der nachträglichen Zurückstellung schulunreifer Kinder.' *Praxis der Kinderpsychologie und Kinderpsychiatrie*, no. 2.
Seyfried, H. (1965) 'Das Problem des Sitzenbleibens.' Unpublished manuscript.
Strebel, G. (1957) *Schulreifetest* (3rd edition). Solothurn.
Wechsler, D. (1956) HAWIK (German version: Hardestie, F. P. and Priester, H. J.). Bern and Stuttgart.
Wurst, F., Wassertheurer, H. and Kimeswenger, H. (1961) *Entwicklung und Umwelt des Landkindes*. Vienna.

GERMAN TESTS OF SCHOOL READINESS: COMPARISON OF TESTS AND RESULTS OF RECENT RESEARCH

RUDOLF MEIS

1. The present situation

The methods and findings of experimental psychology as it existed in Germany during the second half of the nineteenth century have exerted a decisive influence on the development of this branch of science in England and the United States. In 1912 Stanley Hall expressed his dissatisfaction with the lack of originality of American and English psychologists. Hall regretted the fact that experimental psychology was still dependent upon new German impulses. He advised his countrymen to take advantage of the stagnation existing in German psychology at that time, proclaiming 'Back to Wundt!' (Hall 1914, p. 363).

Today we no longer belong to the givers but to the takers, and particularly in the field of educational testing Germany is lagging behind. Being unfamiliar with the material, many German teachers tend to be prejudiced against tests, this applies particularly to grammar school and university teachers. Only in very few cases are tests prescribed by law for diagnostic purposes or for assessing school achievement. As a result, pupils in German schools are subjected to the arbitrary judgments of their teachers to a much greater extent than is the case, for instance, in the United States.

By far the most widely used tests in Germany are those administered to children just starting school. During the past two decades these have been used with steadily increasing frequency. Kern with his Basic Achievement Test, gave the decisive impetus to this movement in 1946. The three main items in this test (copying a short sentence, making a drawing of a child, copying a pattern of ten dots grouped in a particular way) are easily and quickly administered and scored. Even though Kern's Basic Achievement Test does not fulfil the requirements of an objective test, it is still in frequent use. One reason for this is the fact that no special forms are required.

Like Alfred Adler, Kern wanted to preserve children from experiences which might lead to the development of inferiority complexes. Like Adler, he was convinced that aptitude or intelligence is of little importance for school success. Kern's battle was waged against the misery of 'staying down', and even today, as a result of the system of grouping children according to chronological age, this is still a serious problem in Germany. (Approximately 25 per cent of all elementary school pupils have to repeat at least one class.) With the help of his test, Kern hoped to identify those children who were not ready to start school, so that their school entry could be postponed for a year. During this year the children would become more mature and would be more likely to complete their school career without having to repeat one or more classes.

Although in many respects Kern's view of this problem has proved untenable, nevertheless his efforts have contributed to the fact that the question of school readiness has once again come to the fore.

The investigations of school readiness, which, since 1950, have also made increasing use of other tests, have had some very important results. Children under the age of six are now permitted to enter school only if their intellectual development (usually measured by school readiness tests) is considered to be as satisfactory as their physical development. Moreover, many local authorities have established school kindergartens. These are designed to further the progress of children who are not ready to start school, but who would receive insufficient intellectual stimulation if they remained at home for an extra year.

2. History of German school readiness tests: origins and important influences

The German tests of school readiness in use today have been strongly influenced as regards overall conception, outward form and selection of items by intelligence tests (Binet, profile by Rossolimo, Stern, etc.).

The first direct predecessor of present-day German school readiness tests was the Test for the Assessment of School Entrants, which was constructed by Winkler in 1922. Winkler aimed to test the comprehension of form, observation, manual dexterity, motor memory and number comprehension, the same factors which German school readiness tests attempt to measure today. Individual items from Winkler's series, which was intended for individual testing, can still be found unchanged in group tests in use today.

In nearly all group tests which have been developed in Germany since 1950 for the assessment of school entrants the direct or indirect influence of American testing procedures can be clearly traced. Pintner and Cunningham's Primary Test must receive special mention here; in particular, their method of testing children's understanding of situations and speech by means of pictures which have to be marked or placed in a certain order has been adopted by the authors of many German tests of school readiness. The Weilburg Test contains two sub-tests, which correspond exactly to their originals in Pintner and Cunningham's test. The original items from the Metropolitan Readiness Test can still be recognized in some of the newly developed items of the Munich School Readiness Test.

German tests of school readiness

A fourth important source of test material has been the developmental test series by Charlotte Bühler, Hetzer and Schenk-Danzinger. Individual items from these tests, as well as principles of test construction, have been incorporated in a number of German school readiness tests.

3. Types of questions most frequently used in German school readiness tests

As shown in table 1, each of the tests includes items in which the children are asked to copy shapes, figures, numbers, letters, or combinations of these. Very popular, too, is the item asking for a drawing of a man; this appears in five of the tests. Repeat patterns composed of abstract figures, and used in the form of marginal decorations or in a fence-like pattern, are asked for in four tests. The completion of incomplete figures and copying patterns of dots are included in two tests. (In fact, the Munich and the Flensburg tests include two of each of these items.) Three tests use pictures to assess verbal comprehension; two of these require the children to mark the pictures after a story has been read to them, thus assessing both general comprehension and short-term auditory memory. Two tests include sub-tests for the assessment of visual memory, and two attempt to measure concentration by means of a crossing-out test (adapted from Bourdon).

4. Construction data on German school readiness tests

Examination of table 2, in which the construction data of German school readiness tests are presented, shows that important information is frequently lacking.

In the case of the Basic Achievement Test, as well as in the Munich test and the Rheinhauser test, no item analyses have been carried out. For the Göppingen test and the Karas-Seyfried test only the results of analyses of item difficulty are available. In the majority of cases the standard error is either not given or the characteristics of the test make its computation impossible (Basic Achievement Test).

Measures of reliability are available for all tests except for the Rheinhauser, but in most cases these are test-retest or split-half correlations. Parallel forms exist for three of the tests, but for only two of these has reliability been calculated by comparing parallel forms with each other.

It is most regrettable that Nolte has still not published the figures relating to the Flensburg School Readiness Test. These figures have been awaited for more than a decade.

Only for the Göppingen School Readiness Test has a factor analysis

Table 1. Items which are most frequently used in German group tests of school readiness

Copying, drawing in missing parts, free drawing	1. Copying of forms (figures, numbers, letters and combinations)
	2. Drawing a man (e.g. with a tree, a house or as part of a freely chosen theme)
	3. Repeat drawing of abstract figures (marginal decorations, fence, pattern)
	4. Drawing in missing parts of figures
	5. Copying patterns of dots
Comprehension of size and number, comparison of size	6. Drawing, or laying out a given quantity of objects, according to verbal instructions or shown briefly
	7. Indicating familiarity with number concepts
	8. Comparisons of size and quantity
Form identification	9. Selecting and marking figures identical with a given pattern
	10. Marking constituent elements of figures or scenes (or putting together of parts)
Language development	11. Marking of pictures to show understanding of situations described verbally
	12. Marking of pictures to show understanding of a story presented verbally
Memory	13. Visual memory (pictures of objects)
Concentration	14. Repeated recognition and marking of a given figure ('crossing-out test')

Basic Achievement Test	Munich	Weilburg	Flensburg	Göppingen	Rheinhauser	Frankfurt	Karas-Seyfried	Kettwig	
x	x	x	x	x	x	x	x	x	1.
x	x	x		x			x		2.
		x			x	x	x		3.
			x	x					4.
		x						x	5.
x		x			x	x	x	x	6.
x	x			x	x	x	x		7.
	x	x		x					8.
	x		x	x					9.
	x		x		x				10.
		x		x					11.
	x			x					12.
		x		x					13.
				x			x		14.

Table 2. Construction data of German school readiness tests

	Item analysis	Standard error of measurement	Reliability retest	Reliability split-half	Reliability Parallel form	Characteristics
Basic Achievement Test	—	—*	above ·90 N=535	—	—	*Standard error of measurement cannot be computed (characteristic of the test).
Munich	—	+	—	B: ·90 N=500 C: ·946	+	
Weilburg	+	+	—	·84 N=178	—	The author states (verbal communication) that in the retest N was large enough (200); the date of (+) have been obtained but not published. 11 supplementary items available for testing of the lower 40-50%, consisting largely of intelligence test items for Binet and Biäsch; approximate means but no special item analysis are reported.
Flensburg	(+)	(+)	·95**	—	—	
Göppingen	difficulty only	—	·80 N=152	·94 N=87	—	Optional use of supplementary items for individual testing, 11 items of various types, no norms, no item analysis; main test revised in 1965 following standardization and factor analysis.
Rheinhauser	—	—	—	—	—	Nearly all tasks have the character of play; they are derived for the most part from the developmental test of Bühler and Hetzer.
Karas-Seyfried	difficulty only	—	approx. ·90 N=200	—	—	4 individual items for all subjects, based in part on Binet; physical development is assessed.
Frankfurt	+	—	—	—	A:B and A:C =·92 N=350	
Kettwig	+	+	—	—	A:B ·931 N=283	

German tests of school readiness

been carried out. This, however, was not done until 1965, when the test had already gone through thirty-seven editions.

It is clear, therefore, that many German tests of school readiness show weaknesses in construction. It is very much to be hoped that data which is now lacking will be supplied in the near future.

5. Problems of validity

At first glance the validity coefficients for German school readiness tests appear to be perfectly satisfactory. Differences between the reported values are not significant if the confidence limits are taken into consideration. However, careful analysis reveals weaknesses even in the best constructed and standardized German school readiness tests.

Hetzer and Tent (1958, p. 97) using the average of marks obtained for reading, writing and arithmetic as the external criterion, report a product-moment correlation of 0·75 (N = 120) for the Weilburg test. Ingenkamp (1962, pp. 105-6), while pointing out that his investigations should not be regarded as measures of validity for the Weilburg test, obtained product-moment correlations with the general assessment of the teachers for 465 Berlin children. Six months later r was 0·585, after a year the coefficient had fallen to 0·47. Ingenkamp (op. cit., p.106) makes the critical observation that the predictive value of the test was uncertain precisely for those children who only achieved low scores.

The value for r of 0·62 (product-moment correlation) reported by the authors of the Frankfurt School Readiness Test also appears to be satisfactory. Here the overall attainment of 350 children, based chiefly on their marks for reading, was used as the external criterion (Roth et al. 1963, p.37). But despite the fact that this test has been most carefully constructed, an investigation by Kohl showed that when he compared test results with teachers' assessments after six months, 22 per cent of the predictions were faulty. Kohl tested 1,400 children from twenty-five schools in Dortmund. The results of 100 children from five of the schools had to be disregarded, as their scores differed markedly from the average scores obtained by children in their district. Of the remaining 1,300 children 192 were diagnosed as being not ready to start school, or probably not ready. One year later, however, 61 per cent of this latter group showed at least satisfactory levels of school attainment (Kohl, p.183). One must agree with Kohl's conclusion that the Frankfurt test does not discriminate sufficiently at the lower end of the scale.

Schenk-Danzinger (1962, pp.21, 22, 29) reports that 28·8 per cent of predictions were faulty in an investigation using the Munich School Readiness Test, and in the case of those children with the poorest test results the proportion of incorrect predictions rose to 53 per cent (N = 250). Controls extended over two years. On the other hand, in a study of 248 children who were tested individually by Schenk-Danzinger using her Developmental Test for Children of School Age, and whose educational development was followed up for a period of four years, only 16 per cent of the predictions were incorrect

Compared with the 84 per cent rate of correct classifications attained by Schenk-Danzinger with her individual test, Nolte's claim of 98 per cent of correct predictions using the Flensburg test seems improbably high. Since Nolte gives no definite indications of his criteria for incorrect predictions, a comparison is unfortunately not possible. If one considers, however, that in the Flensburg School Readiness Test the 40-50 per cent of children with the lowest scores in the group test are retested with an individual test consisting of eleven items, and that these children are therefore tested with twenty-two items or item groups, one can well understand how this procedure results in a higher percentage of correct classifications than can be obtained by the use of a group test alone.

6. Conclusions and recommendations

There can be no doubt that the best solution of the problem of school readiness in Germany would be to change conditions in the schools and to adapt them more closely to the real needs of the children. While forty or even more children are packed into a classroom the teacher has to assert his authority more strongly than would be the case if he had only twenty-five children to teach (even smaller classes have long been the general rule in other countries), and he has not the time to give individual attention to the children. A preparatory year would also be of great use. This would be particularly helpful to children coming from an unsatisfactory environment, as they would learn to adapt themselves to the demands which the school will later make on them. (Plans for the establishment of such pre-school classes already exist, e.g. in Nordrhein-Westfalen.)

Much time will probably elapse before such ideals can be realized. Until that time comes we must provide teachers with school readiness tests which are easy to administer and which discriminate sufficiently well in the area in which all presently available group tests are apparently weakest: in discriminating between those children who will most probably make a successful start at school and those who will probably fail to do so. In principle, Nolte's combination of a group test and an individual test is the right solution. However, we still lack a short, standardized, individually administered test which fulfils all the necessary requirements and makes it a 'test' in the true sense of the word. Under present conditions the best compromise solution appears to be the use of an economical and reliable group test, given, where possible, to the whole class, followed by individual tests for children who seem to require special attention, and for those whose scores lie within the critical area of probable error (with $p = 5$ per cent). The time which is saved by using the group test can then be used to test doubtful cases over a wide area of activities related to school work.

7. Construction of the Kettwig School Readiness Test

The Kettwig School Readiness Test was designed as an inexpensive test which could be administered to a whole class in the shortest possible time. For this reason it was decided to construct a pencil and paper test. It can be assumed that the average German school entrant has had some experience of using writing and drawing material before starting school. In the case of children coming from an environment where pencil and paper have not been available, the test is, of course, less reliable.

Copying complicated figures (letters, combinations of figures, patterns of dots or hieroglyphics) represents a complex task requiring children to bring all their abilities and skills into play. The interaction of intelligence, ability to differentiate and classify, concentration, comprehension of size and number, application and the understanding of verbal instructions determine the level of performance.

A preliminary form of the test was tried out in 1964, and an analysis of item difficulty was made. Since then the three main sections of the Kettwig test have remained unchanged. Parallel forms were constructed in 1965, and in 1966, following further analyses of discrimination power and item difficulty, two improved editions of the test were published. After standardizing the test for the Federal German Republic and using it experimentally with five-year-old kindergarten children some further improvements were made. In the final form the figures which are to be copied are always printed at the top of the page so that left-handed children are not put at a disadvantage through covering the figure which they are to copy.

Reliability (0·931) is satisfactory (product-moment correlation Form A : Form B, N = 283). Teacher ratings are available for the 603 children who formed the standardizing sample. The correlation of 0·57 can be regarded as satisfactory in view of the fact that eight to nine months after administration of the test ratings made by teachers still tend to be very uncertain.

8. Studies of the construct validity of the Kettwig School Readiness Test

The data pertaining to the test's construct validity include a correlation of 0·85 with Form A of the Frankfurt School Readiness Test, which is based on the scores of 264 children. Since the intercorrelations of the sub-tests of the Kettwig School Readiness Test were fairly high (between 0·569 and 0·752, on the basis of a random sample drawn from the samples used for standardization, N = 200) further analyses are necessary. Some data are already available.

Correlations obtained with the HAWIK test (Hamburg-Wechsler Intelligence Scale for Children) should be mentioned. Of the 234 children whose intelligence quotients were available, 163 remained in the analysis. (As many children were selected as was necessary to achieve a balance between the two distributions. None of the children in the sample was more than seven years old, and the scores obtained in the school readiness test were corrected for age and kindergarten attendance.) The correlation with the HAWIK I.Q. was r 0·810, the performance items correlating significantly higher than the verbal items. Of the various sub-tests of the HAWIK test the mosaic test showed the highest correlation (0·688) with the overall score in the school readiness test. The sub-test 'Mathematical reasoning' correlated 0·623 with sub-test 3 of the Kettwig School Readiness Test, which is also designed to test mathematical ability.

Results obtained from children in the lower classes of special (remedial) schools confirm that intelligence is a very important factor in the attainments demanded by the KST. Since distributions were dissimilar, rank correlations were calculated. The following values, based on the raw scores of the KST and the intelligence quotients, were obtained:

Age in years	N	r_s (or rho)
8–9	23	·508
9–10	71	·324
10–11	62	·434
11–12	46	·569

The correlations are high when one considers the following facts:
  1. Almost all the I.Q.s were obtained a year or even several years previously.
  2. The tests were administered by twenty-six different persons.

3. Besides HAWIK I.Q.s, three different versions of the Binet test were occasionally used.
4. The children who were tested had already learnt reading, writing, drawing and arithmetic for a number of years.

9. Observations on intelligence, school readiness and learning

Although the high correlations between the Kettwig School Readiness Test and the HAWIK test seem somewhat surprising at first sight, nevertheless the results of many investigations confirm that, in general, intelligence is the most decisive factor in the attainment of school success. A brief review of some of these studies follows.

In individual tests with a sample of 115 children who were either not ready to start school or whose readiness was in doubt, Aschersleben (p. 209) using the HAWIK test, found that in only one case could lack of school readiness not be put down to lack of innate ability. Aschersleben (op. cit., p. 215) cites Schenk-Danzinger: 'At least one aspect of school readiness, that of functional maturation, cannot be separated from ability. The gifted child reaches this stage of functional maturity, which is a prerequisite for the acquisition of cultural techniques, at an earlier age than the less talented child'; and in conclusion he states: 'There is no scientific basis for separating the factor of school readiness from that of innate ability, as is frequently done by many authors and uncritically accepted by others'.

Hetzer and Tent (1958, p.106), using the Binet test in an investigation with thirty-three children, found a correlation of 0·74 between results obtained in the Weilburg School Readiness Test and the children's intelligence quotients.

In a longitudinal study of the Göppingen School Readiness Test Paff (p.363) found that the correlations with school marks in arithmetic and and German remained constant over a period of four years. From this he concluded 'that the Göppingen School Readiness Test measures intelligence to a high degree'.

In their investigations of the value of basic attainment tests Kemmler and Heckhausen (1962, p.81) conclude 'that the developmental level of the unpractised ability to arrange and classify is highly dependent on intelligence. This can be demonstrated by measuring the intelligence of children just starting school. Therefore the basic achievement test, if administered at the time of school entrance, is actually a measure of intelligence.'

In a study involving sixty-six children, Votaw and Burdine (1957, pp.3-4) found a correlation as high as that found by Hetzer and Tent between the intelligence quotients and the raw point scores of their Reading Readiness Test (0·74). The authors comment: 'This figure is high enough to indicate the importance of intelligence as a factor of reading readiness, and low enough to suggest the presence of other important factors'.

Hardootunian reports an experiment in which learning ability and intelligence of eighty-eight pupils was measured with the CTMM Test and the Otis Beta. The children were then given the following learning tasks: 'nonsense syllables, number maze, associative learning I and II, digit symbols, mirror reading, cards, mirror drawing'. Hardootunian (1966, p.213) concludes: 'When learning tests were combined, however, the correlation between the learning composite and each intelligence test was almost the same as the correlation between the two intelligence tests. Intelligence and learning have so much in common when the latter is measured by a composite variety of tasks.'

De Boer and Dallmann (1966, p.31) also indicate that in the United States children with average and above average intelligence quotients have better prospects of success in learning to read, and in their opinion: 'If we define the child's intelligence as the rate of his growth at which he is able to learn, we may assume that the rate of his growth in reading is affected by and limited by his intelligence'.

Clearly the correlations with intelligence tests could be even higher if, as is the case in most German school readiness tests, mathematical ability and co-ordination of hand and eye are measured, as well as the ability to learn reading.

10. Further investigations of the construct validity of KST

Further investigations have shown the dependence of performance in the KST on drawing ability, ability to concentrate and comprehension of form.

Two drawing tests, the Wartegg Drawing Test (WZT) and the widely used Draw-a-man Test, were available. Although the WZT is, in fact, a personality test, for the purpose of our investigation it could be used as a test of drawing ability. A psychologist with special experience of the WZT and five experienced primary school teachers rated the children's drawings.

Ratings were made on a six-point scale, and from the six judges each child received a total of forty-eight ratings. The sum of the ratings given to the 212 six- to seven-year-old children taking part in this test were normally distributed, and the product-moment correlation with scores obtained in the Kettwig School Readiness Test was 0·466.

The Draw-a-man Test was scored according to the procedure devised by Ziler. For 194 children who were tested at the beginning of their first year an *r* value of 0·368 (normal distribution) was found between the Draw-a-man quotients and the scores of the School Readiness Test. The correlation was significant, but not as high as had been expected.

With children from the lower classes of special schools some of the rank correlations which were obtained were higher and some were lower. However, if one considers the confidence limits, these values correspond closely with those obtained for children who are just starting school.

Age in years	N	r_s (or rho)
8–9	23	·644
9–10	71	·489
10–11	62	·255
11–12	46	·532

The higher correlation between the results of the WZT and the School Readiness Test can probably be attributed to the fact that in the WZT components of intelligence, imagery and imagination play a much greater role than in the Draw-a-man Test. In the WZT marks are given for productive achievement and originality, while in the Draw-a-man Test the children, for the most part, produced schematic drawings.

Both correlations suggest that drawing ability is probably a factor influencing performance in the School Readiness Test. The greater the extent to which drawing ability is isolated, the lower the correlations apparently become.

The correlations with the test used by Kleinhans (1966) for the measurement of perception of form, and modified somewhat for our purpose, was 0·482 (N = 224). This was lower than had been expected. In the Kleinhans test a figure is shown briefly and must be recognized later when it is shown again together with a number of similar figures (see fig. 1). Speaking with some degree of caution, one can nevertheless say that the perception of form as measured by this test helps to determine the level of performance in the School Readiness Test just as much as does drawing ability. No doubt speed of comprehension and short-term visual memory play an important part in this test. Information available to date is still insufficient to allow a meaningful factor analysis of the KST to be carried out. Investigations will continue as soon as a new group of school entrants becomes available. Correlations with individual school subjects must also be obtained.

Exposed figure

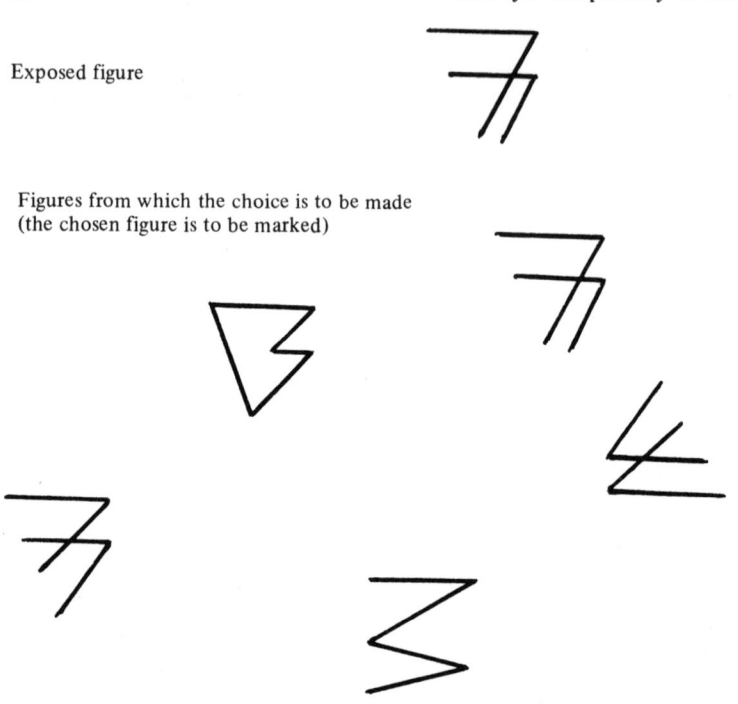

Figures from which the choice is to be made
(the chosen figure is to be marked)

Figure 1. Examples from the Form Comprehension Test of Walter H. Kleinhans

11. Further attempts to raise the validity of the KST

Unfortunately, in its present form as a group test the KST exhibits the same weakness as has been shown to exist in other tests of school readiness—it does not discriminate sufficiently at the lower end of the scale (i.e. where performance is weak). Supplementary items, designed to test the verbal intelligence of children gaining low scores in the group test, are at present being tried out with kindergarten children from the age of five years and six months onwards, with first-year schoolchildren whose attainment is noticeably low and with children from the lower classes of special schools. When item analysis and standardization has been completed, additional information will be available concerning children with poor results in the group test, thus enabling teachers to decide with greater certainty how best to help their weaker pupils.

The need to improve the test becomes clear when we consider the probable percentage of faulty diagnoses which are likely to occur when using a test with a validity of 0·60. Of those children placed in the top fifth on the basis of test results, only about 50 per cent will actually belong to the top fifth on the basis of their school attainment. Of the rest, 48 per cent will belong to the three middle fifths and the remaining 2 per cent to the lowest fifth. On the other hand, of those placed in the lowest fifth on the basis of test results, 50 per cent will actually belong to the lowest fifth on the basis of their attainment, 48 per cent to the middle group and 2 per cent to the top fifth. Of those in the middle three-fifths according to the test results, approximately 16 per cent will belong to the top fifth, 16 per cent to the lowest fifth and 68 per cent will belong to the middle three-fifths according to their school attainment. These figures demonstrate clearly the doubtful value of the practice, so common in Germany, of postponing a child's school entry for a year on the basis of poor results in a group test of school readiness.

References

Aschersleben, K. 'Schulreife und Schulreifeuntersuchungen: Definitionen, Diagnosen und Prognosen.' *Schule und Psychologie,* 11, no. 7. München: Reinhardt-Verlag.
De Boer, J. and Dallmann, M. (1966) *The Teaching of Reading.* New York: Holt, Rinehart & Winston.
Hall, S. (1914) *Founders of Modern Psychology,* German translation by Raymund Schmidt. Leipzig: Meiner-Verlag.
Hardootunian, B. (1966) 'Intelligence and the ability to learn.' *J. educ. Res.,* 59.
Hetzer, H. and Tent, L. (1958) *Der Schulreifetest.* Lindau: Verlag Piorkowski.
Ingenkamp, K. (1962) 'Erfahrungen mit den Weilburger Testaufgaben bei den Einschulungsuntersuchungen in Berlin-Tempelhof.' In Ingenkamp, K. (ed.) *Praktische Erfahrungen mit Schulreifetests.* Basel: Karger-Verlag.
Kemmler, L. and Hechhausen, H. (1962) 'Ist die sogenannte "Schulreife" ein Reifungsproblem?' In Ingenkamp, K. (ed.) *Praktische Erfahrungen mit Schulreifetests.* Basel: Karger-Verlag.
Kleinhans, W. H. (1966) *Stufen der ganzheitlichen Auffassung bei 2- bis 7- jährigen Kindern.* Weinheim: Verlag Beltz.
Kohl, G. 'Die Schulreifeuntersuchungen 1960 in Dortmund.' *Schule und Psychologie,* 10, no. 6. München: Reinhardt-Verlag.
Paff, G. 'Untersuchungen über die Gültigkeit des Göppinger Schulreifetests.' *Schule and Psychologie,* 11, no. 12.

Roth, Schlevoigt, Süllwold and Wicht (1963) *Handbuch zum Frankfurter Schulreifetest* (3rd edition). Weinheim. Verlag Beltz.
Schenk-Danzinger, L. (1962) 'Erfahrungen mit Schulreifeuntersuchungen.' In Ingenkamp, K. (ed.) *Praktische Erfahrungen mit Schulreifetests.* Basel: Karger-Verlag.
Schrader, W. B. (1965) 'A taxonomy of expectancy tables.' *J. educ. Measur.,* June. Relation between standing on predictor and standing on criterion, table 2.
Votaw, D. and Burdine, P. (1957) *Manual of Directions and Interpretations for Reading Readiness Test.* Steck-Vaughn Co., Austin.

TESTING FROM SIX TO EIGHT YEARS

SCARVIA B. ANDERSON

(This paper was introduced with illustrations of test items recently developed at Educational Testing Service for use with children aged 6 to 8. Some of these are reproduced in the appendix, p. 49 ff.)

There are five main questions which all of us who develop such items as you have seen have had to ask ourselves:

1. Why should school people use tests with children of these ages at all?
2. What kind of tests or measures should they use?
3. How should such tests be given in the schools?
4. What conclusions should we encourage teachers to draw from them?

I am sure that each of us comes up with a slightly different set of answers. Let me share mine with you.

In considering the first question (Why should they use tests at all?), my first thought was that if there were one teacher for every child, or even one teacher for every five or so children, there would be *no* need for tests. My second thought was that, even if this Utopian state existed, there would still be several good reasons why tests might be useful. (I am referring here especially to standardized tests.)

First, a teacher may be concerned about how much confidence she should put in her subjective estimates of the ability and progress of some pupils. This is probably especially true of the best teachers, who are the ones who become most sympathetic towards their pupils. Results obtained from an independent and dispassionate measure may amplify, call into question, or at best increase the teacher's level of confidence about her own appraisals of children.

Secondly, many teachers are interested in broadening their perspectives about significant behaviour to look for. Administration and study of good tests made by others may suggest important aspects of observation that the individual teacher may have overlooked or not explored before.

Thirdly, in our present mobile societies, it is not unlikely that a child will be moved from one educational setting to another. We all know that it is important for those responsible for his education in the new setting to have an advance description of the child, in order to be ready with appropriate learning experiences for him. Test results can provide objective descriptions, and can provide them in terms of a standard system of communication.

Fourthly, while the major concern of schools is with individual children and their learning, there is also a need for assessment of groups of children, in order to provide educational administrators with data they need for planning the whole system. If each teacher simply evaluated each of her pupils in an idiosyncratic way, it would be impossible to obtain a comprehensive overall picture.

Unfortunately it is not the case that very many children share their teachers with only three or four children. In the typical situation in the United States where one teacher is responsible for thirty or more youngsters, tests may provide an efficient means of finding out *quickly* about the strengths and weaknesses of children in the class. Then from the beginning, the teacher can orient her instruction in a direction which is reasonably appropriate.

Consider, then, that tests may be useful with young schoolchildren to supplement subjective judgments, broaden local educational perspective, provide data for administrative decisions, and, most important, contribute to selection of appropriate educational treatments. Now, what kinds of tests should they use?

I should recommend tests (including observations) of six kinds of things:

1. Knowledge, ranging from the highly practical (which would contribute to children's safety and ability to get along in the world) to the more abstract (for example, such things as their acquaintance with major figures of children's literature).
2. Understanding, with items expanding on simple memory and knowledge and requiring pupils to classify, apply and translate it.
3. Performance—in the usual skills areas (reading, writing, speaking, mathematical computation) as well as social and artistic performance. So-called 'creative' performance is included.
4. Appreciation, to include appreciations as diverse as of the role of the policeman in the community, of the purpose of attending school, and of a musical performance. This dimension, of course, has a strong affective component.
5. Judgment, involving both the types of preferences they express verbally and their choices for action.
6. Learning modes—how do they learn, what sense modalities are favoured, and what cognitive styles are applied?

Recognizing the limited amount of time which schools can use for testing young children, I should recommend that they concentrate on knowledge, understanding, performance, appreciation, judgment and learning modes with long-term pay-off—in other words, on the kinds of things which seem most crucial to future learning and to personal development.

I think most primary teachers should not fool around with clinically oriented tests of personality or attempts to measure native capacity (as with the so-called 'culture-free' tests of intelligence). The first is downright dangerous. The second is mischievous. Even the potential usefulness of the better intelligence tests is severely limited by the very facts that the name 'intelligence' is applied to them (with its connotation of 'native intelligence') and that performance is reported in terms of an 'I.Q.' By and large, a low I.Q. score is used more as a rationalization for the teacher than as a guide to helping the child. The potential usefulness to teachers of intelligence tests lies mainly in the study of children's reactions to items which tap particular knowledges, abilities, understandings, etc. Thus they would be used as if they were tests of the first six kinds I named.

My third question was how should such tests be given in the schools?

First, they should be given *unobtrusively,* in the regular school setting with the regular teacher as administrator and with as smooth a transition as possible to the other activities of the day.

Secondly, they should be given as *unambiguously* as possible. For example, we should not want to require a child to read a long statement in order to demonstrate his computational skills in mathematics.

Thirdly, they should be given in *full recognition* of the definition properties of tests. When a teacher gives a test, she is in a sense defining the educational objectives she has set for the children. As they get older, they are going to come more and more to take what the tests ask as what is important.

Fourthly, they should be given as *fairly* as possible. Some of the characteristics of the tests we sampled earlier that were designed to make them as fair as possible are these:

a) They include practice experiences before the regular tests are begun.
b) They have no formal time limits.
c) They prescribe repetition of instructions or questions when the repetition would help children fully grasp the nature of the task (and listening comprehension ability is not the specific measurement objective).
d) They seek to use formats and materials which will engage children's interest.
e) They use similar formats and instructions for all the items, so that pupils will not be confused by diverse tasks.
f) They arrange stimulus-response materials in terms of children's usual reading habits.

g) Items and pages are clearly marked so that children can keep their places.
h) Finally, and most important, they use sentence structure and vocabulary suited to the tasks and the developmental levels of the children.

Now, what conclusions should and shouldn't we encourage teachers to draw from such tests as those I have favoured?

In general, barring 'chance' successes, the conclusions to be drawn are that the children can or cannot do the tasks that have been set before them—no less and very little more.

Susie Brown has some notion of what temperature is, but cannot read a household thermometer.

John Jones can read a passage of this type and identify the main point of it.

Hans Schmitt seems to have no appreciation of why reading is important to the individual and society.

Mary Matthews can memorize a short passage quickly when she hears it, but not when she just sees it.

From such tests, teachers must be enjoined *not* to draw conclusions about a child's native capacity, or brain structure and functioning. Nor will test results alone tell a teacher *why* a child is the way he is. But, really, if the teacher knows what some of the skills are that Susie Brown and Hans Schmitt lack, has information on what kind of reading material challenges John Jones, and has some clues about how Mary Matthews learns, isn't there quite enough to keep her busy for awhile?

APPENDIX
LISTENING COMPREHENSION AND MATHEMATICS ITEMS FOR SEVEN-YEAR-OLDS

The teacher says:
   Unless you carry the milk very carefully, you will spill it.

The teacher says:
   Robert had *never* seen a rainbow before.

The teacher says:
   The forest ranger told Dick that trees grow very slowly.
   'You will be a grandfather', he said, 'before these little trees are strong and tall.'

50   *Tests for the primary school*

The teacher says:
   Look at the picture in the arrow. It shows the three balls Rosie put into a can—first the ball marked 1, then the ball marked 2, and last the ball marked 3. If she tips the can, in what order will they come out? ... In what order will they come out?

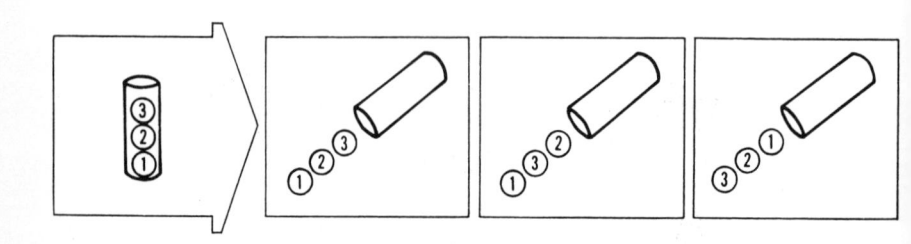

The teacher says:
   Which is *less* than *four?* ... less than four?

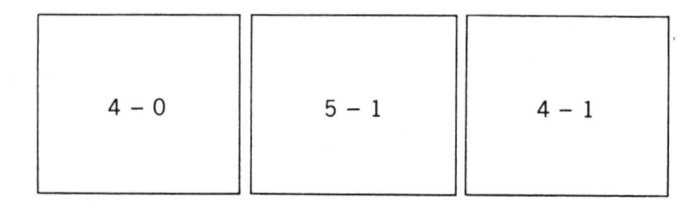

| 4 – 0 | 5 – 1 | 4 – 1 |

The teacher says:
   Look at the picture in the arrow. How many *black* cats are there for each *white* cat? ... How many *black* cats are there for each *white* cat?

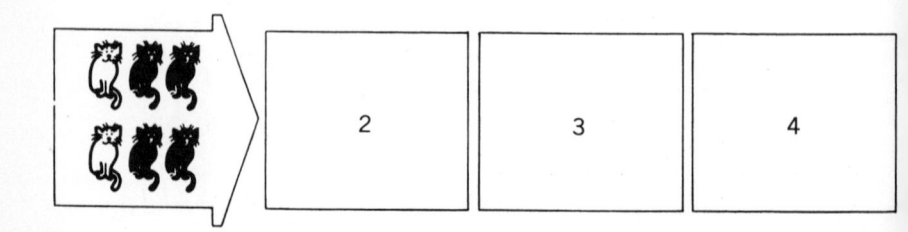

| 2 | 3 | 4 |

Testing from six to eight years 51

The teacher says:
  Which of these would be *best* to measure how *deep* the swimming pool is? ... to measure how *deep* the swimming pool is?

The teacher says:
  About how many *more* flower pots of the same size can be put on this shelf? ... *About* how many *more* flower pots of the same size can be put on this shelf?

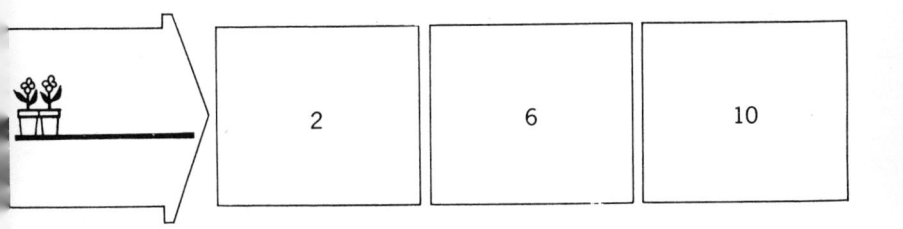

| 2 | 6 | 10 |

THE PREDICTIVE VALUE OF TESTS GIVEN AT SCHOOL ENTRY AND THE USE OF TEST RESULTS IN TEACHING IN READING CLINICS

EVE MALMQUIST

Medical researchers in the field of reading disability do not, as a rule, deny that there are many factors other than a cerebral defect—e.g. environmental conditions—which may influence reading and writing processes. These factors are regarded, however, as 'non-specific', and the types of reading disability they may be assumed to cause are termed 'secondary'. In medical literature the main interest has been directed towards what is considered to be the specific factor—congenital defect or disease of the cerebral cortex, to describe which the term 'congenital word-blindness' is very frequently used.

Educational psychologists, on the other hand, have proceeded along very different lines. They have paid less attention to considerations of cerebral pathology—though, as a rule, they have borne in mind any anatomical and physiological conditions which may be regarded as affecting a case of reading disability—since they do not dispute that in many cases organic defects should be looked upon as contributory to the genesis of reading disabilities. In the great majority of cases, however, they hold that the main cause of under-development in reading ability should be looked for in another direction.

Many investigators have expressed their opinion that only very rarely are reading disabilities due to a single cause. In most cases, a whole complex of factors bearing a relation to reading disabilities are considered to be operative, even if it is not always possible to determine the causal connection (Gjessing 1958, Harris 1961, Robinson 1955). Sometimes it has only been possible to state the symptoms or factors observed in connection with reading difficulties, without being able to determine whether they should be regarded as primary causes of reading disabilities or as a consequence of the disabilities (Malmquist 1958).

Research has largely been concentrated on acquiring such knowledge of the nature of the reading process and reading disabilities as would enable one to make a diagnosis which is of practical use to the teacher who has to look after and teach the child. The information furnished by a research worker that the cause of a child's reading disability is to be attributed to a defect in this or that gyrus of the brain is considered to be hypothesis only, and useless for practical educational work.

Predictive value of reading tests given in the first grade

In order to attempt to acquire an idea of the degree of consistency of the reading disabilities occurring in children, and at the same time to obtain a measure of the predictive value of the reading tests used in my own studies on factors related to reading disabilities in the first grade in the elementary school, I undertook a follow-up study of the reading achievements of those children in the fourth grade of the elementary school who took part in the main investigations in two cities, Linköping and Kristianstad. In this connection I also studied the relation between the results of the intelligence test in grade 1 and reading ability in grades 1 and 4.

Out of the 399 children who took part in the investigations in the first grade I succeeded in tracing 398 in the fourth grade. I was able to obtain, through the school authorities, the marks in reading awarded to these children at the end of the spring term in grade 4.

When grade 1 was investigated, fifty-three of the children were placed in the groups of poor readers on account of their results in the reading tests. Out of the fifty-two children belonging to this group whom we succeeded in tracing when they were in grade 4, only *one* had been given marks for reading which were above the average. Of the children in the group of poor readers, 38·4 per cent had in grade 4 reached a Ba standard, while 59·5 per cent had only reached either a B or a still lower standard. Thus all the children, with only one exception who in accordance with their results in the reading tests in the first grade had been designated poor readers, had remained at a level of achievement below the average of that of their schoolfellows of the same age in the populations investigated.

It should be noted that no special assistance was given to these poor readers in the form of reading and treatment in reading clinics or remedial reading classes.

The following correlations were, among others, obtained between the results of reading tests in grade 1 and marks for reading in grade 4:

$r = 0.622 \pm 0.05$ (Kristianstad, N = 156)
$r = 0.700 \pm 0.03$ (Linköping, N = 242)
$r = 0.659 \pm 0.03$ (Linköping + Kristianstad, N = 398)

The following correlations were obtained between the teachers' rating of the children's reading ability, according to a five-point scale in grade 1, and marks for reading awarded in grade 4:

$r = 0.585 \pm 0.05$ (Kristianstad, N = 156)
$r = 0.611 \pm 0.04$ (Linköping, N = 242)
$r = 0.594 \pm 0.03$ (Linköping + Kristianstad, N = 398)

Consistency in correlation between intelligence and reading ability of various grade levels

Thurstone (1957) reported in her investigations that she found 'a consistent although slight rise in the correlations' between intelligence test scores and reading test scores after certain intervals in time. I have studied the problem, as outlined by Thurstone, in connection with my sample.

I found that the correlations between the results of the different reading tests and the intelligence test scores (Terman-Merrill) in the first grade varied between 0·29 and 0·50. I obtained a correlation of 0·45 between reading ability in the first grade as measured by the composite reading index calculated and the results of the intelligence test given in the same grade. The correlation between the results of the intelligence test in grade 1 and reading ability in grade 4 measured by the marks awarded for reading in grade 4 was 0·47.

Consequently, like Thurstone, I was able to state that no drop in the correlations between intelligence and reading ability took place after an interval of several years, but there was instead a slight rise.

Prevention of reading disabilities: a six-year study

The results and the practical experience obtained in the studies described above have been the starting-point of two further investigations of the development of reading ability at the primary stage, carried out at the National School for Educational Research in Sweden.

The definition of reading ability in these investigations is of an 'operational' nature. The concept 'special reading disabilities' is considered to be relative, and not absolute and fixed. Reading ability has been defined through the method of measurement we have employed. Standardized tests have been applied when delimiting various groups of readers.

In as much as the purpose and the design of these two studies were practically the same and they were both of them of a longitudinal character, they may be considered as parts of a single investigation, extending over a period of six years (1958-64). The main aims of this investigation are as follows:
  1. To find an answer to the question of whether it is possible to prevent the occurrence of special reading disabilities in grades 1 to 3 in the elementary school.
  2. To study the prognostic value of school maturity tests of a conventional type, as very commonly used in the Scandinavian countries, administered prior to the children's entering school.

3. To construct and standardize further measuring instruments both for the diagnosis of children's reading and writing readiness before they start school and at the same time for giving satisfactory prediction of the reading and writing ability of children who have completed grades 1, 2 and 3 of the elementary school.

The theory behind the design of the studies was the following. The occurrence of special reading disabilities is dependent upon a whole complex of factors which are intimately interrelated, and are frequently difficult to separate. In the majority of cases of special reading disabilities there are good prospects of exerting an influence in a positive direction, and at times this may be done to a very considerable extent. In our special remedial reading classes and in our reading clinics many teachers are doing excellent work, entailing considerable self-sacrifice, in attempting to help children with reading disabilities and personality maladjustments, which are often associated with these difficulties.

Ideally, it would naturally be preferable to prevent the occurrence of the reading disabilities in the first place. One of the conditions for an effective programme of this kind would be the ability to diagnose satisfactorily, even before the child begins school, his qualifications for the learning of reading. Another necessary condition is, that it should be made possible for teachers in their methodical planning of instruction to take into consideration the various aspects of various stages of development of each pupil from his very first day at school. How well the teacher may use findings from diagnostic tests and how effectively he may develop a programme based on these findings will naturally be influenced by factors such as his training and experience, the size and organization of the class, the nature of the educational material, etc.

The following main hypothesis was advanced for our investigations: it is possible to decrease, markedly, the frequency of cases of reading disability by a careful diagnosis of the child's reading readiness and general school readiness, and then, on the basis of these diagnostic findings, to establish a teaching situation synthesizing on-going diagnosis—treatment—and teaching for those children who could be expected to experience special difficulties with reading and writing.

The design of the pilot study—diagnostic instruments used—results

In order to test this hypothesis experimentally we first carried out a pilot study, starting in 1958, with a population of first-graders, which was followed up to grade 3 in 1961. Certain organizational and pedagogical arrangements were made.

The four parallel classes of grade 1 at the research school in the school year 1958-9 were matched as far as possible for number of pupils in the class, sex distribution, general intelligence, reading readiness, parents' social and economic status, teachers' competence, etc. Two classes were assigned to the experimental group at random, and two to the control group. In the population studied eight grade 1 classes from the other compulsory schools of Linköping and eight grade 1 classes from rural districts in various parts of the province of Östergotland were included.

The results of the school readiness tests could be expected to give only moderate prognostic value. Supplementary testings of the pupils were therefore carried out, by means of specially constructed reading and writing readiness tests. These tests aim to give an idea of the beginners' level in ability of visual perception, auditive perception, phonetic analysis, sound synthesis and vocabulary. Later on, the pupils' speech, memory span, motor manipulation ability, vision and hearing were tested.

From interviews with the parents of the beginners based on special rating scales and forms, information was obtained about the behaviour and development of the children from birth to the time they started school. Data of this kind were mostly not quantifiable, but it was nevertheless assumed that they might be of some value for the prediction of the children's reading and writing development.

The children in the experimental group, as well as those in the control group, were given a battery of school readiness tests (which may be considered to be a kind of intelligence test) as well as tests of their ability and attainment in reading, writing and arithmetic, before they entered school at the age of seven. The results of these studies have been reported in a special volume (Malmquist 1961).

From the results of the diagnostic instruments used we expected that certain children would suffer from reading disabilities, if no remedial measures were taken. From the very beginning these children were given special help by a reading clinic teacher, in co-operation with the class-teacher, if they were part of the experimental group; but if they belonged to the control group, they were given no help. The remedial teaching was given by a reading clinic teacher who had to take care of pupils with reading disabilities from in all twelve classes at the primary stage. Out of her weekly service time she devoted eight hours to children within the experimental group in grade 1, six hours in grade 2 and five hours in grade 3.

The study was continued until the children had completed the third grade, in 1961.

From the results of the tests given at the end of the first, second and third grades, we found that the experimental group had achieved significantly better results on reading tests, as compared to the control group. The number of cases of reading disability, according to the operational definitions used, was much better in the experimental group than in the control group. The results of this experiment were clearly very promising. Judging by the findings of this pilot study we can expect that this kind of approach might effectively contribute to the prevention of special reading and writing disabilities.

The main study—sample—design

In order to test the results obtained in the pilot study, in 1961 we started a new study of the same character and with much the same design, but on a larger scale. In this study eleven cities with fifty-one classes and a total of 938 pupils fulfilled the conditions put forward for the comparative study in the first grade (control group N = 466, experimental group N = 472). Twelve classes were ruled out from the study during their second and third grade because the local school authorities did not wish to exclude the pupils in the control group from receiving remedial help if they needed it. Two hundred and eighteen children moved to other schools, or were absent from school during test sessions. Complete data for grades 1 to 3 are therefore available for nine cities with a total of twenty-nine classes and 454 pupils (control group N = 230, experimental group N = 224).

Each class was divided into two halves, matched as far as possible for age, number of pupils, sex, intelligence, socio-economic status of parents, etc. The two half-classes had the same teacher. Remedial teaching by a reading clinic teacher was given only to pupils who belonged to the half of the class that was randomly assigned to the experimental group; it was not given to pupils who belonged to the 'control' half of the class.

Statistical treatment of data

Raw scores on the different variables included in the investigation were transformed into standard scores (Z-values, according to the formula: $Z_i = (X_i - \bar{X})/S_x$). Composite indices have been calculated for various groups of variables by the addition or subtraction of standard scores.

We have tested the difference between the experimental group (forty-one half-classes with a total of 472 pupils) and the control group (forty-one half-classes with a total of 466 pupils) by using analysis of covariance. The effect of any initial differences that might remain between the two matched groups would in this way be statistically eliminated. We have also used a special method of covariance analysis not depending on the assumption of common scope for group regression lines, 'the matched regression estimates' method as described in Walker and Lev (1953). A series of multiple regression and correlation analyses were also made, with the purpose of investigating the prognostic value of different predictors as regards the level of reading and writing ability in grades 1 to 3.

By means of these analyses it has been demonstrated that the number of the predicting instruments could be considerably reduced with only a negligible deterioration in prognostic value. A group of three variables has been crystallized, each of which can be expected to contribute significantly to a good prognosis: first, the battery of reading readiness tests; secondly, one of the five visual perception tests (visual letter perception); and thirdly, the battery of school maturity tests. Out of thirty criterion variables registered (ten variables at the end of each of grades 1, 2 and 3) we have calculated, with the use of the transformation procedures mentioned, composite indices for the following three major groups of variables: reading accuracy, reading comprehension and spelling.

Results

a) Prognostic value of the predictors used

The school maturity tests used in this study have notably lower predicting values than the reading readiness tests. This observation applies to each of the three specially studied achievement variables: reading accuracy, reading comprehension, and spelling. Only for the prediction of reading comprehension do the school maturity tests seem to be of some value.

Out of the different predictors studied, the reading readiness variable has throughout given the highest prognostic values, regardless of which criterion variable was examined. The simple pair correlations between reading readiness results and different criterion variables are between 0·48 and 0·55 in grade 1, between 0·41 and 0·51 in grade 2, and between 0·39 and 0·51 in grade 3.

Table 1 summarizes the findings as regards the prognostic values of the three predictors, visual letter perception, school maturity, and reading readiness.

The squared multiple correlation coefficient (R^2) can be interpreted as a measure of the proportion of the total criterion variance, explained by variances of the three predictors. It is obvious that a substantial part of the criterion variance remains unexplained concerning all criterion variables.

Table 1. The prognostic values of the three predictors, visual letter perception, school maturity and reading readiness when used to predict performance in different criterion variables

Criterion				R^2 component due to predictor		
Grade	Type	R	R^2	Reading readiness (1)	School maturity (2)	Visual letter perception (3)
1	Reading accuracy	·507	·257	·183	·043	·031
1	Reading comprehension	·622	·387	·226	·076	·085
1	Spelling	·553	·306	·251	·023	·032
2	Reading accuracy	·421	·177	·148	·007	·027
2	Reading comprehension	·457	·209	·124	·042	·043
2	Spelling	·529	·280	·223	·013	·044
3	Reading accuracy	·400	·160	·130	·006	·023
3	Reading comprehension	·433	·186	·121	·062	·003
3	Spelling	·527	·277	·237	·002	·038

Note: The squared multiple correlation coefficients (R^2) have been divided into their components using the formula

$$R^2_y{._{123}} = r_{y1}\, b_{y1.23} + r_{y2}\, b_{y2.13} + r_{y3}\, b_{y3.12}$$

(Symbols and subscripts according to Walker and Lev, 1953, ch. 13, p. 315 ff.)

The accuracy of prediction decreases with increasing grade level (1 to 3) for all types of criteria. Between grades 2 and 3, however, this decrease is rather small. The prediction of spelling is more accurate than the prediction of the two reading criteria except as regards grade 1. The prediction of spelling also seems to be the most stable in the long run (there is only a small difference noted between R^2 for grade 1, 0.306, and for grade 3, 0.277).

The table also shows the prognostic values of each predictor when used to predict performance in different criterion variables. Under all circumstances reading readiness is by far the most efficient predictor. As regards all the nine criteria, its prognostic value is between 58 and 86 per cent of the combined prognostic value of the three predictors.

The predictor school maturity is evidently of some value as predictor of reading comprehension, but it is of small or no value as predictor of reading accuracy and spelling—especially in grades 2 and 3 (R^2 components between 0.002 and 0.013).

The predictor visual letter perception is obviously of some value as predictor of spelling and reading accuracy in grades 1 to 3. As a predictor of reading comprehension it has some value in grades 1 and 2, but practically no value in grade 3 (R^2 component 0.003).

In relatively long-term prediction (over a three-year period) it seems reasonable to reduce the number of predictors to two for each criterion: namely reading readiness and visual letter perception as predictors of reading accuracy and spelling, and reading readiness and school maturity as predictors of reading comprehension.

b) Stability of different types of criteria through the grades

Table 2 shows the coefficients of correlation between all pairs of criterion variables. Of special interest are the coefficients of correlation between criteria of the same type at different grade levels (these coefficients are found in the 3 × 3 squares along the diagonals of the total matrix).

The criterion reading accuracy is obviously the most stable of the three types, with a correlation of 0.774 between grade 1 and grade 3 measures. This coefficient may, in fact, be interpreted as a long-term retest coefficient, since this criterion is measured by means of the same test battery at all three grade levels.

The criteria reading comprehension and spelling have been measured by means of different tests at different grade levels, and this may partly explain the lower stability (correlation between grade 1 and grade 3 measures: 0.845 for spelling and 0.502 for reading comprehension). The rather low stability of reading comprehension measures may also

Table 2. Coefficients of correlation between different criterion variables

Type	Type Grade	R.A. 1	R.A. 2	R.A. 3	R.C. 1	R.C. 2	R.C. 3	SP 1	SP 2	SP 3
R.A.	1		·829	·774	·848	·734	·471	·659	·682	·637
R.A.	2	·829		·922	·720	·797	·492	·592	·701	·712
R.A.	3	·774	·922		·654	·768	·523	·554	·667	·716
R.C.	1	·848	·720	·654		·745	·502	·661	·626	·555
R.C.	2	·734	·797	·768	·745		·551	·541	·576	·613
R.C.	3	·471	·492	·523	·502	·551		·462	·449	·442
SP	1	·659	·592	·554	·661	·541	·551		·700	·645
SP	2	·682	·701	·667	·626	·576	·449	·700		·785
SP	3	·637	·712	·716	·555	·613	·442	·645	·785	

Note: 1. Coefficients computed from data for control group (N = 230).
2. R.A. = Reading accuracy.
   R.C. = Reading comprehension.
   SP = Spelling.
3. The squares of the diagonal parts of the matrix marked above contain coefficients of correlation between criterion variables of the same type.

be due to an increasing complexity in the set of factors that influence reading comprehension performance. The decrease from grade level to grade level in correlation between reading accuracy and reading comprehension (0·848 in grade 1, 0·797 in grade 2 and 0·523 in grade 3) also seems to indicate that these abilities become more and more differentiated. Correlation between reading comprehension and spelling at successive grade levels show the same tendency (0·661 in grade 1, 0·576 in grade 2 and 0·442 in grade 3). Correlations between reading accuracy and spelling, on the other hand, do *not* show any tendency (0·659 in grade 1, 0·701 in grade 2 and 0·716 in grade 3).

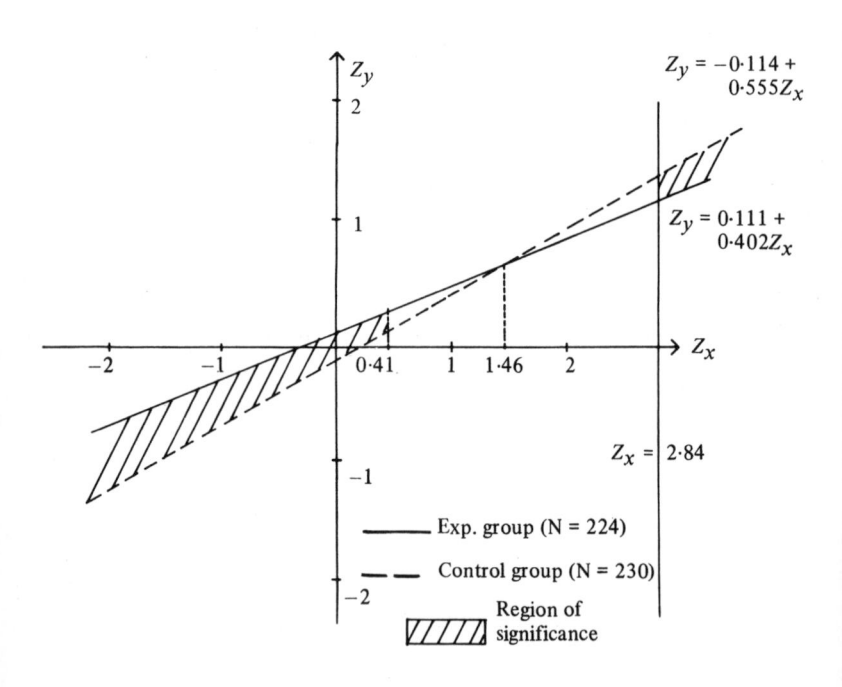

Figure 1. Analyses of differences between the total experimental group and the **control** group regarding the criterion spelling, grade 3 (y), as a function of reading readiness (x)

Note: Z_x values limiting the region of significance and non-significance have been computed according to the method of 'matched regression estimates' as described in Walker and Lev, 1953.

Comment: Two different regions of significance have been found. The upper region contains only one case in the control group and is therefore disregarded. The lower region of significance contains more than 50 per cent of the total number of cases (454). Within this region the experimental group pupils are superior in spelling ability (as measured in this study) in comparison with control group pupils at corresponding reading readiness levels.

It should be noticed that out of the seventy-eight 'reading clinic' pupils in the experimental group seventy-two are found within the lower region of significance.

It therefore seems reasonable to assume that reading comprehension ability during the primary stage becomes more and more differentiated from the two abilities—reading accuracy and spelling, while these two abilities remain quite closely correlated to one another throughout the period.

c) Effects of remedial teaching

Table 3 shows group means and differences as regards the three predictors and the nine criteria studied. The control group was superior in two out of three predictors, although the differences are non-significant. The experimental group was superior in all nine criterion variables with significant differences in five criteria: reading accuracy, grades 1, 2 and 3, spelling, grades 2 and 3.

The aim of the remedial teaching has been to prevent or eliminate reading and writing difficulties among pupils in the experimental group.

The criteria reading accuracy and spelling seem to be most fitted to indicate reading and spelling difficulties at this level. The fact that the analysis of these two types of criteria has yielded significant group mean differences favouring the experimental group in five cases of six strongly supports the hypothesis that the remedial teaching has had the expected effect. The data also supports the hypothesis that there is an additive increase in this effect from grade level to grade level, especially when the criterion is reading accuracy (group mean differences: + 0·191 in grade 1, + 0·236 in grade 2 and + 0·255 in grade 3).

The grade 3 criteria can be regarded as the ultimate criteria of reading and writing performance within this study. Group mean differences in the three criteria have been studied by means of covariance analysis, using all three predictors, reading readiness, school maturity and visual letter perception. These analyses have yielded highly significant F-values as regards group mean differences in reading accuracy (F = 9·44) and spelling (F = 6·96), but a non-significant F-value for reading comprehension (F = 2·94).

As the correlation and regression analyses in some cases yielded lower within-group regression coefficients for the experimental group than for the control group, we have also used a method of 'matched regression estimates' (cf. Walker and Lev 1953), studying reading accuracy and spelling grade 3 with reading readiness as a single predictor. As regards the criterion variable reading accuracy, this analysis did not yield any significance region in the predictor, i.e. the superiority of the experimental group in this criterion is about the same at all levels of reading readiness.

Table 3. Group means, group mean differences and significance of group mean differences (N = 454)

	Variable	Experimental group	Control group	Diff. E-C	Significance
Predictors:	Reading readiness	−·026	·026	−·052	n.s.
	School maturity	·034	−·034	·068	n.s.
	Visual letter perception	−·049	·048	−·097	n.s.
Criteria:	Reading accuracy				
	Grade 1	·097	−·094	·191	$p < 0.05$
	Grade 2	·120	−·116	·236	$p < 0.05$
	Grade 3	·129	−·126	·255	$p < 0.01$
	Reading comprehension				
	Grade 1	·078	−·076	·154	n.s.
	Grade 2	·066	−·064	·130	n.s.
	Grade 3	·060	−·059	·119	n.s.
	Spelling				
	Grade 1	·064	−·062	·126	n.s.
	Grade 2	·104	−·100	·204	$p < 0.05$
	Grade 3	·101	−·100	·201	$p < 0.05$

The corresponding analysis of spelling grade 3 did yield a region of significance (experimental group pupils were better than control group pupils at reading readiness levels *below* + 0.4z) and a region of non-significance (no significant difference between groups at reading readiness levels *above* +0.4z). Thus the total superiority of the experimental group in spelling ability is mainly due to a superiority of experimental group pupils with low or medium initial reading readiness level. As seventy-two out of seventy-eight 'clinic' pupils belong to this category, it seems reasonable to conclude that this finding supports the hypothesis that the remedial teaching has significantly increased the spelling ability of the 'clinic' pupils.

Out of the seventy-eight pupils from the experimental group who received remedial instruction forty-two had initial school maturity test results *above* $-0.5z$. At the final testing session in grade 3 only seven out of these forty-two pupils achieved results in reading accuracy of below $-1.0z$.

Using our operational definition of special reading disabilities, we find that 83 per cent of the cases identified as potential reading disability cases were prevented from occurring. The study further shows that the optimistic hopes of totally eliminating reading disability through remedial procedures such as those used with the experimental group were not fulfilled.

References

Gjessing, H.-J. (1958) *En Studie af Laesemodenhet ved Skolegangens Begyndelse.* Oslo.

Hallgren, B. (1950) *Specific Dyslexia ('Congenital Wordblindness'): A Clinical and Genetic Study.* Diss., Stockholm.

Harris, A. (1961) *How to Increase Reading Ability.* New York.

Hermann, K. (1955) *Om Medfødt Ordblindhed.* Diss., Copenhagen.

Malmquist, E. (1958) 'Factors related to reading disabilities in the first grade of the elementary school.' *Acta Universitatis Stockholmiensis.*

Malmquist, E. (1961) *Studies of the Children's Attainments and Proficiency in Reading, Writing, Arithmetic at the Beginning of Their Schooling in the First Grade of the Elementary School.* Research Reports from the National School for Educational Research in Linköping, Sweden, no. 1 (in Swedish with a summary in English). Stockholm.

Malmquist, E. (1966) *Reading and Writing Disabilities in Children. Analysis and Methodology.* Lund.

Robinson, H. (1955) 'What research says to the teacher of reading. Reading readiness.' *The Reading Teacher,* 8, 235-7.

Thurstone, T. (1957) 'Implications for test construction 1957.' Paper read at the Invitational Conference on Testing Problems, Educational Testing Service, Princeton, N.J.

Walker, H.M. and Lev, J. (1953) *Statistical Inference.* New York.

PRE-SCHOOL TESTS OF CONCEPT DEVELOPMENT FOR CHILDREN FROM DEPRIVED ENVIRONMENTS

L. H. E. REID

In this paper I shall attempt to examine some of the problems associated with measuring conceptual development in pre-school children who are growing up in environments commonly classed as educationally unstimulating. I hope to pay particular attention to the growth of the numerical and spatial group of abilities, and to show that they tend to be minimally developed under conditions of poverty. The possible effects of the quality of language acquirement on these abilities will be examined and assessed. As a postulate, it is suggested that poverty as a state, together with child-rearing practices, exert far more significant effects. It will be shown that traditional middle-class-oriented tests have limited validities in such contexts, and that development of more suitable tests must follow careful research and inquiry in the abilities mentioned above. Directions that these new tests should follow will be suggested.

A great deal of attention is now being focused on the problem of mental growth deficiencies of pre-school children reared in environments which lack the material and social components basic to healthy living. These children are variously described as disadvantaged, underprivileged, or deprived; but whatever the label, it amounts to the same thing—children whose material and social backgrounds are such that it is highly unlikely that they can learn in normal school conditions, unless rehabilitative measures are taken, or highly unlikely that they will ever be able to live fully and adequately in a modern technological society, unless measures are taken to offset some at least of the more significant influences of the subcultures in which they exist. Advanced societies are seriously concerned at the imbalances which exist in their midst: the phenomena of relatively large proportions of their populations existing submarginally and being consequently unable to achieve developmental levels which make it possible for them to move into the main stream of living and to take an optimum part in it. Under-developed societies with considerably larger proportions of their people in this state of poverty are anxious to make the great leap forward economically, and realize that they can hardly do so if large percentages of their man-power continue to atrophy. In the case of the first type of society, some, such as the United States, have embarked on expensive compensatory programmes for the disadvantaged child; but however massive the effort may be, however enthusiastic the proponents of these schemes, success cannot be assured unless those concerned are reasonably aware of the nature of the children's defects, and can identify the deficiencies in mental growth from which they might be suffering. The second type of society, the under-developed, is, in addition, anxious to see that it gets maximum returns from the small amount of money it can afford to spend on education. In either case the need for an adequate definition of the words 'deprived', 'disadvantaged' and similar terms, based on careful research and inquiry, is now very obvious. We must, for example, distinguish between deprivation so severe as to interfere with basic sensory and perceptual development, and deprivation which interferes with conceptual growth, etc., in very subtle ways and for which remedial action can be successful if taken in time. Suitable tests are necessary for the identification of deficiencies as well as for assessing the adequacy of such compensatory programmes as might consequently be attempted.

In this paper I propose to pay specific attention to the numerical-spatial group of abilities, mainly for two reasons. In the first place, I shall try to show that their development is more likely to suffer under conditions of poverty than that of other groups. Secondly, exploitation of their maximum potential is necessary for education which must become increasingly technological, and for living in an age which is overwhelmingly scientific in outlook.

The weaknesses of middle-class-oriented tests when used to measure subjects in other subcultures is too well known to call for any comment. Far more serious, however, is the deterministic manner in which they are generally used. Children are typed, as a result of the scores obtained on these tests, as being marginally educable and incapable of normal school achievement. Defective teaching soon seals their doom, as it were, and they eventually become drop-outs or in other ways completely fail to achieve their potential. Apart from the obvious danger of using pre-school tests for prediction, middle-class-oriented tests can be of little help in the diagnosis of developmental deficiencies. Yet this is the area in which children of deprived environments can derive most help from testing. Existing tests would tend to make us believe that problem-solving abilities are either almost entirely absent in deprived children or, at most, minimally developed. This assumption has been falsely validated through use of unfamiliar tests, which reflect different sources of variance and different cultural background factors. The avowed aim of compensatory efforts on deprived pre-school children is to bring them up to such levels experientially as will make it possible for them to absorb teaching to which 'normal' children are exposed. This assumption that current teaching approaches and the philosophies which underlie them are good for children from lower subcultures has never been validated. One presumes that compensatory efforts involve rehabilitation, which, in turn, would mean effecting some necessary cultural changes. If by that we mean that growth and learning can best take place only within certain cultural and attitudinal contexts, we may be wrong. The very act of having children living in the context of one subculture at home and in the context of another at school could result in such conflict and confusion as to inhibit rather than facilitate growth and learning. It might be that it is necessary to explore the possibilities of adjusting our approaches in education and teaching to match the needs of the lower subcultures, rather than to attempt the reverse. This serves to emphasize the tremendous amount of research and inquiry that is needed to throw light on the problems of educating these children.

If it is suggested that culture-free tests could be helpful, one must remember that no such tests have yet been successfully devised; and, even if they had, the measurement of any component of mental ability separate from environmental effects can hardly be of anything but academic interest. Potential insulated from any environmental context could hardly exist for long.

Language and the numerical-spatial group of abilities

The part language plays in conceptual growth on the whole is well known. We think through language. One can consequently assume that where verbal language is restricted and communication carried on largely in non-verbal media, thinking will be slowed down. The evidence in support of sparse language development in deprived environments is impressive. We can reasonably assume, therefore, that thinking, or at least some aspects of it, will be a laboured process with such children, and that consequently the acquisition of concepts will be proportionately slow. It does not follow, however, that there is of necessity a perfect or even a high correlation between verbal achievement and concept acquirement, particularly in the numerical-spatial ability groups. The ability to make appropriate semantic differentiations among dissimilar but related concepts depends, in the views of Suchmann and Aschner (1961), on how related the concepts have become in the course of the child's experience. Ervin and Foster's (1960) findings are that dimensions such as size, weight, strength, and attributes such as those described by 'good', 'pretty', 'clean', etc., when learned as correlate variables long before the child can clearly differentiate between them, become so linked semantically that the concepts represented by them remain nebulous for the child.

Pre-school tests of concept development

There is also evidence that certain conditions favour the development of verbal ability to a disproportionate extent, at the expense of the numerical-spatial group of abilities; amongst these are restrictive practices in child rearing, emphasis on verbal accomplishment and tense parent-child relations. Bing (1963) shows that discrepant verbal ability is fostered by a close relation with a demanding and somewhat intrusive mother, while discrepant non-verbal abilities are enhanced by allowing the child considerable freedom to experiment on his own. In further support, Ferguson and Maccoby (1966) found numerical ability related to assertiveness, interpersonal competence and an 'appropriate' level of dependency.

Vernon (1965a and b), from a study of West Indian children, found that those whose mental development was handicapped by poor socio-economic and cultural environment, by defective education and family instability, show this to a greater extent in practical spatial and some abstract non-verbal abilities than they do in verbal educational achievements. Though he admits that the relatively high verbal scores of the deprived children might have been the result of mere rote learning at school, the fact remains that, although they showed some facility in use of language, they were comparatively backward in spatial and other non-verbal concepts. In group tests administered to much larger groups of ten- to twelve-year-olds in Jamaica, I found the median scores to be as follows:

	Social groups		
Tests	*Upper*	*Middle*	*Lower*
Verbal	105	97	85
Non-verbal	104	96	72
Significance of difference	<·05	<·05	>·01

Mean = 100   S.D. = 15

The lower group, in which were a very high proportion of children from urban slums and backward rural communities, showed a very significant difference between verbal and non-verbal scores.

Using the WISC performance scale on a group of thirty institutionalized children of 7 to 9 years, I obtained mean I.Q. ratings of only 67. These children had all become physically handicapped over an average period of 2·5 years, and consequently lack of kinesthetic sensing could hardly be advanced as the reason for their low scores. Their disabilities were confined to one or both of the lower limbs; with aids all had learned to move about relatively easily. They were all, however, from relatively deprived backgrounds. On a standardized test of language achievement their mean rating was 84.

In 1965 Caribbean Educational Publications, a part of the Faculty of Education of the University of the West Indies, carried out an extensive survey of the speech structure of five- and six-year-old children of lower income groups, in several Caribbean islands. Word counts and recordings of informal conversations in various unstructured situations were taken. The results showed up the limited nature of their vocabularies compared with those of more privileged groups in the same territories as well as in more developed English-speaking countries. Nouns and verbs used showed a preoccupation with family and other social relations, and with food and clothing, as well as a desire for items identified with higher levels of living. Minimal manipulative contact with the material environment was evidenced by the almost complete absence of relevant words from the lists. These bits of evidence point to two possibilities:

1. There is not necessarily a close correlation between language achievement and concept growth in the numerical-spatial group of abilities.
2. The language of children in deprived environments is, in the main, directed at communication for purposes other than concept growth in this group of abilities.

One can hence reasonably postulate that poverty of experience resulting from little manipulative contact with the material environment can be traced to the effects of poverty as an economic and social state. It has more profound effects on growth than merely depriving children of physical comforts or of parents who can provide necessary educative stimulation. It appears to condition the thinking of the child, and to develop in him negative learning attitudes, attitudes of non-inquiry and but little inquisitiveness. Hunger and material deprivation very possibly inhibit the natural urges of curiosity and inquisitiveness which are important initiators of children's learning. Apart from insulating children from necessary learning experiences, they build up defences against attitudes necessary for learning.

I will here briefly outline studies being carried on in the Faculty of Education of my university, with a view to determining the extent, if any, to which upbringing influences concept growth in the numerical-spatial group of abilities. Data on child-rearing practices are being collected from carefully structured samples of the population in the following behavioural areas:

Pregnancy and early childhood
Agents of socialization in upbringing

Physical aspects of upbringing
Discipline: restrictions and permissiveness
Social relations among children
Sex differentiation in upbringing
Work and play patterns

The sample takes in all strata of the population, including the severely deprived. The interplay of poverty and rearing patterns and their effect on the abilities in question will be studied, and inter-strata comparisons made.

In summary, my hypothesis is that poor language development is not the main contributor to defective growth in these abilities: the state of poverty together with rearing practices have far more direct and significant effects. We must remember that non-language subjects (animals) do succeed in concept learning, albeit by slow and ponderous processes. Deprived children might be none the worse off; their most significant lack may be the necessary stimulus situations.

Numerical-spatial tests

Studies of form perception have revealed that children more readily perceive and discriminate highly complex and irregular objects than they do regular geometrical shapes. Piaget (and Inhelder 1959) found this to be so, and Page (1959) confirmed it. He found pre-school children significantly more successful with haptic recognition of topological forms than with simple regular geometric shapes. In any case, geometric forms occur much less in poor environments than they do in others. 'Educative' toys, such as building blocks and variously shaped articles for constructive manipulation, are less likely to be provided by poor parents than by the relatively privileged. Page thinks that such topological qualities as closure, separation, proximity and continuity provide immediately available cues for young children more readily than do the logical relations in geometrical forms. Performance tests for pre-school children which contain an abundance of plain and solid geometrical shapes—e.g. the Merrill-Palmer Scale—are quite likely to be of doubtful validity when used with deprived children. Many research workers have supported the idea of some degree of performism in perceptual discrimination. This is likely to be minimal in cases of extreme deprivation, which would parallel those of children with such severe physical handicaps that kinesthetic sensing is almost absent, resulting in impaired perceptual growth. Early exposure to particular stimuli obviously renders the child more sensitive to discrimination of forms with which these stimuli are associated. The ability to form new associations apparently develops as a result of experience, no doubt because experience expands the cognitive structure, which, in turn, facilitates the learning of new associations.

It is well known that culture affects perception. Lesser (1965) shows some effects of social-clan and cultural groupings on such specific abilities as verbal facility, reasoning, as well as the numerical and spatial. The subculture of poverty is sufficiently distinct and significantly different from the main cultural stream of a society for it to have profound effects on perception, and consequently on these specific abilities. Poverty, as a psychological state, no doubt exerts insidious influences in devious ways. Until these effects can be identified, interpretation of test results is likely to be relatively unreliable and unhelpful from a diagnostic point of view.

How are concepts acquired by young children?

A knowledge of how concepts are acquired by young children is a prerequisite for making good tests. We know it involves the acquisition of a set of chains (verbal or non-verbal) to representative stimulus situations which exhibit the characteristics of the class that describes the concept. Following this, there must be response to these characteristics in terms of some common abstract property. However, the cultural and psychological factors which facilitate the acquisition of concepts have not yet been adequately identified. There is evidence that very often children who are chronologically advanced and are not otherwise mentally weak are not free from specific stimuli, i.e. have not yet acquired the capability of abstraction nor of generalization. I have found this condition to be reinforced by defective teaching, and this possibly continues into adulthood as a characterizing feature of low-level education. There is no doubt that good teaching assists abstraction and generalizing; in fact, that is one of its basic functions. But we need to learn more certainly how the child acquires his first and fundamental concepts, and, conversely, what factors defacilitate such acquirement. Let us take the concept of conservation. Piaget describes it as developing in three stages: (a) an initial stage in which perception alone determines the judgment of quantity; (b) perception as well as conserving conditions influencing judgment; (c) a stage of complete conservation. There is evidence that in cases of severe deprivation, children tend to remain at stage (b), moving between a stage of conservation and a regression to perception, and continuing in this state well beyond the chronological norm. We are not certain what are the pre-school child's ideas of quantity; one may guess they are ambiguous and amorphous,

Pre-school tests of concept development

for it is unlikely that he demands the same levels of clarity and constancy as the adult. Perceptual cues in quantification might persist much longer than we would assume. In this respect, spatial arrangements of quantities and the quantities themselves may be viewed as a whole. There is so far no evidence that analytic thinking is strongly developed even in the 'normal' pre-school child. Yet our tests assume this to be so. It may be that the chronological stage at which we assume that complete conservation is acquired is far too early. We infer conservation once a child is able to reason logically in concrete situations. This is not necessarily so. These mistaken ideas of developmental progress can possibly apply to other sectors of the numerical-spatial group of abilities. If, therefore, tests are to be helpful, they must in their structure take cognizance of the gradation in concept acquirement, and cease the all-or-nothing approach to assessment.

Further evidence in support is supplied by Lee (1965), whose studies show that concepts of colour, number, form and size have greater salience (probability of being used) for the pre-school child than concepts related to sex-typed objects or similarities based on the component parts of a stimulus. The pre-school child is not inclined to be analytic. He shows a relative inability to group two objects together on the basis of similarity in a component part, e.g. wheels on a vehicle or limbs on a doll. This is also the previously held view of Lamkin and Newhall (1937). Further, they showed that concepts of colour and size have decreased salience for children of six-plus years. This reflects a shift in the importance children attribute to these dimensions as critical in categorizing their environment; they are at this stage paying more attention to form and direction.

What I am trying to show is that the developmental stages followed in the growth of these concepts must be known as a prelude to the construction of good tests. Our concern is largely in the area of diagnosis, not, I make bold to say, in prediction. No attempt to trace weak links in the chain of development can be successful without a sound knowledge of what the whole process should normally be.

In summary, there must be more emphasis on the development of tests indigenous to the subcultures of poverty, and less efforts directed at culture-free measures. The effects of deprivation on the numerical-spatial group of abilities is of crucial importance, the more so because of their importance as a base for general education which must become increasingly scientific and technological; consequently more attention to the psychology of poverty and the light it could throw on learning could be fruitful. There are reasonable grounds for the belief that restrictive practices in children's upbringing generally associated with conditions of deprivation do affect adversely the normal development of the numerical-spatial abilities. It is suggested that measurement of these abilities should not be made on an all-or-nothing basis, but that such assessment reflects the development stages reached by the subject in the concepts being considered. Not unrelated to this is the fact that the intellectual steps required for solving test items should be limited in number, for young children are unable to reason in a sustained sequence. The content of performance tests for deprived children should, as far as is possible, reflect situations and objects that are likely to lie within their experience. Test constructors should consider the possibility of structuring situations which could exist within the limited environment of these children.

Lastly, it should be borne in mind that communication between adults and children is often hampered by verbal confusion in young children as well as by disparate conceptual systems by which adults and children view the same things differently. The same words quite often, however, are used to describe these different percepts. This can be a source of error variance of immense proportions, and re-emphasizes the need for a continuing close relation between child development studies and techniques in measurement.

References

Bing, E. (1963) 'Effect of child-rearing practices on development of differential cognitive abilities.' *Child Dev.*, **34**, 3.

Ervin, S. M. and Foster, G. (1960) 'The development of meaning in children's descriptive terms.' *J. abnorm. soc. Psychol.*, **61**, 271-5.

Ferguson and Maccoby (1966) 'Interpersonal correlates of differential abilities.' *Child Dev.*, **37**, no. 3, 549-71.

Lamkin, J. and Newhall, S. M. (1937) 'Form, colour, size in children's perceptual behaviour.' *Child Dev.*, **8**, 105-11.

Lee, L. C. (1965) 'Concepts of colour, number and form.' *Child Dev.*, **36**, 1.

Lesser, G. G. (1965) *Mental Abilities of Children from Different Social Class and Cultural Groups*. Monograph of the Society for Research in Child Development, **30**, no. 4, 1-115.

Page, E. (1959) 'Haptic perception: a consideration of one of the investigations of Piaget and Inhelder.' *Educ.Rev.* (Inst. of Edn, Birmingham), **2**, 115-24.

Piaget, J. and Inhelder, B. (1959) *La Genèse des Structures Elémentaires de Logique: Classification et Sériation*. Neuchâtel: Delachaux et Niestlé.

Suchmann, J. R. and Aschner, M. J. (1961) 'Perceptual and cognitive development.' *Rev. educ. Res.,* **31**, no. 5, 451-62.

Vernon, P. E. (1965a) 'Environmental handicaps and intellectual development, pt 1.' *Br. J. educ.Psychol.,* **35**, pt 1, 9-20.

Vernon, P. E. (1965b) 'Environmental handicaps and intellectual development, pt 2.' *Br. J. educ.Psychol.,* **35**, pt 2, 117-26.

THE FACTORIAL STRUCTURE AND COMPARATIVE VALIDITY OF SCHOOL MARKS AND ATTAINMENT TESTS*

F. BACHER

In 1961-2, a survey was carried out within a French Département, the Département du Loiret, of all the children who were then in their second year of secondary education (their seventh year of schooling). A large body of information was assembled on 3,124 pupils, in particular school marks and assessments, and the results of attainment tests in French and mathematics.†

For 2,500 of these children information was also available from files started two years before, when they were still at primary school. Each file contained school marks and assessments provided by the teacher, the results of attainment tests in French and arithmetic, and the results of aptitude tests.

The general purpose of the inquiry was to investigate the children's adjustment to their first two years of secondary education. I shall here confine myself to a study of the various school marks obtained during the three years covered by the survey (fifth, sixth and seventh years of schooling).

The group studied at the seventh-year level is, by comparison with the total fifth-year group of two years before, a selected one, consisting of only 46 per cent of that group. The selection (by a board regulating school transfer at the beginning of the sixth year of schooling) was based primarily on school results, though a geographical and socio-economic factor was also present.

There are two types of variable available in this survey: the marks and assessments given by teachers, and the results of standardized attainment tests. Scores are contributed by each of the three years, some referring to French, some to arithmetic, and some to the general educational level.

1. Relations between scores of the various types at the fifth-year level

At this level, the following scores are available:

---

*A preliminary study of this subject has been published: Bacher, F. (1965) 'L'évaluation des resultats scolaires au niveau de l'école moyenne. *Travail hum.*, 28, no. 3-4, 219-30. This contains a summary of the principal results and a supplement covering the factorial structure of the data.

†Bacher, F. and Reuchlin, M. (1965) 'Le cycle d'observation. Enquête sur l'ensemble des élèves d'un departement.' *BINOP*, 21, 3, 149-236.

a) Marks in arithmetic, dictation, questions on dictation, and an overall mark for two examinations taken in December and March.
b) The teacher's assessments of the pupil's abilities in arithmetic, spelling, composition and reading (marks out of 10).
c) Averages over the year for marks in arithmetic and dictation, and a general average.
d) Placements by the teacher into one of four grades, very good, good, average, and poor, for arithmetic and for French.
e) Scores in attainment tests in French and arithmetic (second-year intermediate (3) test: CM 2(3)).

Study of the correlations between these scores showed that the correlations between school marks are in general higher than the correlations between attainment tests and school marks. Thus for French the mean correlation between school marks is 0·46, while the mean correlation between school marks and attainment test is only 0·36; for arithmetic the mean correlation between school marks is 0·62, while that between attainment test and school marks is 0·38.

The greater coherence of the school marks might in part be attributed to the fact that for any pupil all the marks are given by one teacher, several of them at approximately the same time; but it must also be due in part to a basic difference between attainment tests and school marks. The attainment tests, standardized in administration and marking, provide a scale of reference common to all the pupils; school marks, on the other hand, are given within each class and hardly reflect the difference in level between classes, with the result that one of the sources for the variation between test scores is not present in the case of school marks.

This within-class characteristic of school marks is clearly evident from an examination of figure 1, which gives, for French and arithmetic, the distribution of marks (in eleven standardized categories) for each of the groups formed by the teachers' rankings, very good, good and average.

Although the mean scores show a progressive trend across the three groups in both arithmetic and French (a change of about one category between two successive groups), there is also considerable overlap between the three distributions. For instance, in arithmetic the mark 8, which is reached or exceeded by 50 per cent of those judged 'very good' in this subject by their teacher, is also reached by 32 per cent of those judged 'good' and 14 per cent of those judged only 'average'. A far from negligible proportion of the pupils assessed as average thus gave evidence of attainments as great as those of the better half of the pupils assessed as 'very good'.

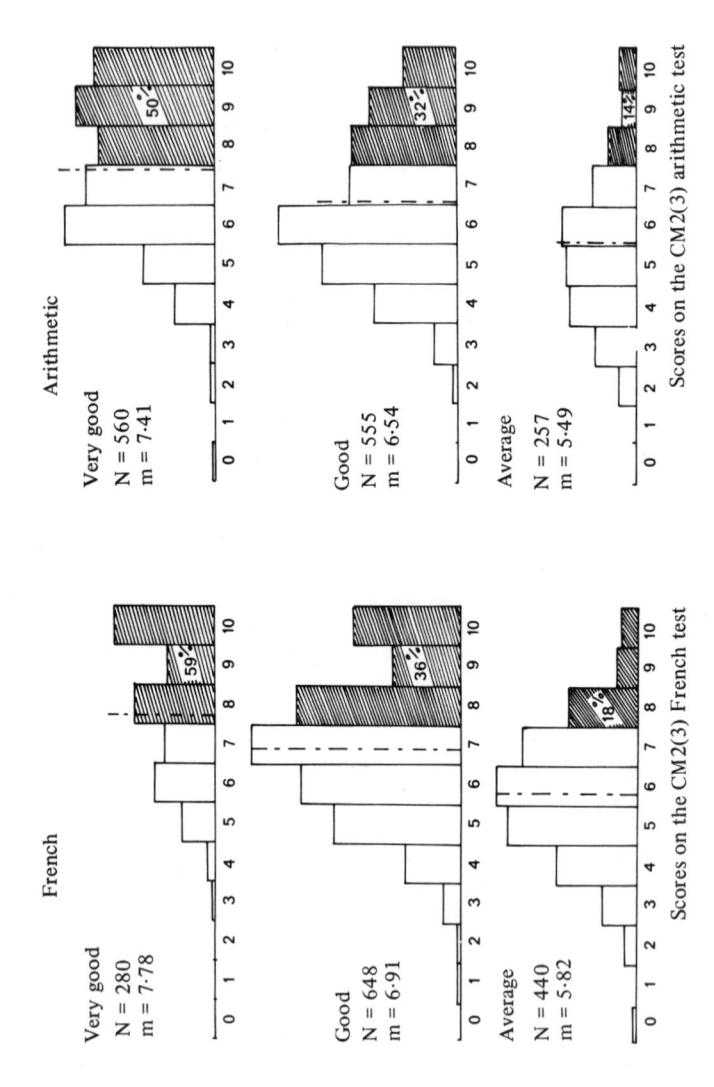

Figure 1. Distributions of test scores for pupils within teacher grades

Factorial structure and comparative validity

2. Validity of fifth-year school marks and assessments as predictors of subsequent school achievement

Various assessments of subsequent school achievement were available, in particular:
   a) The classification of the children into three groups by their teachers, first in the sixth year and then in the seventh.
   b) Scores on attainment tests in French (ICF 5/4) and mathematics (ICM 5/4) given at the end of the seventh year.

It has been shown that scores on the two types of measure can be forecast with similar accuracy by the different predictors, though in general the arithmetic scores correlate slightly less well than the scores for French. Thus the mean correlation of fifth-year school marks in arithmetic with the ICM 5/4 test is 0·27, whereas the marks in French show a mean correlation of 0·31 with the ICF 5/4 test.

A second important observation concerns the relative predictive validity of school marks and assessments on the one hand and of attainment tests on the other. There is, in fact, a marked difference in favour of attainment tests, even if the criterion is not an attainment test but an assessment made by teachers. For example, the mean correlation between school marks and assessments in French and the grading in the seventh year is 0·29, while the attainment test (CM 2(3) French) shows a correlation of 0·44 with the same grading.

In arithmetic, the corresponding correlations are 0·25 and 0·39 respectively.

A third observation concerns the trend in predictive validity against elapsed time. In almost all cases one finds a smaller correlation with a later measure than with an earlier one. Thus, for arithmetic, the mean correlation of school assessments and marks with CM 2(3) arithmetic test, taken the same year, is 0·38; with the ICM 5/4 test, taken two years later, it is only 0·27; the same predictors show a mean correlation of 0·29 with the grading in the sixth year, and of 0·25 with the grading in the seventh year. In the case of school marks in French, the mean correlation is 0·36 with a test taken in the fifth year, but only 0·31 with a test taken in the seventh year; the mean correlation with school gradings in French also falls from the sixth to the seventh year (from 0·32 to 0·29). This decrease in validity appears slightly less marked if we use tests as predictors: the correlation between an arithmetic test taken in the fifth year and the grading in the sixth year is 0·38; the correlation with the grading in the seventh year is 0·39. In the case of French, there is a fall in correlation from 0·47 to 0·44; a composite intelligence test, also taken in the fifth year, shows a correlation of

0·42 with the grading in the sixth year and of 0·39 with the grading in the seventh.

3. Factor analysis of school marks and attainment tests

A factor analysis has been made of the school marks and of the scores on the attainment tests taken in the fifth and seventh years. In the case of the tests taken in the seventh year, marks were available on several sub-tests (in mathematics: quick computation, arithmetic, geometry and problems; in French: grammar, comprehension and vocabulary). These analytic data were used as variables in preference to overall scores. The list of variables used is as follows:

 1. CM 2(3) test—arithmetic
 2. Arithmetic (December examination)
 3. Arithmetic (March examination)
 4. Arithmetic (year average)
 5. ICM 5/4 test—quick computation
 6. ICM 5/4 test—arithmetic
 7. ICM 5/4 test—geometry
 8. Arithmetic (assessment)
 9. CM 2(3) test—French
 10. Dictation (December examination)
 11. Questions (December examination)
 12. Dictation (March examination)
 13. Questions (March examination)
 14. Composition (assessment)
 15. Spelling (assessment)
 16. Dictation (year average)
 17. ICF 5/4 test—grammar
 18. ICF 5/4 test—comprehension
 19. ICF 5/4 test—vocabulary
 20. ICM 5/4 test—problems

a) First-order analysis

A centroid analysis of the correlations between these twenty variables has been carried out.* The four factors extracted were rotated, producing the oblique structure shown opposite.

Factor *A* saturates† the school marks in French, in particular those which relate to spelling and represent an overall assessment for the

*Details of this analysis are given in the appendix.
†The term 'saturates' is retained, as that originally used by Thurstone.

Factorial structure and comparative validity

	A	B	C	D
2. Arithmetic (December examination)	·07	·05	·13	**·42**
3. Arithmetic (March examination)	·05	·02	·07	**·58**
4. Arithmetic (year average)	−·01	·03	·00	**·87**
8. Arithmetic (assessment)	·01	−·03	·08	**·76**
1. CM 2(3) test–arithmetic	·02	·25	**·28**	·34
5. ICM 5/4 test–quick computation	·00	−·01	**·64**	·05
6. ICM 5/4 test–arithmetic	·02	·11	**·64**	−·01
7. ICM 5/4 test–geometry	·04	·12	**·56**	·04
20. ICM 5/4 test–problems	·10	·01	**·57**	·02
10. Dictation (December examination)	**·51**	·12	·12	−·01
11. Questions (December examination)	**·35**	·32	·02	·27
12. Dictation (March examination)	**·55**	·09	·11	·02
13. Questions (March examination)	**·33**	·23	·06	·24
14. Composition (assessment)	**·46**	·14	·01	·08
15. Spelling (assessment)	**·77**	−·02	·12	·03
16. Dictation (year average)	**·80**	·13	−·01	·17
9. CM 2(3) test–French	·21	**·46**	·17	·22
17. ICF 5/4 test–grammar	·13	**·25**	·42	·06
18. ICF 5/4 test–comprehension	−·01	**·45**	·01	·11
19. ICF 5/4 test–vocabulary	·04	**·47**	·11	·00

year. Amongst the other variables, the only one which has a relatively high saturation with this factor is the CM 2(3) French test.

Factor *B* groups the French tests whether taken in the fifth year (CM 2(3) French) or in the seventh year (ICF 5/4). Amongst the other variables, one may notice relatively high saturation of the marks for 'questions on dictation' (December and March examinations) and of the scores on the CM 2(3) arithmetic test.

Factor *C* relates to the mathematics tests. Whereas for French the test taken in the fifth year had a *B*-factor saturation of the same level as the tests taken in the seventh year, the same does not hold true for arithmetic; the saturation of the CM 2(3) test is markedly less than that of the other tests. Amongst the other variables, the sub-test 'grammar' from the ICF 5/4 test is quite heavily saturated with factor *C*.

Factor *D* relates to marks for arithmetic given in the fifth year. As with French, the overall marks for the year show the highest saturation. Amongst the other variables which have relatively high saturation with this factor are the CM 2(3) arithmetic test and the marks for 'questions on dictation' (December and March examinations).

The results of this analysis, therefore, show not only a differentiation between French and mathematics, but also a distinction between the types of origin of the marks (tests or school assessments).

Unfortunately the choice of variables is not completely balanced, for we did not possess school marks for each individual subject in the seventh year. Thus additional comments must relate mainly to the fifth year. At this level, marks relating to spelling have no major saturation except that with factor A; conversely, this factor, though it possesses a slightly wider reference, is basically a spelling factor. The other factors are less clearly defined, as a result, apparently, of the overall character of the arithmetic and French tests.

The French test includes questions involving spelling, and thus approximates to factor A; whilst its inclusion of items of comprehension and grammar may explain why, like 'questions on dictation', it comes close to factor D. This latter factor, although saturating the mathematics marks in particular, probably includes a reasoning element. The arithmetic test seems to include a verbal comprehension element shown by its saturation with factor B (French tests). Lastly, the proximity in time of the school marks given in the fifth year to the results of the CM 2(3) tests must have tended to reduce the differentiation between these two types of measure.

At the seventh-year level, the only isolated saturation of importance is that of the sub-test 'grammar' with factor C (mathematics tests). We can compare this observation with a similar result obtained in an investigation at the ninth-year level. There it was observed that a grammatical analysis sub-test was closer to a mathematics test than to other French sub-tests.

b) Second-order analysis

The above analysis permits correlations between the first-order factors. If one wishes to show what these factors have in common, one can make a second-order analysis of the correlations between the first-order factors. By these means one arrives at an orthogonal structure comprising common factors and second-order specific factors. If one calculates the saturation of the variables with these second-order factors, they can be interpreted as orthogonal factors, some of which (the specific factors) correspond approximately to the oblique first-order factors, while the others (common factors) are more general and represent what is common to the first-order factors.

The method used is that of Thurstone, extended to the calculation of the saturations of the variables on the second-order factors.* Two common factors have been extracted and orthogonally rotated.

*See, for instance, Reuchlin, M. (1964) *Méthodes D'Analyse Factorielle à L'Usage des Psychologues.* Paris: Presses Universitaires de France, pp. 292-310.

	G_1	G_2	a	b	c	d	h^2
2. Arithmetic (December examination)	·34	·07	·10	·03	·10	·39	·29
3. Arithmetic (March examination)	·39	·04	·11	−·03	·04	·53	·45
4. Arithmetic (year average)	·51	·00	·10	−·05	−·02	·79	·90
8. Arithmetic (assessment)	·50	−·01	·09	−·08	−·04	·70	·76
1. CM 2(3) test—arithmetic	·38	·14	·03	·24	**·25**	·30	·38
5. ICM 5/4 test—quick computation	**·47**	·04	−·05	·05	**·53**	·03	·51
6. ICM 5/4 test—arithmetic	**·43**	·10	−·05	·17	**·55**	−·02	·53
7. ICM 5/4 test—geometry	·39	·11	−·02	·16	**·47**	·02	·41
20. ICM 5/4 test—problems	**·40**	·10	·04	·07	**·47**	−·01	·40
10. Dictation (December examination)	·12	·36	**·43**	·13	·08	·04	·35
11. Questions (December examination)	·19	·35	·33	·29	·02	·27	·42
12. Dictation (March examination)	·14	·37	**·47**	·11	·07	·07	·40
13. Questions (March examination)	·20	·30	·30	·21	·05	·24	·32
14. Composition (assessment)	·09	·34	**·41**	·14	−·01	·11	·32
15. Spelling (assessment)	·18	**·45**	**·67**	·01	·06	·10	·70
16. Dictation (year average)	·17	**·52**	**·71**	·12	−·04	·23	·87
9. CM 2(3) test—French	·24	·34	·18	**·45**	·17	·20	·48
17. ICF 5/4 test—grammar	·32	·22	·08	·27	·36	·05	·36
18. ICF 5/4 test—comprehension	·04	·20	−·02	**·43**	·06	·08	·24
19. ICF 5/4 test—vocabulary	·05	·24	·01	**·46**	·14	−·02	·29
Σa_j^2	1·98	1·39	1·81	·99	1·30	1·90	9·38

The calculation of the saturations on the two common factors and the second-order specific factors gives the structure shown on p. 83. If one studies the saturation of the variables on the specific factors A, B, C and D, one may note that the general structure obtained is the same as that with the first-order oblique factors; and that exactly the same comments can be made.

At the level of the common factors, however, the secondary analysis provides additional information. These factors correspond, in fact, to the two subjects investigated: G_1 saturates both school marks and test scores for mathematics, G_2 both school marks and test scores for French. It appears, therefore, that the main differentiation must be between subjects, and that differentiation between tests and school marks is secondary.

Summary and conclusions

In the course of a survey carried out in 1961-2, in a French Département, on adaptation to the first and second years of secondary education, a comparison was made between school assessments and marks in French and arithmetic and the results of attainment tests in the same subjects, obtained by the same pupils in the second year of secondary education and also two years earlier in the fifth year of primary schooling.

First, the various marks given by the teacher in the fifth year of primary schooling were compared. Relatively high correlations were noted between marks and assessments given at roughly the same time for the same subject; on the other hand, the correlations between marks given at different times, or between school marks and attainment tests, were much weaker.

An attempt was then made to assess the predictive validity of the information assembled in the fifth year of primary schooling. The grading of the pupils into three groups (good, average, fair) by their teachers in the first and second years of secondary schooling was one of the criteria. It was found that attainment tests provide a prediction slightly better than that which can be made on the basis of school marks; that the prediction of achievement in the first year of secondary schooling is better than the prediction of achievement in the second; that marks in French have a higher predictive validity than marks in arithmetic. These results were confirmed when other criteria were used (attainment tests taken in the second year of secondary schooling, or an overall judgment on adjustment to the first two years of secondary schooling).

A factor analysis of the attainment tests and school marks produced four factors, the highest saturations being shown respectively by the school marks in French, the attainment tests in French, the school marks in arithmetic and attainment tests in arithmetic; a second-order analysis produced a two-level structure which showed on the first level a differentiation between subjects (mathematics and French). On a subsidiary level, each subject was subdivided into tests and school marks.

APPENDIX

Correlations and residuals

	1	2	3	4	5	6	7	8	9	10	11	12	13	14	15	16	17	18	19	20
1		·39	·30	·42	·32	·30	·29	·38	·47	·25	·26	·23	·24	·08	·17	·26	·34	·11	·16	·28
2	·09		·37	·47	·20	·15	·19	·38	·26	·17	·25	·28	·22	·05	·21	·21	·20	·05	·06	·21
3	−·03	·01		·65	·22	·16	·18	·57	·26	·13	·26	·17	·31	·12	·23	·26	·19	·08	·00	·24
4	−·01	−·03	−·01		·23	·21	·19	·92	·30	·13	·31	·15	·28	·21	·28	·37	·21	·10	−·04	·21
5	−·01	−·03	·00	−·03		·53	·45	·32	·18	·10	·12	·10	·22	·06	·08	·06	·35	·09	·12	·44
6	−·05	−·05	−·02	·02	·03		·50	·24	·28	·14	·21	·07	·15	·13	·11	·12	·38	·12	·19	·44
7	−·03	−·02	−·01	−·02	·00	·04		·22	·26	·12	·20	·11	·20	·13	·13	·12	·34	·16	·15	·39
8	−·03	−·09	−·04	−·08	·03	·02	·00		·21	·12	·27	·12	·24	·25	·27	·32	·16	·08	·03	·26
9	·12	·03	·02	·02	−·06	−·01	−·03	−·04		·33	·37	·38	·35	·24	·36	·46	·38	·25	·27	·25
10	·08	·04	·00	·00	·01	−·01	−·02	·00	·02		·32	·40	·29	·23	·50	·52	·20	·12	·18	·12
11	−·02	·01	−·01	−·03	·00	·06	·03	−·03	−·04	−·01		·29	·43	·41	·35	·60	·29	·15	·24	·17
12	·05	·12	·01	−·01	−·01	−·06	−·02	−·03	−·07	·03	−·06		·31	·26	·54	·54	·20	·12	·14	·21
13	−·02	·00	·05	−·04	−·09	·00	·03	−·06	−·01	·00	−·05	−·01		·30	·34	·48	·23	·17	·12	·14
14	−·07	−·10	−·04	·03	·02	·06	·05	·09	−·05	−·09	−·08	−·09	·00		·46	·52	·19	·11	·21	·03
15	−·03	·00	−·01	−·03	−·03	−·01	·00	−·04	−·02	·03	−·08	·03	−·06	·01		·76	·24	·13	·15	·19
16	−·02	−·05	−·04	·03	·00	−·03	·01	·02	−·03	−·01	−·06	−·03	·00	·00	·00		·23	·13	·16	·15
17	·01	·00	·00	·01	−·01	−·02	−·02	−·04	·03	−·01	−·03	−·01	−·02	·03	·01	−·02		·20	·27	·30
18	−·07	−·02	·03	−·04	·02	·00	·04	·05	−·03	−·02	−·06	·00	·00	−·02	·04	−·02	−·10		·30	·11
19	−·01	−·02	−·01	−·03	·01	·00	−·03	·05	−·04	·02	−·01	−·01	−·05	−·07	·01	−·03	·03	·05		·17
20	−·03	·01	−·04	·00	·00	−·01	−·01	·03	·00	−·04	−·01	−·06	−·02	−·07	−·01	−·01	−·04	·02	−·04	

Correlations (above main diagonal) and residuals after the extraction of four factors (below main diagonal)

Centroid matrix

	I	II	F III	IV	h^2
1	·56	−·20	·07	−·12	·37
2	·46	−·20	−·20	−·07	·30
3	·51	−·27	−·35	−·12	·47
4	·64	−·40	−·55	−·25	·93
5	·46	−·42	·27	·21	·51
6	·48	−·33	·38	·17	·51
7	·47	−·28	·31	·13	·41
8	·60	−·41	−·48	−·16	·78
9	·62	·15	·18	−·17	·47
10	·46	·33	−·02	·16	·35
11	·58	·25	−·07	−·11	·42
12	·49	·34	−·07	·18	·39
13	·53	·18	−·08	−·05	·32
14	·43	·34	−·10	·07	·32
15	·60	·43	−·21	·32	·69
16	·70	·53	−·28	·17	·88
17	·52	−·08	·28	·04	·36
18	·28	·14	·24	−·27	·23
19	·31	·18	·35	−·20	·29
20	·46	−·28	·24	·22	·40

Λ

	A	B	C	D
I	·426	·331	·400	·422
II	·624	·295	−·460	−·338
III	−·224	·470	·523	−·562
IV	·616	−·764	·597	−·626

$$V = F\Lambda$$

	A	B	C	D
1	·02	·25	·28	·34
2	·07	·05	·13	·42
3	·05	·02	·07	·58
4	−·01	·03	·00	·87
5	·00	−·01	·64	·05
6	·02	·11	·64	−·01
7	·04	·12	·56	·04
8	·01	−·03	·08	·76
9	·21	·46	·17	·22
10	·51	·12	·12	−·01
11	·35	·32	·02	·27
12	·55	·09	·11	·02
13	·33	·23	·06	·24
14	·46	·14	·01	·08
15	·77	−·02	·12	·03
16	·80	·13	−·01	·17
17	·13	·25	·42	·06
18	−·01	·45	·01	·11
19	·04	·47	·11	·00
20	·10	·01	·57	·02

$$C$$

	A	B	C	D
A	1·000	−·251	·134	−·291
B	−·251	1·001	−·214	·254
C	·134	−·214	1·002	−·343
D	−·291	·254	−·343	1·000

Factorial structure and comparative validity

Secondary analysis

$$R = D (\Lambda'\Lambda)^{-1} D$$

	A	B	C	D
A	1·000	·187	−·011	·228
B	·187	1·000	·134	−·145
C	−·011	·134	1·000	·295
D	·228	−·145	·295	1·000

Correlations between primary factors

F

	I	II
A	·445	·363
B	·205	·358
C	·517	−·381
D	·387	−·338

Second-order centroid matrix

U

	G_1	G_2	a	b	c	d
A	·104	·565	·819			
B	−·076	·406		·911		
C	·641	·045			·766	
D	·514	−·007				·858

Saturation of primary factors with general and specific second-order factors (G_1 and G_2 were obtained after orthogonal rotation of I and II)

$$\Psi = \Lambda D^{-1} U$$

	G_1	G_2	a	b	c	d
I	·538	·416	·372	·321	·329	·404
II	−·465	·484	·545	·286	−·378	−·323
III	−·025	·098	−·196	·456	·430	−·538
IV	·182	·075	·537	·740	·491	−·599

Unadjusted conversion matrix

· *Tests for the secondary school*

$$\Psi a$$

	G_1	G_2	a	b	c	d
I	·545	·421	·377	·325	·333	·409
II	−·457	·476	·536	·281	−·372	−·246
III	−·030	·117	−·328	·544	·513	−·566
IV	·150	·062	·442	−·609	·404	−·494

Adjusted matrix (arranged orthogonally in rows)

$$G = F\Psi$$

	G_1	G_2	a	b	c	d	h^2
1	·38	·14	·03	·24	·25	·30	·38
2	·34	·07	·10	·03	·10	·39	·29
3	·39	·04	·11	−·03	·04	·53	·45
4	·51	·00	·10	−·05	−·02	·79	·90
5	·47	·04	−·05	·05	·53	·03	·51
6	·43	·10	−·05	·17	·55	−·02	·53
7	·39	·11	−·02	·16	·47	·02	·41
8	·50	−·01	·09	−·08	−·04	·70	·76
9	·24	·34	·18	·45	·17	·20	·48
10	·12	·36	·43	·13	·08	·04	·35
11	·19	·35	·33	·29	·02	·27	·42
12	·14	·37	·47	·11	·07	·07	·40
13	·20	·30	·30	·21	·05	·24	·32
14	·09	·34	·41	·14	−·01	·11	·32
15	·18	·45	·67	·01	·06	·10	·70
16	·17	·52	·71	·12	−·04	·23	·87
17	·32	·22	·08	·27	·36	·05	·36
18	·04	·20	−·02	·43	·06	·08	·24
19	·05	·24	·01	·46	·14	−·02	·29
20	·40	·10	·04	·07	·47	·01	·40
Σa_j^2	1·98	1·39	1·81	·99	1·30	1·90	9·38

THE PLACE OF TESTS IN SECONDARY EDUCATION (ENTRANCE, ATTAINMENT AND TERMINAL) AND THEIR USE IN SELECTING FOR HIGHER EDUCATION

H. G. MACINTOSH

Introduction

Any visitor to Britain studying the educational scene will rapidly discover that there is an immense diversity of educational provision, and that the terminology used is both confused and confusing. I propose, therefore, to talk generally of examinations in secondary schools in England and Wales, adopting the age range of 11 to 18 years as by definition the secondary stage of education. You will note that I have already used the word 'examination' and not the word 'test', but subsequently in my paper the two words may appear to be used indiscriminately. This is a reflection of the fact that both terms tend to be used in the United Kingdom. By habit we refer to 'psychological tests' and to 'mathematics achievement examinations'. In the United States the word 'tests' covers all types, and the adjective 'achievement' or 'aptitude' is added to it.

The English educational system has always been, and is today, full of examinations. We appear to love examinations within the school system, although we are much more reluctant to accept them in industry and commerce for personnel selection. This brings with it advantages and disadvantages both social and educational. I propose, however, to attempt to analyse some of the features of the secondary school examinations before I return to the theme of their aims and purposes and consider how far these are achieved.

First of all, I would like to say a brief word about internal examinations which form a normal part of any teacher's stock in trade. As R. L. Ebel points out in his book *Measuring Educational Achievement* (1965), the most active critics of contemporary school examinations recognize the need for testing within the classroom. Class tests, whatever form they may take, must be part of the classroom situation: they provide a check on the comprehension of lessons already given or activities experienced; they underline gaps in the progress made; they provide a record of progress, and additionally give practice in the necessary skills of marshalling facts, displaying knowledge and exercising judgment. I believe, however, that this activity is essentially part of the teacher's teaching methods and is more directly associated with pedagogy than with the topic of my paper.

External examinations

As I understand it, I am concerned in this paper with examinations relating to entrance to secondary schools; with virtually all tests of attainment or achievement set during the secondary school course; and with examinations taken at the end of the secondary school course which are used both as evidence of the performance achieved within the secondary school and as predictors for selectors, whether these be selectors for further or higher education or for employment.

Transfer to secondary education

The traditional age of transfer in the United Kingdom from primary to secondary education has been the age of eleven, and there can be none of you who is unaware of the controversy surrounding what has become known as the 11-plus examination. This is being dealt with in more detail in another paper, and I will, therefore, only make a few observations here. Let me say straight away that this examination has in the vast majority of cases consisted of an intelligence test very carefully prepared either by the Godfrey Thomson Unit for Educational Research (the devisers of the Moray House tests) or by the National Foundation for Educational Research, or by other experts, and has usually been supplemented by objective attainment tests in English and arithmetic. It is not easy, even today when some of the dust of battle is beginning to settle, to take a detached or disinterested view of this examination, largely because it is very difficult to separate the criticisms made on educational grounds from those more emotional in content, which form part of the case of those who dislike a tripartite system of grammar, technical and modern education. I believe, consequently, that the criticism of the 11-plus is based upon two main factors: first, that the child's future secondary education course ought not to depend upon the performance he must put up in two hours on a selected day, generally a cold wintry day in February; and secondly, that the whole idea of segregation of pupils according to ability is both educationally and socially repugnant. It is, however, ironic that the examination which was more professional in its construction and in the experimental work conducted upon it than the vast majority of secondary school examinations should have been more vilified than all these others put together. The main target of criticism was the intelligence test. This was placed within the examination as a measure of academic aptitude, largely independent of environmental influences. It was no accident that the first local education authority to include an intelligence test in its selection programme was Northumberland. By doing so, the county education authorities hoped to give better opportunities for children who came from small country schools, and who might otherwise have been at a disadvantage when compared with their urban contemporaries. In this they largely succeeded, although this success did them little good. I am not concerned here with spelling out the critics' arguments or with attempting to refute them but with the results, and in particular the overwhelming suspicion engendered concerning a general aptitude test as a predictor of subsequent success in a particular subject area. In addition, there arose a less strong but nevertheless marked suspicion among the teaching profession of the professional test man and the educational psychologist. Both these suspicions have shown themselves in recent months, the one in the attitude of the National Union of Teachers to the use of a general aptitude test in the GCE/CSE monitoring experiment (Schools Council 1966a), and the other in the over-facile assumption, which one hears very often, that objective examinations can be constructed by teachers without the need for expert advice. It may be argued that what has been mentioned above is not fact but prejudice, and therefore has little relevance in a paper such as this. Unfortunately, attitudes are to a great extent conditioned by prejudice, and developments in other sectors of secondary school examinations have undoubtedly been influenced by individual views held of the 11-plus.

I now propose to turn to the two major examinations in the public sector of secondary education in England and Wales, the General Certificate of Education (GCE) and the Certificate of Secondary Education (CSE), and to deal with each in turn, taking the GCE first.

The GCE

It is important to underline immediately the point that the conduct of examinations in secondary schools in the United Kingdom has never been in the hands of a single national examining body. Today the GCE in England and Wales is in the hands of eight boards approved by the Department of Education and Science, each setting papers upon its own syllabuses, which also have to be approved. While there would be little value in a lengthy historical digression in a paper such as this, it is necessary at the start, I think, to sketch in a little background history going back as far as 1911. In that year the Report of the Consultative Committee on Examinations in Secondary Schools was published, in the course of which, incidentally, it set out the good and bad effects of examinations on pupils and teachers in terms which merit the closest attention today. As a result of this report, a new examination was introduced for secondary schools in 1917: the School Certificate, intended for pupils of age 16, and the Higher School Certificate, to be taken two years later. The universities, which in the previous century had become involved in school examinations, and which had taken part in establishing boards for this purpose, were through these boards put in charge of the system. To provide co-ordination, the then Board of Education set up the Secondary School Examinations Council.

The School Certificate examination was a grouped examination, and this had a restricting effect upon the school curriculum. Users outside—the universities, the professional bodies, and national employers such as the banks—came rapidly to accept without question a system of certification which was convenient to them, without any real attempt to question whether it met their requirements. It is interesting to speculate how these users would have recruited staff if such certification had not existed. As a corrective, the point should be made that the population taking the School Certificate examination was a small homogeneous group, consisting as it did of the top 10 to 15 per cent of the population in ability terms and coming in the main from the same social background. Such a system was not particularly likely to welcome change for its own sake, and in consequence the amount of research conducted into the examinations and their suitability and appropriateness was comparatively small. In particular, little or no consideration was given to the question of whether such examinations could really serve the dual role which they had assumed of measuring, on the one hand, achievement at a given moment in time upon a given syllabus, and, on the other, of adequately predicting success in some future university course, career or profession. This duality was later to be carried over into the GCE system. Criticism of the system had already voiced itself in the Spens Report (Board of Education 1938), and this was to be repeated in stronger form in the Norwood Report (Board of Education 1943), some of whose recommendations came to fruition in the 1944 Education Act and led to the replacement of the School Certificate by the GCE in 1950.

Two factors in the new pattern of secondary education arising from the 1944 Act were of particular importance. First, the Act envisaged secondary education for all instead of the few who before 1939 had been able to find places in grammar schools, and secondly it provided for the immediate raising of the school leaving age to fifteen and ultimately to sixteen. These developments inevitably brought about an increased awareness of the importance of the qualifications and certification which followed the successful completion of a secondary school course, and also an increased entry for the new examination. It is worth noting that the Norwood Report recommended for the fifteen- to sixteen-year-old an internal examination under the control of teachers, following a seven-year transitional period in which external examinations would continue. The needs of universities and professional bodies they considered could be met by a separate examination at the age of eighteen. The Report also recommended that every school leaver should be provided with a comprehensive school report containing the fullest possible positive information about his or her abilities and capacities. They suggested, in addition, that objective tests should be set at intervals throughout the secondary stage, the results of which should be recorded in the school records and used for course and vocational guidance. Little attention was paid to these proposals at the time, although they were to be of great importance some twenty years later when the discussions which led to the creation of the CSE took place. Instead, the First Report of the Secondary School Examinations Council recommended in 1947 the establishment of what came to be called the GCE.

This new examination, which was established in 1950, was a single subject pass/fail examination taken at two levels: the Ordinary (originally for age 16 plus, but in practice taken by many candidates today at 15 and some even at 14), and Advanced (17 and 18 years). In addition, Scholarship papers were available until replaced in 1960 by Special papers which could be taken in not more than two subjects. In a Ministry of Education Circular, under the heading 'The main features of the new system', it was stated that the GCE was to be open to any suitable candidate whether at school or not, and that the examination could be taken in as many or as few subjects as the candidate wanted. A certificate would be awarded if only one subject was successfully taken. The crucial word in the first of these two points was 'suitable'. It was the intention of the 1947 Report that the examination should be designed for those pupils who would be completing a five-year selective course of secondary education, although, as will be seen, this was not how it worked out in practice. The administration of the examination was left in the hands of the existing university-based examining boards and was subject as before, through the Secondary School Examinations Council, to control by the then Ministry of Education on the approval of syllabuses and on matters relating to certification. This control was not, however, very clearly defined, and to some extent in practice boards put different interpretations upon their relations with the SSEC, which were in any case not entirely happy.

A marked feature of the years since 1955 has been the enormous increase in the entry for the GCE, as figures for two boards given below will show.

Board	Number of candidates	
	In 1955	In 1965
	(Summer examination only)	
Associated Examining Board	2,409	102,993*
Joint Matriculation Board	72,174	162,506

The equivalent figures for the total candidate entry are as follows:

	In 1955	In 1965
	(Summer examination only)	
All boards	243,109	664,376

(These figures include candidates who took both 'O' and 'A' level examinations in summer 1965. In the figures given for all boards, candidates who sat for the examinations of more than one board have been counted more than once.)

Much of the extension took place among the modern schools, for whom the GCE, as an examination designed for the top 20 per cent in ability range, had not been intended. This increased entry could be met in two different ways: by the expansion of the existing GCE boards, hitherto not concerned with a non-selective school entry, or by the creation of a new examining body concerned to prepare a range of subjects and to consider an approach which would meet the needs of the more diverse range of candidates now presenting themselves. Both these developments took place. The existing boards expanded, although their approach was initially slow to change, and a new board, the Associated Examining Board, was created in 1953 with the approval of the Ministry, and examined for the first time in 1955. This increased entry inevitably presented a far less stable pattern than had been the case before 1950, and highlighted what has been one of the major problems as far as the GCE is concerned—that of comparability between the boards. It could be argued with some justification that this problem is really the tip of the iceberg and that it merely highlights the need for research into all aspects of examinations. With this I would agree, but to the public at large this question is seen in terms of comparability. In a pass/fail examination comparability inevitably gets reduced to emotional terms, e.g. Mary failed with board A and passed with board B, therefore board B is easier. It is curious how very rarely

* It is worth noting that of the Associated Examining Board's 1965 figure, 29,751 came from secondary modern schools.

the conclusion is drawn that board A is more difficult. This simple eye-catching statement, usually followed by a short popular article on the unreliability of the whole system, does not really get to grips with the problem at all. As a rule no evidence is considered on the differences between the syllabuses of the boards concerned; no indication is given of the syllabus the candidate has been studying, nor of the actual result of the candidate in terms of his or her marks; e.g. in a pass/fail examination the difference may be only a mark, and this is largely a meaningless difference except, very regrettably, for the candidate. Unfortunately, not only is this information not usually known to the writers of most articles on comparability, but it has also not been used adequately for scientific study. This again underlines what to my mind has been the greatest defect of the GCE examinations, namely, the comparatively small amount of research that has been undertaken on the examinations. Here we have an examination which holds the key to entry to all universities and virtually all professions in the United Kingdom, an examination, moreover, which is not based upon a clear decision as to whether it is intended to measure achievement at a given point in time upon a given syllabus, or whether it is designed to predict success in a future university course or professional career. Yet this vitally important examination has been conducted, in effect, with an inadequate backing of professional training in statistics and measurement. The greatest pity of all was perhaps the failure of the boards some five or six years ago to agree, at the suggestion of Dr Petch of the Joint Matriculation Board, to a joint research unit. Having said all this, I would now add that the boards throughout this period have done all they can to operate the existing system as fairly as possible—scarcely a scientific principle, I fear. It would also be quite unfair to suggest that the boards have undertaken no research: one has only to look at the work of Professors Oliver and Wiseman at Manchester to give the lie to that statement; but there has been very little research, on the one hand, into the character of the GCE itself and, on the other, upon the work of all the boards considered together. Recently this situation has shown signs of altering with such investigations as the double entry on the 1966 examinations and the proposed 'A' level Physics inter-board investigation in 1968. These, and the increasing development of objective testing within the GCE, serve to give point to a view held by some, both within and outside school examining in England and Wales, that eight different examining boards are a luxury with which we could well dispense.

I mentioned earlier the extension of the GCE entry particularly among the modern schools. At the same time there was a growing demand from teachers, parents, and to a lesser extent from the users of the examination, for the development of an external examination at a lower level than the GCE, a demand which was only in part met by such organizations as the Royal Society of Arts, the College of Preceptors and the Regional Examining Unions. As a result there was a proliferation of local external examinations of which the Reading and Walsall School Certificates are examples. The then Ministry of Education had either to allow this situation to continue to develop, either with or without regulations, or to introduce a new national lower level examination designed to replace existing examinations. It took the latter step in 1961 with the creation of the CSE, and it is to this examination that we next turn.

The CSE

We have seen how the Norwood Report foreshadowed a teacher-controlled examination, ultimately of an internal character. This idea continued to gain ground, reinforced by the effects of the extension of the GCE to the modern school and by the growth of other secondary examinations. The Ministry, however, remained opposed to the creation of any new national examination for secondary schools (see Circular 289, 1955, and Circular 326, July 1957). In this latter circular, however, the Ministry conceded the need for a regionally-based examination for sixteen-year-olds for further education purposes. In 1959, the continued spread of examinations led them to consult the Central Advisory Council for Education, and CACE reported in the Crowther Report (Ministry of Education 1959-60) in favour of external examinations on a regional basis for an experimental period of five years. The work of this committee overlapped with a special sub-committee of the SSEC set up under the chairmanship of Dr Robert Beloe to study examinations in the secondary schools other than the GCE. They reported in 1960 also in favour of regional external secondary examinations. It was this last report, adopted by the Minister in July 1961, which formed the basis of the CSE. The Report set up criteria (seven in number) for the proposed new pattern of secondary examinations. The examination was to be conducted by the regional boards, each controlled by teachers from the local authorities in the areas served by the boards. Of the criteria, no. 6 stated that there should be a central consultative body to co-ordinate the activities of the regional boards and to promote research and development, while no. 7 stated that this consultative body should have the assistance of a small but highly qualified research and development group. Considerable

The place of tests in secondary education

suspicion was aroused about the role to be played in research and development by the Department of Education and Science and the effect this would have upon the freedom of action of the boards. While this suspicion has not entirely died down, it has been to a large extent allayed by the creation in 1964 of the new Schools Council for the Curriculum and Examinations to replace the old SSEC, and by the establishment under it of a CSE Standing Committee (criterion 6) and a Curriculum Study Group (criterion 7). The Department has gone out of its way to emphasize the purely advisory role of the new Council.

The new examination is a graded examination, without pass or fail, designed for an ability range of some 40 per cent below that taking the GCE, that is to say, ranging from the fortieth to the eightieth percentile of ability. Between the issue of the Beloe Report and the actual establishment of the examining boards, a decision was taken on the recommendation of the Seventh Report of the SSEC in 1963 that a grade 1 in the CSE should be regarded as equivalent to a pass in the GCE 'O' level. This decision, which was not part of the proposals of the Beloe Report, has, as I will indicate later, had far-reaching results. It was fundamental to the CSE that teachers should play a more direct part in its organization and control than had been the case with previous secondary school examinations. It is, perhaps, worth emphasizing here that critics of the GCE have tended to underestimate the part played by teachers in that examination. The most distinctive feature of the CSE examination was the introduction of an examination set and marked internally, but moderated regionally as the basis upon which certification was granted. While the normal external examination was available as well, it was hoped that schools would ultimately use internal examinations. The first of the new CSE boards came into being in 1964 and examined for the first time in 1965, so that no board has yet examined for more than two years and most have only had the experience of one examination. It is obviously too early to draw any firm conclusions, and I propose, therefore, to content myself with a few general observations.

It should be said, first of all, that the new examination has had and will continue to have a most salutary effect upon the GCE and the GCE examining boards. Initially it was envisaged that the CSE would completely replace 'O' level, but while it remains true that a considerable number of candidates who were previously entered unsuitably for 'O' level will disappear, future development seems more likely to be concerned with co-existence rather than replacement (Schools Council 1966b). This will ultimately mean the development of a common form of certification for the two examinations. Before this can be achieved, much more research on comparability will have to be undertaken. There will, therefore, be direct effects upon the GCE. Much more important to my mind, however, are the indirect effects. As a result of CSE, examinations are now news; new ideas are being discussed, and the Schools Council is producing an admirable series of booklets on experiments and new techniques. With the creation of the new Schools Council, the GCE boards have been given the opportunity to make their point of view better heard, and have been freed from direct departmental control as far as 'O' level is concerned. All this has created an entirely new atmosphere and can do nothing but good for secondary school examinations.

The opportunities for research and the need for such research have, however, underlined even more strongly the rather anomalous role occupied in this connection by the Department of Education and Science, and poses the question already mentioned above as to whether it is desirable or even necessary to continue to have the number of examining boards we have in this country. The decision taken to establish an equivalence between CSE, grade 1, and a GCE 'O' level pass, taken, one suspects, in the interests of the users and not on its educational merits, has raised the problem of comparability in an even more acute form. So long as national employers use secondary school examinations as the yardstick by which they gauge the suitability of applicants for posts, so long will they want to be assured that a piece of paper from one part of the country represents much the same as another piece of paper from another part of the country. This runs across the basic philosophy of the CSE, which aimed at providing certification at the termination of a five-year secondary course related to the work actually undertaken at the particular school and not awarded upon the basis of an externally imposed examination. Comparability is a difficult enough problem with eight GCE boards; indeed, as I have suggested, the surface of the problem has barely been scratched. How much more difficult will it be with a further fourteen CSE boards? This is not to say that it cannot be tackled, but it will require considerable sums of money and it will require, I consider, a more positive role by the body undertaking the research and development work than has hitherto been assigned to any such body in this country. Here one is on very delicate ground, as the recent controversy over the CSE/GCE monitoring experiment shows. It is also important to stress a curious incompatibility that exists within the CSE boards between, on the one hand, increased experiment and more sophisticated examining techniques—techniques which the necessity to establish comparability have made more acute—and, on the other, increased teacher participation. The two simply do not add up. As examination techniques grow more complicated, teachers may well feel less competent to involve themselves in them. The remedy here lies with training colleges and institutes of education, where a great deal more emphasis should be placed on the fundamentals of educational measurement than is at present the case. Otherwise, far from increased teacher participation, we shall have the measurement experts shrugging their shoulders and saying: 'Teachers! We only use them for public relations.'

The examinations in both CSE and GCE are all achievement tests. In the case of the GCE, the vast majority are based upon external syllabuses presented by the boards. The CSE still uses such an examination, but has, as I have indicated, placed more emphasis upon the internal school-based examination—although even here it should be noted that the school concerned is required to submit its syllabus to the examining board before approval is given. Although oral and practical examinations have been long in use, and although in the last year or two objective examinations have been introduced and increasing use is being made of course work and continuous assessment (developments which will continue to expand), the bulk of secondary school examinations in the United Kingdom remain couched in the essay form. I propose, therefore, to look next at syllabus content and types of examination and question papers, but before doing so I would like to make a brief point concerning the introduction of aptitude testing within the secondary schools for university entrance purposes. Hitherto this type of test has not existed, and university entrance has been based in very large measure on 'A' level results, supplemented on occasion by further examinations set by the university or college and by interviews. Dr Tittle will be describing in her paper the work now taking place to produce such tests, which will be tried out for the first time this autumn. If an aptitude test is generally introduced to supplement the evidence of 'A' level results, it will enable the latter to carry out the role for which they were originally conceived as measures of achievement rather than the role they have been forced to acquire as predictors of future success.

Syllabuses and the problems of their content

As has already been indicated, virtually all secondary school examinations in England and Wales are based upon external syllabuses. Unlike the United States, we live in a syllabus-dominated situation. The writing of a syllabus for a public examination is a task of great importance and considerable complexity. Basically it is a contract between the examiner and the candidate, laying down those areas of study or those skills all of which the examiner is entitled to explore and test, and at the same time limiting the examiner to those defined areas. The syllabus, therefore, must be clear and unambiguous. In practice, however, words and phrases in syllabuses have an accepted meaning almost like a mathematical symbol, and I have seen a complete mathematical syllabus which consisted of two lines—'Elements of statistics and elements of general mathematics'. Since the word used is 'elements' and not 'elementary', the same word might appear in the syllabus at age 16 or 18 or on leaving a university. Such brevity is not, however, customary.

A good syllabus is not necessarily one which on the surface is lively and imaginative, with new projects and new meanings. In a public examination the syllabus should be so framed that teachers can explore with their students their own particular interests and adopt their own attitudes, and be able, while giving rein to inspired teaching, to cover the syllabus for examination purposes. Sometimes, therefore, the more pedestrian a syllabus appears on the surface, the more freedom it may actually give to the teacher in the classroom. In other words, our tradition is to write examination syllabuses and to avoid the writing of teaching syllabuses. This, of course, becomes immediately apparent, as most examination syllabuses are set out in some convenient logical order and do not represent the order in which the topics are introduced to the schools.

One of the major problems of syllabus structure is to define the purpose of teaching a particular subject at a particular stage. For example, we in England are not a nation with adequate knowledge, widely spread over the population, of a second and third language. This is in part due to a failure to decide, for example, for what reason German should be learned by pupils from age 11 onwards. Is it so that they can read German literature? Is it so that they can visit Germany and be able to enjoy the company of German people in conversation? Is it to learn something of the German people by means of studying their history, geography, political organization and culture through the use of their language? Or is it a survival of a view that grammar and syntax in both modern and ancient languages provide the right fare for growing boys? A problem experienced in the writing of examination syllabuses may be summarized in the two words 'breadth' and 'depth'. This is true at all ages. There is real educational value in probing deeply ('deeply' being rationally interpreted in relation to the pupil's age bracket), but there is also real value in the broader survey of a variety of topics and the acquisition of some perspective of the setting in which they are to move. I find that many of the syllabuses with which I am concerned try to solve this problem by dividing the examination into two parts, the first of which is broad and general, and the second of which provides many options from which a choice can be made for a study in depth.

One final word concerning examination syllabuses: they must necessarily be confined to topics which provide examinable material. For this reason in the past they have too often encouraged study only of what is thought to have been examinable material, and this is one of the causes of an over-emphasis on the acquisition of facts in our educational system. I shall attempt later to show that by improving examination techniques we can and should expand the examinable material to the totality of the subject content.

Examination procedures and techniques

The syllabus may be tested or examined in a variety of ways. The majority of secondary school examinations in the United Kingdom are presented to the candidate in essay form, and the candidate is awarded his mark or grade in the main upon pieces of continuous writing. Use has been made of oral and practical tests, and in the last few years objective tests, course work and continuous assessment by the teacher have been introduced increasingly. The purpose of this paper is not to compare the advantages and disadvantages or the merits and demerits of these varying facets of the examination, but to indicate some of their uses and problems. We should concern ourselves first and foremost with our objectives, and then afterwards decide how best we can measure what we wish to measure; to do otherwise is to involve ourselves in fruitless argument.

Written narrative

Until recently no other form of written test would have found general acceptance by teachers in the United Kingdom, and this prejudice is only slowly being broken down. If I disclose a personal view by the use of the word 'prejudice', I must hasten to add that it is founded on a very real and lively fear that the character of the teaching will change and deteriorate, and that the mere acquisition of facts will become an even greater component of too much teaching should the continuous narrative disappear entirely from secondary school examinations. Recent research in the United States, moreover, indicates that continuous writing adds something, in subjects such as English and history, not achieved in any other way, to the picture presented of the candidates through testing. On the other hand, there are subjects such as mathematics and science where an unnecessary amount of such writing can obscure the picture and prevent the candidate from doing full justice to knowledge which the setters of the examination would regard as highly relevant. The main trouble with the written narrative is its highly subjective nature, and ironically it is this that gives it real value, since the candidate is provided with an opportunity to express something of his or her own personality. Serious disagreements can, however, result from the marking, which in a pass/fail examination can have disastrous consequences. One can, of course, overcome many of these differences by an extremely elaborate mark scheme, but this is helping to bring about the very restriction which it is hoped the narrative will avoid. Such an approach, therefore, would seem to have little to recommend it beyond ensuring greater uniformity in the marking. There are three other possibilities: first, multiple marking which is usually, although not inevitably, carried out on an impression or holistic basis; secondly, an increase in the number of pieces of writing upon which the candidate is judged; and thirdly, greater care in the wording of the questions, by this means ensuring that the candidate is guided in his approach to the topic upon which he is questioned. All these create both administrative and educational difficulties, but, used sensibly and in combination, they can do a great deal to improve the reliability of the written narrative. It should not be assumed, however, that these approaches need to be confined to narrative answers in the more literary subjects and in particular to English, although here, of course, the problem is most critical. Research has shown that multiple marking is equally applicable to biology, and the Nuffield Physical Science Project is determined that continuous writing shall form an integral part of their new examinations. It should also not be assumed that the examination as a whole will consist of narrative answers. An examination containing a variety of components, for example, written and objective questions, an oral test and course work, may well be both difficult and expensive to construct, but is likely to provide a fuller and therefore more realistic and positive picture than an examination embodying only one type of assessment.

Objective tests

Very great interest has been created recently in the United Kingdom by objective tests, and considerable work is being undertaken to introduce them into both the GCE and CSE examinations. I think I should say at the outset that it is not yet widely enough appreciated that objective tests can do more than test factual recall and elementary analysis, and in consequence most of their introduction is in fields which require this kind of response from the candidate. The breaking down of this view is, I think, only a matter of time, but it has had the effect of making some people assume that it is comparatively easy to set objective questions; this has resulted in the setting of bad questions which confirm existing prejudices concerning such questions. There is another equally important danger: that by emphasizing the necessity for 'good' items and 'good' tests, and the problems of constructing such items and tests, a mystique of measurement is built up and a belief created that objective examinations can only be constructed by experts. This would be a very harmful development. What is wanted is a middle course: the maximum involvement by teachers and members of examining board staffs, and, at the same time, having available constructive and expert advice from people trained in measurement problems. We seem at the moment to be engaged in rather a wasteful duplication of effort, and there is a good case for all the examining boards co-operating in setting up a common objective test unit which could provide the measurement expertise which the boards will need, leaving them free to develop their own ideas in the way they feel most appropriate to their needs.

Before this can be achieved, if it ever can, there is something far more fundamental that needs consideration, and indeed decision, and that is: what are our motives in England and Wales for introducing objective tests? Are they purely an administrative convenience, designed to save costs in marking an increasingly large number of scripts? Is it hoped that they will improve the reliability of the assessment and shrink the standard error of measurement, or are they merely a new technique which any 'with it' examining board should concern itself? As is so often the case, the motives are confused, and involve, I suspect, all the factors I have mentioned. My own view is that their justification should be in the shrinkage of error that can result from their use, but I do not see objective tests as the only way to achieve such a shrinkage. A lot more can be done to improve the narrative questions by additional marking and greater care in wording. Questions can be objectified without becoming completely objective. I see the GCE examination, in so far as it remains external, increasingly becoming a composite examination involving objective questions, open-ended questions, guided narrative and questions of the narrative type used today but multiply marked. All this is a great deal easier said than done. The balance of such a composite examination is of vital importance; educational and administrative considerations have to be weighed up. It is no use having an extremely reliable and valid test if you cannot issue results until months after the date by which the candidates require them. It is, moreover, idle to assume that such an examination, even after all the research for its initial development has been undertaken, will save money: the reverse will be true. I said earlier 'the GCE in so far as it remains external'. This was deliberate, for I foresee within the next five years a very considerable development at GCE Ordinary level of the internal examination as envisaged in the CSE. With the possible development of a common grading system for the complete range of ability at present taking CSE and GCE 'O' level, it could be that the two examinations will merge. Whether this happens or not, internal examinations will, I believe, increase enormously. So long as examinations continue to be used in this country as they are at present, so long will the problem of comparability be acute. An objective common core achievement test, based not upon a specific syllabus but upon what subject experts think it is reasonable that teachers should cover in their teaching (as practised at present in the United States), would provide one means of monitoring such internal examinations and provide criteria against which the school's own assessments could be judged.

It will not be possible to say much about other types of examination in the scope of this paper, but there are a few points I would like to make concerning orals, practicals, course work and continuous assessment. It should be noted that these are all concerned with the measurement of achievement, and I would regard them as widening the canvas upon which the candidate can paint his picture, thus ensuring a more realistic assessment.

Oral tests

There are in a modern language two aspects to an oral test: aural, which is the understanding by the candidate of what the examiner has said to him in the foreign language; and oral, which is the candidate's ability to express himself simply and coherently in the foreign language. A good examiner has always been aware of these two elements, but considerable research is in hand to identify tests which give credit for abilities in both these elements. These two aspects are, of course, present to some extent in any oral test, although they do not require at this stage the same consideration as in modern languages.

The introduction of oral examinations in subjects other than modern languages and English is a comparatively recent one at the school level, and even in English has not gone as far as many teachers would like. Its great advantage would seem to be in the opportunity it provides for a

The place of tests in secondary education 107

pupil to reveal his general interests in a particular subject—interests which the traditional examination may never disclose. Essentially, therefore, such examinations must be flexible, and herein lies the difficulty. They are time consuming and expensive; they are not easy to conduct fairly for all candidates; they run the risk of creating an artificial situation in a test which ought essentially to be natural; and there are additionally very great problems of standardization.

It is perfectly true that some, if not all, of these objections apply with equal force to written examinations, and it is true that some of them can be overcome by using internal and not external examiners. The increased availability of equipment such as tape-recorders will also help. Moreover, as practice and experiment increase, so will our knowledge. At the moment, however, in subjects like general studies or history the use of an oral examination would seem to pose more problems than it answers, and it would appear that its main value initially would be to provide evidence on these very problems as well as providing additional evidence on the candidates' performance which could be used for border-line decisions.

Practical tests

Traditionally in subjects which involve some practical skill—laboratory work in chemistry, cookery in domestic subjects, wood and metal work in the crafts, performance on an instrument in music—a practical test has been set. In most cases I think this is desirable. In some British universities you can obtain a doctorate in music without any evidence whatever of ability to play a single instrument. In some school examinations candidates sit, and in fact pass, in chemistry who have never in their lives been in a chemical laboratory. Examining boards have, therefore, resisted the removal of the practical test lest it should lead to the abandonment of practical work in the schools or, more realistically perhaps, to a diminution of its importance.

The approach, however, to the practical examination or test in any subject is essentially linked with the view of the teaching of that subject within the schools. For example, more and more teachers are adopting the view that children in schools should not only learn about science but learn what science is. Not so long ago science to many a pupil meant that he or she would be given facts to learn by heart or numerical problems to solve or an experiment to prove something. A candidate could easily fail the examination if he was unable to recall enough facts to satisfy the examiner. Attitudes to science teaching have changed considerably in the last decade, and the Nuffield Science

Teaching Project has done much to encourage this. Although not everyone accepts the Nuffield ideas in their entirety, few would disagree with the view of the Project that science has to be presented to pupils as a way in which they can conduct an inquiry into the nature of things. This approach opens up several possibilities for practical tests in the future, ranging, on the one hand, from the abandonment of the practical as such and its replacement by multiple-choice or open-ended questions designed to test a candidate's ability, and, on the other, to the development of more stimulating 'inquiry' questions in the practical test. There is also the possibility of testing the practical, as is done at university level, by an assessment over a longer period of time. All these methods have possibilities not only in the sciences but in other subjects where practical skill is an essential ingredient. Experiments with these approaches will not only increase the reliability of the practical tests, but stimulate the candidate to produce better work.

Course work

There are obviously subjects in which the examination of course work is essential if the examination is not to be unduly restrictive. This course work can be prescribed by the examining body either in detail or in broad terms, or it can be left to the school to provide illustrations of the candidate's ability in a particular direction which is relevant to the subject concerned. It is generally considered to involve the candidate not in one specific piece of work at one particular time, but in a number of pieces of work over an extended period of time. The varieties are infinite. In some cases the work can be kept in a folio as with art work and be available for inspection. This work can be looked at by an individual and compared with other collections of course work. In other cases this approach is not possible, and the judgment made is more like that considered below in continuous assessment. The problems of establishing comparability in course work are, of course, great, and the following points ought to be considered: the possibility of applying an adjustment factor to take into consideration the fact that the work may not be that of the pupil only and to minimize any halo effect in the assessment; the availability of course work for assessment; the weighting to be given to course work in the final assessment; and the extent to which a good course work mark should be allowed to affect a poor examination mark.

Continous assessment

By continuous assessment is meant an assessment by the educational institution involved of some particular aspect of the candidate's work (e.g. writing ability) based upon work over a period of time. It is, therefore, a teacher's assessment, taking in a wider view of the candidate over a longer period than is possible by an examination. In such an assessment it is vitally important first of all to establish the criteria on which it should be based, and secondly to consider the weighting to be given to the element of continuous assessment within the framework of the examination. The list given below of the possible uses that could be made of the marks or grades given indicates the problems involved. They could be:

1. Combined with marks from an external examination.
2. Scaled on the results of an external examination.
3. Scaled on the results of an internal examination.
4. Used in making border-line decisions.
5. Used to increase marks but never to decrease them.

The danger of the backwash effect from the use of continuous assessment is also important, since it may result in the examination being transferred from one day to as many occasions as are used to provide evidence for the assessment. At present many teachers are reluctant, probably because of their unfamiliarity with the use of continuous assessment in relation to public examinations, to undertake to provide the necessary mark or grade.

Question papers

I have already spoken about the different types of examinations which are possible, but there are certain characteristics of all question papers which we should perhaps examine. Quite clearly there are certain obligatory routines to be observed, such as the fact that questions must fall within the syllabus, must provide a fair sampling of the syllabus, and must be clear and unambiguous in wording. I have referred earlier to the fact that in order to facilitate inspired teaching it may be that the syllabus will appear somewhat arid or stodgy. On the other hand, this does not mean that the pupil is given this impression from the paper. A candidate should find the paper, even in examination conditions, lively and exciting and a challenge, provided that he is interested in the subject and has worked at it. He should feel that it is fair, that it gives him a chance to show his abilities, and that it gives him opportunity to exploit his special interests. This may sound a very tall order, but it is not so—a good paper can give to the good, the average and the indifferent student the opportunity to show his best. This, of course, satisfies one of the most important criteria of public examinations, namely, that they are not designed to catch out the student because of his or her lack of knowledge; they are designed as opportunities to make certain that if candidates can possibly show that they are worthy of a pass they can secure one. At the same time, an examiner in setting a question paper must think carefully about the critical points in his final awarding processes. It may be that there will be three grades, 'pass', 'credit', 'distinction', or there may be, as in the GCE 'A' level, five grades known by the letters A, B, C, D and E. The paper must, therefore, provide for these varying critical limits. There must be sufficient to ensure that the candidate who should pass just secures a grade E. There must also be opportunity to recognize the ability of a candidate who should secure a grade A. This, of course, returns us to the point at which I began, that where an examination serves a single purpose it is relatively easy to design a good paper, but where a paper serves a variety of purposes—and an 'A' level paper with five grades does indeed do this—it becomes increasingly difficult to design a paper and a mark scheme which achieves this multiplicity of objectives.

We ought now, in considering question papers, to consider what kind of standard of pass mark the examiner has in mind. There is, of course, the tradition in Britain that 40/100 or perhaps 45/100 is a creditable performance, and therefore this represents the pass mark. The implications of this view are very far-reaching. It means that papers are set upon which a candidate deserving the bare pass will just reach 40 per cent and neither 41 per cent nor 39 per cent! It would be equally tenable to accept a view that the papers should be set so that the same candidate would reach, for example, 70 per cent and neither 69 per cent nor 71 per cent. Personally I think that public examinations in the United Kingdom have accepted too easily the old university view that fifteen questions were set, and if you answered three, you were given first-class honours; if you answered two, you were given second-class honours; if you answered one, you were given third-class honours; and if you wrote your name on the paper, you were allowed an ordinary degree. It is significant, for example, that when it came to the training of technicians in the Royal Air Force, the type of question paper was such that at the end of the course the pass mark was of the order of 80 per cent or 90 per cent. It is clear that one does not wish to increase examination hurdles, but it does appear that a good deal of research is required into the meaning of a pass so long as we retain the pass/fail concept, and a good deal of research should be undertaken on whether the better method of examining would be to have the more difficult test with a low pass mark or the easier paper with the high pass mark. The whole of the determination, not only of the syllabus content and the nature of the test set whatever the techniques used, but also of the education in the classroom, must necessarily be influenced by any preconception as to the range in which the pass mark will ultimately be fixed. This, in turn, is a reflection of a decision whether to have a simple pass/fail concept, or to have various grades of pass and fail, or to abandon the pass/fail concept and to issue all results in grades so that the total examination result gives, as it were, a profile of the candidates' ability in the subjects for which they have entered.

Assessment

The problem of reliability and validity are too well known to make it appropriate for me to expatiate on them here. Nevertheless, they are at the root of the quality of our examining in secondary schools. I will therefore content myself with a few reflections on points associated with these two concepts.

The first is the traditional view which we have as to what earns a mark in an examination. For example, in mathematics a subsection may be marked on the basis of (a) method–3, accuracy–2, total–5; or it can be marked on the basis of (b) method–2, accuracy–3, total–5. This small difference, particularly if spread over the whole of the paper, means that a chief examiner in one case is giving 60 per cent for method and in another case 40 per cent for method, which will, of course, profoundly affect the results not merely at the border-line but throughout the whole range. Great care is normally given to the preparation and moderation of question papers, and equally great care is given to the determination of the final pass mark and the award of pass or fail and of grades of pass. I think that perhaps too little discussion has taken place concerning the actual detail of mark schemes, which are of such importance in the narrative-type paper, or in the traditional mathematical and science papers. I have referred earlier to the definition of the objectives of an examination containing objective questions where clear decisions must be made in advance on the weighting to be given to the various elements of the syllabus and to such matters as, for example, in mathematics, the marks to be awarded for method on the one hand and for accuracy on the other. It is equally important that similar decisions be taken, whatever the form of the examination and whatever the subject, in order to give the appropriate emphasis.

Secondly, it has become important in the United Kingdom

examinations at GCE level that various grades of pass should be achieved for such purposes as entry to the universities and to the various professions. The grades of pass in the GCE, together with their mark equivalents, are described below:

Advanced level

	Grade	Mark range
	A	70+
Pass at	B	60-9
'A' level	C	55-9
	D	50-4
	E	40-9
	O	25-39
Fail	F	0-24

Ordinary level

	Grade	Mark range
	1	70+
	2	65-9
Pass	3	60-4
	4	55-9
	5	50-4
	6	45-9
	7	42-4
Fail	8	35-41
	9	0-34

It is idle to pretend that in large public examinations equal care can be given to the determination of the critical values in nine grades at Ordinary level and seven grades at Advanced level. No doubt a correct procedure which most boards would follow is carefully to examine the performance and quality of candidates at, say, grades 1 and 6 at the Ordinary level and grades A or B and grade E at the Advanced level, and having done this to determine the intermediate grades on a statistical or *ad hoc* basis.

Thirdly, I believe that we have to examine afresh the whole of what I would call the pass/fail concept. It is a requirement of society that at the end of a medical course the doctor should either be passed out as fit to practise or not. This is true of the professions; it is true at all kinds of levels. But is it appropriate for the secondary school pupil either

The place of tests in secondary education

during his course or at the end of the course? We must examine afresh the whole concept of whether we should think at all about passing or failing, or whether we should, as it were, issue a profile giving in some form or another the candidate's, or rather the pupil's, complete performance in all the subjects which he has studied. It is, I think, because of the pass/fail concept that so many members of the public, parents in particular, are worried about the examination processes upon which so many children's futures depend. There must always be an element of chance in the determination of a clear dividing-line between those who have passed and those who have failed. For example, if an employer wishes to recruit staff and he receives twelve applications for only three vacancies, a dividing-line must be drawn somewhere. There may be little between no. 3 and no. 4 in the selection, but the employer only wants three and he must make an arbitrary decision. This is also true when the time comes to say that an architect has qualified or has not qualified, but is it an appropriate type of decision to apply to the young adolescent leaving school with all kinds of abilities and defects? The examination assessment needs, in my view, a new look based upon a concept not of passing and failing but of accurate preparation of profiles of his abilities, indicating the area of his achievement in the various aspects of his school studies and of his school life.

Use of results

Both in the past and today, examinations, as far as their use is concerned, may be divided into four main categories: examinations for the maintenance of standards; examinations for the provision of incentives; examinations for the provision of guidance to administrators, selectors, parents or teachers; and examinations to provide assistance with the restructuring of society. It should be emphasized that any one examination can, of course, have more than one purpose, or, to put it another way, that the same examination can serve a different purpose for a different person. For example, the GCE examination provides for the pupil an incentive to effort; this also applies in a slightly different way to parents and teachers. For the school administrator it provides at the Ordinary level a device for presenting the sixth form teacher with a relatively homogeneous group of pupils, and for the university selector it provides at the Advanced level a device for selecting a group who will benefit from a university course. In these last two cases it could also serve as a competitive entry examination, if the number of places in the sixth form or the university were limited or the demand exceeded the supply. For the teacher the success or failure of his pupils in the GCE provides one yardstick against which he can measure his success as a teacher, and for the headmaster or local education authority it can also be one yardstick against which the success of the school or authority can be measured. It can be used also by the school to raise entrance standards by providing a target at which to aim. Finally, it can be used as a social tool by identifying the nation's potential leadership and ensuring that the supply is constantly maintained. A mere reading of the above will indicate how inextricably the uses made of examinations are interlinked, and how they affect different people in different ways. In this country we have tended to make our examinations serve many purposes instead of designing them for one specific purpose. This is as true of the 11-plus as it is of the GCE. Nevertheless, the multiplicity of examinations in the United Kingdom is already so great that I think we must accept the challenge and seek a solution to the problem of designing examinations which can effectively fulfil more than one purpose.

Value of examinations

In the opening paragraphs of this paper mention was made of the value of the internal test both for teacher and pupil. The social and educational values of examinations in general, of which the secondary school examinations considered above form but a part, are considered in these closing paragraphs. It is well worth while emphasizing the points for and against by setting them out in full, even though they will be well known to those listening to this paper. For the pupil, examinations give a definite ladder of progression against which he can measure his particular progress against that of his fellows. They compel him to work to a regular timetable in order to produce his best at a given date. Since he is required to answer specific questions, he must marshall and organize his knowledge and then reproduce it in a coherent and comprehensible form. Finally, the pupil is compelled to study some parts of a subject which may not interest him as much as others. But examinations can equally have bad educational effects on the pupil. They can turn him into a mere recorder of other people's ideas; they can make him more concerned with facts than ideas, and can encourage the acquisition of knowledge for the sake of success in the examination rather than for its own sake.

For the teacher, on the other hand, an examination will encourage him to treat his subject thoroughly and as one worthy of study in its own right. The course of study is, moreover, one which must be

The place of tests in secondary education

progressive and aim to cover a prescribed course within a definite period of time. It also enables the teacher to become acquainted with the standards of other schools and other teachers, and to compare his own with theirs. On the bad side an examination may cause a teacher to limit the treatment of his subject; to regard the examination syllabus as his teaching syllabus; and to regard the passing of the examination as the main aim of his teaching. Examinations may, moreover, encourage him to over-value qualities among his pupils that make for success in examinations.

All these educational values and defects are present in some degree for both pupil and teacher in an examination or test, however it is constructed and whatever its components. The aim of those engaged in the construction of examinations in whatever sphere should be the enhancing of the values and the minimizing of the defects. Research is required not only into types of examination but also into purposes—research which I have suggested has not hitherto taken place within the secondary school field in this country. This need for research is heightened by any consideration of the social values of examinations. Important as are the educational values, the social are even more vital. It is clear, however egalitarian a view one may take of society, that society needs methods of selection; if not tests, what else? Nepotism? Quite unacceptable in theory in a democratic society, even if condoned in practice. Interview? Research at Harvard would suggest that as a method taken by itself interview is as unreliable and subjective as any written examination. Record of achievement? This has obvious merits in that it provides a profile taken over a long period of time.

The answer seems to be in a combination of techniques: tests, records of achievement and interviews should all prove valuable as components of the total evidence available to the selectors. Selection, however, does not mean the same thing in all countries at all times. It is clearly wasteful to allow all those who wish to become doctors to enter upon an appropriate and expensive course of training only to discover that they are not capable of completing it. Here one cannot lower the requirements, since society must ensure that those who look after its health reach an acceptable standard of expertise. The selection process must, therefore, act as a sieve, and the more accurate the sieve the more beneficial it will be to all concerned. This approach is necessary for the professions, and many would argue that it should be extended to business and industry if we are not to continue to be inefficient and to waste money. What view, however, are we to take of higher education? Should our selection process here be designed to eliminate the majority of those for whom higher education is considered unsuitable, thus viewing higher education as a means of developing an educational *élite* who will be responsible for the running of the country, or does one take the view that society as a whole will benefit from the extension of education for a longer period to virtually all who wish to take advantage of it? In the latter case, the selection process would become more concerned with the provision of information upon which the receiving agencies could make their choice. A decision as to which course to adopt is fundamental, and is one which must drastically affect our instruments of selection. In the past we have taken the view that the ladders to higher education should be discrete and few in number, and in consequence our selection instrument has been asked to measure the kind of academic success which is likely to make a candidate suitable for the universities or the professions. At the same time, the growth of examinations among secondary school children at age 15 or 16, where they form the end of their course, has caused the same GCE examination to be used as a measurement of achievement which will be valuable to potential employers. The result of this multi-purpose approach is that at present they fulfil neither role very efficiently. They neither predict accurately nor do they provide sufficient relevant information. This confusion is partly a confusion of our society; we do not appear to have made up our minds what kind of higher education we want for our population. Until this dilemma is resolved, it seems likely that we shall ask our examinations to continue to serve more than one purpose. But this should not be used as an excuse for regarding the examinations with any sense of complacency and satisfaction. The necessity for research and development, and the opportunities, are immense. To say this is really to say too little; such work should be obligatory for all who are concerned with selection or with the measurement of achievement, at whatever age or educational level.

References

Board of Education (1938) *Secondary Education with Special Reference to Grammar Schools and Technical High Schools* (The Spens Report). London: H.M. Stationery Office.

Board of Education (1943) *Curriculum and Examinations in Secondary Schools* (The Norwood Report). London: H.M. Stationery Office.

Ebel, R. L. (1965) *Measuring Educational Achievement.* Englewood Cliffs, N.J.: Prentice-Hall.

Harvard University (1945) *General Education in a Free Society.* The Report of the Harvard Committee. Cambridge, Mass: Harvard University Press.

Head, J. J. (1966a). 'Multiple marking of an essay item in experimental "O" level Nuffield Biology examinations.' *Educ. Rev.*, 18, 3.
Head, J. J. (1966b) 'An objectively marked practical examination in "O" level Biology.' *School Science Rev.*, 48, no. 164, 85.
Joint Matriculation Board (1963) *The JMB–What It Is and What It Does.* O.P. 16. Manchester: Joint Matriculation Board.
London University (1964) *GCE London.* London: London University.
Mather, D. R. et al. (1965) *The CSE. A Handbook of Moderators.* London: Collins.
Ministry of Education (1959-60) *15 to 18.* Report of the Central Advisory Council for Education (The Crowther Report). 2 vols. London: H.M. Stationery Office.
Ministry of Education (1960) *Secondary School Examinations other than the GCE* (The Beloe Report). London: H.M. Stationery Office.
Ministry of Education (1963) *Half our Future* (The Newsom Report). London: H.M. Stationery Office.
Schools Council (1966a) *The CSE Monitoring Experiment.* Working paper no. 6, pts 1 and 2. London: H.M. Stationery Office.
Schools Council (1966b) *Examining at 16+.* Report of the Joint GCE/CSE Committee. London: H.M. Stationery Office.
Schools Council (1967) *Standards in CSE and GCE English and Mathematics.* Working paper no. 9. London: H.M. Stationery Office.
Secondary School Examinations Council (1947) First Report. London: H.M. Stationery Office.
Secondary School Examinations Council (1963) Seventh Report. London: H.M. Stationery Office.
Wiseman, S. (ed.) (1961) *Examinations and English Education.* Manchester: Manchester University Press.

SITUATION AND PROBLEMS OF EDUCATIONAL AND VOCATIONAL GUIDANCE IN BELGIUM

J. STINISSEN

If we are to discuss the situation and problems of educational and vocational guidance in the Dutch-speaking part of Belgium, a few words about the *organization of secondary instruction* in Belgium are not out of place, as, I imagine, tests in secondary schools are used in other ways and pose other problems in countries with different educational systems and curricula.

In Belgium secondary instruction normally begins at the age of twelve years and comprises six years of schooling. Pupils have the choice between general education and technical education. General education does not specifically prepare them for a vocation or further studies, and is given in the so-called humanities. The first period of three years is subdivided into two major sections: namely, the Latin section, which from the second year onwards also includes the study of Greek or a more profound study of mathematics; and the modern section with no study of ancient languages. In the second period of three years the Latin humanities are subdivided into three sections: Latin-Greek, Latin-mathematics, and Latin-sciences, and the modern humanities also into three sections: scientific A or mathematics (with seven to nine hours of mathematics), scientific B (with five hours of mathematics and five or six hours of physics, chemistry and biology), and lastly the economics section. These six sections are somewhat different in level. The pupil has no choice between courses or levels of courses within these sections. After graduation he may continue his studies at university or in a higher technical school.

As an alternative to this general education in the humanities, the pupil can have from twelve years of technical education in one of two levels, viz. the more theoretical technical and the more practical instruction, the latter called vocational school. Both sections comprise a lower cycle of four years ending with a specialized certificate, and an upper cycle of three years which follows on the third year of the lower cycle, and again leads to a certificate in some technical or vocational specialization. In all, there is a choice between some 600 final specializations. After graduation the student may continue his studies in a higher technical school, but many enter employment.

I have given this brief description of the educational system in Belgium in order to emphasize that in my country it is expected that pupils and their parents will be given guidance on the choice of a level of instruction and of a specialization or section at least three times: at the end of primary school, at the end of the lower cycle, and at the end of the upper cycle.

Educational advice is given for the first time *at the beginning of secondary instruction*. There are, however, two standpoints and practices in this respect that largely coincide with the distribution between private (catholic) and public guidance centres. In private centres, testing is carried out during the last year of primary school, i.e. before entry to secondary school, with the implicit or explicit assumption that it is possible at this age to give advice on the choice of at least a level, if not a section, of secondary instruction, and that this is desirable in order not to prejudice the gifted children. Pupils who have not had a psychological examination in the primary school are examined at the beginning of the first year at secondary school to obtain a basic psychological file for use in further guidance. Sometimes all the pupils of the first year of secondary school are examined in order to discover if they have greater aptitude for the Latin-Greek or for the Latin-mathematics section, or, on the other hand, for the technical or for the vocational school (the first year of which is common to both). In most public centres, however, psychological examination takes place, not during the last year of primary school, but during the first year of secondary school, and is seen from the point of view of desirability of establishing a common educational cycle of three years (with some optional courses and the possibility of easy transition between them). For these guidance centres the psychological examination is the basis for educational guidance (without immediately giving advice), and mostly leads to an explicit prediction of school marks on the basis of a regression equation. After comparison of estimated and obtained marks, the under-achievers can then be given guidance, while other pupils are transferred to another section.

We prefer the first approach. We find it better not to let gifted children waste their time in heterogeneous classes with a level of instruction below their capacities. Good diagnosis and prognosis will surely prevent too many pupils from becoming under-achievers who will need individual guidance or transfer in the course of their secondary studies. Consequently in the last year of primary school or in the first year of secondary school a rather large battery of group tests is given, which takes a full school day at least. This battery is mostly composed of one or two verbal or verbal-numerical intelligence tests, a non-verbal intelligence test, sometimes a memory or an attention test, an achievement test for language and arithmetic, an interest test and a personality test. The Government—which subsidizes the guidance centres—moreover requires a social inquiry (which may be done by means of questionnaires filled in by the pupil, his parents and his teacher) and a medical examination. If any problem arises out of the analyses of the tests or the questionnaires or from the discussion between the guidance team and the teacher, the examination is completed by individual testing and by interviewing the pupil and his parents.

During the last year of primary school, intelligence tests attain a high level of validity; in schools with an unselected population, verbal intelligence tests such as the Group Intelligence Test of Coetsier (University of Gent) or that of Stinissen (University of Leuven) attain a concurrent validity with school marks of median rho 0·70 to 0·80. In somewhat more homogeneous classes preparatory to the humanities and consequently with a selected population, concurrent validity is still expressed by a mean rho of 0·60 to 0·67. Non-verbal intelligence tests, such as the LV 3 or the Progressive Matrices attain even in heterogeneous classes only a mean validity coefficient of about 0·50. When predictive validity is calculated against a criterion of success three years later (level of education and success combined into a ten-point scale), these verbal and even the non-verbal tests show correlations of 0·52 to 0·58.

An achievement test (called SVT 5678) is usually administered in the heterogeneous classes, but not always in the more homogeneous preparatory classes. In fact, when the counsellor has experience of the grading system in those classes and of that in the humanities of the same school, he often uses the school marks (which in our country are expressed in a percentage of points, in which every course is weighted in accordance with the number of hours it is given, and usually also in a rank within the number of pupils of the class) as a predictor (in a clinical way) for success at secondary school. The value of such school marks is conclusively proved in our country. Spoo (1959) reported a correlation coefficient (corrected for restriction of range) between marks in preparatory class (N = 168) and marks in the first year of the Latin section of 0·91, in the second year of 0·86 and in the third year of 0·83. Swinnen (1961) obtained a biserial r between school marks in the preparatory classes of thirteen secondary institutions and success versus failure in the lower cycle of the humanities (of the same school) of 0·78 for the Latin-Greek section and 0·65 for the modern section (N = 332 and 240). Smet and Stinissen (1961-2) found a correlation of 0·62 between school marks in the preparatory classes of six secondary schools and failure in six successive years of the Latin humanities; only 37 per cent (419 pupils) graduated, but only 21 per cent at the right time, i.e. after six years, whereas the other 16 per cent had to repeat one of two classes. It seems, then, that the use of an achievement test is most necessary with pupils who come from independent primary schools, or with pupils who change schools between their primary and secondary education.

A remarkable test battery constructed by Nuttin and Swinnen (1961) is called the *Humanioratest* (humanities test). It is composed of a general intelligence test (five subjects with multiple-choice answers, adapted from the Cattell Intelligence Scale, plus an arithmetic reasoning test with free answers) and a Latin prognosis test (an adaptation of the Orleans-Solomon Latin Prognosis Test); it uses, moreover, the school rank in the preparatory class as a statistical predictor. This battery yields a multiple R of 0·89 with success versus failure in the lower cycle of the Latin section, and of 0·75 in the modern section. It is interesting to see that the validity of the separate predictors in this battery is as follows for the Latin section: school rank 0·81, aptitude to learn Latin 0·63, verbal ability 0·56, abstract reasoning 0·53, numerical reasoning 0·50. In the modern section the coefficients are lower, and arithmetic reasoning occupies the fourth place, abstract reasoning being the least valid predictor.

Still more recently, a Differential Aptitude Battery was published by Coetsier *et al. (Differentiële Geschiktheidsbatterij,* 1966). The mean correlation coefficients with school marks in thirteen sixth-grade classes range from 0·53 to 0·68 for each of the four verbal and numerical tests (the coefficients are higher for girls than for boys), and from 0·24 to 0·46 for each of the four tests of spatial and mechanical insight, the multiple R being 0·51 to 0·73 (boys and girls, preparatory classes and independent sixth-grade classes taken separately). This battery yields a multiple R between scores and school ranks in the first year of secondary institutions of 0·42 to 0·60 (boys and girls; Latin, modern and technical sections); taking account, however, of the previous school rank, the Rs range from 0·57 to 0·84.

As an interest test the adaptation of the Canadian test by Moreau and Vinette is preferred; it differentiates between four interests (ipsatively tested)—literary, technical, commercial and scientific; such a differentiation seems sufficient at this age level. We are now examining the existence of interest patterns for the first year of the different sections of secondary school.

As personality tests the Aspects of Personality (Pinter) or the Tree Test (Koch) are often used. Also sociometry is frequently used by our guidance centres as a base for helping poorly adapted students. We are now ready with an adaptation of the California Test of Personality for this age level. After two item analyses, fifty-two questions were retained for personality adjustment and fifty-two for social adjustment. The parts have a reliability of 0·88 and 0·93 respectively. They discriminate significantly the well-adapted from the poorly adapted quarter of each class as judged by their teachers. Moreover, both parts differentiate significantly between pupils in the upper and pupils in the lower half of school marks (r_{bis} 0·43 and 0·32).

The second level at which a choice must be made by our pupils is at the end of the lower cycle, i.e. after three years of secondary schooling. At this age level we have more problems, certainly because of the more homogeneous and sometimes highly selected classes. In some schools the mean I.Q. of the Latin humanities is as high as 128, with a standard deviation of only about half that of the age group, in other schools it is only 117; and in vocational schools the mean is as low as 90. Testing has always been more commonly practised in the higher levels of the secondary instruction than in the lower, though guidance is now given to almost all pupils of about fifteen years old.

Again a whole-class testing programme is administered together with a social inquiry and a medical examination, and the testing programme is eventually completed by individual testing and interviewing. At this level we have not much choice of intelligence tests, and the tests are standardized on the population of the different sections and not on age groups. We have only for a few years been able to use adaptations of different tests of Bonnardel, viz. the omnibus intelligence test A, OIT and BV9 and the verbal intelligence test BV 50-16-8N. These tests have concurrent validity coefficients with total school marks or marks in native language of 0·39 to 0·51. A numerical aptitude test (DIT, arithmetic reasoning and completion of digit series with free answers) shows correlations with marks in mathematics from 0·39 to 0·52, whereas the same test (extended at the lower end) yields *r*s of 0·63 for boys and 0·82 for girls with arithmetic in the sixth grade. Another test of numerical aptitude with multiple-choice items yielded a correlation of 0·32 with marks in mathematics, of 0·31 with total school marks in the humanities, and of 0·22 in the technical school. Even after repeated item analyses of representative groups of the level for which the tests are designed, the mean validity coefficients do not rise above 0·50. Of course, these tests may be considered to be more valid for differentiation in the whole population of fifteen-year-olds, but this does not help us very much; for we are asked to give guidance to pupils in the homogeneous classes we mentioned, and we find that we are unable to differentiate well within such groups or, in other words, to make predictions more than 13 per cent better than chance.

At this level non-verbal tests are rarely used; sometimes the

Progressive Matrices (Raven 38) is used, and recently the *Test d'Intelligence Logique* (a Canadian test of fifty multiple-choice items) was tried and yielded a correlation of only 0·25 with total school marks in technical school. The following predictive validity coefficients have been reported between tests applied in the third year of secondary school and academic success three years later (expressed on a ten-point scale combining level of study and credits gained) (N = 60 to 95):

> Verbal group test Coetsier 0·48
> Verbal group test Stinissen 0·25
> Progressive Matrices 38   0·30
> D 48 (a non-verbal *g* test) 0·19

Tests of special abilities have not yet been studied sufficiently in our country. Sometimes a special test (e.g. of the DAT) or a mechanical comprehension test (e.g. of Rennes) or the *Calcul des Longeurs* (Faverge) are used, but without much knowledge of their value. We were able to demonstrate a concurrent validity of 0·21 to 0·41 for different courses in the technical school with an adaptation of the Revised Minnesota Paper Form Board, and we are now working on the field of spatial and mechanical tests and in general on the problem of differentially valid tests. We have not yet found an adequate solution for the construction of tests with differential validity that might predict the specific section and not only the level of instruction for which the pupil has aptitudes. Certainly Mollenkopf's (1952) distinction between differential and comparative prediction is relevant here, the latter being the case when we wish to predict the degree of success in two or more sections and not only to decide the question of which section will assure more success. As many courses are common to many sections, though the level of the courses may differ, the battery should contain a generally valid test and yet be able to predict success in different sections without loss in differential validity. Still more specifically, however, if we construct a test of, say, mechanical information to be administered in the third year of all sections, but used to predict success in the fourth year of the technical school, ought we to select items that discriminate only in the year of the technical school and not in the other sections, in which it is equally applied and standardized, or ought we to select items that discriminate in the total population of the third year of secondary school?

At this level of about fifteen years of age we have no published achievement tests. Work has been done with a Latin achievement test of 100 multiple-choice questions. A split-half reliability of 0·84 was reported, and a correlation of 0·61 with marks in Latin and of 0·47 and 0·54 with total school marks for boys and girls respectively. The construction of a mathematics achievement test yielded after the first item selection a reliability coefficient of only 0·80 for fifty-six multiple-choice questions, and a correlation with marks in mathematics in the humanities of about 0·50. Many counsellors, however, think it useless to give achievement tests to any pupils except those who have changed schools; for students considering going up within an institution, school marks seem to have sufficient predictive validity. Swinnen (1961) showed that the mean of marks obtained in the lower cycle of the humanities correlated 0·78 and 0·79 with the mean school marks in the higher cycle of the modern and the Latin humanities respectively of thirteen schools. Stinissen and Smet (1961) found a biserial r of 0·61 between the mean marks in the lower cycle and graduation with and without repeating one of the three classes in the higher cycle in five schools.

As for interest tests—the adaptation of Irle's *Berufsinteressetest* or of the Kuder Preference Record are most used. We are now studying the existence of specific interest patterns for the different sections of secondary school and of different patterns for good and poor students.

There is not much to be said about personality tests. Some psychologists analyse the pupils' work habits by means of Coetsier's concentration test, which takes half an hour or an hour divided into periods of three minutes; some use the Tree Test or sociometry or some experimental test. Our adaptation of the Heston Personal Adjustment Inventory with six traits showed a critical ratio on the 1 per cent level of significance between mean scores of subjects judged by their principal teachers to represent the extremes of the traits for analytical thinking, emotional stability and confidence, and an r_{bis} of 0·16 (5 per cent level) and 0·21 (1 per cent level) was obtained between analytical thinking and home satisfaction and school marks respectively.

Important, however, for diagnosis and prognosis at this level seems to be the *Studiegewoontentest* by van Hove (Study Habits Inventory 1963), standardized for the first, third and sixth grades of secondary school. It comprises six sub-tests for study techniques and a twenty-seven-item inventory for study habits. The manual demonstrates the discriminating value of the two parts between the extreme quartiles of good and poor students.

The third level at which tests are used in secondary schools is the last year. Students of about eighteen years then receive educational and eventually vocational advice. The main choice they have to make is between a university education (mostly of four or five years, but seven for medicine) and higher technical school (with courses of two, three or four years) or normal schools, unless immediate entry into an occupation seems indicated. At this level we are in great need of tests which demonstrate at least an acceptable level of concurrent validity and preferably a sufficient predictive validity.

The most frequently used intelligence test is a Flemish adaptation of Amthauer's *Intelligenz-Struktur Test*. This test consists of four verbal sub-tests, two numerical and two spatial tests and a memory test. It has been used since 1958, but nothing has been published on the value of the adaptation. On the basis of experience the value of the test was doubted, and data from many centres were collected. Correlations between the different parts of the test or even of the whole test with school ranks in the humanities reached only 0·20 for 2,206 boys and 0·25 for 1,314 girls both for the verbal part and for the whole test, the numerical-spatial part and the memory test yielding only coefficients of 0·09 to 0·15. In the different sections of the technical school for boys mostly non-significant coefficients were obtained, with 0·15 for the verbal part as well as for the whole test in the whole group of 718 boys. In the technical school for girls, however, many significant correlations were obtained for separate sections, some as high as 0·40 to 0·50; yet for the total group of 712 girls the whole test yielded only a correlation of 0·05, this probably proving that the school marks of these different sections cannot be combined into one distribution. The predictive validity of the test is now being studied on this representative sample of students. At present the results are not yet known.

After these disappointing results, an attempt was made to adapt Heim's high-grade intelligence test (AH 5), which consists of a verbal-numerical omnibus test and a non-verbal omnibus test of forty-eight and thirty-six items respectively. After two items analyses, between which the test was supplemented with new items up to more than its original length, only twenty-four and thirty-two items could be retained. The whole test of fifty-four items then showed a split-half reliability of 0·81 and a median correlation with school ranks of 0·28, which was not very encouraging.

In some centres Coetsier's *Algemene Ontwikkelingstest* (a general information test) is used. It shows correlations of 0·27 and 0·25 for girls in the humanities and in technical school respectively, but only 0·15 and 0·11 for boys.

Many psychologists in our guidance centres thought that it was more realistic to use some test of paragraph reading with multiple-choice questions, or to ask the students to précis and synthesize a text read aloud to them or studied by them within a set time. As to the first kind of test, a thorough adaptation of the Davis Reading Test was tried out. After the second item analysis a selection of sixty items gave a split-half reliability of 0·84 and a median rank correlation of 0·30 in twenty-seven classes of the humanities. The test showed a correlation of 0·54 with the adaptation of the AH 5 (N = 209), and also an r of 0·57 with Stinissen's Verbal Group Test administered six years before (N = 85).

As to the second kind of test, a study was made of the introduction of Maria Rosseels' essay *'Het woord te voeren past de man'* ('To act as spokesman suits man, tacitness ornaments woman'), a test of one and a half pages read aloud twice to the students, who have to reproduce the test trying to give the main ideas with their logical structure and relations, and to précis it in one or two sentences. It is clear that the correction of such a test is a laborious and subjective task. One of my students, however, has now elaborated a key comprising eleven discriminating points. By applying this key, the test yielded a normal distribution of scores and an inter-scorer reliability of 0·94 (N = 100). Yet the median rank correlation with school marks was only 0·17 (fifteen classes), the median rank correlation for the Amthauer IST in the same classes being 0·12 for the total test and 0·22 for the verbal part. The scoring of the précis of the text on a three- or five-point scale could be done with an inter-scorer reliability of 0·98 and 0·93 respectively, but it did not show a significant relation with intelligence or school rank. This kind of test does not seem to be any more useful than the more economic tests.

At this level we have no achievement tests.

As an interest test, the Kuder Preference Record is generally preferred. Though the search for interest patterns in the different sections of secondary school and of higher education is still going on, it was already established that computational and scientific interests had significant correlations with school grades in the last year of the humanities, viz. 0·13 and 0·24 for the Latin-Greek section (boys and girls) and for the mathematics section (boys only), but not for the economic section, whereas persuasive interest generally shows a negative correlation, which is also significant in the Latin-Greek and mathematics sections for boys. Also, in technical school the scientific scale seems to be the most predictive and the persuasive scale the most negatively predictive.

As to personality tests, different tests are used, though often in an experimental form, e.g. Cattell's 16 Personality Factors Questionnaire or Thurstone's Temperament Scale (both with too low reliability for their scales), the typological questionnaires of Berger or Gex (activity, emotionality, secundarity) or the Zulliger group or individual test. The Gordon Personal Profile, however, though difficult to adapt because of its forced-choice technique, yields a sufficient reliability for its four scales (0·80 to 0·89), low intercorrelations of the scales, and significant to very significant correlations between the scores of the subjects and the ratings by their classmates.

Very important at this level seems to be an appreciation of the motives and study habits of the students. Van Hove's *Studiegewoontentest 641* appears to be one of the most interesting tests at this level. Though the study techniques part gives only a correlation with school marks of 0·16 for boys (N = 402), it shows an r of 0·31 for girls (N = 323), while the study habits inventory gives an r of 0·35 and 0·34 for boys and girls respectively. The correlations in technical school (on smaller populations) were of the same order. Moreover, the twenty-seven questions of this part are a good starting-point for a subsequent interview about the study habits of the students. A similar but more elaborate questionnaire about study habits including motivation, examination stress, feeling of being able to cope with the demands, etc. (Gellynok), is being studied. Applied in the last year of the humanities, the fifty-seven most predictive questions out of 176 gave an r of 0·30, with success v. failure in the freshman year at the university.

By way of *conclusion*, I should like to stress that severe and repeated item analysis and selection is necessary, and has to be done on the specific population for which the tests are designed. But even then it seems difficult, if not impossible, to construct tests that show by themselves concurrent validities with school marks higher than 0·50 for the more homogeneous groups at the 15-year level and higher than 0·30 at the 18-year level. In the coming years it will certainly be necessary to elaborate multiple regression equations and to establish better the predictive validity of tests in our country. Up to now, some idea of the predictive validity of kinds of tests is gained by studying the concurrent validity of such tests at a higher age level. In the meantime, our psychologists have to use mental weighting of the examined aspects and the clinical approach in order to appreciate more fully the personality aspects that seem to gain in importance over the results of intelligence tests when students reach a higher level of education and become more selected by the grading system in our schools. At every age level school marks appear to be the best predictors of success, at least within the same school.

One further remark is to the point in order not to give the idea that in our country educational and vocational guidance is only a matter of diagnosis and prediction. Collaboration of the teams of our guidance centres—which consist of psychologists, social workers and nurses—with the teachers results in a constant follow-up of the students. Under-achievers and other problem cases are more thoroughly examined (by means of individual intelligence tests such as the Terman-Merrill Scale, the WISC, WAIS, SON, etc., or with projective techniques such as the Rorschach or the TAT) and interviewed in order to find the cause of their problems. They become the subject of individual care and guidance. Improvement of their study methods and their motivation is then attempted, and counselling is given to students and parents in cases of emotional or social maladjustment. If necessary, medical treatment and guidance is also afforded.

References

BIT, *Beroepen-Interessetest* door Dr M. Irle. (1960) Nederlandse bewerking van Dr S. Wiegersma. Groningen: J. B. Wolters.

Cloet, L., van Hove, W. and Vermoere, W. (1961) *Handleiding Schoolvorderingentest 5678.* Brussel: CSBO-uitgaven.

Coetsier, L., Geenens-Thurman, M. and Coetsier, P. (1966) *Opbouw en analyse van een Differentiële Geschiktheidsbatterij voor het einde van het Lager en de aanvang van het Secundair Onderwijs* (2nd edition). Gent: Labor. Toegep. Psychol.

Coetsier, L. (1945) *Nieuwe normen bij het intellegentieonderzoek.* Deinze: Caecilia Boekhandel.

Coetsier, L. (1959) *Praktische handleiding bij het algemeen collectief onderzoek.* Deinze: Caecilia Boekhandel.

De Hertog, W. (1966) *Aanpassing van het Gordon Personal Profile voor leerlingen van het laatste jaar HSO.* Leuven: Niet-gepubliceerde licentiaatsverhandeling.

Depauw, R. (1967) *De aanpassing van de California Test of Personality voor leerlingen van het 6e jaar L.O.* Leuven: Niet-gepubliceerde licentiaatsverhandeling.

Dudal, P. (1968) *Aanpassing van de Davis Reading Test voor het laatste jaar M.O.* Leuven: Niet-gepubliceerde licentiaatsverhandeling.

Handleiding bij de 'Algemene Omnibus-Intelligentietest' (AOIT) (1962) Nederlandse aanpassing door M. Geenens-Thurman en V. Mortier van de V 1.2-test van Prof. R. Bonnardel. Mont-sur-Marchienne: ATM.

Handleiding bij de Collectieve Niet-Verbale Intelligentietest L.V. 3. Brussel: CSBO-uitgaven.

Handleiding bij de Kuder Preference Record. Vlaamse aanpassing bewerkt door de CSBO-Limburg. Brussel: CSBO-uitgaven.

Handleiding bij de test BV 9N (1963) Nederlandse aanpassing van de test van Prof. R. Bonnardel door een werkgroep van PMS-Rijkscentra onder leiding van R. de Froidmont. Mont-sur-Marchienne: ATM.

Handleiding bij de tests 'Beschouwingen': BV 50 en BV 16, en bij de test 'Taalbegrip': BV 8 (1962) Nederlandse bewerking van de tests van Prof. R. Bonnardel door een werkgroep der P.M.S.-Rijkscentra onder leiding van V. Mortier. Mont-sur-Marchienne: ATM.

Hooyberghs, J. (1967) *Aanpassing van de AH5: een collectieve intelligentietest voor het laatste jaar van de humaniora.* Leuven: Niet-gepubliceerde licentiaatsverhandeling.

Mion, A. (1958) *Handleiding voor de gestandaardiseerde aanpassing en bewerking in het Nederlands van de IST, Intelligentiestruktuurtest Amthauer.* Brussel: Editest.

Mollenkopf, W. G. (1952) 'Some aspects of the problem of differential prediction.' *Educ. psychol. Measur.,* 12, 39-44.

Mortier, V. (1962) *Beroepen-interessetest. Aanvullende handleiding bij de Vlaamse Versie.* Brussel: J. B. Wolters.

Nuttin, J. and Swinnen, K. (1961) *Overgang naar het Middelbaar Onderwijs* (2nd edition). Leuven: Leuvense Univ. Uitgaven.

Piron, H. L. (1967) *Belangstellingstest voor 12 jarige jongens naar Moreau en Vinette.* Brussel: CSBO-uitgaven.

Poppe, D. (1966) *Aanpassing van de Heston Personal Adjustment Inventory voor leerlingen van het derde jaar Secundair Onderwijs.* Leuven: Niet-gepubliceerde licentiaatsverhandeling.

Smet, W. and Stinissen, J. (1961-2) 'De uitval tijdens de Humaniora en zijn oorzaken.' *Tijdschr. Opvoedk.,* 2, 73-89.

Spoo, M. (1959) 'Praktijkervaringen in het Lager Middelbaar Onderwijs. *Tijdschr. Studie- en Beroepsoriënt.,* 6, 58-63.

Stinissen, J. (1955) *Collectieve Intelligentietest.* Leuven: Leuvense Univ. Uitgaven.

Stinissen, J. (1967) *Differentiële Intelligentietest-Numeriek deel.* Brussel: CSBO-uitgaven.

Stinissen, J. and Meynaerts, L. (1966) *Handleiding bij de Belangstellingstest voor meisjes naar Moreau en Vinette.* Brussel: CSBO-uitgaven.

Stinissen, J. and Smet, W. (1961) 'De prognose van succes en mislukking in de hogere cyclus van de Oude Humaniora.' *Tijdschr. Studie- en Beroepsoriënt.,* 8, 49-58.

Swinnen, K. (1961) *Prognose van het studiesucces in het Middelbaar Onderwijs.* Leuven: Leuvense Univ. Uitgaven.

Vanden Bavierre, E. (1967) *Studie van een proef voor Intellectuele Maturiteit. Het samenvatten van een tekst en het weergeven van zijn hoofdgedachte (synthese).* Leuven: Niet-gepubliceerde licentiaatsverhandeling.

Van Hove, W. (1963) *Studiegewoontentest 641.* Brussel: CSBO-uitgaven.

SOME EXPERIENCES WITH AN EDUCATIONAL TESTING PROGRAMME AT THE END OF THE SIXTH GRADE

G. J. MELLENBERGH and A. D. DE GROOT

1. The big divide at twelve

Traditionally in Holland, the sixth grade of elementary school has been a critical year. It is after this period—when the child is about twelve—that parents must choose which of three totally different kinds of education their child will, from then on, receive.

The three types of school are:
1. The academic (gymnasium and HBS). The pupils who possess the diploma of this type of school may go to university and to higher professional schools.
2. ULO. This type of school trains for the clerical vocations.
3. LNO. This type of school consists of several vocational and technical schools.

The situation is roughly comparable to the British system, except that 'public schools' of the British type have never existed and that the movement for comprehensive schools is not yet very influential in the Netherlands. A school reform is in operation, but it does not seem likely that the main features of the system will be strongly affected by the resulting changes.

These main features, then, result from and reflect the strong emphasis on selection in the Dutch schools. At every grade of all three types of secondary school there is a year-long 'struggle for life' to be promoted to the next grade. The numbers of students who fail to make it vary from school to school, but the averages are dishearteningly constant and high. For instance, in the academic schools the average percentage of yearly failures is about 25—regardless of grade. In spite of the increase of the secondary school population and many other social changes over the years, this figure has remained constant for nearly a century.

A student who is not promoted to the next grade can do one of three things. He (or she) may repeat the grade all over again, he may change to another school type, that is, be 'degraded' to another educational/social class—in fact, this is generally experienced as a degradation—or he may leave the general educational system altogether. Included in the latter case are changes to vocational schools of various types, a number of which do not require a completed secondary education (diploma).

Selective and competitive as the system is, it confronts teachers and parents of sixth-graders in particular with the very difficult question: 'In which type of school has the child the best chances of succeeding?' Generally, parents tend to choose for their children the most promising of the three possible tracks,* that is, the 'highest' in which they hope the children will survive. In principle, parents have the right to choose, but actually the elementary school-teacher is the most influential person, in two ways: first, in guiding parents in their choice; secondly, in giving the receiving secondary schools information about each candidate's abilities and suitability. In principle, the receiving school is free to decide which candidates it will admit, but this freedom is strongly restricted by various regulations.

2. Amsterdam 1966: introduction of achievement tests

In the city of Amsterdam, up to 1966, recommendation by the head-teacher of an elementary school was practically sufficient to admit a child to an academic school. Candidates not recommended by their head-teacher—a small minority, in fact, of the (25 per cent) sixth-graders who apply—were given an entrance examination. This examination is of the traditional essay type. By a Royal Decision of 1965, however, it was decreed that recommendation by the head-teacher alone was not sufficient to admit a child to an academic school.

In addition, the ability of the candidates for the academic schools had to be ascertained by one of the following four methods:
1. Entrance examination, not only for candidates not recommended by their head-teachers, but for all candidates.
2. A 'trial class': for one week all the candidates are brought together in classes of the academic schools, where they follow a special programme, and are observed and evaluated by the teachers of these academic schools.
3. A roughly specified achievement test.
4. Psychological tests.

It was evident that the number of candidates for the (municipal) academic schools in Amsterdam (about 1,500) was too large for the organization of 'trial classes'. The organization of a psychological testing programme would be difficult, too, for the same reason. Moreover, according to the Royal Decision, psychological testing for this purpose was only allowed with the permission of the parents of each child. Further, there was a rather widespread dissatisfaction with the entrance

---
*Actually, there are many more than three possibilities and all sorts of combinations. There are, however, three main groups.

examinations. In the end, the Council of Amsterdam chose the achievement test method.

The job of constructing the achievement tests for this programme and of organizing the data processing was given to two institutes, both related to the University of Amsterdam.* In January 1966 the contract was signed. The testing was carried out, according to plan, in four morning sessions, on 29 and 30 March and 21 and 22 April. On these days, some 6,000 sixth-grade pupils—of all the municipal schools—were simultaneously tested.

3. The testing programme

The programme consisted of 274 items altogether, divided over fourteen sub-tests. Thirteen sub-tests were of the multiple-choice type; one sub-test ('orthography') was constructed as a completion test. Seven sub-tests tested aspects of knowledge of the Dutch language, five aspects of arithmetic and quantitative relations, two aspects of 'general knowledge' (with subject matter mostly from geography, history and biology).

The children were tested in their own classrooms and instructed by their own teachers. To each class, one representative of some secondary school was, more or less randomly, assigned to oversee the procedure and to help out in case of emergencies. The testees gave their answers immediately on IBM answer sheets, except for one orthography test where the teachers had to correct the pupils' work and to complete their forms.

An adventurous and risky part of the project was, of course, that none of the (6,000) children nor any of the (200) school-teachers had ever done anything like this before. Moreover, the time for preparing both the tests and the organization was no more than a few months. As a result, no briefing meetings could be held; we had to rely completely on carefully written instructions, on some emergency communication by telephone and, of course, on the organizational and supervisory power of the municipal superintendents. The way all this worked out was relatively perfect—in spite of many warnings and predictions to the contrary.

In order to provide the academic schools with the individual data they needed for their selection decisions, six percentile scores were computered for each candidate (in each of which a few sub-test scores were combined):

*The Research Instituut voor de Toegepaste Psychologie (director A. D. de Groot) and the Nutsseminarium voor Pedagogiek (director P. J. Idenburg).

1. Language I (59 items)
2. Arithmetic I (50 items)
3. Total of L I and A I
4. Language II (50 items)
5. Arithmetic II (33 items)
6. Total of L II and A II

'General knowledge' scores were not given to the academic schools. The differences in the elementary school curricula were considered too large to justify any reliance on these scores; they were reserved for research purposes.

In view of the highly experimental character of the whole project, academic schools were urged to accept all candidates recommended by the head-teachers—as they had done in previous years. In the case, however, of candidates who were not recommended, the percentile scores on the achievement tests could be used in deciding whether or not to admit the candidate. So far for the procedure.

4. Reactions and critique

This whole procedure has been strongly and emotionally criticized by many teachers and educationists in the Netherlands. For some time the *Schooltoets* has been a topic in newspapers and professional journals for teachers. In the *Schooltoets* dispute many of the old arguments against the multiple-choice form known from the history of achievement testing in the United States were revived. There were also many people who reacted against the automatization. The headline of one article in a weekly read 'The child in the computer'.

In some cases the consequences of the testing procedure were actually feared: school averages could possibly be compared and *mis*used by the authorities, etc. The latter argument was only rarely voiced openly, it is true. But for many of the, highly individualistic, Dutch elementary school-teachers who do not want the authorities to interfere with what they do in the classroom, this was no doubt a strong underlying motive against the programme. Without objective measuring instruments, comparisons between schools have to remain inconclusive; and that was exactly the reason why many preferred the old situation.

Not all criticisms were irrational or wrong, however. As a result of lack of time the communication with the teachers had been restricted to instructions on what they were expected to do. There had been very little previous contact about the subject matter. Generally, the teachers were not previously informed about the long-term possibilities of the project as the investigators saw them. Apart from the fact that the

Royal Decision had to be carried out, one way or another, the reasons why the investigators were in favour of this particular solution and why they had accepted this hurried job of test construction, could not be sufficiently discussed.

5. The investigators' motives

The latter question must be briefly answered before we proceed.

First, then, the Royal Decision on the selection for academic schools was primarily just an occasion for introducing achievement testing on a large scale. Improving the selection procedure was certainly *not* the primary concern of the investigators. Rather, they wanted to introduce achievement testing as a necessary means for educational research, for educational change and educational management based on objective information; and, in particular, as a means of starting concrete discussions on educational goals and of putting these goals into effect. In Holland, this is a terribly neglected area.

Secondly, in introducing achievement testing the test constructors wanted and had to overcome prejudices. Until quite recently, the majority of teachers and professors of every level in the Netherlands were strongly against objective examinations in general. Most of them had no experience of the method, but, even so, they were against it. At present, this situation is rapidly changing. In this process, the first *Schooltoets* project was a landmark, or rather, it was a surprise capture which was possible precisely because of the hurried nature of the project!

It can now be said that the bridgehead has been maintained; it has extended to a five-year project encompassing all Amsterdam sixth-graders (12,000) and a few other cities as well. Contact with the unknown method has appeared to be an effective way of overcoming unfounded resistance. Now the real discussion can begin: on content, form, on educational goals, on the best uses of the instruments, etc.

6. Some findings

Were the tests satisfactory from a psychometric point of view?

Apart from a few rough statistics derived from the total frequency distribution, test and item analyses were carried out on a systematic sample of 427 subjects. We give some results for the four main (sub-)tests, namely Language I, Arithmetic I, Language II and Arithmetic II (see section 3 above, 1, 2, 4 and 5).

Reliabilities ranged from 0·79 (A I) to 0·89 (A II) according to Kuder-Richardson formula 21 (lower limit), with upper limits, according to van Naerssen 1966, from 0·85 to 0·92.

Testing at the end of the sixth grade

The *intercorrelations* were: between the two arithmetic tests: 0·84; between the two language tests: 0·78; between arithmetic and language tests: ranging from 0·70 to 0·74.

Validities could be computed with one (concurrent) criterion only, namely, enrolment or not—that is, the parents' decision whether or not their child should apply for admission to an academic school. Since in actual practice this decision, while based on a strong parent-school interaction, has always been by far the most influential single selective (self-selective) variable, it can be considered a criterion measure. It reflects largely the old, rather satisfactory situation, and should therefore correlate substantially with the new variables. The biserial correlations were 0·82 and 0·74 for the two arithmetic tests, and 0·72 and 0·71 for the two language tests.

As to the *item statistics*, none of the correlations (phi coefficients) between item and main test scores were below zero, while only five (out of 274) item validities were negative. Generally, the results of the item analysis showed that the test constructors had done a fairly good job.

A *factor analysis* based on the intercorrelations of all fourteen sub-tests resulted, after hand rotation, in a clear-cut structure of three groups of sub-tests:
1. Five tests for 'general school intelligence' (the two 'general knowledge' tests, two reading comprehension tests and one idiom test—loaded on factor I only).
2. All five arithmetic tests (loaded on factor I and II).
3. Four language tests of a more technical nature: orthography and grammar (loaded on factors I and III, and weakly on II as well).

Finally, a few specific questions could be answered. To mention one, the hypothesis that the two orthography sub-tests in the series—one completion, one multiple-choice—measure the same variable, was not confirmed; corrected for attenuation, the correlation coefficient was 0·78.

7. Final comments

As was stated above, the *Schooltoets 1966* has now been transformed into a five-year project. In this project it will also be possible to compute predictive validities with criteria of school success, and so find out whether the tests are good predictors. However, it must be emphasized again that this is by no means the main goal of the investigators. In a system where selection is permanent and where survival is to a large extent determined by non-objective, relative standards and by situational factors, it does not make much sense to try to improve to perfection the selective efficiency at *one* particular point.

In the Dutch system—which cannot be described here in all its complexity—it is, rather, of primary importance to introduce achievement testing as a means of defining educational goals. Apart from the indispensability of achievement tests as criteria in educational research and educational policy, we need them in the Netherlands to stop the present process of arbitrarily relative and permanent weeding out that goes on in our schools. For that purpose, the development of achievement tests is far from sufficient; but it is necessary to have them available.

At present some progress can be reported—the project is one case in point.

VALIDITY STUDIES ON HIGH SCHOOL LEVEL AND THE INTERPRETATION OF INCONSISTENCIES IN RESULTS

Z. SARDI

Over a third of Israel's population of two and a half million attend various educational institutions, and more than 110,000 are at high schools. This is the population with which I am concerned here.

Israel has nine years of compulsory education: one year in the kindergarten (age 5 to 6), and eight years in the elementary school (ages 6 to 14). After that over 80 per cent go on to academic, vocational or— recently established—comprehensive high schools. Most of these schools have a four-year course which leads towards the Bagrut (matriculation) and/or a vocational certificate.

Drop-out rates from high schools are high: of the 20,000 who enter academic high school only about 55 per cent graduate. The others discontinue their studies, mainly because of academic failure. Another 15 per cent of the graduates of the academic high schools fail in the country-wide Bagrut (matriculation) examination. In vocational schools the drop-out rate is somewhat lower. But, even so, only about 25 to 30 per cent of the pupils who enter high school obtain the matriculation certificate, a necessary, though not the only, condition for continuation of studies at university level.

These high drop-out rates have led the high schools (most of which are non-governmental and non-municipal) towards selection of their applicants, in order to avoid economic waste, individual frustration and difficulties in teaching. They have also caused guidance bureaux to lay special stress in the guidance of eighth-graders on the academic aptitudes required by the high schools.

In selecting pupils for the high schools we use only psychometric tests, whereas in guidance these tests are only one—undoubtedly the most important—of several tools, used to predict future high school performance including the chances of obtaining the Bagrut certificate.

Before I can give you the results of two follow-up studies comparing recommendations based on a psychometric test administered to eighth-graders with their Bagrut certificate marks, I must give you more information on our high school system and on the Bagrut certificate.

In elementary school and during the first two years of academic high school, the curriculum is the same for everybody. From the tenth grade onwards students specialize either in the humanities or in the sciences. A year later humanities are split up into social studies, literature and sometimes other fields such as Near-Eastern studies. The sciences are split into biology and mathematics-physics. This is only a general outline, and there are many subvarieties. Bagrut examinations, of course, vary according to the field of specialization chosen, so that at most four of the six examination subjects are common to all: Hebrew language, English or French, Bible studies and mathematics (two levels). The other two subjects are different for each field of specialization. This diversity of criteria makes follow-up studies difficult.

Marks range from 4 (failed) to 10 (excellent). 6 is considered to be the pass mark, though a single 5 in the certificate is acceptable. The marks of the Bagrut certificate are those of the Bagrut examination, modified by teachers' ratings.

The following criteria for success in high school studies were used alternatively:

1. The number of failure marks in the matriculation certificate.
2. The average matriculation certificate mark.

The institute of which I am the director has been engaged in guidance testing of eighth-graders as well as in selection testing of high school applicants for over twenty years. Some of the psychometric tests we use are translated foreign tests adapted to conditions in Israel, but most of them are locally constructed and validated. The battery, which may at the same time serve for guidance and for selection purposes, usually includes two to three verbal, two to three numerical, and two form perception pencil and paper tests, as well as two group performance tests and two to three interest inventories and questionnaires. Pupils are tested in groups of twenty and the testing session lasts about two and a half hours.

The test scores are evaluated and used in different ways for selection or for guidance. In guidance the results of single tests are usually presented in percentile form for easier explanation to teachers and parents. Though the final recommendation is based on the test results, they are freely evaluated. The counsellors take into consideration the testee's social background, year of immigration to Israel, previous scholastic achievements, and other factors. The recommendation is phased as 'fit', 'fit with qualifications', 'doubtful fitness' and 'unfit' for both academic and vocational studies, where:

'fit' means that no failure marks (5 or less) are expected in the Bagrut certificate;
'fit with qualifications' one or two failure marks are to be expected
'fitness doubtful' non-completion of studies, or three or more failure marks in the Bagrut examinations are to be expected;
'unfit' total failure in the early stages of high school should be expected.

The first follow-up study which I shall present was conducted in 1960 on a country-wide sample of eighth-graders tested in 1955; it showed the results given in table 1.

Table 1. The predictive validity of recommendation—testees of 1955

	Accurate prediction	Partial prediction	Conjectured prediction	Failure in prediction	Total
Numbers	126	33	27	13	199
Percentages	63·32	16·58	13·57	6·53	100·00

where 'accurate prediction' means exact correspondence between the recommendation and Bagrut marks;

'partial prediction' means a deviation of one degree in either direction;

'failure in prediction' means a deviation of two or more degrees in either direction;

'conjectured prediction' means the recommendation was 'fit' or 'fit with qualifications', but Bagrut marks are not available ('doubtful' or 'unfit' were classified as 'failure').

A second follow-up study conducted in 1965 on a sample of Jerusalem eighth-graders tested in 1959—a more restricted range than the country-wide population—shows similar results.

Table 2. The predictive validity of the recommendations—testees of 1959

	Accurate prediction	Partial prediction	Conjectured prediction	Failure in prediction	Total
Numbers	141·4	83·4	58·1	35·0	317·9
Percentages	44·48	26·23	18·28	11·01	100·00

It may be concluded that if the results of our tests are applied in this way, rates from high schools and failures in the Bagrut certificate may be cut down from 70 per cent to about 35 per cent. This procedure would bar from entrance to high school two or three probably successful out of every 100 who wish to continue their studies. But it is no mean achievement in four-year prediction, and the greater part of it can be attributed to psychometric tests.

Sometimes when applied to a specific school even better results are achieved. To quote an extreme case: of 122 applicants who over three years were diagnosed as potential failures but were nevertheless accepted, 119 actually did drop out during the four-year course of a particular vocational high school.

I have tried to show how test scores can be used successfully when freely evaluated by counsellors in what we call a guidance situation. Now, how good will the test scores be as a selection tool when used in a purely actuarial fashion, i.e. summarized automatically?

Let us take a field where this procedure is used—prediction of success in the Bagrut certificate by tests administered in the tenth grade of academic high school. As mentioned before, by the beginning of the eleventh grade pupils have to specialize in humanities, biology, etc. The test given at this point must therefore predict whether the pupil will be able to obtain the Bagrut certificate at all. It is selective in that poor matriculation risks have to leave school by the end of the tenth grade. It further has to predict for which trend the pupil is most suited. Here test scores are summarized by actuarial procedure.

Prediction for general success is based on the score in four tests (verbal analyses, Hebrew vocabulary, English vocabulary, and number symbol). This short battery has yielded the following correlations, in a school with three trends:

Table 3. **Correspondence between test score for general success (by trends and in general)**

	(a)					(b)		
Trend:	Humanities	Biology	Math-physics	Total	Trend:	Humanities	Biology	Total
N	22	11	13	52	N	20	22	42
	·390†	·462†	·387§	·533*		·684*	·506*	·486*

Level of confidence
* p = 0·01 or above
† p = 0·05
‡ p = nearly 0·05
§ p = 0·10 all one-tailed

This means that the parameter is about 0·50.
(Note. The correlation coefficients for total populations are evaluated by Pearson's, the others by Spearman's formula.)

These results, arrived at by purely actuarial methods, are not inconsiderable, especially if one keeps in mind that the criteria reliability, i.e.

Bagrut examination raters' intercorrelations, are far from high. They range from 0·50 in Hebrew language to 0·94 in mathematics.

Different correlations might have been obtained, if these two follow-up studies had included all the pupils who dropped out between testing and graduation. They would presumably have been higher, since most drop-outs were due to learning difficulties, and since the test results of graduating pupils were much better than those of drop-out pupils.

As I mentioned, the second purpose of testing at this stage is to find out for which trend the pupils are best fitted. Here follow-up studies are rendered difficult by the small number of pupils in each trend. Since the ninth grade even in a big secondary school usually contains 160 pupils with at most eighty to 100 in the graduating class divided over three to five different trends, one has to deal with populations of twenty to twenty-five. This means using Spearman's correlations, which are notoriously unstable, since incorrect prediction for a single subject may considerably lower the correlation causing divergent results in replications of the study.

Ideally, a test battery for a two-trend school, for instance, should yield a correlation table of the following design:

Bagrut marks	General ability	Psychometric tests predicting success in Humanities	Science
Humanities	High	Very high	Low
Science	High	Low	Very high

Unfortunately, our Institute has not so far succeeded in obtaining such a correlation table, mainly because of lack of discriminating tests for the sciences. At present the picture looks like this (approximations):

Table 4. Prediction of success in trends of study by differential test scores

(a)

Bagrut marks in	General ability	Tests predicting success in Humanities	Science
Humanities	·29	·31	·09
Biology	·31	·35	·27
Math-physics	·09	·06	·09

Table 4 (contd.)

Bagrut marks in	General ability	(b) Tests predicting success in Humanities	Science
Humanities	·38	·23	·44
Biology	·24	·22	·19

It may be mentioned that more than ten follow-up studies in trend prediction, each on a population of fifty to 120 pupils, have shown that differences in general aptitude level may be used as an additional predictor. Using scaling as well as regression-line procedures, it was found that success in the biology trend required a medium aptitude level, between science (higher) and humanities (lower). But general aptitude level cannot, of course, be the only criterion for the choice of the trend. Moreover, since the strict application of the cutting-points causes 14 per cent failure in prediction for those above and—what is much worse—37 per cent for those who fall below the cut-off points, these findings have to be integrated with other indicators.

One of the main obstacles to exact and stable prediction is the perplexing phenomenon of a certain test yielding different correlations with the same Bagrut subject. In different schools it is still understandable, since the teachers' ratings are part of the Bagrut mark. In the same school it is also possible, since the contents of Bagrut examinations change and show low criterion reliability. But different trends in the same school and the same year it is difficult to account for. An extreme example is a 0·78 correlation between English vocabulary in the tenth-grade psychometric test and the Bagrut mark in English in the humanities trend, and a 0·05 correlation in the same school and same year in the biology trend.

Some more extreme instances are taken from selection testing for vocational schools, where test scores are summarized by actuarial methods.

In one of our follow-up studies on ten consecutive yearly class intakes of a four-year school for telecommunication technicians, a well-constructed mathematical problem test yielded correlations ranging from—0·039 to 0·507 ($p = 0·025$). The English vocabulary test yielded a range of 0·092 to 0·571 ($p = 0·025$) or even 0·513 ($p = 0·005$). These different results were obtained under optimal conditions: same school, same principal, stable staff, only a few changes in curriculum. How, then, can such findings be explained, and—what is more important—how can they be nevertheless applied?

I would suggest that the reason for the discrepancies is that even the optimal conditions are far from stable. In most cases conditions are much less uniform. There are different criterion raters, the motivation for certain people in different situations—test and study—are not the same, etc. Moreover, every achievement test, such as the Bagrut examinations, tests a specific sample of the total body of knowledge acquired. In my opinion it is therefore mainly the criterion which causes fluctuation in the correlations obtained. And this can hardly be altogether avoided.

To partially eliminate this drawback I would propose that results of many—even small—follow-up studies should be considered superior to results based on only a few, large-scale studies. A series of correlations between a certain psychometric test and the 'same' criterion should accordingly be treated as a frequency distribution, the median or mean be regarded as the 'true' correlation. Thus, in the example I have given before, the correlation between the English vocabulary test with success in the school for telecommunication technicians should be taken as 0·35 ($p = 0·05$).

In my talk I have tried to outline some of the procedures which our Institute has used for prediction of Bagrut marks in academic high school, and some of the results obtained. The two main problems encountered were:
1. A wide range of correlations yielded by the same psychometric test under similar conditions. A practical solution of this problem has been proposed.
2. Actuarial $v.$ free evaluation of psychometric test scores.

Comparing the predictive power of psychological tests when summarized by actuarial procedures and when freely interpreted shows the superiority of the latter approach. This is somewhat at variance with the general findings on actuarial $v.$ clinical prediction. To me this seems to indicate that the middle way between the two extremes, leaning somewhat more towards the actuarial side, is the best procedure, at least with the psychometric tools which we have at our disposal at present.

The amount of freedom the counsellor may exercise varies, of course, with the proven predictive ability of the test battery or the single test in the specific instance. If the counsellor finds something to account for a certain discrepancy in test results, etc., he is free to interpret them within a certain range. One day we might even be able to incorporate present imponderables in an improved evaluation system. But this day still seems far off, at least for us in Israel, where 60 per cent of the population are recent immigrants from a hundred countries and even more subcultures. For them psychometric tests and interest inventories representing the slowly emerging Israeli culture, and the corresponding school and work requirements, can constitute only a general, though important, common denominator.

A FOUR-YEAR FOLLOW-UP OF SECONDARY SCHOOL SELECTION PROCEDURES IN CENTRAL AFRICA

S. H. IRVINE*

1. Background

This study was begun in 1962 to provide more information about the nature and function of the selection system operating in Rhodesia. At first, only limited follow-up was considered possible, but the study has been extended to follow the progress of African pupils systematically through the secondary school system. A parallel study was begun in Uganda at the same time,† and the possibility of comparison of two systems of education has been realized through close co-operation and detailed planning. This paper concentrates on the central African work; it has two main aims:
 a) The provision of information about the kind of tests used and their utility.
 b) Providing an outline of methods used so that future studies may evaluate the model implied.

It is perhaps appropriate to indicate more detailed sources of information about these studies at the outset, so that they can be followed in detail if necessary. The central African studies may be found in Irvine (1964 a, b, c, 1965 a, b) and the East African studies in Silvey (1963, 1964). Other relevant work in selection in developing countries may be seen in Ferron (1965), Schwarz (1961, 1963), Vernon (1961) and Wantman (1962). Two important bibliographies are Andor (1966) and Hopkins (1962).

2. The first survey

A survey of educational skills and abilities was undertaken in 1962 before the end of the eighth year of education just prior to the secondary school selection examinations. All students took a battery of tests and completed a personal record card. The tests, with all others used at various levels, are given in the appendix. The experimental tests were ability tests in English, a test of reasoning in figural 'non-verbal' context, comprehension, vocabulary and spelling tests. All required

---
*Acknowledgment is made of financial help from the University of Rhodesia and Nyasaland Research Fund, the Ministry of Education in Rhodesia, the Anglo-American and Rhodesia Selection Trust, groups of mining companies, the Ministry of Overseas Development and the Leverhulme Trust, whose senior research award enabled me to return to Africa in 1966 for field work.
†By my colleague J. S. Silvey of the University of Nottingham.

special testing procedures. These were combined with the results of the traditional achievement examination and analysed. The sample consisted of 1,842 students from the schools of a province in Rhodesia selected because its examination results closely fitted national norms. One-third of all schools chosen at random from stratifications by type, quality and geographical location were verified as fitting provincial and national patterns of selection examination results in 1962.

The analysis of this survey included the provision of base-line norms for the experimental tests, estimates of concurrent validity with scaled headmasters' estimates as the criterion, and factor analysis of test content. From the results, the following conclusions were drawn:
1. Experimental tests could add significantly to the concurrent validities ($R = 0.89$) across all types of schools.
2. The main dimensions of ability were reasoning, verbal skills and number skills; and the traditional selection system included tests redundant for prediction purposes, since too many measured the same components.
3. The major influence on the scores was the quality of school attended. Also, males did significantly better than females on verbal tests, especially those demanding information about scientific or social studies. Age (as reported but not verified, since births were not registered by law) was negatively correlated with attainment, even after holding the number of years of education constant. Analyses of variance showed no significant association of scores with level of father's occupation, number of siblings, position in the family, or number of languages spoken.

These results were largely replicated the following year in Zambia with the same basic design and experimental tests (see Irvine 1964b).

Stage one follow-up 1963-4

The utility of the tests was further investigated in 1963 by constructing an achievement battery of objectively scored tests in consultation with principals of secondary schools and officials of the Ministry of Education. They were on 'core' subjects of English language and comprehension, arithmetic processes, algebra, geometry and general knowledge. Headmasters' estimates of performance were scaled on the total of these tests to broaden the base of criterion. All the students (just over 1,000) in the first year of the provincial secondary schools were tested, and of these 291 were identified as belonging to the original sample. Tests of goodness of fit showed the follow-up sample to be representative of the population from which it was drawn. Analysis

Secondary school selection in central Africa

showed that the multiple correlations between the traditional examination and the final global criterion of form 1 total plus scaled headmaster's estimate could be significantly increased by inclusion of ability tests and primary school headmaster's estimate. Once again, the quality of secondary school exerted a strong influence on performance. Pupils rated equal in the selection examinations tended to be differentiated if they went to schools of high, middle or low quality.

It was possible in this phase of the investigation to trace the sample through to the first operational criterion in the survey, the Junior Certificate national examination administered at the end of two years of secondary education. Numbers were by this time reduced to 231, a wastage of nearly one-fifth of the total identified in form 1. The summary of results is included in table 1. Each test, used in 1962, traditional or experimental, was used to make up a battery for multiple regression on core subjects in the examination and on a pass/fail dichotomy. All 1962 tests were re-normed for the 231 pupils involved. The 1963 form 1 tests were treated similarly, and the two sets combined to produce multiple correlations for all available test data. The results showed that the number of tests required to produce a multiple correlation significant at the 0·01 level of probability was considerably smaller than the total used. Secondly, the most consistent predictors of success were ability tests and scaled headmasters' estimates. Thirdly, there were significant changes in subject content from primary to secondary schools that were reflected in the correlations for two key subjects, English and mathematics. However, factor analysis again showed that the major constructs in the tests were reasoning, verbal and numerical skills. Male

Table 1. Predicting achievement in 1964 Junior Certificate (N = 231)

J.C. subjects	1962 tests No. used	R	1963 tests No. used	R	All 1962, 1963 No. used	R
English	3	46	3	59*	3	60
Arithmetic	4	59	3	62	5	67
Mathematics	3	48	5	74*	5	75
History	1	32	4	36	4	42
Geography	3	41	2	35	6	48
Vernacular language	4	50	2	56	3	58
Pass/fail	2	46	4	58*	7	63

*Significantly different from 1962 R. All decimal points have been omitted. Under 'the number of tests used' column is shown the number of tests required to produce the multiple correlation from the total battery available (fourteen in 1962, six in 1963).

aptitude was still present in informational subjects, but it was not nearly so pronounced as in the primary school.

Stage two follow-up 1966

In 1966 the pupils took the final hurdle in the secondary system, the secondary school leaving certificate examination. Just prior to this, in September, I revisited the schools and tested every pupil in them, a total of 340. Of these only eighty had survived from the original 1,800 tested in the primary schools in 1962. A battery of tests of vocational aptitude was administered; a detailed personal questionnaire on background, vocational interests and aspirations was also given. Headmasters' estimates of success in the forthcoming examination were collated, and a follow-up questionnaire on all student drop-outs completed. The data is being analysed at the time of writing and will be related to examination success. Secondly, a detailed study was completed in one secondary school using thirty of the French (1963) battery of factorial tests to give insight into the interaction of such tests across cultures. At the moment a postal follow-up of all 340 students tested is under way to find out what has happened to them since they left school.

Conclusion

What began as an exercise on selection efficiency has now turned into a long-term study of the development and use of high-level African man-power. The opportunities are unique and the information likely to prove fruitful for planners and administrators concerned with underdeveloped countries. When the research in Uganda has been joined with the work in central Africa, the comparisons are likely to be sociologically as well as educationally illuminating.

References

Andor, E. (1966) *Abilities of the African in Sub-Saharan Africa 1784-1963.* Johannesburg: NIPR.

Ferron, O. (1965) 'The test performance of "coloured" children.' *Educ. Res.,* 8, 42-57.

French, J. W. (1963) *Kit of Reference Tests for Cognitive Factors.* Revised. Princeton, N.J.: Educational Testing Service.

Hopkins, J. (1962) 'Bibliographie des recherches psychologiques conduites en Afrique.' *Revue Psychol. appl.,* 12, 201-13.

Irvine, S. H. (1964a) 'A psychological study of selection problems at the end of primary schooling in Southern Rhodesia.' Ph.D. thesis, University of London.

Irvine, S. H. (1964b) (with R. S. MacArthur and A. R. Brimble) *The Northern Rhodesia Mental Ability Survey.* Zambia: Rhodes Livingstone Institute.

Irvine, S. H. (1964c) 'Selection of Africans for post-primary education in Southern Rhodesia.' Pilot survey, June-July 1962. *Bull. Inter-African Lab. Inst.*, **11**, 69-93.

Irvine, S. H. (1965a) 'Selection for secondary education in Southern Rhodesia.' *Faculty of Education Paper no. 4.* University College, Salisbury.

Irvine, S. H. (1965b) 'Adapting tests to the cultural settings: a comment.' *Occup. Psychol.*, **39**, 12-23.

Schwarz, P. (1961) *Aptitude Tests for Use in the Developing Nations.* Pittsburgh: American Institute for Research.

Schwarz, P. (1963) 'Adapting tests to the cultural setting.' *Educ. psychol. Measur.*, **23**, 673-86.

Silvey, J. (1963) 'Aptitude testing and educational selection in Africa.' *Rhodes Livingstone J.*, **34**.

Silvey, J. (1964) 'Selection for senior secondary schools in Uganda.' Mimeograph of the EAISR, Kampala.

Vernon, P. E. (1961) *Selection for Secondary Education in Jamaica.* Kingston, Jamaica: Government Printer.

Wantman, M. J. (1962) *Report on the Malayan Project in Educational and Occupational Selection in West Africa.* London: Oxford University Press.

APPENDIX

TESTS AND INVENTORIES USED 1962-6

CENTRAL AFRICA

NIPR – National Institute for Personal Research, Johannesburg
NB – Normal Battery
Std 6 – Traditional Selection Examination
AIR – American Institute for Research AID Tests, Pittsburgh, USA

Type of tests	Date and number of years of education		
	1962 (8)	1963 (9)	1966 (12)
General ability	Raven 38 NIPR Spiral Nines		AIR Verbal Analogies Higher
English a) Experimental	NIPR NB Compre. NIPR NB Vocabulary NIPR NB Spelling	Irvine English	AIR Reading Higher
b) Traditional	Std 6 English 1 Std 6 English 2		
Number a) b)	Std 6 Arith. (Mech.) Std 6 Arith. (Problems) Std 6 Arith. (Mental)	Irvine Arithmetic	

Appendix (contd)

Type of tests	Date and number of years of education		
Informational a) b)	Std 6 History/Cur. Affairs Std 6 Geography/Nature Study	Irvine G.K.	AIR World and Science Information AIR Mechanical Information
Mathematical a)		Irvine Algebra Irvine Geometry	AIR Graphs AIR Tables
Perceptual a)			AIR Figures
Clerical a)			AIR Names AIR Codes
Estimates	Headmasters' School quality	Headmasters' School quality	Headmasters'
Inventories	Record card		Personal data Follow-up (1967)

SELECTION TESTS FOR SECONDARY SCHOOLS IN MALI

Y. KANE

Introduction: organization of education and guidance in Mali

a) Structure of education

The Act of 17 August 1962, dealing with reform of the educational system in the Republic of Mali, established the broad outlines of a system more in keeping with the needs of a developing state and also set up new forms of organization.

1. Basic education. Children first complete nine years of schooling divided into two periods:
    a) First period of five years, in which the basic skills are acquired.
    b) A further period of four years, undertaken by the great majority of pupils who have completed the first stage. This stage leads to the Diplôme d'Etudes Fondamentales (Diploma in Basic Studies) (DEF), which is a prerequisite for admission to further education in the form of:

2. General secondary schooling, leading in three years to the baccalaureate or to the various vocational courses, which in two, three or five years train those who are to become intermediate executives in agriculture, industry, education, public health and the Civil Service.

3. Higher education, in which the students are trained either in Mali (Ecole Nationale d'Administration or Ecole Nationale Supérieure) or abroad.

b) Stages at which guidance is given

There are three stages at which guidance is given:
1. Between the first and second periods of basic education; no guidance is given at present by the Bureau d'Orientation (Educational Guidance Bureau) at this level.
2. On completion of secondary schooling, when the Educational Guidance Bureau makes its first contribution.
3. On completion of secondary schooling, when a second contribution is made.

c) Characteristics of educational guidance in Mali

In view of the major need for executives, and the necessity for each to be employed, after suitable training, in advancing the nation's development, there was an urgent need for systematic and compulsory educational guidance.

The Bureau first establishes a file and makes a recommendation for each pupil in the ninth year and in the final class, and then hands over the files of all those who pass the DEF and the baccalaureate to the Commission Nationale d'Orientation et des Bourses (National Guidance and Scholarship Committee), which suggests suitable allocations to the Ministry of Education. The Ministry decides the allocations on the basis of which the pupils become the responsibility of the state and scholarships are awarded.

The educational guidance file prepared by the Bureau comprises: (a) an information card, on which the pupil outlines the studies he has completed, his family background, and three choices concerning his future; (b) a record of his marks together with his headmaster's advice on the choice of a career; (c) a record of his scores on tests, and a summary of all the data, forming the basis for a recommendation to the National Guidance and Scholarship Committee.

d) Conditions of work

The testing of young Africans meets certain environmental conditions which make some adaptation necessary, particularly of test instructions. The tests have to be given in a language which is not the pupils' mother tongue. Obviously, these young Mali students are not as familiar with this foreign language as are European pupils, for whom the difficulty does not arise. The pupils' vocabulary, too, is more limited, because of their lack of reading matter other than school books; and they do not recognize pictures of animals as well as Europeans, even when the animals are African. Further, it is difficult to establish the exact age of the pupils, since registration of births has only recently been put into effect. A class in Mali is undoubtedly much more heterogeneous in age than a class of the same educational level in Europe.

These factors justify our practice of giving numerous examples and exercises at the start of each test, and of adapting the items to the experience and vocabulary of the pupils. The interpretation of the tests must therefore take into account these special needs of African pupils.

The use of objective tests is of very recent growth in Mali, and owing to the lack of qualified administrators in the schools themselves the Educational Guidance Bureau is obliged to supervise all the tests, and to see to their marking and the interpretation of the results.

Educational aptitude tests—ninth-year battery

The use of tests in Mali was one of the outcomes of the reform of the educational system. The creation of a system of education in line with national needs involved the preparation of suitable tests. For obvious practical reasons there was no question of devising entirely new tests; this would have been too long and too laborious a process. Nor was it possible to use in their original form tests constructed in other countries. We therefore opted for a gradual adaptation of existing tests used in the United States, Europe or Africa. As I show later, it was primarily the conditions of presentation which had to be modified.

a) Form of the 1966 battery

The 1966 battery comprised six tests:
1. 'Attention'. This test does not, in fact, provide any measurement of attention, but helps the pupils to adapt to the test conditions.
2. Verbal (V), adapted from the PMA V.
3. Spatial (S), also adapted from the PMA, with modified presentation.
4. Reasoning (R), taken without alteration from the PMA.
5. Proverbs (P) is a test of African proverbs.
6. S_6 (calculation of lengths) is an adaptation of Faverge's test.

In 1967 the Bureau tried out a similar battery, with the BV 8, reduced to forty questions, replacing V, and Carrés Pliés replacing S. The items in S_6 were also changed.

b) Preparation of the original battery

The 1966 battery is the result of successive modifications. At the outset, in 1964, when there was no precise information available on the reaction of young Mali students to the tests, a sufficiently comprehensive battery, the PMA, was selected, supplemented by the Faverge S_6. Some modifications were made: an increase in the test time, and the reading of all instructions with the pupils.

A statistical analysis of the tests* for this first year led to the introduction of a familiarization test, A (attention), the addition of visual aids to supplement the presentation of both S and S_6, and the creation of P, with the modification of certain items.

The new battery, as used in 1965, was modified to some extent for 1966 after a statistical analysis; the number of items in V was reduced and major modifications were made to P.

*See 'Compte-rendu des recherches effectues par la section BUS-OSP d'Octobre 1963 a Juin 1966.' Bamako, June 1966.

All these changes are described below.

c) Modifications and adjustments of the test battery

1. Adaptation of V and S. (a) From the first year the results on V showed a high correlation with results in French, but the correlations with the other tests varied greatly for different classes. The girls' results were particularly uneven. In addition, observations during the tests confirmed the hypothesis that difficulties of adjustment to the tests existed in some classes and for certain pupils.

As it was impossible to use more expensive testing methods, it was decided that the tests proper should be preceded by a test intended to familiarize the pupil with methods of answering. Test A gave us the desired result. In addition, failure in this test—a rare event—enables us to express some reservations on the pupils' results. Finally, an analysis of the items in V enables us to reduce the number, which proved rather too great.

b) In the case of S, the results varied considerably with the group concerned. For instance, at the Lycée Technique $M = 22 \cdot 1$; at the Lycée des Jeunes Filles, $M = 10 \cdot 65$. In addition, the proportion of total failures was very high and the general average very low.

We then put forward the hypothesis that there was an educational problem: that the pupils had not been trained to see shapes and movements in a drawing. In the second year, therefore, we introduced visual aids, with which it is possible to demonstrate rotation in a plane.

The general average was considerably higher and the proportion of failures fell heavily, to about 3 per cent for the pupils as a whole. It remains slightly larger for girls.

2. After the first year we thought that the introduction of a proverbs test would strengthen the predictive validity of our battery; but we could not use proverbs alien to the cultural environment, as these raise the same problems as an unsuitable educational system. We therefore tried to construct a test of Mali proverbs. In 1964-5 about twenty proverbs, primarily of Bambara origin, and their meanings were supplied to us by a teacher. The results were uniform over Mali as a whole, except in the Gao region. The sampling of proverbs had been inadequate.

In 1965-6, with a Mali adviser taking part in the research work, we succeeded in obtaining a sample of proverbs from all the regions of Mali, and also in adapting the suggested answers more successfully to the vocabulary of Mali pupils in their ninth year of basic schooling. The results were encouraging from the point of view of uniformity. They were, however, disappointing from the point of view of predictive validity, but here we may be up against problems of marking, which will be discussed elsewhere.

Some attempts at validation on the basis of an essay on a fixed subject may be made shortly.

None the less, the P test played an important part with respect to the attitude of teachers and pupils to the tests; the teachers, finding a test which had been specially devised, were made less distrustful; the pupils felt more capable of succeeding in a field with which they were familiar.

3. Faverge's S_6 test appeared indispensable for the prediction of mathematics results. Based on knowledge acquired in the seventh year of basic schooling, it seemed a test that everyone should be able to tackle.

After the first year, however, we felt that it was essential to read through the instructions with the pupils and check, by using practice exercises, that they had fully understood what was required. Subsequently it proved necessary to reproduce the drawings on the blackboard and supplement words by gestures in order to clarify the explanation.

4. Inter-test correlations. In the first year, the correlations among the PMA sub-tests, with modified times, were very much more comparable with those found by Thurstone. However, V seemed to be rather more closely linked with the other tests. This may well be connected with the fact that testing is not carried out in the native language.

Inter-test correlations 1965-6

	S	R	P	S_6
V	·28	·18	·40	·26
S		·35	·29	·47
R			·31	·46
P				·27

Educational aptitude tests—twelfth-year battery

We thought it essential in this case to find tests which could detect the abilities needed by a higher executive: (a) a certain intellectual curiosity, inspiring an interest in current affairs; (b) the ability to extract the principal ideas from a text; (c) the ability to synthesize and to reach a conclusion, taking into account all the facts known about a situation.

a) Needs met by the 1966 battery

a) TC/MA: Comprehension of texts. Six texts are presented to the subjects; for each text three groups, each of three ideas, are offered, and they have to find, in each group, the one idea belonging to the text. They also have to choose from a list of five suggestions.

b) IG 3/MA/66: General information. This test is inspired by the first AIR IG test constructed at Lagos. The questions had to be adapted to the context of Mali. In addition, the essentially topical nature of some questions entails an annual revision after analysis of the items.

c) BC/MA/66: 'Boxes and cubes'. Based on the French INOP test, this test is preceded by practice exercises in which the subjects are shown how to fit cubes into boxes by applying certain rules.

b) Preparation of the original battery

The original battery did not include the 'Boxes and cubes', but did include the PMA. It was clear, from the first year, that the PMA would not contribute much at this level. In addition, since 1966-7, all the candidates for the second baccalaureate have already been tested in the ninth year of schooling.

The TC test comprised only three texts, which the subjects had to summarize.

The IG comprised fifty-eight questions from the original test and eighteen new ones.

c) Modifications and adjustments of the battery

1. Great difficulty was experienced in the first year over correction of the 'Comprehension of texts' test. Some form of objective marking had to be found. For the second year it was decided, therefore, to suggest nine answers for each text, from which the candidates had to choose three. As the answers could be given more quickly, it was possible to increase the number of texts to six.

The results were encouraging, but an item analysis showed that the test was not very homogeneous. In 1965-6, therefore, the formula of groups of three questions was devised. The subjects had to select one from each group of three. After the item analysis for that year, some were to be modified for the 1966-7 battery.

2. The Mali version of the IG is closely related to current events, and

after a period of one year an item loses its validity. The 1965-6 version included few scientific items, but some items of this type, taken from the Lagos IG test, were added in the 1966-7 version.

Non-verbal aptitude tests

a) In the spring of 1963, a Unesco mission tried out the PM 38 in a number of classes from the ninth to the twelfth year of schooling, with a single special adaptation of the instructions: the presentation of a visual example.

The results were quite good, but, as had already been found in The Cameroons, certain items were invariably failed, particularly those which required explicit knowledge of the laws of geometrical symmetry. To adapt this test, therefore, one would have to study it item by item, in order to retain those which proved most valid.

b) Problem of spatial perception in Africa

Success in this type of test appears to bring two different aptitudes into play: reasoning on the one hand, and spatial perception on the other. As we mentioned above, educational factors affect the spatial aspect. It is not therefore possible to talk of 'culture-free' tests. This is why we preferred to use the R test, where the knowledge required is purely school-based, and virtually 'levelled' at the moment of its use.

c) Testing the PM 47 at fifth-year level

After the Unesco mission's testing of an unfortunately limited sample, the experiment was repeated in 1963-4 on a random sample of fifth-year pupils from Bamako (N = 1,350). The results showed significant differences with age. In addition, graphs of the score distributions for children of different ages who have completed five years of schooling reveal certain distinctive features (see figure). As has frequently been found with the PM 47, two different methods may be used to answer certain items. It seems plausible that the transition to a logical form of reasoning takes place between the ages of eleven and fourteen, but a more thorough study would be required in order to confirm this.

The role of attainment tests

a) Experiments carried out in 1963

Two experiments with attainment tests were carried out in 1962-3:
1. In collaboration with the French IPN, two tests from France, the CM2 (1) arithmetic and the CM2 (1) French test, were applied

Tests for secondary schools in Mali

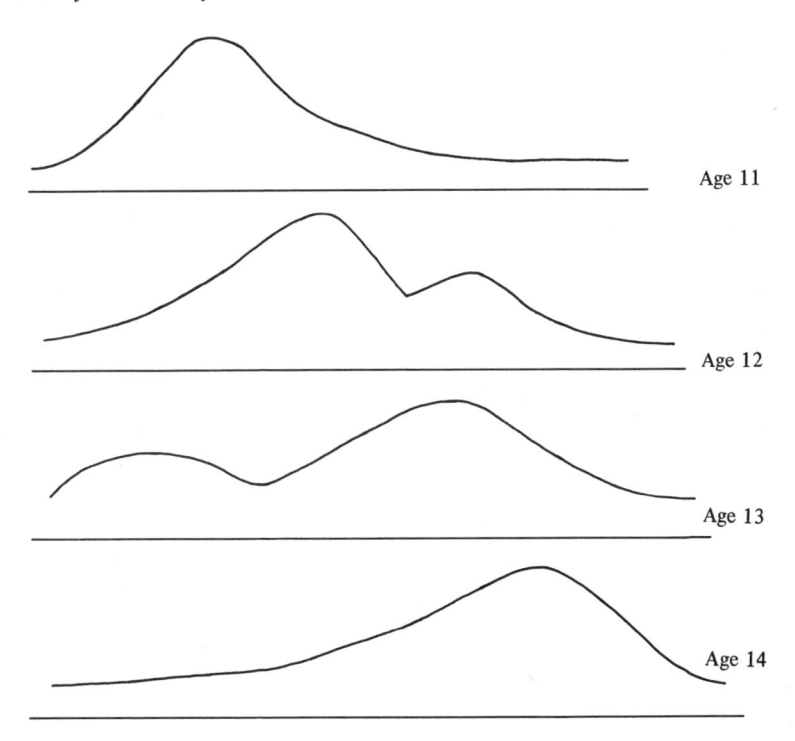

Graphs of score distributions for children of different ages who have completed five years of schooling. Bamako, 1963-4

in sixth-year classes where French syllabuses were still in use. The interesting results were published in *Coopération Pédagogique*, no. 4, 1963.
2. When the syllabuses were changed, the Unesco mission tried to devise very short tests in French and arithmetic for third-, fourth-, fifth- and sixth-year classes. Unfortunately, the sample was limited, and the participation of teachers would have been invaluable for the construction of the tests.

b) The need to devise new tests, in collaboration with teachers, as a result of the reform of the educational system

The construction of new tests at the ninth- and fifth-year levels demands such collaboration. For administrative reasons this has not hitherto been possible, but it is to be hoped that the difficulties will soon be overcome.

c) What could be gained from the use of these tests (maths and French)

The use of attainment tests could be of great service, particularly as marking problems are aggravated in this instance by the heterogeneity of the teaching body.
1. Comparison of pupils among themselves, whatever the class of origin.
2. A standard of attainment could be established at the end of the period, which would, as a supplement to the traditional examination, make it possible to assess which pupils had genuinely acquired the essential basic skills.
3. Similarly, the establishment of a standard of attainment at the beginning of the period would make for better guidance of pupils. It would be possible to give an accurate assessment to teachers of the attainments, and the gaps in attainment, of their future pupils.
4. The inspectors would have a means of checking marks, and would be able to make a summary of the skills actually acquired.

The role of interest and personality questionnaires

Tests of this type would be very useful, in particular at baccalaureate level. However, it seems very difficult at the moment to devise suitable tests, in view of the lack of information on the social/cultural environment and of the rapid development of the evolving Mali society.

Primary education results in comparison with test scores

a) The various guidance criteria

The various factors considered for the purpose of vocational guidance at the ninth-year level are:
1. Age limits: fixed by the National Educational Guidance Committee in accordance with the plan.
2. Labour requirements.
3. The candidates' choice.
4. School results, as shown by marks.
5. Test results.

b) Tests and school marks are complementary, but although the tests facilitate comparison between pupils from different classes, marks raise

Tests for secondary schools in Mali

considerable problems as a result of the heterogeneity of the teaching body, as mentioned previously. For this reason, Spearman coefficients, calculated on the markings in each class, were used. After a test of uniformity an overall coefficient was calculated using a method derived from Fisher. A table of these Spearman correlation coefficients for the tests on ninth-year classes in 1965-6 is given below.

	Spelling	Composition	Maths	General classification
V	·52	·45	·18	·40
S	·11	·13	·28	·22
R	·14	·15	·40	·27
F	·18	·28	·20	·24
S_6	·15	·18	·51	·45

Spearman coefficients between tests and school marks. Ninth-year classes in Mali, 1965-6 (N = 1,972)

c) Test evaluation problems

Faced with the problems of marking, the Bureau carried out a certain number of surveys of marking methods: for the baccalaureate, ninth-year averages, composition and spelling in the ninth year, and the DEF. These surveys were submitted to the authorities, with suggestions about how to achieve a more standardized marking system. The use of attainment tests were also suggested on this occasion.

Guidance tests in secondary schools

a) Lack of continued guidance

Under current policy, there is no continuity of guidance; guidance is provided only at certain well-defined stages. Later modifications are extremely rare, and such cases are studied by the National Guidance Scholarship Committee.

b) Vocational guidance

1. Openings. Mali has at present the following institutions for the training, after the DEF, of intermediate executives:

Productions sector: Institut Polytechnique Rural de Katibougou. (5 years' training for engineers, 3 years' training for technicians.)
Industrial sector: Ecole Nationale d'Ingénieurs. (5 years'. training for engineers.)
Lycée Technique. (3 years' training for technicians.)

Non-industrial sector

Education: Ecoles Normales Secondaires. (3 years' training for teachers of the second stage of basic education.)
Centres Pédagogiques Régionaux. (One year's training (after the DEF) for teachers of the 1st stage of education.)
Institut National des Arts. (3 years' training for art and music teachers.)
Public health: Ecole Secondaire de Santé. (3 years' training for welfare and child welfare workers, midwives, nurses, laboratory assistants.)
Civil Service: Ecole Nationale d'Administration, cycle B. (3 years' training for B-grade officials.)

In each institute the classes are selected each year in accordance with the plan, in order to meet economic needs.

2. To provide guidance on vocational training, the general psychological examination is supplemented by a few more specialized tests, some of which derive from the Lagos AIR. School marks are also used, with emphasis on the subjects most relevant to the particular occupation. The pupils' choices are taken into account to a considerable extent, but here we come up against problems of deeper motivation.

Young people, being ill informed, frequently react in terms of the traditional status of certain jobs—of the Civil Service, for instance, as against technology. Only the provision of information, over at least two years before the time for vocational guidance, laying favourable emphasis on certain occupations and stressing the value to the nation of certain jobs, would produce a valid motivation in the pupils, on terms which are not contrary to the deeper interests of the nation.

SELECTION TESTS FOR SECONDARY SCHOOLS IN KENYA

H. J. KANINA

Introduction

Our educational system in Kenya, and to a large extent in the former British territories, is a product of what the British imported to these countries. It is based on prescribed syllabuses and regulated by prescribed examinations at various defined stages. These examinations act as hurdles which one has to clear before proceeding to a higher grade.

Until 1961 pupils in Kenya schools had to take, and pass well, two public examinations before entering the secondary schools. The first was after four years at a primary school, and the second after a further four years in what was known as an intermediate school. You will note that I do not refer to the age group taking any examination. This is because of the fact that the ages of the children in any one class may vary by as many as four, five or even more years. Thus a child of twelve may be sitting the same examination with another of eighteen seeking to enter a secondary school.

I have decided to talk on a more specific topic rather than deal with generalities. This is because I believe that in outlining the development of the Kenya Preliminary Examination, the most important of all our exams, I could give you an insight of the complexities facing us in Kenya.

As I said earlier, our system of education is still very much British. The success of students, the recruitment for employment, entrance to the next stage of the school system, all depend on the performance at prescribed public examinations.

Background

The population of Kenya is composed of three main racial groups, Africans, Asians and Europeans—the Africans accounting for over 97 per cent of the total of about nine million people.

During the colonial days, i.e. up to 1963, the minority races had far better educational facilities than the Africans. The Ministry of Education prescribed three primary school syllabuses, to be followed by the three different racial groups. Up to 1963, the Africans took eight years to cover their syllabuses, while the other races took seven years to cover theirs. From 1964 the primary school courses became one of seven years for all racial groups.

The history of the Kenya Preliminary Examination up to 1963

shows an incoherent struggle between three factors: (a) setting examination papers (or tests) to test all the work done in the primary schools for the three racial groups; (b) prescribing by examination what work was done; and (c) using the examination as a selection instrument.

I should like to say something about each of the above factors.

a) To cope with the different syllabuses for the three races meant that many papers had to be set. For example, there were seven English papers (or tests), three of them taken in common by African and Asian pupils and four taken only by European pupils. There were three history papers, one for each race; six geography papers, two for each race; five mathematics papers, three common to all three races and two reflecting different syllabuses in algebra and geometry for Asian and European pupils. There were also seven language papers other than English, i.e. Swahili (for Africans); Hindi, Urdu, Gujerati, Arabic (for Asians); Latin and French (for Europeans). In all, the Preliminary Examination up to 1963 required thirty-one separate examination papers.

b) The people charged with the setting of these papers had to rely on the syllabuses for each subject. If they set questions, say, on graphs in a mathematics paper, graphs were taught in schools. Thus they had to be careful, year by year, to set questions on the various parts of the syllabuses to ensure that these parts were not ignored in the classroom.

c) The examination as a selection instrument—of late this last factor, at least in the eyes of the parents and pupils, has overshadowed all the others. The primary school course is designed as if it were a preparation for entry into secondary school for *all* pupils—this in spite of the fact that only about 10 per cent of all primary school leavers gain admission into secondary schools. With the mounting numbers of candidates, the pressure for secondary school places has become very great and the competition for the places very severe. The parents and pupils alike are not content with the certificate which is issued to show that a candidate reached a particular level of performance and therefore 'passed' the examination, but with whether or not he did well enough to enter a secondary school. In fact, pupils who merely get a certificate have begun to consider themselves as having 'failed' if they are not offered a secondary school place. The aggregate of raw scores is used both for selection and certification.

Development of the examination

The number of candidates taking the examination in the last nine years is as follows (in round figures to the nearest 1,000):

1958	19,000
1959	20,000
1960	23,000
1961	29,000
1962	35,000
1963	62,000
1964	103,000
1965	148,000
1966	150,000

The figures show a steady increase up to 1962. The burst forward in 1963 onwards made the multiplicity of papers (the thirty-one mentioned earlier) as well as the type of papers (which were essay) completely unmanageable.

The administrative exercise of mounting a whole week's examination became too cumbersome for so many candidates. Thus from 1964 onwards the number of papers was reduced to three, and the time was reduced to a single day only. The papers were English, mathematics and a general paper. The general paper contains questions on geography, history and science. The papers remained mainly essay-type and the amount of time spent on marking the papers was considerable.

Results

The results are reported on a four-point scale A to D, where A to C are pass grades and D a fail grade.

With the examination being held in November and secondary schools opening the following January, the need to issue the results as early as possible is apparent. This has not been possible because of the amount of time required for marking the papers and processing the results.

An attempt was made to hold the examination in July so that the results could be issued before the end of the year. July is in the second of the three terms into which our school year is divided, and the holding of the final examination in July meant, therefore, that the teaching and attendance in the third term was impaired.

The battle had therefore to be between holding the examinations as late in the third term as possible and issuing the results as quickly as possible. The only answer had to be to design the papers so that the time for marking was considerably reduced.

The papers

As stated earlier, there are only three papers set, viz. English, mathematics and a general paper. With essay-type questions requiring subjective marking, however, it is not enough just to cut the number of papers from thirty-one to three, though this is quite a cut! The call for earlier results to permit surer and quicker secondary school selection has led to the papers being made completely objective as from 1966. I have brought with me copies of the 1966 papers, and those who are interested will be able to have a look at them.

None of the items in the general paper and the English paper were pre-tested. A number of the items in the mathematics paper were pre-tested and analysed.

Problems

a) Registration

Although the examination is held in November, the registration of the candidates starts in March. During this month, forms are sent to every primary school for the head-teacher to enter the names of the prospective candidates. The forms contain printed instructions for the teachers to follow. For each candidate a fee of Sh.10 (i.e. equivalent of £½ sterling or U.S.$1.50) is charged and is collected by the teacher. The forms are then sent to the County Education Officers (there are forty-one counties), then to the Provincial Education Officers (eight of these) and finally to the headquarters of the Ministry of Education. At each stage the entries are checked for errors, etc. They then go to a computer firm which punches the names (and other details such as age, sex, etc.) and puts them on magnetic tape. The lists are then printed, brought back to the Ministry, and sent back to the respective counties for checking. This brings us up to June/July.

The lists then come back from the counties by September and are sent back to the computer for the necessary amendments to be made on the tapes. The computer firm keeps these tapes ready to add the scores when the examination is over.

b) Setting

By tradition, all public examinations which are administered by the Ministry of Education are set by the officers in the Inspectorate Section of the Ministry. The officers are specialists in their own subject areas. An officer may, at his discretion, request other people knowledgeable in a particular subject area to help in submitting questions. This was not common when the examination consisted of essay-type questions, but it is getting more common with the multiple-choice-type questions. The questions are then discussed by a small committee nominated by the head of the Inspectorate, which consists of the inspector of the subject area concerned and three or four others—chosen for their knowledge and experience in the particular subject. The committee can amend or delete a question.

The draft paper is then shown to the Chief Education Officer (Director of Education) for his final approval. After this final approval the papers go to the printers, who may be in Europe. Proof reading is done in June, and the printed papers are ready at the beginning of October. Last year we had over twenty tons of the stuff. (N.B. The lack of people trained in the construction of multiple-choice questions is a great handicap. The fact that we have no testing unit means that the tests are done without pre-testing and any analysis.)

c) Administering the examination

As mentioned earlier, this is now a one-day examination. Every single examination centre (over 3,000 of them in 1966) is supposed to start at the same time and finish at the same time during this one day in November.

During the month of October, officers from the Ministry headquarters travel to all the counties (scattered in over 224,000 square miles) and talk to the invigilators or supervisors who will conduct the examination.

The invigilators are also given printed instructions on what to do on the day of the examination. In 1966 we managed to hold a rehearsal in most centres on the day before the examination. At this rehearsal, the invigilators are able to check on seating accommodation and other facilities at their centres.

The invigilators are given the papers on the day of the examination, the day before or even several days before, depending on the problems of transport to the centre, the weather and the centre's distance from the county headquarters.

In the past we have experienced leakages—caused by some invigilators opening the packets a day or two before to show their relatives and friends. 1966 was the first year when we had no record of a leakage.

When the examination has been administered, the scripts are sent back to the County Education Officer, who delivers them to the Ministry of Education. The Ministry then organizes the marking in centres.

d) Marking

When the examination was essay-type requiring subjective marking, a high calibre of markers was needed and the only source was the staff of secondary schools.

This meant that the marking could not start before the first week of December when the secondary schools closed for the Christmas holidays. These secondary school teachers were paid for the marking, which took three or more weeks to complete with over 500 teachers. The teachers had also to enter the marks on computer-printed marksheets for each candidate.

Although marking schemes were available, the subjectivity of the marking was very varied. The marking centres were also scattered all over the country, making effective supervision very difficult.

In 1966 the marking was very objective and required people of less calibre. Primary school teachers were used and with about 350 of them the marking was over in just over a week.

Future plans

a) If for no other reason, the weight of numbers dictates that the examination be objective. We have had complaints from teachers, who say that pupils should be given the chance to do some pieces of continuous writing. To accommodate this, the last question in the English paper is a kind of 'guided composition'. This does slow the marking and may have to be discontinued in the future.

b) It is our intention, too, to establish a research centre which could help in construction, pre-testing and other relevant research.

It is a pity that, owing to lack of man-power, it was not possible for us to do a complete analysis of the 1966 examination. I am trying to arrange that the items are analysed later this year.

Conclusion

This short paper may have sounded rather too localized for a gathering of this nature, but this examination is a very major concern for our Ministry of Education and the citizens of Kenya.

The merits and demerits of deciding the future of a child (after seven years of school) on a single 3¾-hour examination on one day may be argued. We may have to change the nature of the examination from pass/fail to one of measurement of achievement in the primary school. The fact remains that the examination is with us for some time to come, and our efforts should be to improve the instrument so that it does better the task we want it to do. In particular, there may be a case for an aptitude (scholastic) test for the selection for the secondary schools.

It is also doubtful whether one examination could serve all these purposes. The selection factor is now the most important in the eyes of the pupils and their parents. We have to change—and we are on the way to doing so—from preparing our primary school leavers for a grammar school secondary education, if only because for some time to come only a very small percentage will be able to get places in the secondary schools. We have also to make our secondary school education more diversified.

DEVELOPMENT OF SCHOLASTIC APTITUDE TESTS FOR SELECTION AND GUIDANCE IN SECONDARY SCHOOLS

SABIR ALI ALVI

'How do we know the capacity of a boy or girl for learning? What factors are related to success in a particular program of studies? What is our pool of talent of various kinds in the country? Such questions, and the hundreds more that can be asked, are relevant to one of Pakistan's important tasks—the development and efficient use of the country's human resources. This is a problem of both immediate and long-range significance. This is a problem of extreme complexity, the solution of which will require the best efforts from each sector of the country. This is a problem that must be handled scientifically and humanely' (University of the Punjab, Institute of Education and Research, *Manual for Scientific Aptitude Tests,* p.1).

The concerns expressed in the foregoing paragraph are manifesting themselves in efforts being made in West Pakistan to develop measures of aptitude and achievement, vocational interest, school adjustment, study habits, and attitudes. Much of West Pakistan's interest in psychological measurement is recent, however, and was not strongly expressed until the Commission on National Education in 1959 noted the need for such measures. According to the Commission (Pakistan Ministry of Education 1960, p. 249):

'The construction and use of standardized tests designed to single out special aptitudes has received almost no attention in our education. Although we recognize the limitations of such instruments, we believe that they can and should play an important part in the implementation of any program of talent identification.'

The growing interest in test development at the Institute of Education and Research, Lahore, and to a lesser degree at the Department of Applied Psychology at Punjab University, the Board of Intermediate and Secondary Education in Karachi, the Educational Research Unit at Peshawar University, and other institutions, may be due to the following factors:

1. The country has begun a programme of economic development based on careful planning at national level. There is concern for maximum development of human and material resources. Economic development requires assessment of trained man-power needs and the development of man-power resources. This concern calls for an early recognition of human differences. The construction and use of standardized instruments to measure human

traits is needed to identify these differences and to indicate how the differing potentials can best be developed.

2. Although West Pakistan has considerably expanded her educational facilities—as reflected in a large number of high schools and students, and a greater spending on education the situation is far from satisfactory. The number of secondary schools, and the facilities they offer, fall far short of the needs. It will take many years, perhaps decades, before equality of educational opportunity can be extended to all people. Until such a time, schools will admit more pupils than their resources should permit. Certain categories of schools, like model schools, pilot secondary schools, cadet colleges and many privately managed schools, which maintain higher academic standards, must continue to restrict admission by establishing certain criteria for admission. Selection of students for secondary education is thus a significant problem.

3. Education in Pakistan has been characterized by great waste of youthful vigour, energy and talent. This is reflected in high dropout and failure rates. (The pass percentages in the Matriculation Examinations, at the end of class 10 high school, have usually ranged between 40 and 60 per cent.) The choices of academic and professional programmes are often made with no regard for the student's potentialities. There is need for a guidance programme to help young people identify their powers, interests and limitations, and to make wise decisions concerning their academic, emotional and occupational adjustment. These objectives are now envisaged in the role of Guidance and Testing Services, a project initiated by the West Pakistan Government.

4 For many years until after independence, education in Pakistan had been used largely to train civil servants. To give education a broader function, the Commission on National Education recommended the establishment of comprehensive schools with a wide variety of courses. According to the proposed programme, students could be channelled into vocational schools, polytechnics, commercial schools and professional colleges and universities, after preparation in the secondary schools. The diversification of educational programmes should occur at the following points (stated in terms of class or grade level) in the educational structure proposed by the Commission (Pakistan Ministry of Education 1960, pp. 255-6):

a) At the completion of class 7, when some students will be joining vocational schools for training in crafts.

b) At the completion of class 10 when students will be entering polytechnics to take up prerequisite courses in commerce, medicine and engineering.
c) At several stages in those secondary schools which offer diversified programmes where the student must select a particular area of specialization.
d) At the completion of class 12 when some students will decide to join a college or university and others to enter professional programmes in medicine, law and engineering.

The selection and classification of students by various institutions, and students' choices of future programmes, must rest on a consideration of psychological and social facts. The increasing diversity of educational programmes, the planned development of man-power resources, the need to institute admission programmes in certain types of secondary schools, and the growing concern for academic and emotional adjustment of pupils at school, all require sound selection and guidance procedures. Since the use of tests and other evaluative instruments is vital to selection and guidance programmes, there is an obvious need to develop such instruments. Thus, one of the major research activities at the Institute of Education and Research was a Test Development Project. Initial planning for the following series of aptitude tests began in September 1963.

Scholastic Aptitude Test: Scale I for classes 4, 5, 6
Scholastic Aptitude Test: Scale II for classes 6, 7, 8
Scholastic Aptitude Test: Scale III for classes 8, 9, 10
Mechanical Aptitude Test for classes 8, 9, 10 and pre-engineering
Spatial Ability Test for classes 8, 9, 10 and pre-engineering

This paper describes how the three Scholastic Aptitude Tests (SAT) were developed, and how they will likely be used for selection and guidance in the secondary schools of West Pakistan.

General description of the tests

During the initial planning of the tests, the adaptation of some British and American tests was considered. It was finally decided to develop fairly original tests, although it was assumed that the types of item used would be those common to most existing intelligence tests. The SAT, therefore, resemble omnibus tests like the Otis Quick-Scoring Mental Ability Tests—Beta and Gamma, the Dominion Tests of Learning Capacity—Intermediate and 'Advanced, and the Henmon-Nelson Test of Mental Ability. The content of items written for the tests

Development of Scholastic Aptitude Tests

remained indigenous to the Pakistani culture and was related to the experience of the pupils in their environment. No empirical data were gathered to find if these items—for measuring verbal ability, numerical reasoning, logical reasoning and general knowledge—would constitute the best combination for measuring scholastic aptitude. The *a priori* selection of abilities reflected the nature of current general intelligence or scholastic aptitude tests on the assumption that the structure of 'scholastic aptitude' is similar in different cultures. The SAT were devised to estimate the intellectual level of a person and to afford some objective basis for predicting the probability of success in academic programmes. Four types of items were selected that require mental functioning similar to that needed in school work. These were: (a) verbal ability, (b) numerical reasoning, (c) logical reasoning, and (d) general knowledge.

The *verbal ability* items are aimed at measuring the pupils' language development, including their comprehension of words and concepts. These items are also assumed to measure the ability to generalize and to think constructively. *Numerical reasoning* is tested in such items as number series and quantitative problems. These items are designed to test the student's understanding of numerical relations and facility in handling numerical concepts. Such items also measure the ability to reason with numbers and to deal with quantitative materials. Another mental function which these scales measure is *logical reasoning*, which calls for thinking through a problem using induction and deduction. The item types aimed at measuring this ability are analogies, syllogisms and inferences. In any general intelligence test, a student's performance would naturally be influenced by his general understanding of the environment and of his day-to-day problems. It has, therefore, been felt necessary to include items measuring *general knowledge*.

Scale I of the SAT contains sixty items, Scale II sixty-six items, and Scale II seventy items. Each scale can be administered in about one hour, and the actual working time allowed for the test is forty-five minutes. Each item included in the test series is multiple-choice, offering four choices. Examples follow:

Example 1
    Opposite of *soft* is   1. cotton
                                      2. hard
                                      3. iron
                                      4. hot

Example 2
Which is the next number: 3-6-9-12-15-18-
    1. 19
    2. 20
    3. 21
    4. 22

Example 3
What will thirty watches cost if one costs Rs 60/-?
    1. Rs 1680
    2. Rs 1750
    3. Rs 1800
    4. Rs 1890

Example 4
All intelligent students will pass. Anwar is an intelligent student. Therefore, he
    1. is very clever
    2. is very punctual
    3. will stand first
    4. will pass

Example 5
Which of the following is wrong?
    1. 2-4-6-8-10-12
    2. 6-9-12-15-18-21
    3. 7-11-15-18-23-27
    4. 5-10-15-20-25-30

Example 6
Horse is to *tonga* as engine is to
    1. parts
    2. mechanic
    3. road
    4. train

All items for the preliminary forms of the tests were written by the staff of the Research Wing. Each item was discussed and improved before it was finally included in the experimental form. The number of items written for pre-testing was two to three times the number of items included in the final test. Each experimental form of the SAT was administered to a sample of about 400 pupils stratified for class and sex. Item analyses were facilitated by the use of Chung-Teh Fan's *Item Analysis Table*. The main criteria for item selection were the biserial correlation r and difficulty index Δ. In the light of these analyses some items were further revised and pre-tested before they were included in the final forms. No further analyses of item statistics were undertaken. The size of the biserial correlation and difficulty index were the bases for item selection.

Development of norms

After the final tests has been assembled, they were administered to pupils in classes 4 to 10, from November 1964 to January 1965 for compiling norms. The normative samples consisted of 1,643 pupils for SAT I, 1,676 pupils for SAT II, and 1,655 pupils for SAT III. Grade percentile norms based on these samples are reported in the Manual. The samples were drawn largely from typical schools in the Lahore Region of the province. This region is only one of the many administrative units of the provincial Department of Education. The need to develop norms for other regions of West Pakistan is obvious.

Needless to say, the normative data for the Lahore Region are hardly adequate. It is hoped that schools in the region will develop local norms which will be more useful for their selection and guidance programme. This is especially important because there are no uniform or prescribed admission standards. Since schools are free to set up their own entrance examinations, the use of local norms appears particularly relevant. We should hope that as more schools co-operate with the Institute of Education and Research, it will become possible to develop regional and provincial norms.

Validation of the tests

The validity of the Scholastic Aptitude Tests was judged by determining the extent to which these tests predict the students' academic success. In studies undertaken for this purpose, the tests were administered to pupils in classes 4 to 10, and their performance was later correlated with their final examination school marks. Two to four months intervened between the test administration and the criterion measure, that is, the school marks.

The validity studies reported in this section relate to the prediction of total final examination marks. However, these studies need to be expanded to find how well the SAT can predict students' success in distinct curricular areas like the humanities, sciences, commerce and agriculture. It would be further desirable to plan studies on how SAT III

Table 1. Summary of validity coefficients between SAT I scores and final examination marks *of boys

No.	School	Class	N	r
1.	Government Junior Model School, Wahdat Colony, Lahore	4	55	·62
2.	M. C. Model School, Wahdat Colony, Lahore	4	77	·47
3.	Government Primary School, Kahna Nau, District Lahore	4	65	·51
4.	M. C. Primary School, Muslim Town, Lahore	4	18	·08
5.	Government Middle School, Sharaqpur, District Sheikhupura	4	65	·35
6.	M. C. Primary School, Old Mandi, District Sheikhupura	4	65	·24
7.	New M. C. Primary School, District Sheikhupura	4	112	·35
8.	M. C. Primary School No. 1, Chichawatni, District Montgomery	4	54	·52
9.	M. C. Primary School No. 3, Chichawatni, District Montgomery	4	18	·58
10.	Government Junior Model School, Wahdat Colony, Lahore	5	24	·64
11.	Government Middle School for Boys, Sharaqpur, District Sheikhupura	5	76	·02
12.	M. C. Primary School, Old Mandi, District Sheikhupura	5	59	·12
13.	New M. C. Primary School, District Sheikhupura	5	113	·22
14.	M. C. Primary School No. 1, Chichawatni, District Montgomery	5	68	·38
15.	M. C. Primary School No. 3, Chichawatni, District Montgomery	5	22	·06
16.	Government High School for Boys, Sharaqpur, District Sheikhupura	6	172	·62
17.	M. C. High School, Chichawatni, District Montgomery	6	144	·47

Average r = ·41

*Total marks of classes 4 and 5 include marks in language, arithmetic, social studies, religious education, science and practical arts. Total marks of class 6 include marks in English, Urdu, social studies, mathematics, general science and religious education.

predicts the likelihood of students' success in colleges and in vocations. The validity of these tests is reckoned in terms of pupils' performance on these tests correlated with their final examination school marks. One would, however, question the objectivity and reliability of the latter as a measure of school success. It is quite probable that, given more objective criterion measures, the validity coefficients reported in the present studies might have been higher.

Table 1 gives the summary of validity coefficients between SAT I scores and final examination marks of classes 4, 5 and 6 for boys from various schools in the Lahore Region. The average correlations between test scores and final examination marks for the seventeen school samples is 0·41. The highest validity coefficient for any school obtained by this test is 0·64. The test has low validity coefficients—at least for class 5 samples. This might be due to the fact that the final examination marks were assigned to the students by the Assistant District Inspector of Schools with little regard for sound evaluation procedures. The research personnel engaged in these validity studies found that the

Table 2. Summary of validity coefficients between SAT I scores and final examination marks *of girls

No.	School	Class	N	r
1.	Government High & Normal School for Girls, Sharaqpur, District Sheikhupura		60	·71
2.	Junior Model School, Wahdat Colony, Lahore	4	55	·64
3.	Junior Model School, Wahdat Colony, Lahore	5	22	·42
4.	Government High & Normal School for Girls, Sharaqpur, District Sheikhupura	5	40	·47
5.	Government High & Normal School for Girls, Sharaqpur, District Sheikhupura	6	48	·77
6.	Government High School, Wahdat Colony, Lahore	6	84	·65
			Average r =	·65

*Total marks of classes 4 and 5 include marks in language, arithmetic, social studies, religious education, science and practical arts. Total marks of class 6 include marks in English, Urdu, social studies, mathematics, general science and religious education.

inspectors had given about the same marks to all students in various schools. More objective measurement of the school success criteria would have yielded higher validity indices. Table 1 shows that this scale has, in general, very satisfactory validity coefficients for classes 4 and 6.

The validity coefficients of SAT I for girls, given in table 2, have a wider range than for boys. The correlations indeed run quite high. The average correlation for the six samples of girls from classes 4, 5 and 6 is 0·65. The correlations for most girls' samples are high, thus indicating the strength of the instrument.

Table 3. Summary of validity coefficients between SAT II scores and final examination marks *of boys

No.	School	Class	N	r
1.	Government High School for Boys, Sharaqpur, District Sheikhupura	6	174	·55
2.	Liaqat Memorial High School, Sheikhupura	6	193	·63
3.	M. C. High School, Chichawatni, District Montgomery	6	137	·50
4.	Government High School for Boys, Sharaqpur, District Sheikhupura	7	140	·35
5.	Liaqat Memorial High School, Sheikhupura	7	136	·55
6.	M. C. High School, Chichawatni, District Montgomery	7	161	·76
7.	Government Pilot High School, Wahdat Colony, Lahore	8	35	·48
8.	Government High School for Boys, Sheikhupura	8	121	·57
9.	Liaqat Memorial High School, Sheikhupura	8	99	·41
10.	M. C. High School, Chichawatni, District Montgomery	8	166	·60

Average r = ·57

*Total marks of classes 6, 7 and 8 include marks in English, Urdu, social studies, mathematics, general science and religious education.

The validity coefficients between SAT II scores and final examination marks for ten samples of boys from classes 6, 7 and 8 given in

Development of Scholastic Aptitude Tests

table 3, indicate that this test consistently has been a good predictor of their school success. These validity coefficients range from 0·35 to 0·76 and average 0·57.

Table 4. Summary of validity coefficients between SAT II scores and final examination marks *of girls

No.	School	Class	N	r
1.	Government Girls High School, Wahdat Colony, Lahore	6	142	·85
2.	Government High & Normal School for Girls, Sharaqpur, District Sheikhupura	6	47	·27
3.	Government Girls High School, Wahdat Colony, Lahore	7	106	·62
4.	Government High & Normal School for Girls, Sharaqpur, District Sheikhupura	7	24	·20
5.	Government Girls High School, Wahdat Colony, Lahore	8	103	·60
6.	Government High & Normal School for Girls, Sharaqpur, District Sheikhupura	8	18	·60
			Average r =	·67

*Total marks of classes 6, 7 and 8 include marks in English, Urdu, social studies, mathematics, general science and religious education.

The validity coefficients between SAT II scores and final examination marks for samples of girls from classes 6, 7 and 8 are given in table 4. Comparing these coefficients with those for boys, given in table 3, shows that the test has more validity for girls' high schools. Most of the correlations are indeed high, including the one of 0·85 for a sample of 142 pupils from the Government Girls High School, Wahdat Colony, Lahore. The average correlation for all samples given in table 4 is 0·67.

A summary of validity coefficients between SAT III scores and final examination marks for boys in classes 8 and 9 is given in table 5. The validity indices are less consistent here than for SAT II. Except for three correlations in the table, they are fairly satisfactory. The average correlation for the eight samples in the table is 0·45. Continuing validation studies are needed to furnish more evidence on the validity of the instrument.

It appears from table 6 that the validity coefficients between SAT III scores and final examination marks for girls in classes 8 and 9 are better than those for the boys given in table 5. Except for one low correlation

Table 5. Summary of validity coefficients between SAT III scores and final examination marks *for boys

No.	School	Class	N	r
1.	Government Pilot High School for Boys, Wahdat Colony, Lahore	8	36	·17
2.	Government High School for Boys, Sharaqpur, District Sheikhupura	8	109	·18
3.	Liaqat Memorial High School, Sheikhupura	8	99	·60
4.	M. C. High School, Chichawatni, District Montgomery	8	132	·57
5.	Government High School for Boys, Sharaqpur, District Sheikhupura	9	158	·41
6.	Government Pilot High School for Boys, Wahdat Colony, Lahore	9	154	·26
7.	Liaqat Memorial High School, Sheikhupura	9	120	·54
8.	M. C. High School, Chichawatni, District Montgomery	9	147	·56
			Average $r =$	·45

*Total marks for class 8 include marks in English, Urdu, social studies, mathematics, general science and religious education. Total marks of class 9 include marks in English, Urdu and social studies (common school subjects for science group, agriculture group, etc.).

Table 6. Summary of validity coefficients between SAT III scores and final examination marks *of girls

No.	School	Class	N	r
1.	Government Girls High School, Wahdat Colony, Lahore	8	103	·62
2.	Government High & Normal School for Girls, Sharaqpur, District Sheikhupura	8	18	·24
3.	Government Girls High School, Wahdat Colony, Lahore	9	137	·66
4.	Government High & Normal School for Girls, Sharaqpur, District Sheikhupura	9	25	·80
			Average $r =$	·64

*Total marks of class 8 include marks in English, Urdu, social studies, mathematics, general science and religious education. Total marks of class 9 include marks in English, Urdu and social studies (common school subjects for science group, home economics group, etc.).

of 0·24, they are high. The average correlation of 0·64 for the four samples in the table is also high, and strengthen one's faith in the instrument.

Table 7. Summary of validity coefficients between SAT III scores and Secondary School Leaving Certificate Examination marks

No.	School	Class	N	r
1.	Government High School for Boys, Sharaqpur, District Sheikhupura	10	63	·62
2.	Liaqat Memorial High School, Sheikhupura	10	52	·37
3.	M. C. High School, Chichawatni, District Montgomery	10	99	·70
4.	Government Girls Normal & High School, Sharaqpur, District Sheikhupura	10	21	·42
			Average $r =$	·60

While evidence of the predictive validity of the three scales of the Scholastic Aptitude Tests is based on the correlation between the test scores and final examination marks of pupils in classes 4 to 9, it is interesting to consider how these tests might predict performance of boys and girls taking the *external* Secondary School Certificate Examination of the Board. On the basis of the limited information given in table 7, SAT III could be used for this purpose. If further studies of the predictive validity of this test for class 10 students should indicate similar results, it would then become a useful instrument for academic and vocational guidance.

Reliability

The fundamental index of precision of any scale is the degree to which the performance of the individual remains stable. The split-half method was used to estimate the reliability of the Scholastic Aptitude Tests. The coefficients of reliability thus obtained are given in table 8.

The reliability coefficients range from 0·76 to 0·98, averaging 0·89, 0·83 and 0·90 for Scales I, II and III respectively. In better testing conditions, the reliability coefficients might improve.

Table 8. Reliability of the Scholastic Aptitude Tests, Scales I, II and III

Scale	Class	Number	r	Average
SAT I	4	102	·89	
	5	102	·88	·89
	6	111	·90	
SAT II	6	101	·78	
	7	113	·85	·83
	8	100	·84	
SAT III	8	103	·98	
	9	118	·76	·90
	10	101	·94	

Use of the Scholastic Aptitude Tests

The development of the SAT represents a new initiative in Pakistani education. The ultimate use of these instruments will depend on their demonstrated value in the schools and other situations. Our initial studies give us reason to believe that the SAT series will be useful for understanding, guiding and selecting pupils—and as a measurement tool for a variety of educational research efforts. Moreover, the Scholastic Aptitude Test III, the Mechanical Aptitude Test, and the Spatial Ability Test, which together constitute an integrated Differential Aptitude Tests battery, may become useful instruments for academic and vocational guidance. There is, however, an obvious need to gather more validity data and to extend our knowledge of how these tests will be useful.

The introduction of SAT in schools is a formidable task. Most schools do not have trained guidance counsellors or teachers who can make good use of the results from these measurements. The tests can become lethal instruments in the hands of untrained school personnel. Successful introduction of the SAT in schools, therefore, depends on setting up effective guidance and testing services. Since schools differ in the degree of interest and sophistication in testing, the SAT series might be introduced through a phased programme as follows:

1. First, in government pilot secondary schools which are introducing diversified programmes and have a special interest in helping pupils make suitable choices of programmes.
2. Secondly, in model schools, cadet colleges and some private schools which have academic excellence as their foremost objective and would thus wish to develop sound and rigorous admission testing programmes.
3. Thirdly, in typical schools, both public and private, which admit

most of the school population and share a general desire to offer adequate education to all.

It appears that the thirteen pilot secondary schools are the only type which have introduced some notions of a guidance programme. This has been effected largely by efforts of the West Pakistan Education Extension Centre, and more recently, by the Institute of Education and Research. It is reasonable to assume that these schools can make use of the SAT experimentally, as many are now doing. In view of the greater resources of the second type of schools, in terms of finance and qualified staff, they can be expected to take some initiative in introducing guidance. The third category of schools is less privileged, and it is towards these schools that the Institute of Education and Research should direct much of its attention. The Institute may select a few of these schools to set up experimental guidance programmes. Experience thus gained can then be shared by other schools.

As has been pointed out earlier, the successful introduction of SAT and other measures for guidance and selection depends largely on the supply of trained guidance counsellors and teachers and enlightened school administration. Only then could one hope that guidance and testing services in schools would become operational. The following steps are proposed to help develop these services in schools:

1. In service training of selected teachers in guidance and counselling to enable them to assume the role of guidance teachers.
2. The placing of greater stress on guidance principles and techniques in normal schools and teachers' colleges.
3. An emphasis on guidance in schools during refresher courses for school administrators and supervisory staff.
4. The planning of summer workshops in guidance and testing at the Institute of Education and Research at Lahore in West Pakistan, the Extension Centre, and other institutions.
5. The suitable placement of the Institute of Education and Research graduates who specialize in guidance during their M.Ed. programme.
6. The preparation of brochures, pamphlets and other materials on guidance principles, counselling techniques, the use and interpretation of tests, vocational opportunities, etc.

Successful introduction of the SAT in schools requires these vital steps. The initial success in developing the SAT and other instruments has enabled the Institute of Education and Research to redirect its energies, in collaboration with other institutions, towards the establishment of guidance and testing services. Difficulties which beset the introduction of these tests in schools are slowly being surmounted. A number of pilot schools, cadet colleges, technical schools and general schools are already using these tests for a variety of purposes.

It is becoming apparent that these tests can furnish useful information at critical stages in the academic careers of the learners, and can help channel them into appropriate programmes. It is, furthermore, being recognized that these tests can help discover the range of abilities in schools, help determine the gap between the learning capacity and academic achievement of individuals, and thus enable teachers to adapt programmes to the needs and capacities of their pupils. The school heads are learning the significance of these measures for many of their policies and decisions. It should, however, be pointed out that the expression of such views or philosophies is still limited, and one cannot assume a widely shared appreciation of these views on school testing. It does, however, signify that pioneering work done by the Institute in the study of individual differences, and their implications for education of the individual, is beginning to exercise a healthy influence on Pakistani education.

References

Pakistan Ministry of Education (1960) *Report of the Commission on National Education.* Karachi: Government of Pakistan Press.

University of the Punjab, Institute of Education and Research. *Manual for Scholastic Aptitude Tests.* Lahore.

University of the Punjab, Institute of Education and Research. *Scholastic Aptitude Tests* (in Urdu). Lahore.

DEVELOPING DESCRIPTIONS OF OBJECTIVES AND TEST ITEMS

J. DOUGLAS AYERS

An alternative title for this paper could be 'Adapting Bloom's Taxonomy to a subject area or discipline at the state or local level', but, regardless of how it is labelled, one would think it should not be necessary to explain how to adapt and use a taxonomy. Apparently, it is necessary. *The Taxonomy of Educational Objectives: Cognitive Domain,* edited by Bloom (1956) was first published in 1956, but it is only in recent years that one finds many references to it. Evidence to this effect will be found in two recent annotated bibliographies by Cox and Gordon (1966).

This paper, then, will attempt to explain some of the factors affecting its slow acceptance. It will also report on the procedures that were developed in Alberta, Canada, for putting in the hands of teachers revised and expanded descriptions of Bloom's Taxonomy in each of a number of subject areas. These statements, now available in three subject areas, were developed by groups of classroom teachers and staff of the University of Alberta Faculty of Education.

Role of taxonomy in education

Probably the most striking evidence supporting the contention that Bloom's Taxonomy has gained slow acceptance is that few people have heard about the test folio of seven thousand test items in science, published in 1956 by Educational Testing Service as *Questions and Problems in Science: Test Item Folio No. 1* (Dressel and Nelson 1956). All seven thousand items were classified within sixty content topics as well as by Bloom's categories. Now, where could one find seven thousand items, ready to use, at the bargain price of $25.00, or three and one half cents per item? The items themselves ranged from good to excellent, but this venture was a commercial failure and the last copies of the folio were given away in 1962 or 1963.

The Cox and Gordon bibliographies represent an attempt to list all known references to uses of Bloom's Taxonomy, at least in North America. They are not very extensive, and most of the articles reported are of a general nature or represent validation studies conducted to test the assumption that the Taxonomy categories are hierarchically organized. Moreover, a large number of the references are to unpublished reports. The interesting feature of the bibliography is that most of the references are to reports released in the last few years, which suggests that there are a number of other studies and adaptations that have not been reported. Several such unpublished reports will be discussed below. Further evidence supporting the slow acceptance theme is that there have been few reported adaptations, and yet adaptations should be an outgrowth of its acceptance. Besides the three descriptions in Grade 9 Social Studies, Science, and Literature, published by the Alberta Department of Education (1965, 1966 and 1967), there are only two other reported adaptations of Bloom to subject areas. Sanders (1966), in co-operation with a number of Wisconsin teachers, developed an extremely comprehensive adaptation in the Social Studies entitled *Classroom Questions: What Kinds?*, and the Biological Sciences Curriculum Study group in *Biology Teachers' Handbook* (1963) has reported a rather major adaptation.

I myself have used Bloom so extensively that I am often surprised at how slowly the Taxonomy has been accepted by measurement specialists, school administrators and classroom teachers. This surprise is due, in part, to the fact that the Taxonomy has been found to be extremely helpful to teacher education students in the preparation of objective tests that measure a wide variety of classroom objectives, where before most tests reflected measurement of knowledge objectives. The surprise is heightened when one examines the rationale behind the hierarchy and the accompanying category definitions. They make sense in terms of current cognitive learning theory and development psychology. Finally, a factor-analytic study of items within an achievement test suggests that the classifications in the Taxonomy may need some revision, but the essential hierarchical nature of the Taxonomy will probably not require substantial modification for some time (Ayers 1967). In my view, then, teachers, school administrators and curriculum development experts are missing an opportunity to improve both instruction and evaluation by not developing rather specific subject-oriented descriptions of objectives and items.

Problems associated with preparation of descriptions

There are two problems involved in the development of statements of objectives and items that may need clarification because they have important implications for what is discussed later. They have to do with the appropriate degree of specificity for objectives and the so-called threat of restrictiveness on the teacher when objectives are specified in behavioural terms and illustrated with questions and items.

Nowadays, we are frequently exhorted to define 'specific behavioural objectives', but how should this be done? Krathwohl (1965) clearly distinguishes among three main types of objectives. Those objectives found in courses of study or curriculum guides are typically very

Developing descriptions of objectives

general, whether in the introduction to the guide or associated with a particular unit. Admittedly, such objectives are general and vague because, even at the local level, it is extremely difficult to obtain agreement on the methods for implementing general goals. 'To develop citizenship' is a general goal on which it is possible to obtain universal agreement as to its worth, but there is little agreement, even in the same community, on how to teach or measure it. Such general statements of goals, then, meet an important need, but they are completely inadequate for the teacher who must describe the desired pupil behaviours in more objective terms for purposes of instruction and evaluation. Krathwohl suggests that objectives for these purposes be defined at an intermediate level of specificity as illustrated by the statements found in the Bloom or Krathwohl (1964) taxonomies. Why the intermediate level of specificity should be used will be explained more fully below. Very specific objectives such as those used in programmed instruction and computer-assisted instruction for describing terminal behaviour exemplify the third type. Such statements typically specify not only the objective, but also the content and degree of achievement, all in great detail. At most, such descriptions may be useful in preparing sequences of programmed instruction material, but they are much too restrictive for delineating the objectives of classroom instruction and evaluation.

Most of us are familiar with the complaint often made in popular magazines and newspapers and frequently used by teachers, that external examinations and standardized tests restrict the teacher's freedom to teach a subject for its own sake. Such complaints are also extended to courses of study and prescribed textbooks. The contention is that external tests and examinations require that students and teachers prepare for them as if this, in itself, were inherently bad. What is overlooked is that students still prepare for a test, but it is the individual teacher's or professor's test, instead of a common one. Apparently, this is different in some unexplained way. There are also a number of other arguments against objective external examinations that have to do with learning poor study habits, memorizing, and so on. These complaints, of course, miss the essential function of tests, which is to determine the effectiveness of learning or instruction towards pre-assigned objectives. What is surprising is that the persons who complain the most, be they classroom teachers or university professors, generally administer tests and examinations that are much more restrictive of the student's intellectual development than most external examinations, particularly those developed in recent years. Teachers and professors have not kept up with the times. In fact, a study of the

Alberta descriptions of objectives and items in science and social studies, together with copies of state-wide external examinations, would indicate that teachers are fairly free to teach the subject for its own sake. At least 60 per cent of the items measure objectives in the intellectual skills and abilities categories which cannot readily be taught directly by the teachers. Additionally, many of the statements of objectives in the knowledge categories of Bloom are not completely specified; for example, Bloom's 1.20 categories, 'Knowledge of ways and means of dealing with specifics', which have to do with knowing concepts and abstractions and with their manipulation. Charts 1 and 2 (in the appendix) show that the statements of objectives and the sample items are intended as illustrative and not prescriptive.

As a further indication that the overall tone in the descriptions is one of encouragement to experiment, the introductory sections to these descriptions (not illustrated here) emphasize that the best preparation for an external examination is 'to teach science for science's sake'. Also, in the introduction it is pointed out that the more complex abilities in the higher categories of the cognitive domain require far more sophisticated learning experiences than communication of the correct version of a concept or abstraction to the students, and that the course must emphasize the higher mental processes if the students are to be affected to any significant degree. In addition, teachers are encouraged to develop the unifying ideas of a discipline, to stress precise and accurate definition, to emphasize similarities and differences between related concepts and abstractions, and to have students reformulate new propositions in their own words. They are urged to foster thinking by encouraging students to recognize and challenge assumptions underlying new propositions, and by having them distinguish between facts and hypotheses or between warranted and unwarranted inferences. It should be noted that nearly all of these statements represent paraphrasing of the objectives found in the Taxonomy under 'Intellectual skills and abilities', including Comprehension, Application, Analysis, Synthesis and Evaluation. Charts 3, 4, 5 and 6 present some examples of objectives and test items for the more complex intellectual skills and abilities.

Illustrations of items from an external examination are provided in charts 7 and 8. Some of these items are based on novel situations and these cannot be prepared for directly.

Perhaps this sampling of illustrations from the Alberta descriptions may provide the reader with some appreciation of the excitement engendered because of their obvious usefulness. The Alberta High School Examination Board believed that the published descriptions

Developing descriptions of objectives

would not only improve the quality of the external examinations, but also have a direct and desirable effect on classroom instruction and measurement.

Procedures for developing taxonomy descriptions

Based partly on the experiences gained in developing the Alberta descriptions and partly on the reported experiences of others, there are certain general guidelines that might be helpful to groups, if groups or committees of teachers, measurement specialists and subject matter experts are to develop adequate descriptions of objectives and items.
 1. The committee should have a draft description or model. A draft description might be prepared by a group of students in a measurement course. An alternative is a model in another subject, such as has been described and illustrated above.

It should be noted that while models are very helpful, if they are too detailed or prescriptive they may have an inhibiting effect on the adequacy of adaptation. For example, a group of teachers in British Columbia, familiar with the Alberta Grade 9 Science description, suggested weighting the objectives within each major category (Mason 1966). They also did not lack imagination in attempting to use the idea of the underlying theme in works of literature at several levels of the Taxonomy. Such an adaptation appears to represent an inappropriate attempt to include aspects of both the substantive and the syntactical structures of literature in the description itself. Such an innovation is important, provided that it is consistent with the intent of Bloom to maintain a hierarchical organization of objectives.
 2. One member of the committee should be a measurement specialist. Comprehending the intent of Bloom's Taxonomy requires experience that is probably best gained in teaching a measurement course in which the Taxonomy is used by students to prepare, analyse and revise unit tests.

This experience provides background required to explain the subtleties involved in defining categories and in distinguishing between categories, particularly adjacent ones.
 3. One member of the committee must understand the substantive and syntactical structure of the discipline and preferably have some background or experience in measurement.

This person is most likely to be found at a university.
 4. Several members of the committee should have experience in the writing and revising of questions and items. Personnel with backgrounds in curriculum development and revision may also prove to be useful members of the committee.

Another caution might be inserted at this point. Too much structure can be provided by models, and too much assistance can be given the committee. The main job of the chairman is to explain and clarify, in addition to providing encouragement. In the initial stages the tendency is for the committee members to feel that very little progress is being made, particularly when no model is available. As a result, the measurement specialist tends to do more than explain, clarify and encourage.

Some additional observations

It is difficult to determine to what extent departures from Bloom represent significant change or improvement. Admittedly, both individuals and groups should be encouraged to experiment with and create new categories and combinations. At our present state of knowledge, one cannot really determine if a significant improvement has been effected. What follows are references to some adaptations with a brief comment on each.

1. The Biological Sciences Curriculum Study (1962, Klinckman 1963) group has made a rather violent and unnecessary reorganization of the higher categories of Bloom. As it is difficult to find a university graduate in the biological sciences with a knowledge of Bloom to defend the adaptation, it would appear that the BSCS group did not fully comprehend Bloom.

2. The School Mathematics Study Group has outlined a very interesting adaptation of Bloom which, at least on the surface, makes sense (Romberg 1966). Final evaluation of its adequacies must await a description of the objectives and test items that would be included under each of the categories.

3. Bloom's Taxonomy was used quite extensively in Project Talent in California. In fact, six thirty-minute movies were produced showing teachers using the objectives in each of the main Bloom categories.*

4. Chart 9 shows how a group in Grossmont, California, has extended the meaning of the Bloom categories together with suggestions on how the Taxonomy can be used for instruction and evaluation.

5. Finally, in Portland, Oregon, Doherty (1967) has reported on a Carnegie project which encouraged teachers to adapt the Taxonomy in the preparation of curriculum guides. The concomitant objectives column in chart 10 was apparently added to show the wide variety of objectives including those from the affective domain that teachers

*Acme Film Laboratories, Inc.
1161 North Highland Avenue, Los Angeles, California

should consider in teaching a unit. It would appear that this group has neither understood the hierarchical nature of the Taxonomy nor appreciated the importance of separating content and objectives. They have not only confounded content and objectives, but have failed to specify the objectives clearly. What they have done is show the essential concepts, themes, relations and principles—the substantive structure which, of course, is desirable in the preparation of instructional guides.

It was the intent of this paper to provide sufficient background information and references that other measurement specialists with knowledge of Bloom's Taxonomy would be encouraged to develop descriptions of objectives and test items to meet local conditions and needs. Moreover, until it can be shown that Bloom's Taxonomy is inadequate, it should be used as it is or with only minor adaptations, with the view to improving communications and having a standard conceptual model for research into the process dimension of learning.

References

Alberta Department of Education (1965) *Summary Description of Grade 9 Science Objectives and Items.* Edmonton: Alberta Department of Education.

Alberta Department of Education (1966) *Summary Description of Grade 9 Social Studies Objectives and Items.* Edmonton: Alberta Department of Education.

Alberta Department of Education (1967) *Summary Description of Grade 9 Literature Objectives, Test Items and Blueprint* (1st edition). Edmonton: High School Entrance Examinations Board, Alberta Department of Education. Mimeographed.

Ayers, J. D. (1967) 'Justification of Bloom's Taxonomy by factor analysis.' (Accepted for publication, *J. educ. psychol. Measur.*)

Biological Sciences Curriculum Study (1962) *Biology Teachers' Handbook,* chap. 16. New York: Wiley.

Bloom, B. S. (ed.) (1956) *Taxonomy of Educational Objectives, Handbook I: Cognitive Domain.* New York and London: Longmans.

Cox, R. C. and Gordon, J. M. (1966) *Validation and Uses of the Taxonomy of Educational Objectives: Cognitive Domain.* A select and annotated bibliography, mimeograph of the University of Pittsburgh, School of Education, with Cox, R. C. mimeographed 8-page addendum.

Doherty, V. W. (1967) *Objectives Revisited.* Report of the Administrative Research Department, Portland School. Presented to the California Test Bureau Institute, 12 April.

Dressel, P. L. and Nelson, C. H. (1956) *Questions and Problems in Science.* Test item folio no. 1. Princeton, N.J.: The Cooperative Test Division, Educational Testing Service. Out of print.

Forness, E. and Lochthowe, C. (1966) *Approaches to the Study of Cultures through Anthropology and Sociology.* The Carnegie Progressional Growth Programme.

Klinckman, E. (1963) 'The BSCS guide for test analysis.' *BSCS Newsletter,* **19**, 17-21.

Krathwohl, D. R. (1965) 'Stating objectives appropriately for program, for curriculum, and for instructional materials development.' *J. Teacher Educ.,* **16**, no. 1, 83-92.

Krathwohl, D. R. *et al.* (1964) *Taxonomy of Educational Objectives, Handbook II: Affective Domain.* New York: David McKay.

Logsdon, J. and Tarr, D. (1962) *World Geography Test Bank.* Grossmont Union High School, California.

Mason, G. (ed.) (1966) *Statement of Objectives and Items, English 10 Literature.* Faculty of Education, University of Victoria.

Romberg, T. A. (1966) *Development of Mathematics Achievement Tests for the National Longitudinal Study of Mathematical Abilities.* Mimeographed report.

Sanders, N. M. (1966) *Classroom Questions: What Kinds?* New York: Harper & Row.

APPENDIX

Chart 1. Grade 9 Science objectives and items in knowledge of ways and means category

*Some objectives**

1. Recognizes when precision of measurement given is of a degree warranted by the nature of the problem. For example, the rule for 'rounding off' numbers.
2. Recognizes causal interrelations of a series of specific events such as which valve is open when the piston of a lift pump is moving downwards.
3. Recalls nature of process, for example, change in energy involved when water evaporates.
4. Recalls or recognizes classifications which structure and systematize physical and chemical phenomena such as types of energy or classes of compounds.
5. Knows criteria for judging the adequacy of an experiment.
6. Knows the procedure for the laboratory preparation of oxygen or the destructive distillation of coal.

Some items

1. Magnetic poles are usually named

   A. + and −
   B. red and blue
   *C. north and south
   D. anode and cathode

Items 2 to 5 involve simple machines. For each item select from the key the type of machine it illustrates.

Key

   A. lever
   B. inclined plane
   C. pulley
   D. wheel and axle
   E. screw

---

*In all categories of the taxonomy, supply type items (completion, short-answer, short- and long-essay) can be made by rewording the objectives. In the lower categories of the hierarchy the items will be of the completion or short-answer type, then as one moves into the intellectual skills and abilities, they will be predominantly of the short- or long-essay type.

2. ramp
3. block and tackle
4. human arm
5. rotary egg beater

Keyed answers are 2 (B), 3 (C), 4 (A), 5 (D).

Chart 2. Grade 9 Social Studies objectives and items in knowledge of ways and means category

Some objectives

1. Knows the relevant symbols and conventions used in reading maps.
*2. Knows trends and sequences such as the development of responsible government in Canada.
3. Knows cause and effect relations such as the social effects of the Industrial Revolution.
4. Recalls or recognizes the fundamental classifications, divisions and arrangements. For example, the various types of government or the various forms of business ownership.
5. Knows the criteria by which facts and principles are tested or judged, for example, the factors which influence climate.
6. Recalls or recognizes the methods of inquiry, techniques and procedures employed in the social sciences to investigate particular problems and phenomena, for example, methods of graphing or the time-line procedure.

Some items

1. Match each symbol in the right-hand column below with the appropriate term in the left-hand column.

Term	Symbol
A. isotherm	1.
B. isobar	
C. snow	2.
D. rain	3.
E. wind	
F. cloud	4.

    Key: (1) A, (2) F, (3) C, (4) B.

2. Following the North-West Rebellion, the trend in Canadian federal politics was towards

Developing descriptions of objectives 195

  A. conservatism
  *B. liberalism
  C. annexationism
  D. separatism

3. The factor which had the *least* effect on starting the Industrial Revolution in England was

  A. availability of capital
  B. availability of resources
  *C. government planning
  D. labour supply

Chart 3. Examples of Application and Analysis items

The following are some of the basic principles upon which our federal government has been built:

  A. majority rule
  B. the federal government has primary responsibility only in certain areas
  C. responsible government
  D. other principles not listed above

For each of the following practices (items 9 to 12) indicate the principle involved. Mark D if none of the above principles are involved. Then, in the second step, indicate if the practice agrees with the principle or not by marking

  E. for agreement with the principle
  F. for disagreement with the principle

9. Mr Pearson as leader of the Liberal Party is Prime Minister.
10. The federal government provides unemployment insurance.
11. The federal government collects excise taxes.
12. The governor-general may request the leader of the opposition to form a government.

Key: (9) A, F; (10) B, F; (11) B, E; (12) D, E.

Note: The above block of items is just one example of an almost unlimited variety that can be developed for classroom quizzes. Such blocks are less appropriate for external examinations because of the two-step procedure involved in responding, and because some items may be open to several interpretations. However, they do provide an excellent basis for measuring Comprehension, Application and Analysis, and they serve as a basis for classroom discussion. In the above block the first step involves Application and the second step Analysis.

Chart 4. Examples of Application items

Some items

Study the map of the imaginary continent and use your knowledge of geography to answer questions 1 to 5 below.

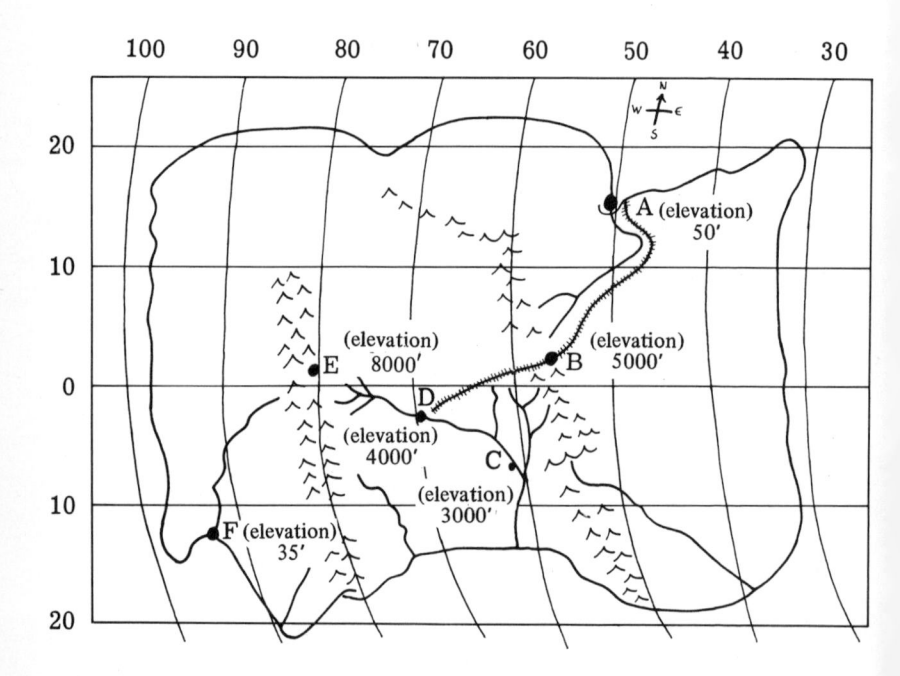

Choose the appropriate letter to complete each of the following statements:

1. The greatest annual precipitation occurs at
2. The least annual precipitation occurs at
3. The coolest year-round temperature occurs at
4. Banana plantations are found at
5. The cattle industry is centred at

Key: (1) A, (2) F, (3) E, (4) A, (5) D.

Developing descriptions of objectives 197

Chart 5. Examples of Synthesis objectives and items in Social Studies

Some objectives

1. Selects, relates and organizes material in a report or talk.
2. Contributes to discussion with material from experiences.
3. Prepares an essay outline.
4. Plans a programme, T.V. show, panel discussion or field trip.
5. Proposes ways of teaching hypotheses.
6. Formulates hypotheses to explain interrelated social events or data.

*Some items**

1. Design a mural symbolizing the ethnic origins of Canadians.
2. Examine and explain this statement:
'Trade takes place in response to demand which varies with differences in people, their desires and their abilities. It also depends upon differences in geographic factors, neutral resources, location and accessibility.'

Key to item 2

The exchange of surplus materials is known as commerce or trade. Trade is the response of countries to give of their surplus in order to be able to obtain necessities and luxuries. No modern country has all of the products that are desired; thus trade has become a necessity.

The human resources of a nation have a great effect on its trade. The people must have a desire to obtain necessities and luxuries which they are unable to produce. Furthermore, they must have the technical knowledge and skills to produce the natural resources which are available and, when possible, manufacture them into finished products which will be most desirable for trade.

Chart 6. Examples of Synthesis objectives and items in Social Studies

Marked differences in climate, land forms and natural resources from place to place have led to regional differences in the activities of men and in the products of these activities. Particular climates favour particular occupations; thus regional specialization occurs.

Nearness to water and other transportation facilities assist in carrying on trade. The location of a country in relation to other trading centres encourages or discourages trade. Thus Canada is ideally situated for

*It is extremely difficult to write objective items to measure Synthesis and Evaluation. Bloom provides several additional examples.

trade, as it has good harbours on both east and west coasts which are readily accessible to Europe and Asia. Trade depends on the development of natural resources and on import and export policies.

3. The best way of testing the proposition, 'The bonds holding together the OAS are becoming weaker', is to

   A. compare the number of members in 1965 with that in 1955
   B. examine changes in the Canadian government's statements on the OAS
   C. examine the trend in power of Castro's régime in inciting revolt in other countries of Latin America
   *D. study the trend in settlements of disputes among member nations

4. Organize your class for a discussion of Bolivar's proposal that the Spanish-speaking republics should join together to form a United States of South America. One person can be designated to represent Bolivar and other students to represent different South American countries. You should provide some arguments in favour of the proposed federation for the student playing the part of Bolivar and some arguments against the federation for students playing the other parts.

Key to item 4

This exercise calls for synthesis of the views of the Latin-American countries after the defeat of the Spaniards and the liberation of all South America from Spanish control in 1824.

The plan for the discussion in the form of role playing would involve first of all an explanation of the setting: Panama City, 1826, just after the final liberation.

Simon Bolivar is in favour of the federation of the countries to achieve a United States of South America.

Chart 7. Sample items from Grade 9 Science

51. The principle which most directly underlies the operation of mechanical refrigeration is that

    A. evaporation is a cooling process
    B. cooling results when vapour expands against the attractive forces between the molecules
    C. the volume occupied by a given mass of gas is inversely proportional to the pressure applied
    D. none of the above applies to refrigerators

Developing descriptions of objectives

52. Air which escapes from the valve of an automobile tyre feels colder than the surrounding air because

   A. the air condenses moisture on one's hand
   B. the air absorbs heat as it expands
   C. the air in the tyre is colder
   D. forceful blasts of air feel cold

53. The rate of evaporation of water may be increased by all of the following steps except

   A. placing the water in a pan of larger diameter
   B. increasing the humidity of the room
   C. decreasing the pressure over the water surface
   D. increasing the molecular motion of the water

54. The heat required to raise the temperature of 50 lbs of water from 40°F. to 80°F. is

   A. 40 BTUs
   B. 2000 BTUs
   C. 10 BTUs
   D. none of these

Below is a diagram of a tank of water with thermometers placed at W,X,Y and Z. The temperature of the water is 70°F. A block of ice is placed as shown. (Use this diagram in answering questions 55 to 57.)

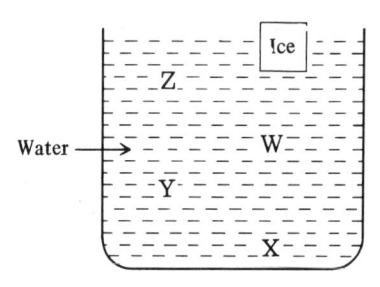

55. In the above diagram, which thermometer would be the first to show a drop in temperature?
   A. W
   B. X
   C. Y
   D. Z

56. In the above diagram, which thermometer would be the last to show a drop in temperature?

   A. W
   B. X
   C. Y
   D. Z

57. In the diagram above, which type of heat transmission is the most important in cooling the tank of water?

   A. conduction
   B. condensation
   C. convection
   D. radiation

58. A room thermometer graduated in the Fahrenheit scale reads 70°. Outside the window a Centigrade thermometer reads 15°. The temperature difference in Fahrenheit degrees between the inside and outside is

   A. 55
   B. 43
   C. 30
   D. 11

Chart 8. Sample items from Grade 9 Social Studies

77. The recent general election in the United Kingdom resulted in the election of the

   A. Conservative government with an increased number of seats
   B. Conservative government with a decreased number of seats
   C. Labour government with an increased number of seats
   D. Labour government with a decreased number of seats

78. The Lieutenant-Governor of Alberta is

   A. J. Percy Page
   B. Ernest Manning
   C. Georges Vanier
   D. Grant MacEwan

79. The Vice-President of the United States is

   A. Hubert Humphrey
   B. Robert Kennedy
   C. Lyndon Johnson
   D. Dean Rusk

80. The Commonwealth's only woman Prime Minister is Madam
    A. Ayub Khan
    B. Indira Gandhi
    C. Patrice Lumumba
    D. Sirimavo Bandaranaike

81. The Federal Government Cabinet Minister who was most influential in the establishment of the Canada Pension Plan was
    A. Guy Favreau
    B. Paul Hellyer
    C. Paul Marsh
    D. Judy LaMarsh

82. In an attempt to make Rhodesia relax its stand on Negro representation in government, all the following pressures have been imposed *except*
    A. military
    B. diplomatic
    C. press
    D. economic

Items 83 to 86 contain a pair of statements which are either in agreement or not in agreement with each other, and either or both of the statements may be true or false. Study the pair of statement and mark

    A. if statements I and II are both false
    B. if statements I and II are both true
    C. if statement I is true and II is false
    D. if statement I is false and II is true

83. I. The United Nations is faced with financial problems.
    II. The USSR has not paid its dues.
84. I. The number of member nations in the United Nations at the end of 1965 was over 110.
    II. Communist China gained a membership in 1965.
85. I. The number of votes in the General Assembly is granted on basis of the population of a nation.
    II. The African-Asian lands form the largest block in the world organization when they agree to vote together for a particular purpose.
86. I. The United Nations sent a peace-keeping force to Viet Nam.
    II. Canada is a member of this peace-keeping force.

Chart 9. Analysis of factors in the learning process*

TYPES OF LEARNING

	Knowledge	*Comprehension*
A. What students do Activity	Responds Absorbs Remembers Rehearses Covers Recognizes	Uncovers Details Lists Dissects Explains Demonstrates Translates Extends Interprets
Tangible outcomes (Objective tests)	Objective test results Completes programme learning sequences	Objective test results Experimental write-ups Précis
B. What teachers do Activity	Directs Tells Leads Shows Delineates Enlarges Examines	Demonstrates Listens Reflects Questions Compares Contrasts Examines
Tangible outcomes (Objective tests)	Programmed materials	Objective tests Essay tests
C. Appropriate organization and location		
Methods used by teachers and students	Lecture Drill Recitation Objective test Homework	Objective test Essay test Recitation Socratic dialogue
Materials used by teachers and students	Textbooks Programmed materials	Audio-visual materials Television Natural phenomena
Times used by teachers and students	Formal regularized	Formal regularized
Places used by teachers and students	Large group classroom	Classroom typical group

*Grossmont Union High School District, Grossmont, California. 1962.

Chart 10. Sample page from Curriculum Guide (from Forness and Lochthowe 1966)

Suggested learning activities	Concomitant objectives	Evaluation	Organization
I. Use of inquiry process—Observe pictures of various peoples throughout the world. A. What common traits or ideas are depicted through the pictures which you have seen? B. List these common facts as a group. C. What similarities do you see in kinds of food, in manners of dress and of eating, in homes and in recreation? D. What differences do you see in these human problems and needs? E. Through what subjects have we been approaching the field of social studies? F. Are there other sciences through which the study of the culture of man could be approached? List. G. Show the guide sheet prepared to give teachers an overall view of the disciplines used in social studies. H. Define the disciplines.	To enable teachers to help children arrive at the following concepts: 1. That all people need food, shelter and recreation. 2. That all people need some form of training in order to exist in their particular culture. 3. That they should help children develop a deep appreciation of and a sympathy for all people. 4. That they should help children to understand what people do and why they do it.	1. Observe how teachers have become aware of one anthropological concept, that human beings have the same fundamental needs. 2. Observe that teachers have become aware that there are other approaches to the study of cultures besides geography and history, and that they can improve the teaching of social studies by their use. 3. Observe through discussion the reading done by the teachers.	1. To acquaint teachers with the concept that human beings everywhere shape their beliefs and behaviour in response to the same fundamental problems and needs.

(Continued on p. 204)

Chart 10 (contd)

Suggested learning activities

II. Using the anthropological and sociological approaches to the study of culture, what are some words to be defined? List.
   A. Copy. Define in terms which children might understand.
   B. Have children make a dictionary of their own, defining the words, using words in sentences, illustrating if possible.
   C. Have children categorize words into lists.
   D. Develop other methods to use with children to aid in the understanding of words to be used.
   E. Read Pelto's *The Study of Anthropology.*

A CRITICAL APPRAISAL OF ONE NATIONAL TESTING PROGRAMME

JOHN M. DUGGAN

The College Entrance Examination Board (CEEB) is a non-profit membership association of colleges, universities, secondary schools and educational associations. It is not, to my knowledge, supported by the CIA, but largely by test fees paid by students. It has a relatively successful history of service to secondary schools, colleges and students. Founded in 1900 by school and college leaders who recognized the need for an organization that would help provide direction and co-ordination in helping students move from secondary school to college, the association has grown steadily until today there are 707 colleges and universities, 232 secondary schools, and 88 associations in membership. The member institutions, large and small, public and private, represent a cross-section of American education, and, regardless of an institution's kind or size or prestige, each member has a vote in policy decisions.

The major activity of the Board is an extensive programme of examinations for guidance, college admissions and course placement. The college admissions testing programme, in the beginning, was similar to the British examining system in scope and style. During the 1920s and 30s psychological testing was tentatively introduced to the Board's programme, particularly in the development of an aptitude test of scholastic ability. During the 1940s, the Board s testing programme moved from a written series of tests to an objective set of multiple-choice aptitude and achievement tests. Last year the Board administered its most widely used test—the Scholastic Aptitude Test—to approximately one and a half million students. More exactly, Educational Testing Service administered this and other tests on behalf of the College Entrance Examination Board. All of the Board's testing programmes and many of its other services are conducted under Board policy control by Educational Testing Service, an independent, non-profit, testing agency founded in 1948 by the Board and two other educational associations.

To explain how the College Board works, it is necessary to describe the context within which it operates. One feature of United States education to keep in mind is that we have developed many more college facilities proportionate to the population than any other nation. There is, as a consequence, a great deal more diversity in the kinds of colleges. It is not that we have developed a higher proportion of able students, but going to college has become an inexorable social pressure so that the demand for educational experiences after high school has been met by a rapidly changing definition of the word 'college'. About 90 per cent of the sixteen- and seventeen-year-old youngsters in the United States are now enrolled in secondary school; the figure was about 68 per cent twenty years ago. About half of those graduating from secondary school continue into college of some sort. There are, at the last count, 2,230 institutions of higher learning in the United States. Of these, 154 are universities, 817 are liberal arts colleges; there are 186 teachers' colleges, 55 technological schools, 207 theological institutions, 134 other professional schools, 622 junior colleges and 57 semi-professional schools. All kinds of admissions systems operate in these institutions; there are perhaps 150 that are highly selective. There is a large group of colleges that accepts virtually all high school graduates within the state. In many of these colleges academic demands force out those students who are not able to handle the work. There is also a very large group of 'open door' institutions that fit their programmes to the abilities of their students.

All these colleges, though diverse in purpose and kind, are considered equally collegiate as a convention. Many of them are ideologically committed to open enrolment, and many others practice open enrolment by necessity. Therefore, admissions decisions by selective colleges are not ultimately very crucial within the total system. Therefore, also, the test score that is part of the information imbedded in the admissions decision receives much less pressure, bears much less responsibility, and reveals much less in the way of faults than would be true if a test score alone determined whether or not a youngster could continue his education.

But my purpose today is not to describe the system of secondary and higher education. Nor do I intend to trace the founding and evolution of the College Board. My purpose is, however, to describe the strengths and weaknesses of the one national testing programme I know best. Fortunately, for my own vocational well-being, and I believe for the well-being of students, schools and colleges in the United States, the strengths far outnumber the weaknesses. But I am not suggesting that our testing programme should be exported wholesale anywhere. I wish only that you understand it on the chance that it may contain lessons, good and bad, for you to consider as you develop, implement and gain support for your own testing activities. I do not pretend that the College Board should be a model to be emulated everywhere, but I do believe our programme has some eminently worth-while features which should only knowingly be disregarded, and some built-in problems which should be scrupulously avoided.

I think of the CEEB as a four-legged animal. It has the mobility to keep pace with the rapid development of higher education in the United States, and it moves fairly smoothly between secondary school education and higher education. (I would be less than objective, though, if I did not report that there are those who see it as more of a plodding elephant than a sleek gazelle.) The four legs are: a good testing programme, a comprehensive research programme, a broad variety of educational programmes in support of or in addition to tests, and a broad membership base that includes the voices and votes of secondary school representatives.

The testing services of the College Board, particularly the Scholastic Aptitude Test, are as good as years of careful development and scrupulous attention can make them. The SAT is a three-hour, multiple-choice test of basic ability to understand and use words and numbers. It yields two scores—a verbal reasoning score and a mathematical reasoning score. When its scores are considered in conjunction with grades earned by students in secondary school, it provides a pretty fair prediction of achievement in college (as measured by instructors' grades). This test, as with all College Board tests, is developed under the supervision and direction of a committee of experts from the teaching profession. In the achievement testing programme, a series of one-hour specific tests in fourteen different subjects, the use of committees ensures that the test development process is attuned to what is actually going on in secondary schools. The purpose here is to keep the tests relevant to what the classroom teacher is trying to develop in the way of skills and understanding within the subject matter areas. I commend to you a wide involvement of the academic community in your test development work and a set of procedures open to the view of the academic community and even of the public in order to reduce the danger of a poorly understood 'testing mystique'.

I mentioned earlier that the tests are used in conjunction with the high school record for admission to college. If American education used tests alone to sort students, the use of tests in college admission probably would have had a lot of very serious faults which either do not exist, or are virtually unnoticed in our context. I mean, particularly, that in almost no other educational system does anyone representing higher education pay much attention to the secondary school record, or even to the less formal testimony of secondary school teachers, principals and headmasters. Therefore, when a test is used, it must carry the full burden of the decision and cannot be corrected by the weight of other evidence, suggesting that for some reason the test is not working correctly or justly. The high school record and teachers' recommendations are used in the United States in conjunction with the tests, and in this way, extra attention and emotion, which might otherwise be focused on the examination, are focused on all of the pertinent evidence in total composition. If we did otherwise, the current criticism of testing would be far more serious than it is.

Tests in conjunction with the high school record normally predict average grades at the end of the first year of college, on the order of $R = 0.50$. Through the Validity Study Service of the College Board, or the research service of the American College Testing Program, colleges are encouraged to provide data for a multiple regression analysis, in order to determine how the various predictors of college success should be combined in admitting or sorting their students. Virtually thousands of such studies have been done, so that the use and interpretation of tests and other predictors in college admissions rest on an empirical base.

This analysis of the validity of tests and their use in admissions is an essential element to a successful testing programme, but should be part of a larger research effort. The College Board annually spends about 5 per cent of its total expenditure of just under $20 million on its research programme. The purpose of the College Board's research programme is to develop easy and rational access to higher education for students by using the techniques and resources of the social and behavioural sciences. Our research programme operates on three distinct levels. One level consists of the broad questions facing those who make educational policy, and our purpose here is to help governing boards make decisions that take full account of existing impediments to education. These activities include determining the adequacy of educational facilities, projecting the numbers of students who will be in schools and colleges nationally and regionally, understanding the social forces that impede or impel higher education, identifying potential economic resources, and evaluating admissions systems. The second level of research is concerned with the development of techniques that would improve present practices in identification, guidance, examinations, admissions, financial aid, and placement of students. The purpose of the third level of research is to maintain the quality of our programme. This monitoring of services through research techniques provides for additions, deletions and refinements of existing activities.

A random listing of some current research and development projects might give you some flavour of our broad-based research programme:

    A study in four states of the flow of students from ninth grade through college admission with analyses of the distribution of ability

The development of an academic interest measure
The study of college financial aid awards as a function of socio-economic status
Effect of teaching methods on College Board language test scores
The content validity of achievement tests as judged by teachers
Differential weighting of item distractors
Testing literary comprehension at the advanced level
Studies of cultural differences in test scores
Development of an environmental index to measure college atmosphere
The development of a listening comprehension test with seventh-grade disadvantaged youngsters
Study of the educational problems of Mexican-American children in the south west
Career perception and college performance
Study of candidate overlap among colleges

The Board's research programme, once confined to test development, now includes a wide variety of concerns, ranging from the ability of farm families to pay college expenses to a study that describes students' perception of vocational choice. Much of this research is conducted on behalf of the Board by Educational Testing Service. Slightly more than half, however, is contracted with individual research workers or teams on university faculties or with research centres at universities.

The third leg of the College Board is its associational nature. The fact that the Board is a membership organization in which the members exercise a vote in policy matters means that its services cannot veer very sharply from its educational constituency. Complete involvement with users helps to insure relevance of our services and programmes. On any given day or with any given issue the professional staff may tend to feel restrained by the membership, but over the years the wisdom of restraints is clear.

This membership aspect also leads the Board to provide a forum through the sponsorship of meetings, conferences and seminars on problems of access to higher education. The Board sponsors: an annual meeting wherein the membership votes on actions presented by committees; training sessions for secondary school counsellors and college admission officers; conferences on curricular change; and various forums where school and college representatives may discuss problems common to them. In addition, there is a sizable group of some 100 publications providing information to students about college admissions and supporting all Board programmes. These include score interpretation leaflets, profiles of college norms, a quarterly magazine providing information about current work of the Board, and a variety of publications dealing with various aspects of college admission, curriculum development, counselling, financial aid, and related topics.

Each of the Board's programmes, and I will mention each only briefly, is managed by a professional staff with the advice of a committee of educationists with special competence in each of the programme areas. These programmes serve to broaden the scope of the Board and to support its testing activities. In addition to the admissions testing programme, there is a guidance programme that provides information about college opportunities and a test called the Preliminary Scholastic Aptitude Test available to juniors in secondary school for guidance purposes; an advanced placement programme in which able students do college-level work in secondary school and validate their competence by examinations in order to receive advanced placement and credit in college; a college-level examinations programme to provide institutional evaluation and to serve students who have done college-level work independently or outside the main stream of higher education and who wish to receive college credit by examination; a programme in which families provide information about their financial status to colleges for the purpose of determining the amount of scholarship aid needed, and, hopefully, awarded; and a new programme in international education whose activities include the development of a Spanish version of the Scholastic Aptitude Test, maintaining an operational office in Puerto Rico, and, in conjunction with Educational Testing Service, offering a new test of English as a foreign language for students from abroad. Each of these activities, and a good many other special projects, heavily involve schools and college teachers in a way that prevents the Board from becoming an organization external to American education. I commend this type of broad-based service to you.

The press in the United States has steadily contained a small amount of criticism of college entrance tests. This has not been very respectable criticism, however, because it is not very helpful to those interested in the virtues and defects of the system, simply because the criticism rarely addresses itself to the tests as they really function. What is of practical importance is that the objective, multiple-choice form of the tests, which is responsible for many of their virtues, necessarily generates a certain amount of unrest in academic circles, as well as among the general public. This is the bane of objective testing. And this criticism is over and above the fact that *any* test will generate some criticism and can be picked to pieces by those who want to speculate about how some hypothetical candidate might deal with some particular question. Our own history is full of examples of bitter battles even over our older form of essay examinations. The point, though, is that the characteristics of our testing programme that make for precision and economy and fairness are the very characteristics that make the tests seem unattractive to some college professors and many articulate laymen. This is a fault in the system, no doubt, but, as with most of the faults I am describing, it is probably more of a dilemma.

A scant thirty years ago colleges exerted, through the influence of admissions tests, virtual control of the secondary school curriculum. The development of the present tests, with their objective, multiple-choice format and opportunity for wide sampling of ability, have virtually freed secondary schools from curricular restrictions by colleges. The SAT, in particular, has allowed students to follow a variety of patterns of course work in secondary school. In fact, the SAT as it was first developed in the late 1920s and early 30s was a liberating device to enable a student to show what he could do with his mind to the exclusion, to the extent possible, of where he lived, who his parents were, what courses he studied, and the like. This ideal, while never completely realized, none the less made it possible for colleges to select students from the increasing number and variety of youngsters continuing through secondary school. Forty years ago, for example, the prestige institutions in the United States were admitting students relatively similar to one another in socio-economic indices, but representing a wide range of academic ability. The situation today is just the reverse. Students in highly selective institutions represent a relatively high level of academic ability and, at the same time, a broad spectrum of backgrounds, geographic, social and economic.

Another dilemma in the Board's history surrounds the question of predicting academic success. Tests and other predictors are validated against college grades. But the use of freshman grade-point average as a criterion means that grades tend too often to be translated into the symbol of college success. It would, in my opinion, be more appropriate if competing criteria were well developed for validating tests, including measured satisfaction, growth in abilities (even using other tests as criteria), ratings by fellow students, leadership ratings, creativity ratings, values, attitudes, and anything else that would broaden the current and unhealthy emphasis on grades.

We have not found a way, except in small volume programmes such as the advanced placement programme mentioned earlier, to provide enough opportunity for students to use free response in tests, including short answers as well as longer written responses. There seems to be no feasible and economic way in a system that tests a million and a half students and reports scores to colleges, on a timetable that typically involves testing in December of the senior year followed by admissions decisions several months later, to provide an opportunity for essays to be written and graded with acceptable levels of reliability. While many of you envy our sophisticated technique with objective testing and machine scoring, we, in turn, envy some aspects of your written examinations. One cannot help but wonder about the impact of multiple-choice testing on the teaching and learning of writing at every educational level in the United States.

Testing has done less than was hoped, especially hoped for standardized testing, in fitting together the parts of the educational process through a positive definition of necessary sequence in education. While standardized testing has helped in articulation in the sense that it has allowed us to clear away unrealistic and restrictive admissions requirements as, for example, specific numbers of units or credits, it has not contributed much information concerning the positive things that should be done to prepare for college. By that I mean to suggest that testing has not revealed much about necessary continuities in the education of the managerial, professional and technical members of the work force or of liberally educated human beings generally. A college in the United States can now be perfectly secure in admitting students who have not studied Latin, for example, but it gets not much guidance from tests as to what the student should have done apart from develop his verbal and mathematical reasoning. In other words, tests have not communicated adequately with anyone concerning the real outcome of education at any level.

In addition, tests have been less effective than was originally expected in supporting democratic values through discovery and encouragement of talent in lower socio-economic strata where encouragement of the able is particularly needed. This is partly because theoretical problems such as, for example, culturally neutral testing, have not been solved, but also because testing intended for 'talent searching' has often been misused or has not really been used at all once the tests are given and the scores reported. At first glance, this seems not to be the fault of testing *per se*, but of people who could, but do not, employ it. On the other hand, the crucial test of any system may be what corruptions it readily lends itself to. It may be that testing—as an essential characteristic—lends itself to the particular corruptions of misunderstanding and of filing and forgetting. If adequate use of tests turns out to require a really large body of highly trained personnel, the results of testing are not worth the effort required. On the other hand, when we see results of tests used by personnel who are highly trained, but not in the use of tests, and who are heavily burdened by other important responsibilities, we must say that testing is, so far at least, a failure in doing what we thought it could do improve access to opportunity.

Nor has testing made the contribution to science that was once expected, although science applied to testing has proceeded remarkably far. The test as an instrument for making scientific observations has never reached the expectations once held. Science expects to progress in quantum jumps as better means of making observations are devised; the series of steps from the naked eye to the electronic microscope is a clear case in point. Standardized tests were once regarded as a very powerful new way of observing human behaviour, which, when coupled with mathematical analysis, would lead to new fundamental understanding of mental and even emotional processes. However, when we look at tests today, we see that they are enormously improved and sophisticated versions of the tests that were there almost from the beginning and that a theoretical structure of the intellect has not been greatly revealed.

The difficulty with tests, as now developed, is that they present a relatively narrow view of what it is that students can do. They tend to obscure a student's individuality and appear to many to be too highly saturated with the conventional skills of reading ability and number facility. Our programme, in the interests of simplicity and economy, does not offer any extremely wide range of options for students to demonstrate a variety of skills, abilities, interests and attitudes. This concern has been voiced about large testing programmes that require all students to run the same race. The dilemma appears again: fairness and economy to all on the one hand and lack of sensitivity to individual strengths and weaknesses on the other.

What is needed in our programme, and in every other programme I know about, is the provision of better descriptions of relevant differences and needs of individuals. Educational systems should not only tolerate, but actively encourage, individual differences other than those traditionally labelled as intelligence. It has been suggested that the tasks set for youngsters by a large-scale testing programme such as ours and some of yours are roughly analogous to requiring the Olympic athletes only to be weighed to determine their rating on a common scale, rather than have the runners run, the swimmers swim, and the jumpers jump. Testing ought to keep pace with developments in education that reject the concept of bringing students up to a certain common level in favour of a concept of developing the diverse interests and abilities of students. Testing should even take the lead in helping us to recognize, even cherish, diversity of talents.

Finally, testing, if it is to be a reasonable instrument in educational planning, ought to lean much more heavily in the direction of helping individuals understand and make decisions about themselves as opposed to providing the means for decisions to be made about them by others. Admittedly, institutional self-interests and the individual's self-interest, in college admissions, for example, do not always coincide. But only to the extent that institutional will is visibly, gently and fairly imposed can colleges retain their selective role, if that is the role they choose, in the face of public expectation and, sometimes, raw hope. Poor tests, narrowly defined in scope, badly researched, if at all, and used with indiscretion, provide a vulnerable and visible target for valid criticism of the whole system. Only to the extent that tests are well constructed and fairly used in an open, defensible and well-understood system will they be worth the considerable effort required.

A SCHOLASTIC APTITUDE TEST AND EDUCATIONAL CHANGE

C. TITTLE

Overview

This paper will present some implications of introducing a change into an educational system through a scholastic aptitude test. In order to achieve this, a survey is provided of a scholastic aptitude test project which is currently being carried out in Great Britain. There is a summary of the main points related to the project which were put forward in the Report of a Committee on Higher Education in Great Britain. A brief review of the English literature related to the problem of selection for university entrance follows, with a summary of current project plans. After this introduction to the scholastic aptitude test project, the project is placed in the context of a model of change processes in education. In looking at an educational test within a change model, it is helpful to distinguish between the *product,* the physical development of a scholastic aptitude test—its test booklet, manual, answer sheet, etc.—and the *set of ideas, practices* and *research methodologies* which accompany the use of the product in its original setting in the United States. The distinction between the product and its accompanying ideas or practices is useful in suggesting how well in England (or any other country) such a project may succeed in providing for the diffusion and adoption of a scholastic aptitude test. Some suggestions are made which might be useful, particularly in the adoption phase of the project. These suggestions point to the possibilities in the project for the use of an educational test as an agent of change. The limitations of an educational test are seen in the distinction made between the product and its accompanying ideas and practices: failure to recognize this distinction may limit the usefulness of a scholastic aptitude test in a new setting.

A history of the scholastic aptitude test project

The Robbins Report

In 1963 the report of a Committee on Higher Education was published. The report was the result of a three-year study to review the pattern of full-time higher education in Great Britain, and to make recommendations regarding the future development of higher education. The Committee was under the chairmanship of Professor Lord Robbins, and the report is popularly known as 'The Robbins Report'. The report includes a survey of the setting of the system of higher education in

Great Britain, notes that higher education is rightly a matter of public concern (since a large part of the finance is public), and assumes that courses of higher education should be available for 'all those who are qualified by ability and attainment to pursue them and who wish to do so' (Ministry of Education 1963). Data is presented showing that in 1962 over 8 per cent of the age group began full-time courses in higher education. (The 'age group' is a weighted composite, but mainly nineteen-year-olds.) The report includes a comparison of the British system of higher education with that of continental, Soviet Union and American systems (op. cit., chap. 5). Features which appear distinctive to the British system include:

1. Fundamental differences before entering higher education. The degree of specialization in sixth forms is the exception among secondary systems of education preparing students for higher education.
2. A high degree of selection among those who wish to enter higher education. The most comparable situation of highly selective admissions occurs for the Soviet Union, in contrast with western European countries' tradition of the Abitur, baccalaureate or equivalent as passports to higher education. The United States represents a mixture: some institutions are highly selective, but many state universities are required to admit high school (secondary school) graduates.
3. A greater proportion of students studying part time. In Britain approximately 40 per cent of students take courses of part-time study; comparable data for the United States is about 15 per cent. Only the Soviet Union shows a higher percentage (over 50) in part-time courses.
4. A higher proportion of students provided with financial assistance in Britain. Coupled with the higher proportion of assisted students is a greater proportion of students living in accommodation associated with their university.
5. A greater minimum length of courses in other systems: four years in the USA, five years in the Soviet Union, four or five years in most western European countries—contrasted with three years in Britain.
6. A smaller proportion of the age group admitted to institutions of higher education in Britain; a relatively more favourable picture obtaining when percentage completing higher education is considered.

In considering the provision of opportunities for higher education, the committee rejected the concept of a fixed 'pool of ability', and

A scholastic aptitude test and educational change

based its projections on the likely increases in demand for university places—due to such factors as the result of increased national prosperity, improved general level of education of the population, and better primary and secondary education, etc. Rejection of the fixed 'pool of ability' concept is likely to result eventually in a more flexible approach to educational problems and an acceptance of the potential impact social changes and education may have in developing the individual pupil's abilities (Ministry of Education 1963, Appendix V, pp. 79-89, Vernon 1963).

The Committee also considered the problem of selection for higher education. Noting that selection was bound to continue and that competition to enter the more favoured institutions could not be eliminated, the concern shifted to *how to select* and the need for promoting greater understanding between institutions of higher education and the secondary schools. Consideration was given to the necessity of providing information about opportunities for higher education in the three main sectors (universities, teacher-training institutions, and colleges of advanced technology and regional technical colleges). Problems of selection were to include investigation into methods of aptitude testing. The Committee recommended that co-operation between schools and higher education be furthered by forming a Schools Council within the Department of Education and Science, with representatives from all parts of the educational world, including universities (Taylor 1966). The Council was to be concerned with school curricula as well as examinations.

The scholastic aptitude test* project in England has been started as a result of the Robbins Report and the formation of the Schools Council.

Financing for the project has come from the Department of Education and Science and the Schools Council. The finance is given to the Committee of Vice-Chancellors and Principals of the Universities of the United Kingdom. The Committee of Vice-Chancellors and Principals in turn has established a Steering Committee for the Project (officially titled the Investigation into Supplementary Predictive Information for University Admission). Responsible to the Steering Committee is a Project Directorate, established in 1966 for implementation of the project and responsible for its technical aspects. The Project Directorate has established two working parties for different aspects of the investigation; a working party for test development and a working party for data gathering and data processing.

---

* The test has been officially named the test of academic aptitude.

Data used in selection for university

While there is some variety in the data used for selecting students for higher education in Britain, several reviews and studies (Drever 1963, Furneaux 1961, Himmelweit 1963, Iliffe 1967, Kelsall 1963, and Vernon 1963) indicate the main sources of data to be the following:

1. School records, and in particular headmasters' reports (since most school records are not systematically collected and/or summarized).
2. Ordinary level General Certificate of Education.* External examinations set by eight GCE boards, almost exclusively essay examinations, covering a wide variety of subjects, usually taken at ages 15 to 16. Ordinary level is sat to provide a certificate for those leaving school or as a preparation/selection for sixth form work.
3. Advanced level General Certificate of Education. External examinations set by the eight GCE boards, almost exclusively essay examinations, covering a slightly narrower range of subjects, mainly related to specialization preparatory to further education. The Advanced level GCE is usually taken at ages 18 to 19 for university entrance purposes, or to obtain a certificate useful in gaining employment.
4. Interviews held at the university.

In addition, some studies (notably Himmelweit 1963 and Furneaux 1961) have used psychological or educational tests as predictive data.

The studies to date are generally unencouraging with respect to the use of headmasters' reports and interviews, unless particular effort has been made to develop a content analysis of the headmasters' recommendations (as in the Himmelweit studies). Headmasters' recommendations as usually received show a very low or zero relation to university success. Interviews, while used extensively, have also yielded slight relations with success in the university. As is stated by Kelsall (1963), 'Research over a long period of time and in many countries has established the point that generally interviews conducted by those with no special aptitude in such matters, are a highly ineffective means of bringing to light quality of character or temperament. . . .

The results of predictive studies of Ordinary level GCE results are equivocal. Some studies show a slight positive relation with type of degree obtained. One analysis (Barnett and Lewis 1963) examined the

---

* Now broadened to include an alternative examination at the same level, the Certificate of Secondary Education (CSE)—an examination system set by fourteen regional CSE examining boards.

canonical correlation between GCE 'O' and 'A' level results and degree obtained at university. The correlations in this study, which included other variables such as age, number of subjects studied, as well as mean GCE scores, ranged from 0·36 to 0·54. This data undoubtedly capitalizes on the error variance available in both degree and examination results, and did not use a 'hold out' or cross validation sample as is usual in multiple correlation work. Since the study was not replicated, it is hard to know whether the same variables would yield as high correlation or canonical weightings in a second study.

In view of the uncertain status of most currently used information for university selection, the Robbins Report (1963) recommended that:
1. More attention should be paid to school records, and attention should be specifically drawn to the assessment of performance over a period of years and a clear indication of the candidate's aptitude for the work of the institution for which he or she is applying.
2. Investigation should be undertaken into methods of testing aptitude with the view towards two innovations: (a) if some of the predictive load could be shifted from examinations (i.e. Advanced level GCE), the pressure upon candidates to cram for them would be less; and (b) selection is likely to be more efficient if based on performance in more than one type of test.

We recommend experiment and investigation here, rather than a frontal attack on the present system of selection.

Present plans for an SAT project

Following from the recommendations of the Robbins Report, the structure described earlier was established to implement study of both sources of data: school records and a scholastic aptitude test. The formal statement of the Committee of Vice-Chancellors and Principals envisaged that the investigation will include,

> 'the assembly of information on methods of supplementary predictive testing already in use,
>
> 'the development of tests as may be necessary for use in a British university context and their application to selected groups of candidates for entrance, with the subsequent extension of tests to large numbers, and a continuous process of evaluation of the results.
>
> 'It has been accepted that to be fully effective the investigation would involve research into the other main instruments of the

selection process—"A" level examinations, school assessments and university interviews' (Letter of 31 January 1966 from the Vice-Chancellors Committee to the Permanent Secretary of the Department of Education and Science).

The project is proceeding in several phases. In order to begin the evaluation of a scholastic aptitude test as rapidly as possible, Professor Oliver of the University of Manchester offered the Vice-Chancellors Committee the use of a scholastic aptitude test he had devised. Professor Oliver's aptitude test is generally modelled on the College Entrance Examination Board's Scholastic Aptitude Test, providing separate verbal and mathematical aptitude scores. Professor Oliver had developed his aptitude test for a study of abilities in sixth form pupils. His test will be administered in October 1967 to a sample of sixth formers sitting the Advanced level GCE examinations of the University of London Entrance and Schools Examinations Council and the Joint Matriculation GCE Board (plus a smaller sample from several other GCE Boards). At the same time, a set of newly written items will be pre-tested to provide the basis of a second form of a scholastic aptitude test, similar to those of Professor Oliver and the College Entrance Examination Board, providing two scores: of verbal and of mathematical aptitude.

The students tested in October 1967 will be followed up after they leave school in July 1968. For those who enter a university, additional follow-up is planned for their entire university careers; intermediate results should be available by the autumn of 1969. SAT scores will *not* be available to the universities at any time until the university follow-up studies are complete. For this group of students, Ordinary level and Advanced level GCE grades, biographical data and the aptitude test results will be available for analysis.

In another phase of the project, several volunteering universities will administer Professor Oliver's test during October 1967 to their complete intake in a few departments. Follow-up of these students will permit some evaluation of the predictive validity of a scholastic aptitude test by autumn 1968. Again, 'O' and 'A' level GCE results and biographical data will be available for analysis. SAT data will not be available to universities at least until it is related to the end of first-year university results, and probably not any individual score data until graduation.

During October 1968 an SAT will be administered to another group of students, and additional follow-up studies are planned. This group might comprise a sampling of the entire sixth form planning to take the Advanced level GCE examination in order to provide more general normative data. Probably the same plan of encouraging selected institutions to administer an SAT to their intake for some departments will again be followed, in order to disseminate experience with the aptitude test. This study should incorporate collection of headmasters' reports and interview results in order to permit a comparative evaluation of an SAT with data currently used in selection.

It should be noted that there has been a postponement for one to two years of the investigation of the development of school records into a form suitable for assessment as to validity and reliability. Also, it is unlikely that data will be available during the first year's testing in selected institutions to permit comparison of the use of interviews and/or school reports in their present form.

The SAT and educational change

I should like to turn now from this brief sketch of an SAT project to consider its probable impact as a part of the process of a change in the educational system. The problem can be put into context by indicating that:
1. The current data used in selection for admissions seem often to be of dubious value when evaluated in the studies of the selection process.
2. The focus in higher education will be on answering the *demand* for education made by candidates of suitable ability and attainment.
3. Points 1 and 2 are likely to bring into sharper focus the 'criterion' problem.

Point 3 refers to the university examination, first-year pass/fail, or other variables at which the predictor data is aimed. It means that a university must be able to assess how adequately it is doing its job of higher education,* and, in effect, be able to start to describe what abilities and attainments are necessary for the goals the particular institution has set for itself. In some instances this type of analysis has been started in the United States.† In order to select and predict, the criterion must be defined, and an SAT may force an earlier consideration of the criterion (as defined by the educational goals of

---

* It should be noted that the Society for Research into Higher Education has started work on the problem of examinations in higher education (see Cox 1966 and *Universities Quarterly*, 21, no. 3, 1967: ' Examining in universities').

† As indicated by *The American College* (1962), originated by the Society for Psychological Study of Social Issues. Particularly relevant are Sanford's opening chapters and Fishman's comments on a theoretical framework for selection studies.

the institution) than might occur 'naturally' as the impetus for change builds up out of the innovation which is occurring in the primary and secondary schools in England. A 'sign of the times' in this direction may be the demand by a speaker at a British National Union of Students Conference for a full investigation into the best ways of assessing people. One speaker, commenting on students' failure, asked, 'How many other unions would accept their workers being thrown out if they had to be judged on three hours of work done on a factory bench at the end of a year?'* 'Ready-made' criteria in the form of end-of-course grades are not usually available in English institutions, as they are in the schools and universities of the United States.

A model of change processes

The recently developed classification scheme of Clark and Guba (c. 1965) provides a good model for considering the processes for change. Their schema incorporates four major processes as related to and necessary for educational change: research, development, diffusion and adoption.

To relate an SAT project to these change processes, it may be helpful to divide the project into two aspects: (a) that of developing a product —a standardized group test with accompanying practice booklet, test manual, answer sheet, etc., and (b) the ideas or practices which are an integral part of the use of the SAT in its original setting in the United States.

It is important to distinguish between the product and the accompanying philosophies, ideas and research practices or context within which the educational test functions. There is always a danger that something that has been developed and successfully applied in one educational system may not function in the same way when transferred to another system. It should not be assumed that the preparation of an educational test (or product), with the accompanying manuals and so on, will lead to the same level of operational practices in a new system as in the system from which the product is being adopted. Keeping in mind the distinction that the SAT in its original setting involves both an educational product and a set of ideas and practices, the SAT project in England can be placed within the schema of change processes.

1. Research. The research phase, in its basic sense, is past for the product and for many of the ideas which can be implemented in relation to an SAT. Taking a long-term look at the experiences in the United States (for example, see Fishman 1962 and Lavin 1965) it is possible to evaluate

* From 'Scrap "sudden death" exams, say students.' *London Daily Mirror*, April 1967, p.10.

these experiences and conclude that research has demonstrated the value of an SAT (or similar predictor) on an individual institution level. What about the accompanying ideas of guidance, selection and placement, and even the general concept of evaluation? While there have been varying amounts of research in these areas, the ideas of guidance, selection and placement seem to have been accepted as having value, although not necessarily on the basis of research. For the more general idea of evaluation it seems that there is a fairly wide-spread acceptance of the *idea* of evaluation in the United States.

In terms of the English project, acceptance of research on the product is demonstrated by the beginning of an SAT project. It is likely, however, that in accepting the product, it may have been viewed only as a technology, with insufficient consideration being given to the philosophies, ideas or the research practices themselves which accompany the product in its original setting.

2. *Development.* The development process involves two stages—invention and design. The SAT project in its present form is in the development phase of the change process. While the SAT is modelled on the American test, it is a new solution to a problem in the English setting: that of providing additional information which should be predictive of university success. The design of the product follows fairly closely that of the American SAT in providing two aptitude scores, verbal and mathematical.

The project as it is planned will fulfil several of the criteria for evaluation of the product in the development phase. Clark and Guba describe this evaluation as typically being called field testing. The field testing will primarily assess the feasibility of the design by administering the test in schools; by checking out methods of pre-testing items for new forms; by examining the adequacy of the test specifications, and so on. The project will, in its first three years, learn something about the way in which the sheer mechanics of the testing programme can be implemented. The problem of how *generalizable* the application of the testing programme is will be examined in a few limited institutional settings for several years.

While this evaluation of the development phase in the English setting will take place over the next three years, the current planning does not yet include consideration of the *diffusion* and *adoption* phases of the change process. The project itself seems to have taken the form of a 'classical' educational research study, and the plans extend as far as the typical prediction study.

The Robbins Report recommended trying out an SAT. They did not intend 'a frontal attack on the problems of selection' by directly encouraging institutions to evaluate their selection procedures or by evaluating the impact of higher education itself. It would seem difficult to encourage the diffusion and adoption stages in the change process without recognizing that the development and field testing of an educational test will not necessarily lead to wide-spread adoption of the ideas and practices which accompanied it in its original setting. The very practices which the Robbins Report did not want to 'frontally attack' will not be adopted or changed just by making an SAT available. The heart of the use of the SAT in the United States is in studies of the selection process and in guidance of individual pupils within the secondary schools. The SAT has been available as a model for many years with few English universities studying the use of educational or psychological tests in their selection procedures. Even where the selection procedures have been studied (as at the London School of Economics, Himmelweit 1963), there has not been a corresponding shift in selection procedures to using psychological tests as recommended in line with the results of the study. However, in certain colleges and departments use is made of psychological tests, though on a small scale.

The limitation of the present educational testing project lies in the lack of consideration of the total system in which the test operates in its original setting—a setting in which the trial and adoption are done on an individual institution basis, with a set of procedures and practices developed over the last twenty years, and in which a systematic collection of secondary school assessments is always provided to balance the use of test results.

3. Diffusion and adoption. The problems of planning for diffusion and adoption of both the product and its accompanying ideas/practices can be considered together. Here a second dimension can be added to the Clark-Guba schema for processes necessary for change: the parts of the educational system which are affected by the change—the introduction of an SAT. Possible steps which might be taken to aid the change process at each level of the system are suggested.

a) The secondary school pupil. The pupil receives a practice test booklet, takes a test and then, under the system as it operates in the United States, receives his test results back. The results are presented to him along with a booklet which is intended to give him guidance in interpreting the scores in a very general fashion, and to encourage him to talk over his educational or vocational plans with his teacher or guidance counsellor. Under the best of circumstances, the guidance personnel will be aware of opportunities for higher education in a variety of settings. Counsellors will also have available the complete high school grade record of the student, results of any other specialized tests or interest blanks, comments from individual teachers, etc. The College Board will also have provided a manual which gives distribution of scores and high school ranks for entering freshmen in a number of institutions. (In the American College Testing Program, predicted first-year college grades are computed, when criterion data have been developed for the colleges of the student's choice.) In theory, the counsellor and student will both be aware of as much information about the student as is relevant to the decision-making process. It is, however, the *student's decision* process, and *not* the counsellor's.

What will happen in the English context at this stage? Few schools will be equipped with personnel trained in the guidance function. The Robbins Report recommended that information on opportunities in higher education be systematically disseminated; there is no machinery at present to serve this function. It is unlikely that the model of the SAT practices in the secondary schools in the USA can be readily installed in the English setting, but plans can be made to encourage these practices. One step which could be considered for feasibility in overcoming the shortage of guidance personnel is that of carefully building a set of self-instructional materials related to education/career guidance. Little is known systematically about the effects of knowledge of test results on the individual; an SAT project has a responsibility to consciously plan the adoption or rejection of American practices of making scores available to students and the emphasis on the individual student's decision-making process.

In view of the changes occurring in education, particularly in the Government's decision to try to implement comprehensive schooling, it would seem important to plan a conscious adoption of guidance practices and to develop self-instructional materials to try to reach as wide an audience of individual students as possible. While it is unlikely that the method of 'selection by orientation' or guidance—as described by Bowles can by implemented in England,* some steps in that direction could further the usefulness of an SAT and reduce the importance of examinations in determining entrance to higher education.

b) The secondary school—teachers and/or career masters. While some

---

* Bowles (1963) notes three conditions for selection by orientation: a diverse programme of higher education to offer a variety of choices; competent advisors in the educational system; a student capable of making decisions in accordance with the facts presented him. He recommends control of student entrance through guidance 'advice based on student performance, judgments of student ability and expressions of student preference. . . .' This is analogous in some ways to recommendations for allocation rather than selection models in admission (see Cronbach and Gleser 1965, Finney 1965).

publications at the pupil level, developed in a simple self-instructional style, should be helpful, the results of an SAT in terms of the potential guidance function of the results will be limited without support from the teacher. In some of the English schools there are teachers who function as 'career masters'; their role has not been widely extended to the majority of schools, and has largely been aimed at vocational information for school leavers at age 15.

As there will be limitations on the amount of material which can be reasonably expected to be assimilated by the student in the form of self-instructional materials, it is important that the teacher be made aware of an SAT and how to interpret scores (or, more important, how not to over-interpret the scores). There are several possibilities at this level. Awareness could be developed by working through professional organizations which exist, such as the educational psychologists. There are few educational psychologists, however, and most serve such large numbers of pupils that they seem an unlikely source of help for this guidance function. Other alternatives would be to work with representatives of teachers' professional associations to develop a special programme. The programme would, through a series of conferences or localized meetings, be aimed at developing two or three teachers within a school who would be informed about an SAT and who would provide guidance only in the sense of being a source of information of career materials and opportunities in further and higher education.

It would seem a dubious practice to report scores to students even with accompanying guidance materials, unless some provision is made to develop skills of teachers related to the guidance process. Planning for the development of this aspect of SAT practices could be started through appointing another working party within the current structure of the project. This working party would examine the feasibility of reporting scores to students and schools, in what manner, with what accompanying materials, etc. It could plan for education of teachers in the guidance area and it could also be the start of a committee to relate secondary and higher education practices relevant to university entrance.

c) University entrance officers/registrars. When the SAT programme comes into effect, the scores of the SAT could be readily available to the personnel of university entrance requirements departments of the student's application form for the university. There is an established organization—the University Central Council for Admissions (UCCA)—which provides central assembly of application forms and distributes the forms to as many as six universities of the student's choice.

The present role of the university entrance requirements is mainly one of setting a minimum hurdle for applicants. For example, London

University requires three 'O' level GCE passes, plus two 'A' level GCE passes. These five passes must be in five different (acceptable) subjects. Beyond this minimum, the individual colleges (schools) of the university set their own requirements, and these may vary for each degree programme within the colleges.

The results of the Ordinary level GCE examinations are available at the time the student applies to a university. For most applicants the 'A' level GCE is not taken until the June of the year which they enter a college. The grades of the 'A' level are not available to the student or university until sometime in August.

The procedure for an applicant is to make application to several colleges through the UCCA. With a good recommendation from his headmaster, plus good 'O' level results, he will be given a 'conditional' acceptance at a college. This acceptance is conditional on attainment of certain grades in a specified number and/or set of subjects in the 'A' level GCE. Not until August does either the university or the candidate know how successful or unsuccessful he has been. If a candidate who was given a conditional place dependent on two Bs in his 'A' levels receives an A and a C, he will find that both he and the college are in a further quandary. The decision on his admission may have to wait until the college finds out how many applicants meeting the two Bs requirements have accepted. If spaces remain, the college may then reconsider those who did not succeed in attaining the required marks in 'A' levels.

The reliability of the GCE examinations is not known, but it is likely that errors of measurement in any examination are large enough that the student who received an A and a C could as easily have made two Bs, depending how close his actual marks were to the cutting-points for the grade categories (see Valentine 1967). The pressures of time, unawareness of the standard error of measurement and the desire for any additional 'measure' of students' ability may lead to unrealistic use of an SAT. There is a danger that any SAT results might be used to set preliminary rigid cut-off scores. This procedure could be harmful from two viewpoints:

1 It would mean that SAT results would not be balanced by systematic school reports or GCE Advanced level results (if used for rejection when administered in October/November nine months before entrance). An SAT is a fallible measure, as are the other pieces of data being used to select for university entrance. As Thresher (1966) has pointed out, we do not know a great deal about what is important for university success in terms of student characteristics. A purely predictive approach would place emphasis on selecting the 'best' student in terms of the measurements available without trying to decide what is 'best' for the

institution or for the larger society in terms of the institution's responsibility for education. Universities such as Harvard could easily select students only from the top 1 per cent of the SAT score distribution, yet deliberate, conscious decisions are made to encourage diversity in the characteristics of its entering classes. The SAT alone does not determine entry to Harvard, and candidates with a relatively low SAT (for Harvard) will be considered if they show other signs of promise.

2. There are limitations to the use of general ability tests yielding only one or two scores. Cronbach (1965) states the problem in terms of a decision-theoretic model: the problem is not one of the success of university entrants only, but of trying to maximize social benefits. The decision is one of recommending 'treatment' (i.e. further education/training) for each person. It is a problem of allocation rather than selection. For testing, it is a matter of inquiring 'what predicts differential success under various educational methods or about how different types of schooling modify aptitudes'

English education prior to entry into higher education is more specialized than that in the context in which the SAT was developed in the USA. It is also a more specialized education after entry into higher education. Can an SAT help with problems of differential allocation?

These comments are mainly cautionary, but they are intended to indicate that there is a need to ensure that university entrance personnel do not arbitrarily and rigidly establish cut-off scores on an SAT.

As with the secondary school guidance function, there is a problem of effectively educating or, in effect, developing what amounts to a 'professionalization of admissions or entrance practices'. The problem includes education in the techniques of selection and placement studies, and incorporating attempts to reach a more theoretical approach to the selection problems which will encourage a more effective evaluation of the criterion used in predictive studies. Fishman (1962) points out the importance of going beyond the personnel selection concept (which assumes a fixed individual and, for effective prediction, a fixed environment and little impact of the education system). He suggests focusing upon studies which assume that the individual will deliberately be changed as a result of being in the educational environment. If one accepts Fishman's model of developmental change in the individual and environmental differences at the institutional level, it becomes important to focus on the development of more adequate criterion measurement and on the role of guidance within the university also. The 'professionalization' of these university selection, placement and guidance functions may be aided by the development of an SAT.

At the university entrance officer/registrar level it would be possible to bring representatives (selected from different types of institutions) together to begin discussions of an SAT and its possible aid in university entrance procedures. These discussions would have several aims: first, to improve understanding of an SAT and to inform regarding the results of the developmental stages of the project; secondly, in view of these results to consider the methods which could be used to disseminate the results obtained. Can special publications be prepared which will aid other university personnel in evaluating an SAT? Alternatively, would it be better to present results in professional journals? Would a series of regional meetings encourage admissions personnel to plan how an SAT could be used in their institutions? Is a combination of these and other methods needed?

d) Departmental admissions personnel. The actual acceptance into the university is often made on a departmental (degree-offering) level. This means that in contrast to the original setting of the SAT (where admissions are made on a general university level), the dissemination and adoption of the ideas and practices which accompany an SAT will usually need to be on a department by department (or degree-offering) basis. This extends the problem of 'informing' about the SAT results and ways of instituting studies of these results.

What are some steps which could be taken to try to aid the dissemination and adoption of SAT results at the university?

Going beyond plans for dissemination to university entrance personnel, dissemination to departmental personnel could be on a within-institution basis or could be formulated between institutions (such as all mathematics selectors from a number of universities). At the very minimum, the departmental personnel responsible for selecting students will need to be aware of the characteristics of SAT scores and how to interpret them.

The problem may turn out to be as with the 11-plus examination, to prevent a rigid application of the test results in terms of some cut-off scores or arbitrary selection which focuses on picking out those candidates with the highest score from the pool applying to any department. Vernon rightly rejected the concept of a fixed pool of ability. An SAT will provide only a limited measure of general ability, and measurements which are fallible. The methods which are used to disseminate and try to persuade people to adopt the use of SAT scores will have to carefully put these scores in a proper context from a measurement and validity standpoint.

Summary

The decision to develop a scholastic aptitude test can be subject to many limitations, unless a project includes plans to introduce some of the ideas and practices which accompany the SAT in its original context. If these ideas and practices are not to be adopted, reasonable alternatives need to be found within the context of the new setting for an SAT. On an institutional and individual level, the majority of the concepts of selection research, guidance and placement based on test results, *on an applied level,* are foreign to the English educational scene. They will be a long time being assimilated if there are not systematic attempts to integrate them into English education through professional meetings, special courses and teacher training. Examining an SAT project in the context of processes related to educational change may help us to realize both the possibilities and limitations of an educational test.

References

Barnett, V. D. and Lewis, T. (1963) 'A study of the relation between GCE and degree results.' *J. royal stat. Soc.,* Series A, 187-216.

Bowles, F. (1963) *Access to Higher Education,* vol. 1. Unesco and the International Association of Universities, p.212, and chaps 1 and 2.

Clark, D. L. and Guba, E. G. (Undated, *c.* 1965) *An Examination of Potential Change Roles in Education.* Bloomington, Ind: The National Institute for the Study of Educational Change.

Cox, B. (1966) *Examinations and Higher Education: A Survey of the Literature.* London: Society for Research into Higher Education. Duplicated.

Cronbach, L. J. and Gleser, G. C. (1965) *Psychological Tests and Personnel Decisions* (2nd edition), p.347. Urbana: University of Illinois Press.

Drever, J. (1963) *Prediction, Placement and Choice in University Selection.* Godfrey Thomson Lecture, University of Edinburgh.

Finney, D. J. (1965) 'The statistical evaluation of educational allocation and selection.' In Cronbach, L. J. and Gleser, G. C. *Psychological Tests and Personnel Decisions* (2nd edition), pp.182-229. Urbana: University of Illinois.

Fishman, J. A. (1962) 'Some social-psychological theory for selecting and guiding college students.' In Sanford, N. (ed.) *The American College,* p. 1034. New York: Wiley.

Furneaux, W. D. (1961) *The Chosen Few.* London: Oxford University Press.

Guba, E. G. (1965) 'Methodological strategies for educational change. Paper presented at the Conference on Strategies for Educational Change, Washington, D.C., in November, p.37.

Himmelweit, H. T. (1963) *Student Selection, Implications Derived from Two Student Selection Inquiries.* Sociological Review Monograph, no. 7, p.79-98.

Iliffe, A. H. (1967) *The Foundation Year in the University of Keele.* Sociological Review Monograph, no. 12.

Kelsall, R. K. (1963) *University Student Selection in Relation to Subsequent Academic Performance: A Critical Appraisal of the British Evidence.* Sociological Review Monograph, no. 7, pp.99-115.

Lavin, D. E. (1965) *The Prediction of Academic Performance: A Theoretical Analysis and Review of Research.* New York: Russell Sage Foundation.

Miles, M. B. (ed.) (1964) *Innovation in Education,* p.689. New York: Teachers College Press, Columbia University.

Ministry of Education (1963) *Higher Education,* Report of the Committee on Higher Education (The Robbins Report). London: H.M. Stationery Office.

Sanford, N. (ed.) (1962) *The American College.* New York: Wiley.

Taylor, P. (1966) 'Curriculum reform in England.' In *Emerging Strategies and Structures for Educational Change,* pp.67-79. Toronto: The Ontario Institute for Studies in Education.

Thresher, B. A. (1966) *College Admissions and the Public Interest,* p.93. New York: College Entrance Examination Board.

Valentine, J. (1967) 'The comedy and tragedy of errors in the GCE—an American view.' *New Educ.,* 3, no. 2.

Vernon, P. E. (1963) *The Pool of Ability.* Sociological Review Monograph, no. 7, pp.45-57.

METHODS OF SCREENING BY HIGHER EDUCATIONAL INSTITUTIONS

KAZUHIKO NAKAYAMA

The term 'higher educational institutions' includes (a) those institutions which grant a bachelor's degree, and (b) university preparatory institutions, when referring to Japanese higher education before the educational reforms carried out after the Second World War (1949).

The main purpose of this paper is to review the past and present methods used for admitting students to universities in Japan, and to discuss their results. I will also give my own ideas on possible methods of screening for higher educational institutions in the future.

Purpose of screening

It is a world-wide phenomenon that the number of applicants to institutions of higher education is increasing every year, and that the number is beyond the capacity of the existing institutions. Japan is no exception to this trend. In theory one of the solutions to the problem might be to increase the capacity to meet the number of applicants, but in practice this would be very difficult. In Japan, the capacity has been increased every year by authorizing the establishment of new universities and colleges, and by increasing the enrolment quota of individual institutions. But the increase in the number of applicants has been so rapid that such measures have not been very effective.

One of the reasons for screening, then, results from the small enrolment capacity in proportion to the large number of applicants. Hence, universities will select those applicants with the ability to master all the necessary courses of study for graduation within certain levels of performance and with personality suitable for the university. In addition to this need at the university level, there is also a need for screening at the national level. That is, from the stand-point of securing talented men for the national interest, it is necessary to enrol as many applicants as possible who are able to pursue university education, regardless of their economic or social background. In other words, no one who has the potential should lack the opportunity to receive higher education because of economic and social inequality. To meet the second need, there should be a national policy of assistance for talented children and examination for national merit scholarship. This paper, however, does not deal with them.

Patterns of screening

Whatever the purpose of screening might be, the function of the screening done at present is to limit the number of applicants to be admitted to higher educational institutions. The methods used may be classified into two types: the first is to select, at the secondary level, those qualified for higher education; the second is to screen students at the time of application to higher educational institutions.

The difference between these types is largely due to the difference in educational systems. The first type is administered in such countries as England, West Germany and the Soviet Union, where the number of graduates from secondary education is limited, thus limiting the number of those who aspire to higher education, or where students take a qualifying examination while still at secondary school, thus limiting the number of those who will qualify for higher education. The second type of screening is practised in Japan, where all young people are encouraged to receive secondary education, and anyone graduating from an upper secondary school may be expected to have qualifications to enter an institution of higher education. The United States of America also follows this system, although the American system differs slightly from that of Japan in the actual procedures used for admitting students to higher educational institutions.

Methods of screening at the time of application

At present, one of the following three methods, or a combination of them, is used for screening at the time of enrolment:
1. Students take entrance examinations prepared and given by individual institutions.
2. Students take one examination prepared and administered by one organization.
3. The universities base their judgment on students' high school grade records, the number of credit hours and kinds of course earned.

Although all three methods are used in the United States, most major universities follow the second method: that is, students have to take the SAT and achievement tests given by the College Entrance Examination Board. In Japan, however, all universities, with almost no exception, use the first method. Certain private institutions which have their own 'attached' high schools or which are of very low standard, apply the third method to graduates from the attached high schools or to other applicants. This does not mean that there has not been any attempt to administer a common examination to all the applicants throughout the nation. There are also, at present, attempts being made to use in screening the results of nation-wide testing of high school graduates administered by one organization, Educational Test Research Institute (ETRI); but these attempts have not yet been successful.

History of screening in Japan

In 1867, by the Meiji Restoration, Japan changed from its feudalistic state into a modernized nation. At that time, the advanced techniques and culture of foreign countries were introduced into Japan. Higher educational institutions were also established, based on European models. As a natural consequence, they inherited the European system of screening, and have been screening the applicants chiefly by achievement tests. Such screening examinations have been carried out by each institution since 1867. Over this period, differences in levels arose among the institutions, and more and more persons began to apply for the higher standard institutions. In order to avoid having able persons fail the screening by applying to an institution with a large number of applicants, the nation tried twice (for six years from 1902 to 1907 and for two years in 1917 and 1918) to screen applicants on a national scale by setting a uniform examination for all applicants throughout Japan and placing them in appropriate institutions according to their performance on the test.

In order to minimize the evils arising from preparation at secondary schools, it was decided in 1927 that test subjects, which had been fixed, should be decided each year and announced only two or three months before the examination.

In 1941, high school grades and the results of interviews and physical check-ups were added to the results on achievement tests in making decisions of screening. At public institutions throughout the country the same paper and pencil test was given, being constructed by the Ministry of Education.

A few years after the end of the Second World War, the education system in Japan was radically and extensively reformed. Naturally there was a change in the method of screening applicants by the higher educational institutions. On the advice of Civil Information and Education (CIE) of the Occupation Army, the Ministry of Education issued a directive to all the higher educational institutions that they should give equal weight in screening to the results of (a) SAT, (b) achievement tests, and (c) the high school record, with reference to the result of a physical check-up. This SAT was constructed by a specially formed committee in the Ministry of Education, and was administered on the same day throughout the nation. However, opposition to SAT gradually became strong. Most of such opposition resulted from lack of understanding of the SAT. The major points made by its critics may be summarized as follows:

1. It is not a good thing to put heavy weight on the SAT, or to let it and the high school record be the basis for first screening, and not to let students take the achievement tests given at second screening.
2. The SAT's form of asking and answering questions is too simple and uniform to measure the student's true ability.
3. Students and teachers become more and more active to prepare students for the SAT. Thus, the students' load was doubled, preparing for achievement tests and for the SAT as well, and this might interfere with the regular high school curriculum.
4. Though it was originally planned to give equal weight to the SAT, achievement tests and the high school record, the universities did not positively use the SAT, but gave it less weight or neglected it almost completely.
5. Difficulties of administering the SAT arose because of the heavy burden on those universities where the SAT was administered and, especially, because of the small remuneration to the test administrators.

For these reasons, a request to discontinue the use of SAT was submitted to the Ministry of Education by the National Association of High School principals, the Association of National Universities, and other bodies, and a special committee was formed to examine the matter. After their study, the nation-wide administering of SAT was abolished in 1955, and it was decided that individual institutions should administer one if they needed it. At present, only one institution out of a total of 759 institutions in Japan administers its own SAT—the International Christian University (ICU), to which I belong.

Since 1955, the final decision of screening has been based on written examinations, the high school report and the physical check-up report. However, only one department of one institution among all the national universities uses the high school record for screening. All the other national universities carry out screening only on the results of the written achievement tests. Although, as I reported in the last section, a few institutions select students only on the basis of the high school report and recommendation by the principal, among the high-ranking private universities without attached high schools only ICU makes use of the high school reports.

It has been common practice for almost all institutions in Japan to give only one entrance examination in a year to a given faculty of a given institution.

Achievement tests—type, subjects and levels

From 1867, when institutions of higher education were first established, to 1940, all achievement tests were of essay type, testing one's memorized knowledge. In the nation-wide tests, constructed by the Ministry of Education between 1941 and 1946, objective testing was first introduced, though being a small portion of the total test items, the majority being subjective.

In 1947 on the recommendation of the Occupation Army that tests should be of the achievement type and that the form of testing should be objective, the Ministry of Education drew up a handbook with detailed examples of questions, and distributed it to each institution. Since then all tests for entrance devised by individual universities have been of the objective type. To this many criticisms and expressions of disapproval have been made, chiefly by professors at higher educational institutions, by mass-communication media, and by other sources. As a result, among the entrance examinations given in 1967, essay-type tests and free-answer-type tests (these are subjective) were included.

The areas and number of subjects to be tested in the entrance examinations to the national universities are prescribed by the Ministry of Education. According to the regulations, students who aspire to enter a faculty of natural science should take examinations in two subjects in science, one in social studies, Japanese language A, mathematics I to III, and one foreign language. Those who aspire to enter a faculty of literature or social studies should take examinations in one subject in science, two in social studies, Japanese language B, mathematics I and II and one foreign language. At private universities, the areas and the number of subjects to be tested differ at different institutions and in different faculties, though the most commonly observed practice is to let applicants to science faculties take examinations in one or two subjects in science, mathematics I, II and III, and English, with applicants to faculties of literature taking one or two subjects in social studies, Japanese language and English.

Though in the subjects tested there are differences among institutions and faculties, the levels to be tested should be in accordance with those prescribed in the high school Course of Study. The University Entrance Examination Council, an advisory organ to the Ministry of Education, collects copies of all the questions asked in entrance examinations at all the institutions and colleges every year, and investigates them. The result is printed in a pamphlet that is sent to each institution. Institutions which asked questions that were outside the prescribed range of test levels or that were considered inappropriate are warned by the council. However, authorities of upper secondary schools have often proposed to

Methods of screening by institutions

the university authorities to ask reasonable questions for entrance examinations, that is, questions which are within the scope set by the Course of Study and in agreement with the objectives of teaching stated therein. As this phenomenon shows, in many cases universities ask questions of a higher level not only than high school study, but also than the freshman or sophomore year study at university.

As already mentioned, all entrance examination tests given at all universities are achievement tests. The only exception to this are those given at my own university, the ICU. From the time of its establishment in 1953, ICU has given unique learning efficiency tests with the scholastic aptitude test and English language proficiency tests.

Testing and processing the results

In most universities, test constructors, who are professors of each university, read and score the answer sheets of all the candidates. The scores in each subject are then totalled for each candidate by means of an abacus. The candidates are ranked according to the total scores they obtained in the examination. Starting with the highest rank, the examiners choose the required number of examinees as successful candidates.

In the last few years, some universities have come to use electronic computers for processing the results. One of the reasons for this is that the results of a very large number of candidates should be processed and announced in a very short time, usually within several days. Different institutions use computers in different ways. They may be classified into the following three types of use.

In the first type, a man checks and scores the answers. The scores are then punched on to cards by a puncher. The computer is used to obtain a sum total of scores for each individual, rank candidates and then print out the name, the seat number and scores of each candidate according to the rank order. In the second type, the computer scores the answer cards that have been punched on to cards by a puncher, and does the remaining processes, from calculating the sum total of scores for each individual to printing out the final report, as in the first type. The third type has so far been adopted only by ICU. A computer with a specially designed optical card reader reads and scores the answer cards, converts the raw scores into T scores, and prints out a profile report of total score, rank order and other data for screening.

In brief, the method used at ICU is as follows:

A student writes on a name card his name, his school of graduation and other necessary information. The puncher punches them on a card. According to the report sent from the applicant's high school to ICU, the average score in each subject area for three years is calculated and written in a table, which will then be punched. A computer checks the data so far and corrects the errors, if there are any. The university sends to ETRI the cards with applicants' seat numbers for ETRI's test, and asks them to send back the results of the test both on magnetic tape for the computer and in paper form. With the results of the ETRI test and the high school report, a profile is made for each applicant, based on which the university carries out the first screening. As a result, the university invites twice as many applicants as the final number to be admitted to take the second screening test, which consists of the scholastic aptitude test which the university has constructed, learning efficiency tests and English language tests. The answer cards of these tests are read by an optical reader and recorded on magnetic tape. Using the tape, the computer scores the results: first the raw scores are calculated, and then these are converted into T scores. After processing the data, a final report is typed out in a profile. The screening is done on the basis of this report.

Predictability of results on entrance examinations

If the main purpose of screening is to select students who would be able to master all the courses at a given institution, as stated before, the screening test should be one yielding a high predictability of college grades.

Though there are not many studies in Japan concerning the predictability of college grades, the results show the following correlations: between the sum total of scores at entrance examination and college grades $r = 0.08$-0.51, between the high school report and college grades $r = 0.11$-0.57, and between the scholastic aptitude test, given by the Ministry of Education in the period 1947 to 1954, and college grades $r = 0.21$-0.31. At ICU, the correlation between college grades and the SAT is 0.04, with the learning efficiency test 0.02, and with the high school report 0.50.

The reasons why high school reports are not used in most institutions, though they have the highest predictability, are that professors think that (a) there is no guarantee that the reports are free from falsification, and (b) there are differences in level among schools and equal weight cannot be placed on the reports. According to my survey in relation to reason (a), there are false statements in approximately 25 per cent of all the high school reports received each year at the ICU. Concerning reason (b), there is a wide range in school averages on ETRI tests from 65 to 35 in terms of T scores. Thus the reasons the universities have for not using high school reports are not without basis.

Problems caused by admission tests and its process

The problems here discussed may be peculiar to Japan.

1. Problems caused by the lack of balance between the number of applicants and the capacity of universities

The number of students newly enrolled in higher institutions in 1966 was 329,850 from the total of 1,757,779 applicants, although there are included in this total those who applied to more than one institution. The number of persons who sought admission was not accurate, but it was estimated to be about 649,000, including 531,000 new graduates from upper secondary schools and 118,000 repeaters for entrance examination.

This brings out the following problems:
   a) There are many persons who failed the entrance examination. To avoid failure in the entrance examination, the upper secondary teachers tend to put emphasis on preparing pupils for entrance examinations, and in giving them skill and training for answering the entrance examination. Consequently, students do not learn what they are expected to learn at the upper secondary school. The school itself has become like a preparatory school for higher educational institutions instead of completing the education at the secondary level. Most of those who fail the entrance examination attend preparatory schools, not legally accredited, to master the techniques of taking university examinations. They will be repeaters the following year, and some of them repeat again and again. The number of repeaters for 1968 is estimated to be about 230,000.
   b) One person takes several entrance examinations in a year. According to upper secondary school teachers, one pupil generally takes about five entrance examinations for different courses in a university, or for different universities. A great deal of money for entrance examination fees and time and energy are wasted.

It is thus not only desirable for the individual concerned, but a big loss of man-power for a nation to let many persons concentrate on years of preparatory study in the period of their life when they are best able to develop their talents.

2. Problems caused by attitude towards tests

The following are common ideas among university professors about university entrance examinations and national tests by ETRI.

Whatever purpose it may have, the actual function of an entrance examination is to screen a few successful candidates from a large number of applicants. Thus, difficult questions should be asked. They think that multiple-choice and matching-type tests cannot measure the applicants' scholastic achievement and ability, and that they should be asked written-answer-type and, more desirably, essay-type questions. The only reliable data for screening are scores on examination tests given by their own universities, and all other data are unreliable. The screening and decisions concerning the successful applicants are the responsibility of the Faculty Meeting, and no one else should transgress this authority.

They feel they should not use a nation-wide test in order to preserve the authority of their university, because a ranking of universities would be made possible by the test results, which is not at present clear. Also, a nation-wide test may be used by the State for controlling education. Therefore, it should not be used. At private universities, the entrance examination fees occupy a large part of the annual income of the university. So any attempt that may lower this income—that is, the number of applicants—is not acceptable.

All these ideas do not consider the interests of the applicants, and thus they result in forcing the students to make idle preparatory study.

It is also a natural consequence of professors' ideas about testing that they do not dare to use high school reports and scores on ETRI national tests for screening, and to set up an admission office to study and carry out entrance examinations.

Low predictability and the need for other information

It is said in Japan that entering a university is very hard but that graduating from it is easy, and that college students do not need to study as hard as high school students and should enjoy life. These facts occur because very few drop out because of low grades, and almost all who entered the university can graduate in a maximum of eight years of residence.

The grading is on a four-point scale (good, average, pass and failure). Usually the failure grade is not recorded in the original record. There are professors who give the 'good' grade to nearly 80 per cent of the class. Thus, it is generally more important what university a student has graduated from than with what grades he has graduated.

These facts, together with the nature of the entrance examination, may naturally lower the predictability of the examination scores of college grade. Predicting college grades for scores on the entrance examination is theoretically a difficult task. For instance, at a certain

Methods of screening by institutions

university, students who were successful in one out of every four applicants (which is a typical rate of competition for a ranking university) show a correlation of 0·30 between their scores at entrance examination and university grades. If we assume that all the applicants of this group had enrolled in the university and that their scores and their grades were normally distributed, the correlation coefficients for those who passed the examination is that for a selected portion of the population. The estimated correlation coefficient for this population is 0·54. As long as the successful applicants are a selected group, we might not be able to expect a high correlation between entrance examination scores and grades after entering the university.

What, then, are the factors which control scholastic achievement? A survey of this is now in progress for university students, and so not much can be said as yet. However, there is a report that study hours, among the four variables of the scholastic aptitude test, scores on entrance examination, high school report and study hours, had the highest correlation with grades at the university. A senior thesis, 'A study on personality factors related to academic achievement', was written by a student under my supervision, and the Japanese trial edition of the Edwards Personal Preference Schedule was administered to upper secondary school students. The thesis showed a correlation coefficient of 0·27 between scholastic ability and achievement test scores, 0·33 between achievement motivation and achievement test scores. The correlations between interview scores on the ICU entrance examination and grades at the university is higher than any correlations between other tests.

The results indicate the importance of personality factors in influencing scholastic achievement. The above mentioned results are from studies in Japan. Studies on university students made in the United States also indicate the importance of personality factors in scholastic achievement.

From the findings of those studies, I propose the hypothesis that scholastic achievement is a function of the three variables: (1) scholastic aptitude, (2) scholastic achievement at a given time, and (3) personality factors.

This hypothesis explains why in all cases the high school report, which itself is a function of the variables, had the highest predictability of university grades.

A proposal for screening

From the study of the present situation in Japan, I propose the following as a method of screening. There may be countries where all or part of the points are done, or where screening is done by an entirely different

system. I shall welcome criticisms by the participants of this conference.
1. Screening for higher education should be done as late as possible from the standpoint of children's development.
2. Sufficient educational and vocational guidance should be given to avoid vain competition and to prevent the loss of human resources.
3. Achievement tests for screening should be made in co-operation with high school teachers and specialists in evaluation and testing with university professors, who are subject specialists, rather than by professors alone.
4. To carry out the second and the third proposals, an institute should be established to provide nation-wide testing of scholastic aptitude and achievement.
5. The individual universities should use the results of such testing by the institute and give tests only when they need to give their own. In that case, the number of applicants should be limited to some reasonable size before giving the additional tests.
6. In order to make better use of high school reports, individual universities should calculate the coefficients for each high school from students' grades at the university or from the results of nation-wide tests, and multiple high school grades by these coefficients to correct the differences in level among high schools.
7. An inventory of personality factors related to academic achievement should be constructed and used as one of the data for screening. The development and administration of this inventory should be made by the institute mentioned in proposal 4.
8. In order to make full use of the data, an electronic computer should be introduced to process the data, as well as to score the tests.
9. Follow-up studies should be made to check the validity and predictability of data used for making decisions in screening. The results should be fed back to improve the screening methods and decision making in the following year.
10. The proposals made above are beyond the ability of the Faculty Meeting. Therefore, a specialized admissions office staffed with a full-time officer should be established.
11. It is desirable that a joint organ should be made of admissions offices of individual universities, and that this joint organ and the testing institute co-operate to study and improve screening methods.

THE ONTARIO TESTS FOR ADMISSION TO COLLEGE AND UNIVERSITY: WHAT BACKGROUND? WHAT FUTURE?

VINCENT D'OYLEY

Both on the provincial and on the national levels, Canadian educationists have bestirred themselves to ponder the need for a common university entrance examination. Because there had been no such system heretofore, our universities have had to place considerable emphasis on the average marks in matriculation examinations as the means of screening their applicants. The great variation in high school curricula across the country poses a problem to admissions' officers who wish to evaluate fairly every applicant's high school record. This problem was thrown into bolder relief a few years ago by the sharp increase in secondary school enrolment, which had shortened the time span between the publication of matriculation marks and the date on which universities must make their final decisions about whom to admit. Then, at the beginning of this decade this issue was complicated further by the fact that our students began applying to more than one university to a greater degree, and thereby made the phrase 'multiple applications' a bogey for admissions' officers.

This paper presents a bird's-eye view of the background of a few large-scale testing programmes for university admission in the United States, to some aspects of developments in Ontario with descriptions of the present role and the future directions of the Ontario Tests for Admission to College and University.

In the last six decades there has been in the United States the development of large-scale testing programmes aimed at standardizing the evaluation of university candidates. These programmes are operated by bureaux with varied funding and backgrounds—the New York Regents, over a century old, the College Entrance Examination Board, the Educational Testing Service and the American College Test Service.

Oldest of the three American testing programmes presented here is the *New York Regents' Examinations.* Their achievement tests, administered thrice yearly, cover forty high school subjects studied in grades 10 to 12. The Regents' Examinations were begun in 1865 when the New York area responded to the need for a standard evaluation of candidates entering her public academies, later, they began to be used not only for the selection of candidates but also for the evaluation of schools and for the determination of the financial aid each school required or deserved. They were graded locally until 1870, when a central system began to emerge. In 1878 the New York Regents administered the first academic exam for admission to college; that exam determined entrance to college, and was also used as a basis for granting school leaving certificate to the graduates of the public academies.

Since 1900 the Regents' Examinations have tried to keep pace with the rapidly developing techniques of standardized testing. The superintendent's exams at the end of grade 8 have become obsolete, and the local schools are now responsible for issuing the Regents' Certificate at this level. As a result, there is more flexibility in the curriculum in grades 7 to 9.

Teachers and administrators from the New York school system develop the Regents' Examinations, and this factor has helped to ensure that the instruments remain a reflection of current practices in the classrooms of that state.

The College Entrance Examination Board, established in 1899 by co-operative effort on the part of member colleges and secondary schools, envisioned a national system of examinations to evaluate applicants to the colleges. Their early efforts were highly unreliable. In the article, 'The future of the College Entrance Examination Board', Thorndike (1906) suggested that the exam results could be put to better use as informational device for strengthening the curricula in the secondary schools instead of as a means of determining the qualifications of applicants to colleges, so that qualifications for all the candidates would be equal by virtue of standard past training. 'The establishment of the College Entrance Examination Board in the Middle States and Maryland was an advance in the management of the admissions of students to college, not only because it made the practice of many colleges more efficient, but also because it instituted an authoritative committee through which future evaluation may be wisely directed' (ibid., p. 470). The original series of tests were designed to evaluate the candidate's ability in English, mathematics and the classics.

In the 1920s, Professor Carl Brigham designed and standardized the Scholastic Aptitude Test, an objective measure of the candidate's verbal and mathematical aptitudes, as opposed to his academic achievement in these fields. The Scholastic Aptitude Test has since been refined to such an extent that it is now one of the better predictors of scholastic success available anywhere.

Achievement tests, objective in nature, are offered in a wide variety of subjects, and are administered five times yearly so that prospective applicants to a university may write them when they feel most qualified to do so. In the mid-50s the College Entrance Examination Board, at the request of many secondary schools, instituted the Advanced Placement Program, a series of tests designed to evaluate the achievement of high school students in university level courses offered by their schools. Member colleges may grant credit to students in some subject areas where the applicants demonstrate both capability and proficiency. The Educational Testing Service, 'the operating arm' of the College Entrance Examination Board established in December 1947, is now engaged in curriculum research and reform, and in studies and workshops in the guidance area.

A new and rapidly expanding series of examinations was begun in Iowa in 1959. This series, the *American College Testing Program** (the new organization and its affiliates Science Research Associates, Inc. and Measurement of Research Center, Inc.), has expanded to such an extent in its brief existence that in 1962-3 it served 725 American colleges, and provided information to influence decision making on admission, guidance, scholarship awards and loans.

The programme offers essentially a four-part test battery purporting to measure the candidate's background in English, mathematics, social studies and the natural sciences. The English examination is geared to measure the candidate's understanding and use of the skills underlying effective writing: the mathematics exam aims at measuring the candidate's mathematical reasoning ability, and includes some achievement items on the mathematical techniques studied in the high school curriculum; the Social Studies Reading Test is designed to evaluate the candidate's ability to comprehend and analyse reading passages from the social sciences, and the Natural Science Reading Test purports to measure critical reasoning and problem solving in the area of the natural sciences. The programme requests the candidate to supply his most recent high school grade in each of these subject areas, and to fill in a personal information form stating his past interests, special accomplishments and future ambitions. All of this information is passed to the colleges requesting it. The tests are administered four times a year at participating colleges and centres. Scores are reported to the colleges in the form of a standard scale from 1 to 36 with a standard deviation of 5 to 6. Included on the report form are predictive grade indices and also a weighted combination of ACT scores and junior high school grades (American College Testing Program 1965, pp. 1-2, 11).

The Ontario background

For some years now, the residents of Ontario have been questioning

* Based on the old Iowa Placement Associates.

their upper high school programme and the examination pattern embedded in it. The complaints and the search for improvement led the Minister of Education to appoint in 1964 the Ontario Grade 13 Study Committee which sought answers to some problems such as the thirteenth year's reputation as a cram year, Ontario's thirteen-year system *vis-à-vis* the United States' twelve-year system and the twelve-year system in some other Canadian provinces. The Committee reported in November 1965. Their report, based on 149 letters and briefs and 76 working papers in combination with 1,281 questionnaires filled out by grade 13 students, stated that these communications 'contained a full measure of criticism and recommendation for improvement, with very few bouquets either to the course, its examination or its teachers' (Watson and Lyle 1965, p. 125). It was clear, too, that there existed definite confusion about what could be done to improve the nature of the final year and its examinations. The students criticized the examinations, charging that they engendered anxiety, placed a premium on factual recall, and were no true estimate of their ability to work at university level. The most vehement protests dealt with the failure of the final year to provide 'challenging courses stimulating creative, original thinking' (ibid., p. 30).

Another real pressure for change in the system has been the rapid increase in enrolment in grade 13 in the past few years. In 1959-60 there were 18,447 students in grade 13 throughout the province; in 1964-5 the number was 37,692, an increase of nearly 100 per cent in five years. A complete table of enrolment from 1919 to 1965 inclusive can be found in the appendix.

Late last year, C. A. Brown commented (1966, p. 10): 'The announcement that no grade 13 Departmental examination will be provided in 1968 undoubtedly brought considerable relief to many people in Ontario. The unreasonable pressures and the inherent evils of the examination will be replaced, it is confidently expected, by a system of student assessment which is based on sound educational principles . . . the responsibility for conducting the school leaving examinations at the grade 13 level will be turned over to the schools.' With the elimination of the grade 13 Departmental examinations imminent, some means whereby universities, schools, parents, the Department of Education (and the students themselves) may receive a standardized estimate of a student's academic ability and achievement had to be found.

The national scene

On the national level, Canadian educationists examined the need for a

The Ontario Tests for Admission to College

common college entrance examination for students. Very active planning was engaged in for nearly two years with a view to establishing a Canadian body to administer scholastic aptitude and achievement tests that could be used throughout the nation as one criterion for selecting students for admission to Canadian universities (Department of Measurement and Evaluation 1965). The Board of Directors of the Association of Universities and Colleges of Canada and the Ministers of Education of the provinces approved in principle a proposal to establish a Service for Admission to College and University. It was envisioned that one primary function of such a council should be to assist universities and other post-secondary institutions with procedures and the solution of problems connected with the admission of secondary school students. The inaugural meeting of SACU was held in Ottawa in April 1966, when Mr Colin McDougall, Registrar at McGill University, was elected President. Since that time, Mr Leon Lamontagne, Dean of Letters at Laval University, has accepted the appointment as Executive Director of SACU.

The Ontario Tests for Admission to College and University

In Ontario, with the discontinuation of the grade 13 examinations, the universities and the grade 13 year will be freed from their dependence on the grade 13 exam, which served both as school honour graduation and as the main university entrance requirement. The secondary schools will be at liberty to establish the proficiency level required for their own school graduation,* and OACU, then, will make it possible to establish tests of a standardized nature for the specific purpose of admission to university. The year 1967 will serve as a transition period during which both the traditional grade 13 examinations as well as the Ontario Tests for Admission to College and University will be administered.

The Measurement Department of the Ontario Institute for Studies in Education has been commissioned by the Ontario government to develop and administer the Ontario Tests for Admission to College and University. For 1966-7, four tests will be given:

Ontario Scholastic Aptitude Test (OSAT)—26 January 1967

Ontario Physics Achievement Test (OPAT)—27 April 1967

Ontario English Composition Achievement Test (OECAT)—4 May 1967

*The Grade 13 Committee of the Ontario Teachers' Federation is studying the future of the grade 13 year.

Ontario Mathematics Achievement Test (OMAT)—11 May 1967

Each test will be administered only once, and all grade 13 students have been encouraged to write OSAT and any or all of the three achievement tests, according to whether or not those subjects are included in their study programmes.

The results of the tests will be reported in the form of a percentile rank for the province and a standard score. The results will be sent to the Ontario universities, the Ontario Department of Education, and to the schools for their own records and for the candidates. The candidates will learn their results from the schools. The universities will receive the scores of all the candidates, as it will not be possible, this year, to supply the universities with a separate list of specific candidates applying to their institutions. OACU results will be released to the schools and the universities after the Department of Education receives the teachers' marks from the schools (i.e. after 5 June). The individual candidate will not receive his results until he has completed his grade 13 examinations.

The four instruments are the product of interaction between (a) the College Entrance Examination Board and its operating arm, the Educational Testing Service of Princeton, New Jersey, and (b) the Ontario Institute for Studies in Education. Dr Frances Swineford, Head of the ETS Test Analysis Department, worked at OISE for two months at the beginning of 1966 helping to assess the applicability of CEEB tests to the Canadian student population. OISE has been permitted to draw, not only upon the expertise and item polls of the ETS, but also upon the energy and enterprise of the Ontario universities and Ontario teachers. OSAT, OPAT and OECAT will carry the inscription, 'Adapted by special permission from . . . the College Entrance Examination Board, New York'.

Eight Ontario scholars, teachers and measurement specialists served on the committee for the development of each of the three achievement tests, and four on the Ontario Scholastic Aptitude Test Committee. OSAT, OECAT and, to a lesser extent, OPAT are essentially adaptations of their CEEB originals. Each committee began its work by examining Frances Swineford's *Evaluation of Performance of Some Canadian Students on College Entrance Examination Board Tests,* a series of six detailed reports and one summarizing document. On the OECAT, one type of item which did not discriminate effectively among Canadian students has been revised drastically; in OPAT, too, there has been a considerable amount of item revision and refining of

The Ontario Tests for Admission to College

distractors. But it was on the OMAT that the greatest departure has been made. Driven by necessity, the Mathematics Committee has developed a genuinely new test based upon the new mathematics curriculum introduced this year at the grade 13 level in Ontario. OMAT is designed to measure and evaluate the ability of the students to understand and apply what they have learned rather than the ability to memorize facts, rules and formulae. The test is designed for those students who are enrolled in Mathematics 13A.

Because these tests are to be used for university admission purposes, they must be *secure*. To achieve this end, a new series of regulations has been drawn up in consultation with relevant groups of Ontario educationists. The present advisory board which helps with the planning of the general instructions for the administration of the tests includes representatives from (a) four secondary school groups—directors of education, superintendents of secondary schools, secondary school headmasters, and secondary school teachers, (b) school trustees, (c) the Ontario Department of Education, (d) directors of admission in the universities of Ontario, (e) the Ontario school trustees, and (f) the Measurement Department of OISE. The instructions are succinctly stated in the brochure entitled *General Instructions for the Administration of the Ontario Tests for Admission to College and University* now in the hands of the school principals and superintendents. The Measurement Department has been fortunate in obtaining the services of Dr Corbin Brown (formerly Registrar at the Ontario Department of Education) as Liaison Officer for test development. Ontario principals communicate directly to Dr Brown on all OACU problems.

The advisory board will be asked to constitute a Research Advisory Board which would draw on representatives from the same six groups just mentioned above, but will no doubt add a few university teachers. The Research Advisory Board will meet possibly twice yearly to review the results of the most recent test administrations and to raise questions about the plans for research into varied aspects of the measurement programme.

What future?

The Ontario government has requested that OACU be administered again in 1967-8, and Ontario universities have been enthusiastic in their acceptance of this programme. One achievement test might be added to the series in 1967-8. We are undertaking preliminary negotiations for a gentleman's agreement which would see the College Entrance

Examination Board in 1968 administering in Ontario only such tests as are not included in the OACU programme.

The programme will survive: (a) if it remains a co-operative venture with development staff drawn from within and without OISE and always with a substantial concentration of Ontario university and high school personnel, aware of the value of large item pools; (b) if it preserves links with other university admission programmes, notably CEEB/ETS,* benefitting from their expertise and traditions, but seeking new patterns for the solution of the special problems facing the young people desirous of entering Ontario universities: (c) if it recognizes a responsibility for the improvement within this province of competence in both the use and interpretation of test results by administrative staff (both university and high school), guidance counsellors and teachers, and sets out a strategy for reducing the communications gap on problems of test theory and test construction between the test users and the test specialists. Both the advisory and the research boards must play crucial roles for the constant updating of the programme.

OACU should encourage the already recognized need on the part of some of our universities for validity studies for their local educational and vocational situations.

Finally, OACU is not designed to forestall the proposed national body, SACU; on the contrary, OACU must provide some worth-while training and experience for the benefit of SACU, which will need to move with alacrity and caution towards the solution of the many admission problems now resting on the doorstep of Canadian universities.

References

Brown, C. A. (1966) 'The problem of standards.' *Ontario Education*, 1, no. 1, 10-11.

Department of Measurement and Evaluation (1965) *Test Letter*, no. 2. Toronto, Ontario: Ontario Institute for Studies in Education.

Reports of the Minister of Education (1920, 1925, 1930, 1935, 1940, 1945, 1964, 1965) Toronto, Ontario: Ontario Department of Education.

Technical Report (1965) Iowa City, Iowa: American College Testing Program.

---

*CEEB/ETS have already given invaluable guidance and support to the programme.

Thorndike, E. L. (1906) 'The future of the College Entrance Examination Board.' *Educ.Rev.*, **31**, 470 ff.

Watson, C. and Lyle, P. (1965) 'Ontario Grade 13: three studies. *Bulletin*, **23**. Toronto, Ontario: Ontario Institute for Studies in Education.

APPENDIX*
SOME HIGH SCHOOL[1] AND UNIVERSITY POPULATION DATA, ONTARIO 1919-65

Year	Grade 12	Grade 13	Total high school	First-year university	Total university
1919-20	8,170[2]	1,522	42,952		9,240
1924-5	17,665[3]	4,576	77,870		
1929-30	12,003(1)[4]				
	7,586(2)	5,126	65,903		12,047
1934-5	13,583	9,451	111,848		
1939-40	15,795	8,893	73,102		12,410
1944-5	10,504	8,022	73,866		
1946-7	17,694	9,415	121,911		
1949-50	17,576	9,457	130,041		23,207
1954-5	23,846	10,799	173,296		
1959-60	38,697	18,447	261,417		
1960-1	42,266	21,482	297,769	8,345	32,947
1961-2	46,776	23,750	330,106	8,676	36,927
1962-3	55,731	26,262	359,033	10,006	41,092
1963-4	64,418	32,770	380,649	12,164	43,325
1964-5	67,282	37,692	392,980	14,176	48,794
1965-6				17,124	57,840

[1] The high school totals include high schools, collegiates, continuation and vocational schools.

The high school totals do not include schools where pupils were not assigned to grades.

[2] Schools in three grades only: lower, middle, upper (on table middle is listed under grade 12, and upper under grade 13).

[3] Schools are in a four-grade system: lower; 1, 2; middle; upper. Vocational is in a five-year system with fourth and fifth combined—listed under grade 13 total; third year is listed under grade 12.

[4] Schools are in a five-grade system: lower; 1, 2; middle; 1, 2; upper. Populations of vocational schools are listed as in 1924-5. Middle (1) and middle (2) are listed under grade 12.

*Report of the Minister of Education, Ontario, Ontario Department of Education, 1920, 1925, 1930, 1935, 1940, 1945, 1964, 1965.

Refs: Department of University Affairs, Ontario.

UNIVERSITY SELECTION PROCEDURES IN CHILE

E. GRASSAU

As the listener will realize, the title of this lecture is rather inadequate. In fact we in Chile cannot really speak about selection procedures in use, because we are at this moment at a turning-point: the selection procedures used until 1966 have been abolished by law, and new requirements have been established for 1967. Perhaps, then, a better title would have been: 'Causes which led to the abolition of essay entrance tests for the first time'. But this might have led the listener to infer that selection procedures in Chile had been altered because of a general awareness that the methods employed were out of date. This was not the case. Perhaps, therefore, the best title would be: 'The problem of selecting university students in Chile'.

I think that our experiences in Chile may be of interest. Whether we are at the beginning of any real improvement in our selection procedures remains to be seen; but the members of the audience may be able to draw their own conclusions after listening to this report.

Description of the admission procedures existing before 1967

If a student wished to apply for any institution of higher education, he had to fulfil the following requirements:
1. Successful completion of secondary school education. This had to be proved by a certificate given by the schools, listing the qualifications he had obtained during his last three years of study, and by a secondary school graduate certificate *(Licencia Secundaria)* given by the Ministry of Education.
2. *Bachillerato* degree granted by the University of Chile* after having successfully passed a *Bachillerato* examination. This examination was administered by the Faculty of Philosophy and Education.
3. Besides these general requirements, many schools and faculties of the universities gave another set of examinations, called entrance examinations. These examinations varied from one university to another, from one school to another within the same university, and from one year to another within the same school. This meant that a student had to take in December the final examin-

---
*Before 1957 this degree was only granted by the University of Chile, but then the Technical University provided a Technical *Bachillerato* degree for its students, and the Catholic University of Valparaiso included its own *Bachillerato* examination in its selection procedures.

University selection procedures in Chile

ations of the last year of secondary school, in January the *Bachillerato* examinations, and, at the end of January or at the beginning of March, the entrance examination required by the school he had applied for. These three sets of examinations had to be passed one after another. Failure in one set prevented the applicant from taking the next. At the end the total marks obtained were combined and the student rejected or accepted, depending upon the criteria of the school.

The *Bachillerato* examinations which constituted the first stage in the selection procedure consisted of two parts. The first, or 'general' part, was compulsory for all students. This included a listening comprehension and composition test, and a test of ability to understand a written foreign language (the student could choose from among the languages he had studied at school). The second, or 'special', part of the *Bachillerato* examinations included three tests in the fields in which the student had chosen to be tested: mathematics, humanities or biology. Mathematics included attainment tests in mathematics, physics and chemistry, biology included tests in biology, physics and chemistry, and humanities included tests in Spanish literature and grammar, history and geography. All these tests were essay-type, and all claimed to measure writing ability, comprehension and reasoning

In the 'general' part of this examination the students were required to listen to a short lecture on a philosophical or psychological topic, write a brief summary of it, and answer two or three questions on the subject matter. In the foreign language test, the students were given a passage to read and some questions about it in the foreign language, which they had to answer in Spanish.

In the 'special' part of the *Bachillerato* examination, three written tests, one in each subject, were administered. Each test consisted of five questions at most. These questions dealt with a group of topics randomly selected from the ones studied at secondary school.

All these tests were given within a period of five days, at the same time, in sixteen different centres throughout the country. The same questions were put to all students taking the same field, and the tests were graded by one professor on a scale ranging from 10 to 70. The final score was obtained by adding together the marks of the five tests. To qualify, a minimum of 180 points, from a maximum of 350, was required.

The scoring of the papers was quite interesting. Each question included in the test dealt with a particular topic, and comprised four or five sub-questions. Each sub-question was allocated a certain number of points. In chemistry, for instance, three of the sub-questions earned one point each, and the remaining two questions earned two points each.

The total score for all items correct was therefore seven points. The instructions stated that these seven points correspond to the mark 7. The final score of the whole test was obtained by multiplying the mean of the items answered by 10.

The entrance examinations required by many schools and faculties consisted of essay tests in the field of studies which the school considered basic; sometimes, too, the candidates were given an interview, or tests of general ability or special aptitudes were administered. Scoring procedures and the weighting of each requirement were decided by the individual schools and varied a great deal. No technical advice in educational measurement was needed for it.

The existence of the *Bachillerato* degree granted by the University of Chile was due to the fact that until 1927—when the Department of Secondary Education of the Ministry of Education was created—secondary education came under the control of the University of Chile. In spite of a clear statement in the University's regulations that the *Bachillerato* examination was a university entrance examination, the degree was in fact considered a final secondary studies degree. Moreover, this degree was usually required of applicants for certain kinds of jobs.

The increase in the number of secondary school leavers meant a larger demand for university places, and therefore the universities were forced to reject more and more applicants. Besides this, the failure rate at the universities became quite substantial. This caused criticism both by the public and by the university authorities. At this time, two investigations showed the weakness of the *Bachillerato* examinations as a selection instrument, and showed, too, that there was tremendous gap between the level of achievement at secondary education and the level required by the universities (see Grassau 1955, Salas and Orellana 1960). From that time on, there was no doubt that the absence of the most able students from the university was due to insufficiency of the secondary education and to the evaluation system then in use, which did not allow a proper selection.

Thus there came into being a distrust of the *Bachillerato* examination and a distrust of the secondary school grades. All these facts had several effects:
  1. As there was a general demand for a change in the admission procedures, the committee in charge—convinced of the necessity of improving the examinations—made some changes in the procedural details; but this, unfortunately, did not bring about an improvement in the academic standard of the students nor in the prediction efficiency of the methods of selection. The effect observed was that the failure rate went down—possibly this was

an unconscious way of avoiding criticism from the public and of reducing the number of applicants rejected by the universities. In fact, the failure rate in the *Bachillerato* had been going up in the period between 1942 and 1949; from then on, it went down. Strong criticism from the public through the press started in 1948. Parallel to it, there was an increase in the proportion of students getting the minimum pass marks and a decrease in the proportion of those with higher scores; and the correlation between *Bachillerato* and the university grades became lower. In my own opinion, the only improvement worth mentioning was that more precise instructions were given to the examiners in an effort to obtain a more objective method of scoring. If this was achieved, it can be detected by looking at the scoring procedures employed; these were mentioned before.

2. Entrance examinations were established at those university schools with the highest demand. Until 1960 these were mainly essay-type achievement tests. In 1961, however, the Board of Deans of the University of Chile—aware of the similar content in the entrance examinations, the *Bachillerato* and secondary school grades, and taking into consideration investigations which showed that these examinations did not improve selection—suggested that the schools replace the achievement tests with measurements of the candidates' personality characteristics, interests, general ability and special aptitudes.

1967 selection procedures

In 1964 and 1965 the criticism of the *Bachillerato* examination became stronger. Everyone was against it, and even the Faculty of Philosophy and Education wished it to be abolished; on the other hand, in the view of the Institute of Statistical Research (ISR), its abolition could turn out to be very dangerous, since, they thought, if selection procedures were left entirely to the university schools, the possibility of establishing a central admission department would be lost. That would take us even further away from the possibility of having uniform standards for admission to university. Knowing that the entrance examinations were no better than the *Bachillerato* examination, and aware of the lack of trained staff and the impracticability of this procedure from the students' point of view, the ISR proposed, in 1965, a plan to replace the listening comprehension test (which showed no correlation with university studies) with an academic aptitude test, and to change the 'special' part of the examination from the essay-type to objective-type tests. This was refused. In September of the same year, the Institute asked permission to administer the academic aptitude test, for research purposes, to all *Bachillerato* examination applicants, in addition to the traditional examinations; this was also refused. In April 1966 when it was clear that the abolition of the *Bachillerato* examination would be approved by Parliament, the ISR put forward to the Council of Rectors of Chilean Universities new regulations for admission. Their main proposals were these:

1. The Academic Aptitude Test should be made a general requirement for entry to any university.
2. The 'pass/fail' system should be changed to a system of selection based upon the relative position of a student in his group, in accordance with a combination of requirements.
3. The same objective tests should be administered at all the schools which needed to measure their applicants in the same subject fields. These tests were to be constructed by a committee of professors of the faculties that would use the test, in collaboration with outstanding secondary school teachers.
4. Secondary school grades should be taken into account when selecting the applicants. Measures should be taken to ensure the reliability of the information supplied by the secondary schools.
5. The students should be given the opportunity to apply for at least three different university schools.
6. These antecedents, which only take into account factors from the cognitive domain, should be the only ones used in January 1967; no other information about the students was available.
7. The system should be improved and broadened permanently in order to obtain more and better information on the students; and continuous and careful research should be assured, in order that a real improvement in selection procedures should be made.

The universities accepted the Academic Aptitude Test as a common requirement. The mean of the last three years of secondary school grades was also considered; each university and even each school within any university could administer a set of specific achievement or aptitude tests. Objective achievement tests in biology, mathematics, physics and chemistry were constructed. They were requested by the faculties of science, who stated that a maximum of two achievement tests should be required by each school. With the exception of the School of Architecture, the Faculty of Music and the School of Arts, no university school used specific aptitude tests. The weighting given to each requirement in order to obtain a final score for each applicant was decided by the schools, but they had to take into account that the

Academic Aptitude Test and secondary school grades should have at least a weight of 30 per cent each.

The new selection procedures meant an improvement on the old ones in these respects:
1. The use of objective-type tests and the acceptance of the mechanical scoring.
2. Objective achievement tests were constructed by a committee of professors from the faculties which needed them.
3. The change from the pass/fail system to a system that ranks students according to their relative positions in each of the requirements. The schools established a certain number of vacancies which were filled by the applicants with the highest scores.
4. The candidates were allowed to apply for more than one school, with a maximum of five applications, in the University of Chile. In former years, multiple application was forbidden; indeed, when cases of this were discovered, some schools even annulled the applications.

Analysis of admission procedures before 1966

Investigations of the qualities of the *Bachillerato* examinations were carried out for the first time in 1953. This research was started as a seminar in educational statistics at the School of Education of the University of Chile, and was continued by the staff of this course. The study referred to general aspects of the *Bachillerato* examinations from 1942 to 1951, including data about the number of applicants, failure rates and a more careful analysis of the 1950 examination, such as the qualifications obtained and comparison with secondary school grades and university performance in the Schools of Agronomy, Architecture, Law, Engineering, Medicine, Veterinary, Pharmacy, Dentistry and Education. Another study of the entrance examination of the Schools of Agronomy and Social Service and the History Department and Physical Health of the School of Education, was carried out by the same group. The School of Medicine, too, made its own research on its entrance examination.

The conclusions drawn from these studies were these:
1. The *Bachillerato* examination had a different prognostic value for most schools; the correlation coefficients were all positive and were not higher than 0·45.
2. The correlations between secondary school grades and university grades were about the same—in most cases even lower than those between *Bachillerato* and university grades.

3. The correlations between secondary school grades and *Bachillerato* scores were much higher than the former, ranging between 0·57 and 0·68.
4. The combination of school grades and *Bachillerato* scores did not improve prediction. The highest multiple correlation coefficient *(R)* was obtained by the Schools of Engineering and Medicine, 0·45 and 0·39 respectively.
5. The entrance examinations did not show a better correlation with the criteria than the *Bachillerato* examination with university grades. The correlation between the *Bachillerato* and these examinations was very high, about 0·70.

Fortunately, in 1957 an institute devoted to educational research and statistics in higher education had been created at the University of Chile; this made it possible to continue with the studies on entrance examinations. In 1959 a sample was taken to study the correlation between the *Bachillerato* scores and university performance. The results did not show any improvement on the former investigations. Moreover, this study showed that the 'general' part of the *Bachillerato* examination had no correlation with university grades. Only the 'special' part of it had a slight correlation.

In 1960 investigations were made in order to see whether rank in class was a better predictor than secondary school grades. No difference was found in the sample of 954 students. The multiple correlation coefficient between secondary school grades, *Bachillerato* examination and university grades was now 0·38. As in the 1950 study, this multiple correlation was in some cases practically the same as the correlation between *Bachillerato* and university and, in some other, like that between secondary school grades and university grades. These low validity coefficients could be partly accounted for by the unquestionably low reliability of these examinations caused by the type of tests used and the way they were scored.

Surprising enough were the rather low correlations between secondary school grades and university grades, ranging from 0·12 to 0·41. Analysing the distribution of the secondary school grades, we could demonstrate that the shape of the distribution had not changed at all. In a seven-point scale marking system, the mean of the last three secondary school years has always been 4·5 with a standard deviation of 0·6. About 82 per cent of the candidates got marks of 4 and 5. The university applicants show, as always, a mean of 4·8 and a standard deviation of 0·5. Ninety-five per cent of them had the medium qualification. It is interesting to note that 86 per cent of the group of secondary school leavers with a mean of less than 5 (4 is the minimum pass mark), 60 per cent of the group with a mean of 5, and 80 per cent of the group above 5·5 applied to the university.

Fifteen out of a hundred students with a secondary grade mean of 5·5 failed at the university. (In lower average, chances are about half and half.) The problem is, if the university restricts its entrance to this group of students, university schools would not fill the vacancies.

When we examine the qualifications obtained by the students at the university, we can again observe the restricted range of marks and a high percentage of low grades. The seven-point scale is not used in its full range. Undoubtedly, the restrictive range of both secondary school and university grades affects the correlation coefficients obtained. Moreover, the poor quality of the university applicants measured with secondary school criteria would also explain the university rejection rate and the high failure rate in the first year of university studies.

Convinced of the necessity of taking into account other factors besides school performance, my collaborators and I have been studying, since 1949, the possibility of improving selection procedures by including psychological tests. The Minnesota Paper Board Test showed some validity for the careers of architecture, dentistry and engineering. The results of the Verbal and Numerical Differential Aptitude Tests, administered to students at the School of Agronomy and Veterinary, and the results with the Amthauer Intelligence Test, administered at the Catholic University, showed that it would be a good plan to start thinking about the construction of a general aptitude test for university entrance. This was carried out after attending a seminar on test construction at ETS. This visit to ETS, besides providing us with a broader view of the problem and with invaluable material, gave us the courage to embark, for the very first time in Chile, on the construction of our own tests.

The possibility afterwards offered by CEEB of collaborating in the construction of the Academic Aptitude Test for Puerto Rico led us to devote most of our time to this project. A grant from the Ford Foundation made it possible to establish a testing department at the Institute of Statistical Research.

This General Aptitude Test, besides adding a new antecedent to the selection procedures, would help to discriminate the applicants better, and would provide a common scale by which to interpret the students' other prerequisites, in order to rank them. As I stated in my first paper, the marking system in Chile is a absolute marking system with a low discrimination rate.

Our final purpose when we embarked on the Academic Aptitude Test was, on the one hand, to produce some effective changes in the obviously inadequate procedures used in the entrance examinations, and, on the other, to demonstrate objectively—as we could not do using the information then available—that the academic standard of the candidates was going down year by year, in order to convince teachers of the need to take some effective action to improve our educational outcomes.

1963, 1964 and 1965 were devoted to the development of an Academic Aptitude Test. We used this test for experimental purposes in some schools of the State University and the Catholic universities. The results were promising: by adding the Academic Aptitude Test to the other antecedents we could improve our prediction efficiency for selection. Our efforts were better rewarded with the results obtained at the School of Medicine; besides raising the multiple correlation from 0·33 to 0·65, we earned enthusiastic approval for our recommendations, and the School of Medicine selection procedures came to be considered the best in Chile.

The Academic Aptitude Test for university selection (AASU)

The test was constructed by the Institute staff. Items were also provided by the students of the seminars of test construction held at the Institute. Up to now, seven parallel forms have been used. The content of the test, the type of items included, and the assembling of the test are similar to the Scholastic Aptitude Test (SAT) of the CEEB.* The verbal section comprises ninety items and the mathematical section sixty. Scores are given in standard scores with a mean of 500 and a standard deviation of 100.

The first experimental form was tried out in October 1962 on a sample representative of the last year of secondary school; from this tryout the 1963-4 form was obtained. This form was administered in 1963 and 1964 to a group of 4,830 students, which included applicants to the Schools of Agronomy, Education, Psychology, Social Service, Sociology, Pharmacy and Veterinary, applicants to the Catholic University of Valparaiso, and first-year students of economics, engineering, law and medicine.

During 1965 and 1966 parallel forms of the test were administered for research purposes to university applicants and first-year students, at those schools that requested it. In 1966 some schools were permitted

---

*The CEEB and the ISR have been considering the possibility of including a certain number of common items in their forms, for future comparisons. The Chilean version of the SAT has been used successfully at the School of Administration in Lima, Peru; this made us consider the possibility of getting into closer touch with the Latin-American universities.

Table 1. Verbal part

Test forms	No. of students	Scaled score statistics(1) $\bar{x}$	σ	Raw score statistics $\bar{x}$	σ	Reliability (2) (3)	Mean item difficulty(5)	Mean item biserial r	Error of measurement R S	S S
AASU 63–4	4830	497	109	40	12	·95	12·06	·45	3	24
AASU 65–A	2288	513	104	47	14	·91	11·62	·49	4	31
AASU 65–B	1878	475	97	37	14	·91	11·87	·48	4	29
AASU 66–A	3004	528	66	42	12	·89	12·40	·45	4	22
AASU 66–B	5386	454	82	33	13	·91	12·45	·47	4	25
AASU 67–A	12607	480	93	24	13	·89	13·25	·41	4	31
AASU 67–B	17069	491	98	26	13	·89	13·14	·44	4	33

Mathematical part

Test forms	No. of students	Scaled score statistics(1) $\bar{x}$	σ	Raw score statistics $\bar{x}$	σ	Reliability(2) (3)	Mean item difficulty(5)	Mean item biserial r	Error of measurement R S	S S
AASU 63–4	4830	494	103	15	10	·96	15·56	·54	2	21
AASU 65–A	2288	542	89	24	12	·94	13·02	·62	3	22
AASU 65–B	1878	462	90	15	11	·94	13·34	·62	3	22
AASU 66–A	3004	506	100	19	12	·93	13·83	·59	3	25
AASU 66–B	5386	485	107	15	11	·92	13·77	·59	3	27
AASU 67–A	12607	482	100	16	10	·87(4)	13·37	·49	4	33
AASU 67–B	17069	495	108	17	11	·89(4)	13·61	·54	4	32

(1) Up to 1966 scaled scores are expressed in AASU 63.64 units. For 1967 scaled scores were not equated.
(2) With exception of 63.64 all r_{xx} are estimated on items included in the test according to the results obtained on experimental try-out.
(3) Computed with Gulliksen formula: $r_{xx} = \dfrac{k}{k-1}\left[1 - \dfrac{\Sigma \sigma_i^2}{(\Sigma r_{it}\,\sigma_i)^2}\right]$ $\sigma_i^2 = pq$ (item variance)
    k = number of items
    r_{it} = point bis.r between item and total score
(4) When calculated with K–R 20 r_{xx} became 0·91 and 0·92 respectively.
(5) Expressed in Δ (mean 13, $\sigma = 2$).

to use the test results as a requirement in selection; but these schools were advised that the test score should not be used to reject a student.

In 1967 the test was administered to the total population of university applicants: 29,677 students.

In tables 1 and 2 some statistical information about the test is given.

Table 2

Test forms	Equating equations
AASU 65–A M	Y = ·96 X − 2·74
AASU 65–B M	Y = 1·06 X − 2·84
AASU 65–A V	Y = 1·13 X − 8·36
AASU 65–B V	Y = ·85 X + 7·13
AASU 66–A M	Y = ·94 X − 3·40
AASU 66–B M	Y = ·83 X − 1·42
AASU 66–A V	Y = ·86 X + 3·15
AASU 66–B V	Y = ·86 X + 6·49

Y = Raw score 1963-4
X = Raw score of the corresponding year

Until 1966, the standard scores are expressed in 'AASU 63.64 units' The standard scores for the 1967 group have not been equated, because of the substantial difference observed between this group and the earlier groups. Doubtless, some factors that were not present in the previous years were operating in the 1967 administration. It looks as if it will be convenient to change our reference group to the 1967 group; but a more careful study has to be made. The first analysis showed that the 1967 group has lower abilities than the other groups. The reference group we have been using was a sample taken only from school leavers coming out from general secondary education. As the technical universities agreed to use this test in their selection procedures, students coming from the secondary schools were also included in the 1967 group. Furthermore, it is possible that the age distribution of the 1967 group will differ from the reference group; 1967 regulations did not impose restrictions on those who had failed in the *Bachillerato* examination in former years, so that the proportion of candidates who had left school years ago and took the examination this year was high (46 per cent). This was foreseen, and it was recommended that these applicants should be considered apart from the 1966 school leavers; this suggestion, however, was refused by the local authorities.

Though a remarkable difference was clearly seen, the shape of the distribution obtained by this 1967 group was similar to the former ones. The frequency distribution of the verbal section presented a normal distribution, while a moderate positive skewness was shown in the mathematical section.

The Academic Aptitude Test as a predictor for first-year university grade mean (UGM) in comparison with secondary school grades (SGM) and Bachillerato scores

The results of the Academic Aptitude Tests have been carefully analysed. These studies included, for each student group taking the test, a detailed analysis of the score distribution and correlations between each predictor (antecedents) and the criteria. Secondary school grades were studied for each subject. The same was done with *Bachillerato* scores and first-year university grades.

The conclusions we can draw from the data available at present are the following (the figures refer to the results in 1963-4 and part of 1965 in the Schools of Medicine, Engineering, Economics, Education (English Department), Agronomy and Law):

1. The AASU shows differences in ability levels among the different professional schools. The Schools of Medicine and Engineering show the highest values. This is in accordance with the facts: these schools attract the best students, and have the highest rejection rate. Moreover, table 1 shows that the group which answered the A forms in 1965 and 1966 achieved the highest mean AASU scores. This group comprised the applicants to the schools just mentioned. The group that answered the B form, on the other hand, consisted mainly of applicants who had failed in examinations in December or January and who had obtained the lowest AASU scores.
2. Multiple correlation *(R)* became higher if we added AASU scores to secondary school grades and the *Bachillerato* scores.
3. The predictive efficiency did not change significantly when R was computed from the SGM and AASU scores alone, without the *Bachillerato* grades among the antecedents.
4. Multiple correlation became higher whenever the scores in the *Bachillerato* 'special' part were considered instead of the total score on both parts.
5. There is no doubt that all these multiple correlations must be affected by the narrow range of secondary school and university grades. In all the schools we studied secondary school grades ranged approximately between one sigma below and above the mean. Moreover, the result also suggests that there is not a marked relation between the abilities measured by the AASU and those

evaluated by university grades: AASU measures reasoning ability, while most of first-year university examinations are mainly based on memory. Nevertheless, it is interesting that in one of the schools studied (Medicine), a higher R was obtained with second-year university students; this may be explained by a change, on the part of the students, towards a less passive attitude in their studies.

Besides this, the Rs were computed for the group staying at the University up to the end of first year (about 30 per cent had dropped out before this time for reasons which could not be discovered). Looking at AASU results in most schools, the group of students who got to the end of the year showed higher AASU scores than the group of students who dropped out.

6. To obtain UGM, the different subject grades were transformed into standard scores in a scale with a mean of 50 and a standard deviation of 10. The UGM was the mean of these transformed scores. This had to be done because there were enormous differences in shape and difficulty level between one subject and another. For example, while in the School of Engineering, 3·5, the lowest pass mark, corresponded in two courses to the mean, in the other three courses it corresponded to 1 or 2 standard deviations below the mean. The failure rate ranged between 3 per cent and 52 per cent. Correlations between the subject grades varied from 0·3 to 0·8.

All these facts raise the question whether the UGM represented a true picture of the students. A more detailed study of this is now being carried out.

7. The AASU showed the highest correlation with the grades obtained in those courses with a rather low failure rate and a wider variability. In the courses where objective tests were used to evaluate students, higher correlations were also obtained.

A summary of some of our findings is presented in the tables below. They include: (a) single antecedents as predictors for first-year university grade mean (table 3); (b) mean and standard deviations of predictors (table 4); (c) correlations between predictors (table 5); and (d) multiple correlation coefficient for predicting UGM (table 6).

Objective achievement tests versus essay-type tests in university selection

In our proposal for admission in 1967, we recommended that objective tests should be used when specific achievement tests were considered indispensable. We based our recommendations in the following facts:

Table 3. Single antecedents as predictors for first-year UGM

University schools Variables	Medicine	Engineering	Economics	Law	Agronomy	Psycho-logy	Education (English)	Others	Total university
SGM (1)									
H	·41*	·22*	·25*	·45*	·29	–·16	·27*	·08	·22*
S	·38*	·10	·24	·40*	·07	·26	·59*	·59	
	·42*	·36*	·26	·48*	·07	·03	·53*		
Bach. (2)									
G	·24*	·11	·09	·18	·00	·33	·18	–·00	·38
S	·14	·07	·09	·12	·07	·36	·11	·30	
	·34*	·23*	·02	·13	·04	·16	·25		
AASU									
V	·34*	·25*	·37*	·16	·23	·35	·10(3)	·32(3)	·35*
M	·36*	·33*	·34*		·37*	·40			·25*
									·31*

(1) H = SGM of humanities courses
    S = SGM of science courses
(2) G = *Bachillerato* examination, 'general' section
    S = *Bachillerato* examination, 'special' section
(3) Verbal + mathematical scores

* = Significant

Table 4. Mean and standard deviation of predictors

School of		Medicine $\bar{x}$	σ	Law $\bar{x}$	σ	Agronomy $\bar{x}$	σ	Psychology $\bar{x}$	σ	Economics $\bar{x}$	σ	Engineering $\bar{x}$	σ	Education $\bar{x}$	σ	Total university $\bar{x}$	σ
SGM (1)	Total	5·4	·6	4·79	·6	4·7	·6	4·6	·49	4·9	·52	5·31	·52			5·02	·65
	H			4·99	·62	4·88	·65	4·68	·51	4·99	·61	5·2	·6				
	S	5·4	·7	4·52	·64	4·65	·57	4·44	·52	4·90	·54	5·48	·52				
Bachille-rato (2)	Total	5·3	·5	4·82	·51			4·85	·44	4·39	·50	4·93	·59			4·5	·5
	G	5·7	·8	5·03	·78	468	·78	3·59	·41	5·1	·86	5·03	·7				
	S	5·1	·7	4·53	·61	383	·62	4·44	·65	3·99	·67	4·83	·52				
AASU (3)	V	619	78	561	82	538	83	558	70	529	77	540	89			568	87
	M	614	65	—		512	72	483	95	569	57	650	63			588	82
AASU (4)	V			504	92	508	90	523	84	525	80	551	84	474	90	497	101
	M			...	...	503	68	456	86	567	61	650	62	404	75	494	102

(1) H: SGM of humanities courses
    S: SGM of science courses
(2) G: *Bachillerato* examination, 'general' part
    S: *Bachillerato* examination, 'special' part
(3) Of students staying up to the end of the first year
(4) Applicants

Table 5. Correlations between predictors (1)

	Bachillerato	AASU. V	AASU. M
SGM	−.13 .34*	.03 .24*	−.28 .22*
Bachillerato		.00 .37*	−.10 .31*
AASU − V			.25 .52*

(1) Presenting the lowest and highest r obtained in the different professional schools

Table 6. Multiple correlations for predicting UGM

	Medicine (N=143)	Engineering (N=78)	Economics (N=67)	Agronomy (N=51)	Law (N=91)	English (N=39)	Psychology (N=32)	Total university (N=527)
SGM+*Bachillerato*	·42*	·27	·28	·08	·45*	·30	·44*	·38*
SGM+*Bachillerato*+AASU	·60*	·32*	·61*					
SGM+AASU	·55*	·37*	·55*	·56*	·45*(1)	·59*	·39	·37*
SGM+AASU +*Bach.S* (2)	·63*	·43*						
SGM+AASU+*Bach.S*+EE(3)	·65*	·48*				·68		

(1) AASU verbal section only
(2) *Bach.S* = *Bachillerato* examination, 'special' part
(3) EE = Entrance examination

1. The predictive efficiency of the antecedents used was higher when the 'special' part of the *Bachillerato* was considered.
2. There was a lack of standardized objective achievement tests in the secondary school.
3. Our experience at the School of Medicine proved that it was possible to construct a test with an acceptable reliability in a rather short time.

In fact, the results obtained in the School of Medicine are worth commenting upon, because they showed how the change from essay tests to objective tests based on the same educational objectives made possible a better discrimination, while improving the scoring procedure.

A multiple-choice test of 120 items was constructed by a committee of the Medical School professors advised by members of the ISR staff. The test had three sections of forty items each, corresponding to the fields of chemistry, biology and physics. The test obtained had an item difficulty mean of 62·5 per cent (delta 11·5) and a reliability coefficient of 0·90; correlation with UGM was 0·39. The distribution of the scores presented a moderate positive skewness, as expected. By combining this test result with secondary school grades and AASU and transforming each into standard scores, a multiple correlation of 0·66 was obtained.

The former essay tests used in selection at this school included four items, one on physics, one on biology, and one on chemistry; the fourth was supposed to measure vocational interest. The first three questions, which were intended to measure comprehension and application, included five sub-questions in each subject. A maximum of 120 points for each item was laid down, but no instructions were given to the examiner on how to score each question. There was no correlation between these three parts of the test. The distributions were skewed; the difficulty level was different, the means obtained were 41, 9 and 55 in physics, chemistry and biology respectively. In chemistry 83 per cent of the group did not reach the mean, and in the other two subjects 50 per cent was below the mean. There was no correlation between the final score obtained by adding the scores of each part of the test and the UGM. It is interesting to note that if they had used the sum of standard scores of the three parts of their test, the correlation with UGM would have been 0·20.

Final comments

What does our experience show? The strength of social and political factors in promoting educational changes and the importance of continuous educational research. In fact, the abolition of the *Bachillerato* examination was due to social and political factors: the increase in the number of secondary school leavers who did not enter the universities and the current political slogan, 'We need changes in order to progress'.

The establishment of the AASU as a requirement for university entrance was mainly due to the conviction that it was a test constructed at a Chilean research institute, that it was based on a scientific study, that scoring methods would be objective, and that nobody would fail.

The criticisms after the administration of the test were mostly favourable. A few of them pointed out that there was a danger of dehumanization of the university selection procedures, but all agreed that there was no technical or scientific objections to the methods employed.

According to the opinion of some authorities, the possibilities of survival of the 1967 selection procedures will depend upon the policy of the universities and the Ministry of Education. The most difficult problem is to obtain co-operative action between secondary education and university, which is indispensable if selection is to be improved..

References

Grassau, E. (1955) 'Análisis estadístico de las pruebas de Bachillerato. *Ediciones Anales de la Universidad de Chile.*
Grassau, E. (1957) 'Análisis de resultados de la restricción de matrícula y selección de alumnos en la Escuela de Medicina.' *Boletín Estadístico de la Universidad de Chile.*
Grassau, E. (1957-66) 'Estadística del Bachillerato de 1957-58-59-60-61-62-63-64-65-66.' *Boletínes Estadísticos de la Universidad de Chile.*
Grassau, E. (1959) 'Característica del Bachillerato considerado como Instrumento de Medición.' *Boletín Estadístico de la Universidad de Chile.*
Grassau, E. (1966) *Examen de Admisión a la Universidad.* Publication of the Instituto de Investigaciones Estadísticas, Santiago.
Grassau, E. and Orellana, E. (1962) *Report on Admission to Higher Education in Chile.* International Study of University Admission, Santiago
Grassau, E. and Segure, T. (1961) 'El rango ocupado por el alumno durante los estudios secundarios como indice de predicción para los estudios universitarios.' *Boletín Estadístico de la Universidad de Chile.*
Grassau, E. and Segure, T. (1964) 'El problema de la comparación de los puntajes de Bachillerato.' *Boletín Estadístico de la Universidad de Chile.*

Grassau, E. et al. (1967) *Informe Técnico sobre la Prueba de Aptitud Académica 1967.* Publication of the Instituto de Investigaciones Estadísticas, Santiago.

Landsberger, H. et al. (1964) 'Rendimiento escolar en la Escuela de Economia de la Universidad de Chile 1959-1962.' INSORA. Facultad de Ciencias Económicas, Universidad de Chile.

Lopez, A. and Molina, G. (1965) 'Acerca de un examen de selección.' Thesis, Universidad de Chile.

Salas, I. and Orellana, E. (1960) *Correlación entre el Liceo y la Universidad.* Publication of the Instituto de Investigaciones Pedagógicas, Universidad de Chile.

Vargas, S. (1965) 'Análisis estadístico de la batería de selección de la Escuela de Medicina de la Universidad de Chile en 1964.' Thesis, Universidad de Chile.

Viel, B. et al. (1956) 'Análisis de resultados de la restricción de matrícula y selección de alumnos en la Escuela de Medicina.' Facultad de Medicina, Universidad de Chile.

TESTING FOREIGN STUDENTS FOR ADMISSION TO UNIVERSITIES

ROY ADAM

Since their earliest days, universities have opened their doors to foreign students. From the Middle Ages, all great universities have included in their membership students and teachers from other countries.

During the past few decades, the tremendous expansion of university education has been matched by an astonishing growth in the number of students seeking education abroad. The latest Unesco figures suggest that there are at least 300,000 students working in countries other than their own. It is possible that the total may be even larger than this estimate. There are difficulties in collecting reliable figures of private students who have no government sponsorship, and particularly of those who may have lived in the host country for a period prior to university enrolment.

The number of students who seek admission to a university in a foreign country is many times larger than that of students who actually enrol. It is with applicants, and not only with enrolees, that university admission officers must deal. It is applicants who must be tested for admission.

One may guess that more than 100,000 students each year undergo some form of testing with a view to seeking admission to a university in another country. This number will presumably increase during the next decade. In developing countries, secondary education is expanding more quickly than university education, and the number of students wishing to enter their home universities but unable to do so will inevitably grow larger. Many of these African and Asian students will seek university places in Europe or America.

At the graduate level, the tradition of further study abroad is strongly established, and the number of graduates is growing rapidly. It may be expected that increasing numbers of them will travel abroad for post-graduate study.

While universities welcome students from foreign countries, they are becoming deeply concerned about methods of selecting students for admission. While the numbers of foreign students were small, and applicants came mainly from institutions which were well known to the host university, few problems arose. A form of accreditation or mutual recognition of qualifications avoided the necessity for formal testing. For larger universities, the situation is now very different. Applications are received from school pupils with qualifications which are meaningless to admission officers. Graduate students come from new universities whose very names are unknown to those who must assess their ability to cope with post-graduate study. There are now single universities which draw students from more than fifty foreign countries.

It is pertinent to note also that some Asian and African countries have different concepts of the standards and role of a university from those which are accepted in the older countries. This is probably a highly desirable situation: traditional concepts of a university may be meaningless in the new nations. It does, however, make the interchange of students very difficult, since it gives different values to examinations and qualifications carrying the same names and titles.

It would be possible for the host university to require all students seeking admission to enter the country and take the same matriculation examination as local students. This attitude has been adopted by some universities. It permits immediate comparison between the results of local and foreign students.

Most universities, however, regard this as unnecessarily harsh, and feel that it tends to destroy the study-abroad tradition which they see as an essential part of university life. (They have also observed that, surprisingly enough, failure rates among foreign students are not greatly reduced when they take the same admission tests under the same conditions as local students.) Universities are therefore prepared, often at considerable cost, to arrange special testing procedures for foreign students.

The equivalence of examinations

The first problem in such arrangements is to decide on equivalence of examinations. How is it possible to say that two examinations, particularly when set in different countries by different authorities, measure the same attainments or qualities? Few people would be confident that any examination conducted in the same country by one authority maintained identical standards from year to year.

It must be recognized at the outset that any statement of equivalence is approximate rather than exact. The search for perfection in this matter is a waste of time and effort.

Admission officers are wise to err on the side of requiring higher rather than lower standards in overseas examinations. The varied pressures of adjustment difficulties demand a higher level of ability from a student from a foreign country than from a local student. Any inclination towards a sympathetic lowering of admission standards for the foreign student can only result in increasing the probability of his failure in the university.

International and local examinations

Despairing of finding in overseas countries local tests suitable for their matriculation requirements, some universities have arranged to set their own test, or to use some international examination for all overseas candidates. The candidate is then able to take the test at a centre close to his home. Examinations set by the Cambridge University Syndicate have been widely used in Asia and Africa for this purpose. These excellent examinations have served a useful purpose for universities in other countries, but inevitably there is a clash of objectives with them, or with any examination not set specifically for the selection of university students. A university cannot expect to find an international examination used for a variety of other purposes by employers and school authorities wholly satisfactory.

The problems of using examinations taken in one country for admission to universities in another are complicated by the rapidly changing pattern of local examinations in many parts of the world, and particularly in the developing countries. In West Africa, for example, independence has meant the introduction of many new school examinations. It will be difficult, during the next decade, to stabilize these examinations. Universities in Europe and North America will not find it easy to assess their standards or values during this period of fluctuation.

When a university decides to set its own entrance examination and allow it to be taken in foreign countries, a great deal of administrative work is involved. The co-operation of diplomatic representatives may be required. There is the major problem of selecting the body of material to be examined. Even in short-answer prediction tests, the previous academic and cultural experience of the student may falsify results, and give an incorrect evaluation of his potential.

In surveying the various possibilities, it would appear that recognition of some local assessment is likely to prove as effective and as economic as any other procedure. It is doubtful whether a special examination, set either by the university concerned or by a national or international examining body, will predict more accurately the future academic success of a student than a careful study of his local school and public examination record. This latter approach implies more knowledge of overseas education conditions than is usually possessed by university admission officers. Regular visits by these officers to the

countries concerned are highly desirable, as is also continuing study of education in developing countries.
Whatever system is used, comparison between different countries will be unsatisfactory. Each case must be judged on its merits.
It is through better understanding and evaluation of foreign testing arrangements rather than a superimposition of new tests by universities that the best hope lies of a workable system of university admissions of foreign students. This approach is admittedly somewhat crude, and likely to result in some wrong decisions. It is advocated here because it is considered at least equal to other methods in its predictive value, and superior to them in convenience and economy. There is an added advantage in the additional status accorded to the examinations of developing countries, and to the assistance to examiners in these countries which is likely to result from recognition of their efforts by overseas universities.

Language tests

The greatest single difficulty encountered by foreign students is language. Even those who have been educated throughout their school life in a second language have been found to be handicapped when they attempt university studies abroad. The extent of the language burden carried by foreign students has not been fully appreciated because there has been inadequate documentation and research on this subject. The few studies of reading speed among foreign students (only one of the language difficulties they encounter) suggested that the length of private study time required by foreign students is often two or three times as long as that needed by local students to cover the same material.

The implication for university admission testing procedures is that special attention is required for assessment of the competence of foreign students in the language of instruction. There is evidence that present procedures are generally unsatisfactory with regard to language testing. Reports indicate that otherwise well-prepared and able students are failing at the university through poor language ability.

It has only recently become evident that foreign students who pass the same entrance test as local students may nevertheless have an inadequate command of the required language for satisfactory study in the university. This has caused some surprise (and even disbelief) among academics who have little contact with overseas students. It is, however, now generally acknowledged among advisers to foreign students that a pass in the final examinations of a secondary school may be achieved through intensive memorization and reasonable competence in written aspects of the language. It is not necessary for these students to have more than an elementary knowledge of the spoken language, or even the ability to read with good speed and comprehension. In short, it is unwise to rely on ordinary school examinations for prediction of language competence at the university level.

In the English-speaking countries, most institutions of higher education require additional evidence that a foreign student has a good command of English. Universities in the United States make extensive use of a test of spoken and written English developed in the University of Michigan. The existence of a United States National Council for the Testing of English as a Foreign Language gives an indication of the seriousness with which this matter is treated in America. The help of American Consulates in many countries is enlisted in testing English ability by means of standardized tests.

In the United Kingdom, the British Council's English-teaching experts have experimented with tests of English ability for foreign students, and several universities have worked in this field. The Commonwealth Office of Education in Australia has recently been supplying Australian diplomatic officials in Asia with a newly developed comprehensive test of spoken English. It is being used to help in measuring the suitability of applicants for places in Australian universities and colleges.

In spite of the proven value of these various British and American tests, experts in this field are far from satisfied with the tests as predictions of competence in university or technical studies. Such basic questions as the relative importance of the listening, speaking, reading and writing skills in higher education, or the value of early training in specialized subject vocabularies remain unanswered. Until research can reveal more about the abilities required, testing cannot be entirely satisfactory.

It has been suggested that responsibility for general academic testing might be passed back to schools and colleges in the home countries of the students. This cannot be done in the case of language testing. It is unreasonable to expect school examinations in Asian or African countries to predict success in the use of English in universities in the United States, Britain or Australia. The answer lies in thorough research into the language needs of a foreign student in higher education, followed by the construction of better tests to fulfil these needs.

Even then, the matter will not be finalized. A test maker cannot ignore the conditions under which his test will be administered. They must be constructed, in this case, for administration by relatively unskilled personnel in many different countries. All this represents a formidable research task, but it is one which cannot be avoided. To fulfil their function, and to assist developing countries, universities and colleges must accept foreign students. If these students are to have reasonable chances of success, a reliable measure of their language competence is necessary.

An aspect of these tests which has not yet been mentioned is their impact on the schools in Asian and African countries. Any responsible person who writes an educational test must ask: what effect will this test have on the content of courses and on methods of teaching?

For many years, the predominantly literary tests of English required for entry to British and American universities have encouraged teachers in the developing countries to concentrate on literature. This has had a very bad effect on language teaching generally. The tests now being used place strong emphasis on the oral aspects of language. Overseas universities may now have the satisfaction of knowing that these tests, in addition to selecting students more likely to succeed, will hasten the growth of new techniques for language learning which will be of great benefit to the schools in Asia and Africa.

Co-operation among universities

The admission of foreign students to universities or colleges is a matter which affects the whole nation. In recent years, there have been serious repercussions in international relations from incidents involving foreign students. It is natural, therefore, that governments should be deeply interested in the decisions which universities make about applicants from other countries. Most governments have been of great assistance to their universities in the selection of foreign students. They have also tried to arrange co-operation among the universities and the adoption of common policies.

It is obviously undesirable for universities to act alone in this matter. Students and authorities in foreign countries become confused about entrance requirements. Research is piecemeal and ineffective.

There is a real need now for large-scale research on the best procedures for testing foreign applicants and on testing techniques, particularly in language. There is a need to analyse the political and economic implications. The numbers of foreign students have grown to very large proportions and will continue to increase. They are providing a problem for educational administrators, and they offer a challenge to those interested in educational testing.

PROBLEMS INVOLVED IN SELECTION AND PLACEMENT OF UNIVERSITY STUDENTS IN DEVELOPING COUNTRIES

IRAJ AYMAN

The problems involved in the selection and placement of university students in developing countries are varied and numerous, but they have not yet been studied in a comprehensive manner for cross-cultural comparison. This paper is devoted to the presentation of some of these problems; it is based on my own experience and observations in a number of developing countries. The subject matter, however, is so vital and the problems so acute that it deserves a cross-cultural survey aimed at the development of a world-wide system of technical co-operation.

Rapid increase in the number of applicants

The number of applicants for higher education in developing countries is increasing at a very high rate; this is mainly because of the following factors:

1. A general growth of the population due both to lower mortality and to the lack of proper birth control.
2. The spread of general education, bringing literacy and schooling to those segments of the population which were traditionally deprived of any aspiration towards higher education, either because of a lack of educational facilities or because of the absence of financial means. For example, the number of high school graduates in Iran has been doubled during the past decade, and is now increasing at a much faster rate.*
3. A new awakening among the less privileged families due to their discovery that education is the best break-through for fast moving from the lower to higher strata of society, for getting better jobs and earning more money, and, last but not least, for successful entry to the world of politics.

Depending on the ratio of the number of vacancies to the number of applicants, the competition may get very tough, and quite often there are between ten to twenty times more applicants than there are vacancies. This type of situation is in itself a further motivation for citizens to join the crowd and rush to the universities.

---

* 20 per cent per annum at the time of writing.

Quality of applicants

Applicants interviewed at the time of the entrance examinations are often vague as to why they are applying for enrolment. Their answers are usually general statements repeated in the society and the schools. They do not know what is the nature of the education they are going to get, and how that education can help them to have a better life. Above all, a good many of them are already employed, and are in line for careers which could provide them with a better future than they could get out of the education they are seeking in the college.

Because of the rise in the cost of living, many of the applicants either are interested in evening courses so that they can obtain some employment during the day (if they are not already employed) or they hope for some part-time job, or merely to register at the college and try to be absent often enough to carry on with their jobs and so earn their livelihood. The number of scholarships are very limited and hard to distribute properly. Not infrequently you find students who are living and working in one city and are registered at the university in another city, travelling long distances back and forth to keep up with both engagements.

In the usual way, the applicants are graduates of the high schools, but they have not all graduated recently; there is therefore a wide age range among the applicants. Besides this, many of the high schools they attended were not adequately equipped and administered, so that, although all the applicants possess a uniform and officially recognized certificate, they form a very heterogeneous group from every point of view.

The universities' position

Faced with an increasing number of applicants, and handicapped by inadequate staff and facilities, the universities in the developing countries are in a very difficult position. Many of them are run by the State on a very tight budget, or, if they are private institutions, the income available to them is very limited. Moreover, the more promising and well-trained compatriots are usually attracted to more interesting positions abroad, or to more appealing opportunities in industry or the Government. The ratio of lecturers to students is unbelievably low; indeed, there are faculties, even universities, with very few qualified lecturers.

At the same time that the universities are so ill equipped and poorly prepared for executing their duties, they are under pressure to accept as many students as possible. The pressure from those in positions of power to use favouritism is bothersome. Under the prevailing pressures, universities tend to adopt one of the following procedures:

1. To cut down the number of applicants in order to be able to accommodate them.
2. To establish some order of merit so that the better candidates are accepted.
3. To select those who are qualified in accordance with the capacity of the institution.

No matter which one of these procedures is adopted, there are two ways of getting the job done: (a) by using essay-type examinations and/or interviews; and (b) by administering more objective-type examinations such as tests. The tendency to use test-type examinations is not always caused by a full appreciation of the values and functions of the tests. But in order to be in better control of the situation and to prevent favouritism, the best solution is to use objective examinations. The use of tests for student selection and placement is therefore the easiest way of reducing the large numbers of applicants to a manageable minimum with some order of merit, in such a manner that those in charge of selection will not be bothered by outside pressure, either in the form of asking for a favour or complaining of injustice.

This is not, of course, an invariable rule. There are everywhere in developing countries certain institutions of higher learning which do their best in applying the best available techniques in order to select qualified students.

Selection and placement

There are two major problems involved in the entrance examinations for the universities: one is the process of elimination of the applicants; the other, which is no less troublesome, is the distribution of the acceptable ones among the different branches of the university. Both these problems are hard to tackle, even if tests are used.

As far as selection is concerned, every candidate tries his luck at as many colleges and universities as possible. This means over-crowding in the examinations, unnecessary expenditure and difficulties in the final selection and enrolment. This last point is interesting and should be emphasized. Capable candidates usually appear on many lists at different universities, and for some time no one knows which students are definitely enrolled in each university. The less famous or respected institutions are left with a bunch of poorly qualified students. The dilemma in the selection of the students lies in the fact that developing a nation-wide system of selection is too ambitious and difficult to operate. On the other hand, a completely decentralized system artificially increases the number of applicants for each institution to such a great extent that it makes the selection of students an extremely difficult job to do properly.

The selection of the students is much easier to handle than their placement or distribution among the different branches of study. There are a number of ways that one can screen the candidates, establish some order of merit, and make sure that those who are accepted are of better calibre than those who are rejected. However, it is not as easy to assign the students to different programmes in the universities.

First of all, there are no comprehensive and reliable man-power studies which indicate the distribution of trained man-power in different disciplines, and which give a workable estimate of the future needs in various fields. For the majority of applicants, what is important is merely a university education with some academic degrees. As things are developing at present, the higher the degree the more possibilities there are for better opportunities in careers. The candidates' knowledge of the nature of the education received in each field, and of the job possibilities related to those fields, is so incomplete and misleading that the vocational interest of the applicants cannot be a sound basis for their placement. As a result, everyone tries to get a higher degree in a discipline which seems to him to be enjoying more prestige in the society. However, if it is impossible to work in those fields, they usually settle for just any other subject. Experience has shown that, regardless of the discipline and the nature of the programme offered, there are always more applicants than it is planned or possible to accommodate, provided that the course leads to a degree.

When it comes to the placement of the student, first of all, the traditional type of examination and interviewing cannot be very helpful; developing a battery of tests which would be sufficiently useful for this purpose is difficult or sometimes impossible. The administration of such testing programmes is costly, and needs facilities and planning beyond the reach of most of those institutions. The result is that we usually end up with a group of students enrolled in courses of study in which they have no interest. Furthermore, they usually have no aspirations for the type of activity which logically follows that type of education. The group is so heterogeneous in ideology and aspirations that proper teaching and learning cannot easily take place.

Problems of validation

It is very difficult to select suitable criteria for the validation studies of the tests developed for student selection and placement at the universities. As the immediate goal of this selection and placement, we are interested in predicting successful completion of studies. This means evaluating aptitude for scholarship. In reality, however, many of the students are not properly prepared for university education. Most of the members of the teaching staff are not adequately trained for the job, and do not agree with each other on the teaching methods that should be followed. They demand various types of academic and intellectual exercises which require a variety of aptitudes not necessarily predictable by one system of evaluation. It is sometimes misleading, therefore, to use the class records as criteria for validation.

In other words, there is very little relation between the type of aptitude measured by psychological tests and the demand of the class work as it is exercised by the lecturers. That is why in certain studies in developing countries we find that school records or the traditional type of examinations are nearly as good a predictor as psychological tests. This is due to the fact that there is a more fundamental relation between the former criteria and what actually takes place in the university classroom.

However, we cannot say that selection for successful completion of studies is the only objective which should be followed. In certain cases, what are more important are the requirements of the profession for which the person is being trained. In other words, in the selection of students we have to consider not so much the academic subjects as the type of activities these students will have to engage in when they embark on their careers.

In the universities, where teaching is done on the classical pattern, there is sometimes very little relation between the requirements of academic studies and the demands of the ensuing profession. Therefore, a successful selection and placement for university education is not necessarily a successful selection for a profession. This creates a problem in deciding on the criteria for validating the tests or test batteries. To this one has to add another prevailing difficulty, which is the future occupation of the university graduates. There is often very little relation between the two. This means that the career a graduate chooses is not necessarily based on his professional training, but rather on a number of other considerations, including having a university degree, knowing one or two foreign languages, having special

Problems of selection in developing countries

connections in business or the Government, possessing some kind of leadership or supervisory ability, and the like. The scarcity of trained man-power in developing countries is such that usually the least important qualifications are all that are taken into consideration. Very often what is searched for is a college graduate who knows a certain foreign language. Such a person after some period of working with a so-called foreign expert becomes a national expert in the same field and develops a very successful social or political career in that area.

This type of development is not only detrimental to professional education; it makes the job of selection and placement very difficult. Almost any rational and scientific plan of action faced with the realities of the situation seems too sophisticated and extravagant for the authorities to endorse and finance. When we are forced either to forget about the validation or not to do a good job of validational studies, we are practically following the first and second procedures in these entrance examinations, which means a process of elimination and establishing some order of merit.

Scarcity of know-how

We are generally faced with two sources of demand for test development and testing for the selection and placement of university students: (a) authorities sufficiently learned and convinced of the advantages of a sound testing programme; (b) authorities who ask for testing programmes either to solve some of their administrative problems or because of their ignorance. They believe that testing can do quite a lot more than it actually can. No matter where the demand comes from and provided that sufficient time and money is available to do a good job, the actual difficulty is the lack of know-how. There are so few individuals available with enough practical and academic knowledge of test development and testing that the demand is not often properly met. Sometimes the failure is due to the fact that the authorities concerned are not aware of the operational requirements of test development and testing; and therefore the test technicians remain poorly supported and equipped in their work. The failure to conduct satisfactory testing programmes creates more doubt and antagonism among the responsible authorities who should patronize the proper development of scientific testing.

It would seem a much better approach to introduce test development and testing for the selection and placement of university students in developing countries simultaneously with the proper training of necessary technicians and some models or plans for overcoming the major administrative and operational problems mentioned in this paper.

Conclusion

Psychological testing, although the best solution for student selection and placement in the developing countries, especially in economy and conservation of limited man-power resources, is faced with some major operational handicaps. These problems are often beyond the power of psychologists and test technicians to overcome. As a result, testing programmes for the selection and placement of students are not progressing satisfactorily in nearly all the developing countries. It is therefore suggested that urgent consideration should be given to the development of practical solutions to these problems, and that these solutions should be brought to the attention of the university authorities in the developing countries. Perhaps a team of experts could be recruited and appointed to investigate the situation, and to assist the universities of the developing countries to do a better job of selection and placement. This will probably be one of the most important types of assistance to the future social and economic development of these countries. We all know that there can hardly be any sizable achievement in national development programmes without a parallel development of highly trained man-power; and proper selection and placement of university students is the key to the preparation of a pool of trained man-power for the operation of plans for national development.

Furthermore, we need to have an international consulting service to give technical support and to advise both the technicians and the authorities who ask for testing services. In view of the fact that most of the tests can be quite easily adapted for use in different languages and cultures, such an international centre might also recommend certain tests or test batteries for adaptation.

The centre could also serve as a clearing-house for the exchange of information, to encourage a more rigorous scientific approach to testing in developing countries and to maintain a higher international standard of performance.

TESTING AT THE INTERFACE BETWEEN MODERN AND ANCIENT CULTURES: VERBAL AND NON-VERBAL TESTS IN ETHIOPIA

CHARLES R. LANGMUIR

Testing needs, practices and problems in Ethiopia, as elsewhere, derive from the educational structure. Traditional education in Ethiopia consists of four years of instruction offered in churches, taught by priests, and is, of course, primarily religious. The language is usually Ge-ez, a very ancient language related to Amharic and some other Ethiopian languages as Latin is to English. No one knows how many of these church schools exist. One hundred and five are recorded in the school census because they follow the Ministry of Education curriculum. These schools enrolled 17,000 pupils in grades 1 to 6 in 1966 (4 per cent of the total enrolment in the Empire). There are 550 mission and private schools enrolling 40,000 pupils. 283,000 pupils are enrolled in a thousand Government schools. It is significant to note that fewer than one half of the Government schools are complete in the sense of providing all grades 1 to 6, and the actual number of complete primary schools, Government and others, is 552, less than one-third the number of all schools. These facts reflect the recent and continuing rapid expansion of the Government school system. Over a period of the last ten years the enrolment in grade 6 increased from 5,400 to 20,000.

The attrition or wastage is very large. Forty per cent of the pupils who enter grade 1 do not enter grade 2; two-thirds of the pupils have dropped out before grade 4. In 1959-60, 65,000 pupils were enrolled in the first grade in Government schools. Six years later 16,000 were in grade 6. For all types of primary schools, public and private, the attrition is similar. 82,000 school starters resulted in 19,000 reaching grade 6, and 15,000 will complete grade 8 this year.

The secondary system is largely new. The first secondary school was founded by Emperor Menelik II in 1908. There are now forty complete secondary schools, twenty-nine Government and eleven private. Half of all these schools are in Addis Ababa, reflecting the fact that education in Ethiopia is an urban phenomenon in a country that is largely rural isolation. Isolation and the associated difficulties of communication are dominant characteristics of the Empire. Eighty-five per cent of the population lives more than ten kilometres from any kind of road.

Retention in the senior secondary schools has improved in the last five years. In 1965-6 there were 2,061 students in grade 12, approximately one half of the class that entered grade 9. The secondary system is expanding rapidly. Nine thousand students entered grade 9 in 1965, a figure three times the enrolment in 1960. Twelve thousand places in grade 9 are expected in 1967.

The Haile Sellassie I University is the newest ornament in the Empire's educational system. It was established by the Emperor in 1961 by bringing into one administration several separate and recently established post-secondary-level faculties. Bachelor degree programmes are now offered in arts, science, engineering, education, business administration, public health, law, agriculture and theology. University tuition is free for Ethiopian citizens, and essentially all students are subsidized by a monthly stipend. One thousand first-year Ethiopian students are budgeted for admission in September 1967. This is a reduction from 1,250 admitted in 1966.

In addition to this formal organization of education, there are twenty-seven technical and vocational institutions which are essentially at the secondary level. These include teacher-training institutes, hospital schools of nursing, public health and community services, agriculture and junior technical programmes. Furthermore, there are an unrecorded number of Government and semi-official organizations concerned with defence, telecommunications, highways, airlines and commercial enterprises which run training programmes. These are important in the total picture of formal education because they recruit largely from the tenth and eleventh grades. The opportunities are attractive because they are subsidized and imply guaranteed employment. The number of such annual recruitments is not known. Possibly as many as 1,000 secondary school leavers are involved, but what effect this drainage has on the output of the secondary schools is not known.

From the total man-power utilization point of view, the tap-off perhaps makes no difference. But from the point of view that a Ministry of Education should take in a society that seeks and demands the fastest possible transition from an ancient stable tradition to something new and expanding, the attrition and the irregularities in formal progress through school require full understanding. Some kind of standardized testing and pupil achievement accounting is clearly needed. The concept seems to be acceptable to younger officials in Ethiopia, but the necessary action enjoys executive malaise.

Examinations in the Ethiopian schools are of the British-European convention. In the grades they are 'set' by teachers, presumably reviewed by school directors, and graded by teachers on a percentage scale. By various and incomprehensible schemes the pupils in elementary schools and the students in secondary schools are ranked.

Formal Ministry-set and supervised examinations are used at the end of grade 6, grade 8 and grade 12.

At grade 12 we have the Ethiopian School Leaving Certificate Examination. This is modelled on the Cambridge and London overseas examinations, and the papers are set in the same manner by the University establishment, and read and graded in the manner conventional to that system. I am told by persons intimately experienced with this basically British system that they are equivalent to the 'overseas' certificate examinations used elsewhere in the former colonial world and especially in Africa. More about these ESLC examinations later.

The formal grade 8 leaving certificate examination has been officially abolished, but some procedure is nevertheless required to choose 10,000 to 12,000 pupils from the 15,000 to 18,000 who seek places in grade 9. This year an examination consisting of a set of objective school subject achievement tests and a more general verbal-numerical academic aptitude test will be used in 250 centres for 15,000 to 18,000 candidates. These examinations will be constructed by hunch and judgment uninformed by any prior statistical experience.

The grade 6 examination I will not elaborate on, because I am sure that what is not done in using and evaluating the results of the grade 8 and grade 12 examinations is also not done at grade 6. Furthermore, I cannot even examine the examination at all. The language of instruction in grades 1 to 6 is Amharic.

The facts about language, scholastic achievement and by implication academic aptitude in the primary schools raises a problem of absorbing interest in Ethiopia and I think of equal interest throughout the whole realm of transitional societies.

In Ethiopia there are at least forty-five identifiably different languages. The population is about twenty-two million. Most of these forty-five different languages are without the mechanics of writing, and are inconsequential in the educational system except as their existence exhibits the language problem faced by pupils and teachers. By Government policy the national language is Amharic, properly called Amarinnya. This language derives from ancient Ge-ez, and is the first language of less than a third and possibly as few as one-fifth of the population. There are three or four other languages of numerical consequence—Tigrinnya, spoken in the north, and Gallinnya and Guraghinnya. This situation leads to the fact that about two-thirds of the pupils entering school have to learn Amharic as a second language.

English is taught beginning in grade 3, and English becomes the language of instruction in the secondary school beginning in grade 7.

The extent to which language is the major problem in Ethiopian education is further revealed by the facts about teaching staff and the conditions in which they work. One-third of all primary school teachers have seven or eight years of formal schooling. One-fifth have lesser formal qualifications. Those who teach English have never been exposed to a native speaker of English. Text materials are skimpy and teaching aids are virtually non-existent. Paper is a rare and hard to obtain commodity anywhere outside the cities. Classrooms are small and the number of pupils is frequently huge. Classroom groups of seventy-five or more are not uncommon.

The circumstances in the secondary schools are different, but not necessarily better. In 1966 there were 1,600 teachers in all types of secondary schools. Sixty per cent of the teachers are expatriate, about half of them Peace Corps Volunteers and the other half largely Indian nationals employed on contract. The variety, quality and quantity of text materials is even more serious. It is routine for several sections of forty students each to share ten or twenty books. Frequently the teacher will have the only textbook. Two-thirds of the secondary school teachers are teaching in English, which is not their native language and which they do not speak correctly and cannot read with minimal competence. It is small wonder that emphasis at all levels of education is placed on memorization of textbook materials frequently copied into notebooks from the blackboard.

Students who complete the twelfth grade sit for the Ethiopian School Leaving Certificate Examination. They write five, six, seven or more half-day examinations from a group of sixteen secondary school subjects. Any candidate who obtains five passes at the C level including Amharic, English and mathematics or an average of C in five subjects and no failure in the three required subjects is automatically admitted to the University.

The certificate enjoys enormous prestige, partly because the examinations are the prime basis for university admission, and partly because employers use it as a screen to reduce the number of job applicants. The enormous prestige is matched by enormous anguish, and there is ample dissension among parties with official interests in the system. Those with vested interests in the examination ardently claim that the existence of the certificate, and especially the form of the examining procedure, is the last bastion—the ultimate guarantor—and the only hope for maintaining and improving standards in the schools. Others who are less enthusiastic point out that the information obtained is not used and has no visible impact on the schools, the teachers or the curriculum. It is frequently said that a School Leaving

Certificate is not a suitable basis for admission to university. Some change is inevitable if only because of the rapidly increasing costs of administration and marking, and shortage of staff to do it. In 1965 the number of examinations was 13,200 and the cost, excluding salaries and overheads, was Eth. $48,000. In 1966, 18,000 examinations cost Eth. $60,000. The real costs are much greater.

The fact that the examination results have no impact in the schools may be attributed to a number of circumstances. The results of the examination are so consistently dismal that it is understandable that teachers might give up and simply forget the whole business. A more important factor, and one which could be corrected, is the lack of communication among the persons and agencies concerned. There is no effective communication between the examining board in the University and the teachers, the school directors, or Ministry officials. Effective communications with schools and teachers are a problem everywhere, but they are particularly severe in the emerging societies and perhaps extremely so in Ethiopia. A single example will suggest what might be accomplished if the ESLC examining board could hurdle the traditional barriers and reach the teachers.

Every year the chief examiner in each subject writes a detailed report on the results, including comments on the errors and difficulties found in the candidates' papers. The reports are issued annually as a public document. For the last few years the English examiner has discussed the problem of hyphenation of words at the end of a line of writing. The problem arises to a ridiculous extent in Ethiopia as a consequence of the structure of Amharic writing. In the written Amharic language there are 275 characters, each of which represents a syllable. Words are separated by a punctuation mark something like a colon. A full stop is either a question mark or a double colon. There is no hyphen, and words are divided anywhere. Every letter is a syllable. An Ethiopian naturally inserts a hyphen or splits a word between lines anywhere. English text composed, edited, proof-read and printed in Ethiopia exhibits this characteristic in newspapers, magazines, books and all other printed materials. Locally printed English is a model not to be emulated. The English examiner annually writes in his report this simple recommendation. He tells the teachers, 'Tell your students never, never, never divide an English word'. The instruction is simple. Any teacher could learn to do it, and any student could learn it and do it. But the message never, never, never reaches the teacher.

This example is perhaps amusing, but it is also a true characterization of a very fundamental problem in testing, educational measurement, and any applied research or inquiry at the interface between modern and ancient cultures or western and traditional societies.

Of course, in any educational organization, even the best, more research findings can be generated, reported and filed than can be effectively disseminated. But in the long run information does effect change in policy, procedure, administration and planning. There are people who are interested. Reports are available; and they circulate; and the discursive and data-reporting literature is abundant. As a consequence, information and relevant ideas do percolate upwards, filtrate downwards and diffuse outwards. Active workers may reasonably hold that the process is slow, but the process *is* continuous and it works.

In Ethiopia reports are filed in the standard manner, but with a difference. Once filed they are inaccessible. There is no diffusion, no filtration, no percolation. As a consequence of the lack of information, there is little real dialogue. Dialogue and the critical study of facts and their implications are replaced by interminable speculation without the essential verification. There is a major element in what is often referred to as the 'managerial crisis' in emerging Africa.

In the domain of educational measurement the notion of learning from experience is accepted only as an abstract concept and not as a concept to be successively applied. For example, a two-hour aptitude test consisting of seven timed sections was used in grade 8 throughout the Empire in 1962, 1963 and 1964. This was handled with the most stringent security precautions. Every test book was returned, and they now fill a large cabinet all in carefully sealed and certified envelopes. The answer sheets are non-existent and no one knows anything about them. There is not one bit of information, even hearsay, about the results. No rosters, no frequency distributions, and no summary statistics. Absolutely nothing after three consecutive years of a costly national programme.

In circumstances such as these, the introduction of any kind of pupil accounting or system evaluation using even the most primitive measurement is a major operation. It will be many years and possibly many decades before any standardized testing will be achieved in the primary schools. Studies sampling urban schools which are economically accessible are conceivable and could be immensely productive. But in the existing administrative circumstances the probability of any support for any inquiries involving testing in the primary grades is zero. Nevertheless, some preliminary steps will be undertaken at the University Testing Centre. It is proposed to assemble a file of examinations used in the Addis elementary schools to serve mainly as a source of information about what the actual curriculum is.

The development of some rudimentary standardized testing in the Ethiopian secondary schools is a more likely possibility. The Ministry of Education has continuing and increasing need for greater objectivity in the selection of eighth-grade graduates for admissions to the senior secondary schools, for the guidance for students into the several programmes of the planned comprehensive schools, and for recruitment for the various vocational programmes outside the regular school system. If the recently established University Testing Centre proves viable, the required technical, research, and data-reporting services will be available.

The only application of measurement technique has occurred in the University and, of course, arises in the problem of University admissions. The University admitted 1,250 students in September 1966. Actually 387, 19 per cent of all candidates for the ESLC, qualified for admission by the official University doctrine requiring five passes at C level. An additional 102 were acquired by a supplemental certificate examination given at the end of a special summer session. Obviously the University is forced to modify its admissions doctrine in order to make full use of its facilities. Some testing of grade 12 students is urgently desired to identify students who have academic potential, but have not acquired a satisfactory secondary education. Finding a practical solution to this problem is the main task of the University Testing Centre.

The Faculty of Education annually recruits 250 students for teacher-training degree programmes. These students are selected from the eleventh grade, and are brought to the University Laboratory School for the twelfth grade. If they are successful in their grade 12 programme, they are admitted to the University, thereby bypassing the ESLCE formality.

In the process of this recruitment in March 1966 the Otis Self-Administering Test of Mental Ability, Higher Level, Form A, was administered to the twelfth grade in nearly all high schools and to all eleventh-grade students in almost all schools. Standard thirty-minute time limits were used. This 1966 testing produced the first recorded test data on secondary school students other than the annual reports of ESLC examinations. As a result of this experience the April 1967 laboratory school recruitment programme used the lower-level Otis Quick-Scoring Mental Ability Tests, Beta, Form A. This test was administered with specially prepared directions; the time was extended from thirty minutes to forty minutes. The Otis test was supplemented with a two-hour school subjects test (129 objective questions).

With the generous co-operation of the College Entrance Examination Board, the Special Scholastic Aptitude Test, Form LAF, sometimes known as ASPAU (an acronym representing African Scholarship Program in American Universities) was administered to all freshmen in the University in November 1965. The surviving students are now sophomores in the University. In April 1966 the same ASPAU Scholastic Aptitude Test was administered to all regular—that is, grade 12—student candidates during the ESLC examination week. Presumably most of the students admitted to the University in September 1966, the present freshman class, took the Special SAT at that time. I use the word 'presumably' because we do not know the facts, for reasons which will be detailed shortly. For the university freshmen tested in November 1965 we have frequency distributions for students by faculty enrolment, but we have not yet achieved confidence in untangling individual identity and associating an individual test record with the same individual's university record.

In Ethiopia there are no family names. A person receives a given name, and his additional name is his father's given name. A published answer sheet, in the space for recording names, asks for last name first. Even with extraordinary attention to this problem in administering tests there will be a number of candidates who will record their names backwards, especially if the group is large where proctors cannot cope with everybody at once. In English, family names are sufficiently distinctive to indicate highly probable corrections. Since there is no tradition of distinct family names in Ethiopia, there is no way to estimate even in a probabilistic sense whether a name has been reversed. In English, Brown Robert and Robert Brown can be easily clarified. In Ethiopia Hailu Admasu is just as probable as Admasu Hailu.

When we seek to resolve these uncertainties by comparison of dates of birth and addresses, we run into other cultural differences. Many students do not know their date of birth. Furthermore, the Ethiopian calendar differs from the Gregorian calendar by seven years, not quite large enough a difference to make certain whether the date recorded is Gregorian or Ethiopian. And curiously quite a large number of students, when they attempt to fill in spaces marked month, day and year, will claim they do not know whether they were born on Monday, Tuesday, or what day. Some will just guess without raising the issue.

Comparison of addresses is useless. There is no mail delivery anywhere in Ethiopia, and there are no addresses of the western urban type. I live in a compound of six five-storey modern apartment buildings. The best address I can give is, 'From Meskal Square proceed to the buildings in back of Africa Hall'. Another more typical example

Verbal and non-verbal tests in Ethiopia

is quoted from the *Ethiopian Herald*: 'For Sale. 1966 Ford Mustang. Contact Miss L. McCoy at Mexico Circle behind the Russian Hospital, in front of the Ethiopian Policemen's Hospital down the dead-end road with the transformers on top of the telegraph pole'.

Thus I hope to make evident that the acquisition of usable psychometric data by group testing in the senior secondary schools and in the University is a task that requires much more than usual attention at the point of planning the administration and writing the directions. The time required to distribute material, write in the name and identifying data, and work through directions and example questions is at least two and more probably three or four times the expectation as estimated in a publisher's test manual. This situation does not derive solely from the necessity of simplifying the language of directions by elaboration and repetition or the time required to be sure that everyone understands the mechanics and format of the questions. Generally the students have had some experience with multiple-choice questions and separate answer sheets. There are, however, two important characteristics of Ethiopian students partly associated with language difficulties, but probably even more deeply associated with culture.

The first of these two cultural factors is what I term the decision time constant. Perhaps we should name the phenomenon the indecision time constant. Whatever term we use, it is very noticeably large.

In administering group tests, in any group larger than some small number, say ten persons, there will be a noticeable and continuous problem to get students to follow the simplest of directions and act upon them. This is not simply a problem of English language comprehension. It is observed widely throughout the culture, whether the instructions are in English, Amharic, by pantomime or other communication including individual demonstration. One cultural element found in any group situation in Ethiopia is a social distraction factor. For centuries and possibly for millennia the interpersonal social contexts of a group situation have dominated, whatever other content permeates the circumstances. The effects of this traditional characteristic are evident in testing groups. Attention to an examiner is peripheral. Other ego-centred social concerns are central.

The second cultural characteristic that is observable in administering tests also has importance in the design and format of tests for use in Ethiopia. Ethiopians do not read in any language. This is not a matter of literacy. It is a cultural characteristic, and perhaps reflects educational values quite different from those of the modern West where ideas and dialogue about ideas are prevalent. In Western society not only has literacy been increasing, but for 200 years reading for all purposes has been increasing and availability of reading materials of all kinds has been phenomenally abundant.

In Ethiopia it is essentially true to say that reading materials, whether books of any kind, magazines, pamphlets or newspapers, are simply not available. Of course, some waiting-rooms, barbers' shops, and doctors' surgeries have various out-of-date picture magazines in Italian, German, Swedish, French, English, and sometimes Chinese and Japanese. There are three small book stores in Addis primarily supported by the large international community. There is a Ministry of Information newspaper in English and another in Amharic with a circulation of a few thousand. I have never seen a news-stand in Addis. *Time, Newsweek, Life* and the newspapers are sold by street urchins. The fact is that reading material in any language, including Amharic, is effectively unavailable to the Ethiopian population.

The limitations of available reading material in the schools and outside the schools not only restricts students' (and teachers') opportunity to develop English comprehension abilities which we are concerned with testing, but it has other effects which must be allowed for in designing tests. Ethiopians have so little experience in reading varied kinds of material that they cannot scan. Even the simplest instruction, 'Now turn to page 3 and begin', is fraught with difficulties associated with finding page 3. Some of the difficulties are manipulative-mechanical. These young people have never had the kind of repeated experience from earliest childhood in handling paper, magazines or books that Western children can hardly escape. But the problem is also lack of the visual experience of reading. A change of format in typography is likely to cause difficulties. A change in format of the test questions, especially if it is accompanied by new directions, is certain to disturb many students, and variations in an answer sheet can be extremely troublesome. For example, the Differential Aptitude Tests, Form L, were administered to all first-year university students in October-November 1966. The Digitek answer sheet was used. The answer spaces for the eight parts are areas spanning the width of the page; thus there are two or three parts or sections on each of three sides of the answer sheet. The names of the parts, verbal reasoning, numerical ability, and so on, are printed along the long edge in adequately large capital letters. Of course, when the answer sheet is viewed normally these captions are vertical in the left-hand margin. Many, and perhaps most, Ethiopian students do not see the caption titles. With this understanding you can easily imagine the proctorial problems following the direction, 'Turn your answer sheet to page 3 and find the place for space relations. Put your finger on it.'

We will next consider the result of testing secondary school and university students in Ethiopia. The findings are detailed in the appended statistical tables.

APPENDIX

Table 1. Otis Self-Administering Test of Mental Ability, Higher Level, Form A: frequency distribution of grade 11 and 12 scores

	Grade 12, 25 schools			Grade 11, 34 schools		
X	f	cf	c%	f	cf	c%
67-68-69	2	1211	100·0			
65	0	1209	99·8			
62	2	1209	99·8			
59	5	1207	99·7			
56	5	1202	99·3	1	2173	100·0
53	10	1197	98·8	4	2172	99·9
50	10	1187	98·0	3	2168	99·8
47	12	1177	97·2	9	2165	99·6
44	38	1165	96·2	18	2156	99·2
41	56	1127	93·1	27	2138	98·4
38	66	1071	88·4	39	2111	97·1
35	113	1005	83·0	66	2072	95·4
32	134	892	73·7	138	2006	92·3
29	167	758	62·6	198	1868	86·0
26	178	591	48·8	284	1670	76·9
23	158	413	34·1	338	1386	63·8
20	123	255	21·1	402	1048	48·2
17	75	132	10·9	338	646	29·7
14	42	57	4·7	188	308	14·2
11	13	15	1·2	93	120	5·5
8	2	2	0·2	23	27	1·2
5	0	–	–	3	4	0·2
1-2-3	0	–	–	1	1	–

N	1211		2173
Median	27·8		21·4
Mean	28·7		22·8
S.D.	8·96		7·56

Table 2. Otis Self-Administering Test of Mental Ability, Higher Level: distribution of scores of seventeen-, eighteen- and nineteen-year-old students in grade 12

(from the publisher's manual dated 1928)

X	f	c %
72	18	100·0
67	181	99·8
62	466	98·2
57	743	94·0
52	1601	87·3
47	1928	72·9
42	2257	55·5
37	1914	35·2
32	1122	18·0
27	541	7·9
22	242	3·0
17	56	0·8
12	18	—
7	13	—
2	4	—

N	11104
Median	43·14
Mean	43·34
S.D.	10·06

Table 3. Otis Quick-Scoring Mental Ability Test, Beta, Form A: distribution of grade 11 applicants for laboratory school.

42 schools—April 1967

40-minute time limit

X	f	cf	c %
70-71-72	1	1182	100·0
68	2	1181	99·9
65	5	1179	99·7
62	3	1174	99·3
59	11	1171	99·1
56	26	1160	98·1
53	51	1134	95·9
50	79	1083	91·6
47	85	1004	84·9
44	114	919	77·7
41	159	805	68·1
38	158	646	54·7
35	147	488	41·3
32	128	341	28·8
29	100	213	18·0
26	50	113	9·6
23	36	63	5·3
20	16	27	2·3
17	8	11	0·9
14	0	3	
11	0	3	
8	1	3	0·3
5	1	2	0·2
1-2-3	1	1	0·1

N	1182
Median	38·5
Mean	38·7
S.D.	9·1

Table 4. Special Scholastic Aptitude Test (ASPAU), Form LAF: frequency distribution of HSIU freshmen

November 1965

Verbal score				Maths score		
CEEB scale equivalent	X	f		CEEB scale equivalent	X	f
	62-63	2				
	60-61	0				
	58-59	1				
	56-57	1			44-45	2
	54-55	1				
	52-53	1			42-43	1
600	50-51	3			40-41	5
	48-49	2			38-39	12
	46-47	6			36-37	9
	44-45	7		600	34-35	14
	42-43	4			32-33	24
500	40-41	8			30-31	30
	38-39	20			28-29	36
	36-37	16			26-27	49
	34-35	23		500	24-25	45
	32-33	24			22-23	45
400	30-31	39			20-21	63
	28-29	33			18-19	57
	26-27	44			16-17	64
	24-25	57		400	14-15	53
	22-23	64			12-13	40
300	20-21	72		350	10-11	27
	18-19	66			8- 9	21
	16-17	51			6- 7	6
	14-15	35			4- 5	3
	12-13	17				
	10-11	6				
	8- 9	3				
	N	606			N	606
	Median	23.2			Median	20.5
	Mean	24.9			Mean	21.3
	S.D.	8.7			S.D.	7.8

Table 5. Percentile rank norms for the Differential Aptitude Test

(875 freshmen degree candidates entering September 1966)*

Percentile rank	Verbal reasoning	Numerical ability	Abstract reasoning	Clerical S & A	Mechanical reasoning	Space relations	LU-I spelling	LU-II grammar
98	35-50	39-40	43-50	67-100	53-68	42-60	94-100	45-60
95	32-34	38	40-42	59-66	48-52	36-41	90-93	41-44
90	30-31	37	38-39	55-58	45-47	31-35	88-89	39-40
85	28-29	36	36-37	53-54	43-44	29-30	87	37-38
80	27	35	35	51-52	42	27-28	85-86	36
75	25-26	34	34	50	41	25-26	84	35
70	24	33	32-33	48-49	40	23-24	82-83	33-34
60	22-23	32	30-31	45-47	38-39	21-22	80-81	32
50	21	30-31	28-29	43-44	36-37	19-20	77-79	30-31
40	20	29	26-27	40-42	34-35	17-18	73-76	28-29
30	19	27-28	25	38-39	33	16	71-72	27
25	18	26	24	36-37	32	15	69-70	26
20	17	25	22-23	34-35	30-31	14	66-68	25
15	16	23-24	20-21	32-33	29	13	63-65	24
10	15	21-22	17-19	29-31	27-28	12	59-62	22-23
5	12-14	17-20	11-16	23-28	24-26	10-11	49-58	18-21
2	0-11	0-16	0-10	0-22	0-23	0-9	0-48	0-17

Raw scores

*Tested in October, November and December 1966.

ECONOMICAL AND OBJECTIVE PROCEDURES FOR THE CONDUCT OF INTERMEDIATE EXAMINATIONS AT UNIVERSITIES

ERICH HYLLA

Up to the present time intermediate examinations taken during a course of study have not been customary at universities in the Federal German Republic, except in the case of certain subjects. These exceptions include medicine, where an intermediate examination *(Vorphysikum)* is taken, and mathematics, the natural sciences, physics and technological subjects, where a pre-diploma examination is usual. Although the exact nature of these examinations has differed from one university or technological institute to another, their form has remained traditional. They consist of a supervised written examination and an oral examination. The written examination consists of one or more essay-type questions, the marking of which demands a considerable expenditure of time on the part of relatively highly paid academic staff. The grading obtained in the oral examination depends not only on the knowledge and ability of the student but also on the goodwill, or at least on the individual characteristics, of the examiner, as well as on a number of other factors which are difficult to define. The form taken by the examination as a whole is left to the discretion of the head of each department. The value of gradings given by different departments of a faculty are not comparable, and comparisons between similar faculties or departments of different universities are quite impossible. In the humanities intermediate examinations, or other methods of exerting some measure of selective control, hardly exist.

This situation is likely to change as a result of the reforms proposed by the major German advisory bodies, the Scientific Advisory Board and the Educational Advisory Board, and adopted by the Conference of West German University Rectors in February this year. Intermediate examinations, usually to be taken at the end of the fourth semester, or at the beginning of the fifth, will become compulsory in all subjects, including the humanities. The results of this examination will decide whether the student will receive a higher grant (in the form of a major scholarship, based on the Honnef model). As a result of these measures a certain degree of selective control can now be expected. A considerable number of students who have little prospect of success will discontinue their studies more or less voluntarily, and some will transfer to other fields of study better suited to their abilities. This should have a favourable effect on students in general and should reduce the burdens borne by the bodies responsible for the financial support of the universities.

Examinations, including intermediate examinations in the subjects where these are a requirement, already make considerable demands on the time of the academic staff. These demands will increase steadily, since the number of university teachers relative to the number of students will not increase for many years to come. The reason for this is partly due to financial factors and partly to lack of suitably qualified candidates for university posts. In arts departments the intermediate examinations will now place additional burdens on the academic staff. In these departments the position will be particularly difficult, since the estimated student-teacher ratio is considerably higher than in mathematics and the natural sciences. This becomes evident when one considers the future teachers of all types, most of whom are reading arts subjects, and especially the tremendous number of elementary and secondary modern school teachers who are being trained in colleges affiliated to or incorporated with universities or institutes of technology, or which have been raised to university rank.

If all intermediate examinations take the form which is usual today in mathematics and natural science subjects, a considerable number of additional lecturers will be required, especially in arts departments. This will inevitably lead to even higher demands for increased financial support than the universities are already making at present. If the efficiency of the universities is to be maintained, expenditure can be limited only by rationalizing methods of instruction and of examining.

The rationalization of the process of university teaching need not concern us here. The development of more rational examination procedures is of at least equal importance, since this would lead to a saving of time and energy which lecturers could then devote to teaching.

The need has long existed for more objective examinations with greater comparability; such examinations would provide a more accurate assessment of candidates. This is becoming particularly important in the case of intermediate examinations, for, according to a resolution of the Conference of West German University Rectors, intermediate examinations taken in a particular faculty of one university will be recognized in the corresponding faculties of all other universities. Thus comparability of examination results will become an essential factor not only as between different departments of one faculty, but also on a much broader basis.

As far as I can see, there is no alternative to the course which has long been followed by more progressive countries, namely, the introduction of written group tests. Such tests, however, should not completely replace the present examination methods. The way to such a change has been opened by the resolution of the Conference of West German University Rectors. This resolution states that each faculty is free to develop its own intermediate examinations as it sees best.

In Germany there is still a considerable degree of prejudice against group tests in some quarters. The major argument against their use is that group tests can assess knowledge, but fail to test understanding, insight, reasoning power, critical thinking, independent judgment and similar intellectual qualities which ought to be tested in examinations at university level. Experience has shown that it is certainly easier to develop satisfactory group tests for elementary schools, grammar schools and vocational schools than for universities and similar institutes of higher education. But it is possible to produce such tests; numerous examples have been constructed in other countries and at least a few convincing examples exist in the Federal Republic. These German group tests have been developed for a more advanced level than the intermediate examination, namely the final examinations *(Staatsexamen)* of medical faculties. In the particular instances in which the tests were used the results did not affect the results of the final examination as a whole. These group tests have been used in two German universities—once in Heidelberg and twice in Munich.

The Heidelberg experiment will be described first. Here a group test was administered by one of the departments of the Faculty of Medicine, the Department of Internal Medicine. Approximately 190 candidates took a six-hour examination which consisted of about 140 questions constructed by a study group composed of lecturers from this department. The test results were compared with the marks obtained by students in the oral examination. Exact figures concerning the correlation between the results of the group test and the oral examination marks are not yet available. But it can already be said that the majority of the examiners, as well as almost all the students who took this examination, have been won over to the idea of group testing. The examiners, however, have become aware of the difficulties which are involved in producing a suitable test booklet. They have realized that it is impossible to produce a satisfactory booklet without the help of experts in test construction methods.

The Munich Test was developed by Dr Hannes Kapuste, of the Munich branch of the Study Group for Research in Medical Education.*

---

*This group has other, more far-reaching aims. It hopes to investigate and compare the success of medical training in universities in different countries, including non-German-speaking ones. This, however, will not be discussed here.

By constructing this test Dr Kapuste has done most valuable pioneer work. The description which follows is largely based on his reports.

The Munich Test consists of two parallel test booklets, each containing 220 questions. Five possible answers to each question are given, and the correct, or the best possible answer has to be marked on the answer sheet. Some of the questions relate to pictures or diagrams shown in the test booklet. The questions are drawn from six major areas of medicine (internal medicine, paediatrics, pathology, surgery, pharmacology and gynaecology including obstetrics), with a comparative weighting, according to the relative importance of each of these areas, which is based on the opinion of numerous medical experts. The panel of experts suggested many more than the 400 questions required, and the final choice of those which were to be included in the test was made after thorough preliminary investigation. In these studies careful attention was given to the necessary requirements of a group test, such as validity, reliability, correlation, etc. On examining the two parallel test booklets even a person without medical knowledge recognizes at once that memorized facts alone will not be sufficient to enable students to choose the correct or the best possible answer. Insight and understanding, the ability to generalize, to solve familiar and unfamiliar problems, to size up a situation correctly—in fact, higher intellectual abilities—are required to answer the questions correctly. What a group test cannot test is a student's ability to handle patients, and his capacity to present the facts of a case in a coherent, clear and systematic form. These factors, however, can be assessed sufficiently in the oral examination and in the medical reports written by the student.

Some general statements can now be made on the results of the group test, which has now been used twice to examine medical students in Munich: (a) the test discriminates clearly between weak, average and good students; (b) the tests could be marked very quickly by clerical assistants using calculating machines; (c) students consider group tests to be a fair and objective method of examining. Of 200 students questioned so far, 90 per cent have stated that they would gladly take such an examination again at any time. Obviously a decisive role is played here by the fact that students can see from their results where their strengths and weaknesses lie, and can prepare themselves accordingly for their final examination.*

To sum up the results of these experiments: it can be said with

---

*The test was taken prior to the final examination, and the test results were not taken into account in the mark awarded in the final examination.

certainty that the use of group tests for final examinations at university level is practical, and in many respects desirable. There is therefore no reason to doubt that they could be used successfully at intermediate level.

For use in intermediate examinations a good group test of sufficient length, with items well distributed to cover the whole syllabus, has certain distinct advantages.

1. The results obtained by each student can be compared with the observations made by his teachers during his first four semesters, and in this way chance inconsistencies in the test results can be corrected.

2. The strengths and weaknesses shown by the student in the different parts of the test can be used as a basis for advising him. Such guidance is important not only for the students who pass the examination and who are grateful for any advice that they are offered concerning their further studies; it is equally important for those who fail the examination. These may be advised to fill the gaps in their knowledge during an additional semester and then to take the examination again, or to transfer to a different course of study more suited to their abilities, or even to abandon their university studies and take up work of a more practical nature. The results of the group test might give some indication of the type of practical work most suitable for a particular student advised to take this latter course.

3. The predictive value of the test and the effectiveness of the guidance given can be checked by administering a second intermediate test and by noting the progress made by students during the second part of their course.

4. It will often be possible to dispense with the oral examination in the case of students obtaining very good or very poor marks in the group test. A considerable part of the time now spent on oral examinations will therefore be saved.

5. For the very large number of future teachers an intermediate examination in test form offers a further advantage: it forms a good basis for an introduction to the use of group tests in their future work in schools. Basic courses and practical work in the use of tests in all types of school should nowadays form an integral part of the training of every teacher.

At present, however, there are no group tests ready for use in intermediate examinations. The universities or faculties which wish to use group tests will, for the present, have to develop their own tests. This is consistent with the principle of academic freedom and with the fact that during the first four semesters of a course the curricula of corresponding faculties at different universities may differ considerably.

Academic standards are also far from uniform. The test items which lecturers of each university construct for their own intermediate examinations must be adapted to these circumstances. However, for the construction of test booklets it will be essential to seek the co-operation of experts in this field. These can nowadays be found in the psychology departments of almost every university. Where such assistance is not available locally, it must be obtained from other universities. Certain specialist organizations would also be glad to help with advice, and would possibly collaborate directly in the development and use of tests. Among these organizations are: the Department of Psychology of the Education Centre (Pädagogisches Zentrum, 1 Berlin 31, Berliner Strasse 40), the Test Department of the German Institute for International Research in Education (Deutsches Institut für Internationale Pädagogische Forschung (6 Frankfurt/Main W 13, Schloss Strasse 29) and the Munich branch of the Study Group for Research in Teaching (Arbeitsgemeinschaft für Ausbildungsforschung (8 Munchen 5, Müllerstrasse 55).

Mutual co-operation and exchanges of experience between similar departments at different universities would be highly desirable. This would probably lead to a certain measure of standardization both as regards lectures and practical work during the first four semesters, and of the content of the intermediate examinations. In view of the recent decision that intermediate examinations taken at one university should be recognized at all other universities, this would be most desirable, since it would give students greater freedom to move from one university to another. All faculties would be strongly advised to start a collection of test items suitable for intermediate examinations. Such a collection would increase steadily and would be a useful source of examination material. The exchange of items between similar faculties of different universities would greatly facilitate the construction of test booklets and would lead to a gradual standardization of curricula. Sooner or later the need will probably be felt in Germany for the establishment of organizations similar to the long-established College Entrance Examination Board or the Educational Testing Service in the United States. The tests which are constantly being developed by these institutions save the universities a great deal of work, but have by no means led to a complete uniformity of standards. Virtually all universities in the United States require students wishing to enter a course of study leading to the Ph.D. examination to take the Graduate Record Examination developed by the Educational Testing Service. But in making their decisions on the admittance of candidates and the award of scholarships, the universities consider not only the test results, but also much other information, such as school reports, evidence of preparatory academic study, particulars of social and financial circumstances, health certificates, and so on. Thus it is by no means unusual to find that a student with a particular test result has been rejected by one university, but accepted and even offered a scholarship by another.

THE INFLUENCE OF TESTS ON THE LEARNING PROCESS

MOTIVATION TO STUDY FOR ESSAY AND MULTIPLE-CHOICE TESTS

JOHN W. FRENCH

What it is that motivates school and college students to learn is, indeed, a very varied collection of things. Some parents make a desperate attempt to develop strong academic goals in their children. Their success is sometimes fair. The schools and the teachers also make an attempt to motivate their pupils. Their success is small, but it does exist. Small as it is, it is worth while. The tests that a student faces represent only one kind of incentive that the teacher uses for motivation. It appears, then, that tests can account for only a small corner of the environmental press upon most school and college students; but motivation produced by tests seems to exist, and it has the advantage of being highly controllable. It has justified a great deal of thought by educationists, some research, and a lot of test construction.

Important at least to educated people is a motivation to achieve, need-achievement or 'n-ach' in the parlance of David McClelland. Social pressure from parents, teachers and peers have some influence on this. Personal feelings of pride are important, and practical pressures best represented by the desire for money are also responsible. Perhaps for some students the cumulative influence of working for high grades on tests in school is instrumental in developing a habit of trying to achieve. A generation ago it could be said that a need for achievement in school was a real force in the first two decades of life, but one cannot say that now. Those of you who have talked to present-day American students about their academic motivation will have strong feelings about this. American students today realize that it is fashionable and also quite sensible to question the desirability of expending effort in certain ways just because their elders request it. Most teachers will deplore this as an impediment to learning, but it is not necessarily such. Students will learn, understand and make use of ideas that have justifiable importance far more rapidly than ideas that are simply pushed at them by requiring them to take a test.

Let me describe two researches that involved study activities motivated by the requirement to take certain kinds of tests.

The first has to do with essay testing. The use of an essay test as a part of the College Entrance Examination Board's test of English composition has been an up-and-down controversy for many years. Teachers of English would persuade the Board to include an essay because of the obvious reason that you cannot measure ability to write unless the student is called upon to submit a sample of his writing. Then the psychometricians would persuade the Board to drop the essay because of obvious statistics proving that a multiple-choice verbal test is even more valid for predicting essay scores than is another essay. Well, people are happy now with the use in the English Composition Test of a very brief essay reliably scored by several readers. One of the interesting arguments put forth by the teachers of English during this controversy was that students could be expected to learn to write, if they expected to have to write an essay on their college entrance examinations. Why should a student practice writing, if he could demonstrate his skill merely by blackening little squares on an answer sheet?

A controlled experiment was set up in order to find out whether expecting an essay test rather than an objective test would in fact affect the kind of studying that students do. At two public and two private schools, eleventh-grade students took an objective and an essay test of English composition in October. At two of these schools, the students were told they would take another objective test in January. Actually both kinds of tests were given in January to the students at all four schools. A questionnaire given to the students on the occasion of the January test revealed that only 14 per cent of the students did anything special to prepare themselves for the expected test. The test scores of all students in each school and those of the students claiming to have undertaken special study were analysed. The school groups expecting an essay or objective test did not make consistently larger gains on the expected test than did the groups not expecting the test. The students who indicated that they prepared specially for the test did not make greater gains than those who failed to prepare themselves or those who did not expect the test.

It is of interest to look into just what the 14 per cent of students did to prepare themselves for the expected test. For the objective test they 'did some work in my grammar book'. When an essay test calling for a discussion of books was expected, the answers were more variable, but most of the students who did any special study at all mentioned doing some extra reading or reviewing the plots of books they had read, so that they would more easily be able to cite specific examples from books in writing their answers to the essay questions. A few students claimed to have worked harder on their regularly assigned school compositions. None, repeat, none did any *extra* writing. This study does not say what would motivate students to learn to write. Maybe prizes for the best essays would do it, or publication of essays in a school paper, or reading essays in front of the class. This study does say that the mere threat of a certain kind of test has minimal effect.

Before leaving this research concerned with essay writing, I would like to describe the results of a questionnaire we sent to 224 teachers of English in 224 different secondary schools, asking them about their instruction in essay writing and about what effect an essay test in the College Board programme has had on their own teaching. I think this comes under the heading of how a test influences a student's learning, because, if the test influences a teacher's teaching, it will, we hope, influence the student's learning.

Only very few teachers admitted that their teaching practices were influenced by the college entrance examination. About 10 per cent in schools deeply involved in College Board testing said they gave more drill in grammar, because of the multiple-choice examinations. About 15 per cent said the current college entrance examinations influenced them to assign more writing practice to the students. However, this result may be open to suspicion, because the same percentage in schools not involved with College Board tests indicated this influence. When asked what would influence them to assign more written work to their students, a majority of the teachers mentioned smaller classes and less competing activities for the students. Less than one-third thought that putting essay tests into the college entrance programme would also be a factor. A few of them, however, did plead for college entrance essay testing, so that they could use it as a goad to persuade students to take their writing assignments seriously.

There seems to be evidence here that teachers are more influenced than students by the kind of tests the students will have to take. Indeed, it was ever thus. The older generation is more ready to do things for the younger generation than the younger generation is to do things for itself!

The second research that I should like to describe, actually a series of research studies, has to do with the effect of coaching on the multiple-choice verbal and mathematical College Board Scholastic Aptitude Tests (SAT).

Unlike the situation described above where it was *hoped* that the test would give direction to a student's efforts, coaching for college admission tests is a problem, because it might interfere with the validity of the test. British studies reveal substantial rises on intelligence test scores brought about by coaching. If some students are coached and others are not, a considerable number of errors in college admissions might be made. No accurate figures are available, but in the United States thousands of secondary schools give students specific coaching, not intended to educate the students in areas covered by the tests, but specifically directed towards performance on the special kinds of test items that the students will face. Hundreds of schools exist solely to coach for college entrance tests, charging $35 to $150 for their services, and dozens of different books are sold as a help in 'beating the tests'. The College Board and Educational Testing Service have carried out an extensive series of researches aimed at estimating what effect this coaching has on test scores.

In the first study two large and very similar private secondary schools took part. Both gave one form of the SAT to their seniors in September for equating purposes. During the autumn one school gave its students weekly coaching sessions based on specially prepared exercises consisting of test items exactly like those on the SAT: mathematics problems, verbal analogies, completion items, antonyms, etc. General instructions for taking multiple-choice tests were reviewed, and techniques for most efficiently solving each kind of item were practiced. For example, take the following analogies item where the subject is to select a pair of words having the same relation to one another as the words in the given pair.

QUIET:NOISE— 1 darkness:night   2 calm:depth   3 sun:day
4 rest:sleep   5 darkness:light

The given words, 'quiet' and 'noise', refer to sound, the absence of it and the presence of it. Answer number 5, darkness:light, is correct, as it also refers to the absence and presence of something. Just as this item concerns absence and presence, the others are concerned with such relations as opposites, part and whole, corresponding parts of speech, cause and effect, etc. Subjects in the experiment were made aware of such possibilities, so that they would recognize them in new items.

All subjects in the coached school and in the uncoached school then took the regular SAT for college entrance. After corrections had been made by means of analysis of covariance for differences found at the time of the first testing, there still remained some differences in average test scores presumably due to the coaching. The coached students did five points better on the verbal test and thirteen points better on the mathematical test. These differences are significant but very small. The score scale goes from 200 to 800, and the standard error of measurement in the test score is about 25, far larger than the effect of coaching.

Some very cogent comments about this study lead to further researches in the series. Somebody said, 'Private school students are tested a great deal. They are already test wise, and so the coaching is not as important to them as it would be to others.' Therefore, we repeated the experiment on public school students with a similar significant but very small result. Somebody else said, 'Your coaching was only one class period each week. What would happen with more intensive coaching?' We tried that too: intensive individual coaching, two sessions a week with lots of homework. A similar significant but very small effect was found. A coaching school protested against our studies, saying, 'You don't have the coaching experience we have; we give our students a real boost on the test!' The College Board then co-operated in a study with the coaching school. Despite the boasts of the coaching school, the average gain for the coached group surpassed that for a control group by only the usual small amount, eleven points, and this time the difference was not even statistically significant. Finally somebody wondered whether it would be effective to coach students for a college entrance *achievement* test, even if it is not very effective to do it for the aptitude test. A coaching study was, therefore, directed at the College Board's English Composition Test. At that time this was strictly a multiple-choice test of grammar, writing style and organization. In the six schools that co-operated, the score differences in favour of the coached groups ranged from near zero to seventy-three points, indicating that some schools had substantial success in preparing students for this achievement test. Ten months after the experiment was completed, another form of the English Composition Test was administered to the same students. This time the scores on the experimental and control groups were almost identical. The coached groups had lost almost all of their advantage!

The conclusion of all this experimentation on coaching seems to be that the type of test *does* influence learning . . . learning of dubious value by thousands of misguided students who devote much time and money to it. The learning in connection with coaching for aptitude tests is too small in amount to make much difference. Reading a good book might boost test scores even more! The learning in connection with coaching for achievement tests, if well designed, may help substantially to pass the test but will then fade away.

In summary, we have found that tests influence a student's practice in writing not at all; they influence the behaviour of the teachers, but even this is very secondary to other things; they influence a lot of students to take coaching courses, but the courses have little effect or the effect is quickly lost. It seems abundantly clear from all of this that we should not *try* to influence students' learning by threatening them with various kinds of tests. Tests can be used to measure how much a student has learned. They can be used to predict how much he will learn. They can even be used to summarize to the student what you want him to learn. However, the real influence motivating the student to learn certain things cannot be tests. It must be persuasion of the students that the material being offered is really worth learning. Society, the school, the teachers and the parents must all take part in this effort of persuasion. Once fired with a desire to master the material, learning will be rapid.

INFLUENCE ON A STUDENT'S LEARNING OF THE TYPE OF TEST TO BE ADMINISTERED

E. PAUL TORRANCE

At least since the days of Plato there has been some recognition that students tend to learn and develop along whatever lines they find rewarding. Several of you have expressed such a view at this conference. In *Rewarding Creative Behavior* (Torrance 1965), I have described a series of experiments which show that the way in which performance is evaluated influences various kinds of creative functioning. In another source (Torrance 1967a), I have attempted to summarize data that I believe show how changes in ways of measuring achievement bring about changes in how predictor measures operate, and how changes in methods of instruction result in changes in the operation of predictors, using the same criteria.

Since performance on achievement tests is generally the basis on which students are rewarded, it is to be expected that their learning will be influenced by the type of test to be administered. Since a particular kind of test tends to call into play predominantly certain mental abilities and skills and not others, there is a danger that the exclusive use of a certain type of test such as the recognition-type multiple-choice test will not only discriminate against certain kinds of students, but will result in a general failure to produce certain kinds of achievement required for success outside schools and colleges.

It is true that some students hold to their own objectives, preferred ways of learning, and the like. Since the rewards associated with school and college grades are themselves powerful determiners of opportunity for many kinds of success, it is only natural that students develop skills for identifying clues concerning 'what counts' in the teacher's grade book. A major source of such clues is the nature of the tests the teacher administers. Thus, it is to be expected that the type of test to be administered will influence the student's learning, with certain kinds of learning being emphasized to the neglect of other types.

In this paper, I shall summarize a series of four experiments in graduate and undergraduate courses in educational psychology at the University of Minnesota and the University of Georgia. In these experiments, I have tried to find out if there are differential relations among mental abilities and degree of success on different types of tests, if the kind of mental set used in reading for an examination influences the degree of success on different kinds of tests, if the kind of test on which a student is to be graded will influence his performance on other types of test on the same content, and if students thoroughly conditioned to taking multiple-choice tests are influenced by shifts to other kinds of test.

1. Different predictors and different criteria

Let us examine first some rather simple statistics that involve two types of predictors and several types of criteria in an educational psychology course in personality development and mental health. The predictors were scores on the Miller Analogies Test, taken as part of a battery required for admission to candidacy for the master's degree and a composite score derived from a forty-minute battery of creative thinking tests. This composite score was the sum of the fluency, flexibility, originality and elaboration scores on one form of the Ask-and-Guess Test, the Product Improvement Test, the Unusual Uses Test, and the Circles Test. (Since that time I have stopped working with composite scores, but I still believe that there are times when one is justified in obtaining a composite score from these tests.) Four types of examinations were given in the course: (1) a rather traditional multiple-choice test requiring recognition of a correct answer, (2) a completion and short-answer test requiring recall, (3) a test of creative applications requiring divergent productions, and (4) a decision-making test requiring evaluation and judgment.

In a class of 110 students, Bentley (1966) obtained the following set of coefficients of correlation from these data:

Achievement measure	Torrance Creative Thinking	Miller Analogies Test
Recognition	·03	·47
Memory	·11	·41
Productive thinking	·53	·37
Evaluation and judgment	·38	·27

In addition to the course examination, students were required to develop an original idea. Judges evaluated these original idea papers according to two sets of criteria. First, they were evaluated in terms of how well they described the idea, the process by which it occurred to them, the psychological rationale behind the idea, how the idea could be tested, and what consequence the idea might have should it be found valid. This was called the convergent rating. The second evaluation was based on criteria very similar to those used by the United States Patent Office: (1) the extent to which it is a step forward, (2) its potential usefulness, (3) the creative intellectual energy required to produce and develop it, (4) its surprisingness, and (5) its newness. This was called the divergent or inventivlevel rating. The convergent rating tended to correlate more highly with the Miller Analogies Test score than with the creative thinking score (0·33 and 0·16), while the inventivlevel rating tended to correlate more highly with the creative thinking score than with the Miller Analogies score (0·25 and 0·19).

2. Different reading sets and performance on different criteria

Another experiment (Torrance and Harmon 1961) was designed to test the differential effects of memory, evaluative and creative reading sets in handling assignments in a graduate-level course in personality and mental health. The 115 subjects were arranged alphabetically and assigned to one of three groups. Each group was assigned in turn each of the three reading sets to be used in the assigned readings for a week. At the end of each week, a twenty-minute test containing recognition, memory, creative thinking and evaluative items was administered. Subjects also estimated their degree of success in maintaining the set, difficulty in maintaining it, the number of minutes spent on the Friday's reading assignment, and their semantic reactions on nine polar-adjective pairs.

Analyses of variance indicated that the three sets produced differential effects on most of the tests for all three weeks. Those operating under the creative set achieved the highest mean each week on the creative applications (table 1). Those operating under the evaluative set achieved the highest mean on the evaluative or decision-making problem when such a problem was given (second week only) (table 2). Those

Table 1 Three reading sets and performance on creative application items for each of three weeks

Week	Set	Mean	Fratio	Level
1	Memory	4·25		
	Evaluative	5·43		
	Creative	6·18	12·496	<·01
2	Memory	4·45		
	Evaluative	4·94		
	Creative	7·96	16·149	<·01
3	Memory	6·88		
	Evaluative	8·37		
	Creative	8·60	13·763	<·01

Table 2. Three reading sets and performance on evaluative (decision-making) test items

Set	Mean	F-ratio	Level
Memory	5·88		
Evaluative	7·34		
Creative	6·70	11·469	<·01

Table 3. Three reading sets and performance on memory items for each of three weeks

Week	Set	Mean	F-ratio	Level
1	Memory	6·04		
	Evaluative	6·24		
	Creative	5·78	2·226	n.s.
2	Memory	7·32		
	Evaluative	6·65		
	Creative	7·20	2·543	n.s.
3	Memory	8·30		
	Evaluative	8·15		
	Creative	7·54	3·429	<·05

Table 4. Three reading sets and performance on multiple-choice items for each of three weeks

Week	Set	Mean	F-ratio	Level
1	Memory	6·21		
	Evaluative	6·52		
	Creative	6·33	0·893	n.s.
2	Memory	4·03		
	Evaluative	3·32		
	Creative	3·43	5·537	<·01
3	Memory	4·68		
	Evaluative	5·06		
	Creative	4·42	3·797	<·05

operating under the memory set achieved the highest mean on the memory tests (completion) during the second and third weeks (table 3). The differential effects on the memory items were not statistically significant during the other weeks (table 4). Differential effects on the recognition items were not consistent. Those operating under the memory set achieved the highest mean during the second week, and those under the evaluative set led during the third week.

Subjects reported that they found it easier to maintain the memory set, and rated themselves as more successful in maintaining this set than the other two. There were no differential effects on the estimated length of time spent on the reading assignment. On the semantic differential, subjects under the memory set tended towards *fast, cautious, old* and *boring*. Those under the evaluative set tended towards *slow,* and those under the creative set, towards *rush, new* and *interesting*.

During the second week subjects generally reported greater success in maintaining assigned sets than during the first and third weeks. On the semantic evaluations, there was a consistent and significant drift towards *fast* and *boring*. The three original groups did not differ significantly, giving no evidence of the differential effects of the three sets.

3. Instructional sets for four types of test items

A third experiment (Torrance and Harmon 1962) was designed to determine the effects of the psychological sets produced by an assignment to prepare for a particular type of test. Subjects were 134 students enrolled in a graduate-level course in personality and mental health. Four types of examination items to be included in an examination on a book assigned as required reading were described in one of the first class meetings. These included recognition (multiple-choice), memory, creative applications, and critical evaluation items. All subjects ranked these four types of items on the basis of 'how they would like to be assigned' to corresponding study sets and which type of items they would prefer their grades to be based upon. Subjects were then assigned randomly to one or another of the four instructional sets.

The examination was administered about two weeks later. The examination contained all four types of items, but the score that determined a subject's grade was that score which he attained on the sub-test corresponding to the instructional set to which he had been assigned. Each subject kept a record of the number of hours he had spent in preparation for the examination, and estimated on a five-point scale his success in maintaining the assigned set.

The mean rankings of the four kinds of test items in terms of preference were:

Recognition	1·68
Memory	3·12
Creative application	2·76
Critical evaluation	2·55

The differences are significant at the 0·001 level of significance, the most popular type of item being the recognition, multiple-choice type and the least popular being the memory item.

The relation between preferred type of test item and assigned type of item was not statistically significant, indicating that the randomization was effective in eliminating bias from this source.

The relations between amount of time spent in preparing for the test and both preferred type of test and assigned type of test were studied by means of analysis of variance. The relation between preparation time and assigned type of test was not statistically significant. The relation between preparation time and preferred types of test, however, is statistically significant at the 0·01 level of confidence (table 5). Subjects who had been assigned to a type of test that they had previously ranked either third or fourth spent considerably more time (about three more hours on the average) in preparation than did those subjects who had ranked the type of test to which they were assigned either first or second.

Table 5. Preferred type of item and number of hours spent in preparing for test

Assigned set	1st	2nd	3rd-4th	Total
Multiple-choice	9·6	7·3	12·0	9·7
Memory	10·8	7·8	11·7	10·6
Creative application	8·3	6·9	10·7	9·2
Evaluation	10·3	9·4	12·3	10·7
Total	9·7	8·1	11·6	10·1

F-ratio (rank given assigned set) = 5·84. Significant at 0·01 level.

Analysis also indicated that those subjects who had been assigned to types of tests which they had previously ranked as third or fourth reported less success in maintaining a set for that type of test than did subjects who had been assigned to types of tests they had ranked as first or second (significant at between the 0·01 and 0·05 level of confidence). Differences in reported success among the subjects assigned to the four different types of tests were also significant at between the 0·01 and 0·05 level. The four types of tests ranked in the following order of preference: first creative applications, second recognition, third evaluative, and fourth memory.

Overall, the relations of success on the multiple-choice, recognition-type test to assigned and preferred sets were not statistically significant. The interaction effect, however, was significant at between the 0·01 and 0·05 levels (table 6). Those who preferred the recognition-type test and were assigned that type of test scored higher than any other group.

Table 6. Instructional set and performance on four types of test items

Assigned set	M-C	Memory	Creative	Evaluative
Multiple-choice	14·75	6·66	15·41	13·84
Memory	13·47	9·21	17·03	13·60
Creative application	13·37	7·68	21·33	13·18
Evaluative	13·69	7·69	11·69	19·69
F-ratio	0·78	5·24	11·32	14·82
Level	n.s.	<·01	<·01	<·01

On the memory test, the analysis of variance yielded results statistically significant for assigned type of test at the 0·01 level of confidence and approached significance at the 0·05 level of confidence for degree of preference for the memory-type test. Those who were assigned the memory-type test, as expected, had the highest mean scores; those assigned the recognition-type test attained the lowest mean score.

On the creative applications test, the results of the analysis of variance revealed highly significant differences (less than 0·001) for assigned type of test. Those assigned the creative set attained a mean of 21·3 compared with 17·2 for the memory set, 15·4 for the recognition set, and 11·3 for the evaluative set. Preference for the creative-type test did not have a statistically significant effect.

On the evaluative test, both assigned set and degree of preference for the evaluative type of test item were found to be related to degree of success at the 0·01 and 0·05 levels of significance respectively.

The final course examination covering quite different substantive content also contained recognition, memory, creative application and evaluative items. To evaluate the possible effects of the earlier assigned reading sets on final examination performance, four one-way analyses of variance were completed. In no case was the F-ratio statistically significant. Thus, having been assigned to one or another reading set for one set of material made no difference on the corresponding sub-test on a different set of material. Similar analyses were made for degree of preference for type of test item. Only in the case of the evaluative set was the F-ratio significant at better than the 0·05 level. Subjects expressing first or second preference for the evaluative type of test item performed better on the evaluative sub-test than subjects ranking this type of item third or fourth in preference.

4. Influence of limited practice on taking a specific type of test item

An experiment just completed (Torrance 1967b) was designed to avoid some of the obvious limitations of the foregoing studies. I was anxious to carry out the experiment in eight equally divided sections of our undergraduate course in introductory educational psychology at the University of Georgia, and to vary the type of test item throughout a quarter and actually to determine grades on the basis of the assigned type of test item. Since all the instructors of these eight sections are quite thoroughly sold on the recognition-type, multiple-choice test there was too much resistance to conduct such an experiment. Co-operation was obtained, however, to conduct the experiment over a three-week period on the psychology of learning unit. Three chapters in the textbook (Garrison *et al.* 1964) were used as the basis of the tests. Two sections were assigned randomly to the recognition-type multiple-choice tests, two sections to the recall- or memory-type item, two sections to the creative applications type item, and the other two sections to a different type item for each of the three chapters. An assistant and I constructed all of the tests and scored them, using predetermined scoring keys and guides.

At the beginning of the experiment, all subjects were asked to express their preferences for type of test item. During the experiment they were asked to keep a record of the amount of time spent in preparing for each of the three chapter tests that were administered one at a time upon completion of the chapter. The test over the three-chapter unit contained all three types of items and was given unannounced two days after the completion of the unit. The scored chapter tests were returned to the subjects before the final test. Complete data were available for 345 subjects.

One-way analyses of variance were run for each of the four measures on the final test (table 7). Although there was a consistent tendency for

Influence on learning of the type of test

Table 7. Type of test item given and performance on test containing three types of items

Type of item given	M-C	Type of item in test Memory	Creative
Multiple-choice	54	50	43
Memory-recall	53	51	50
Creative application	43	47	54
Combined series	53	51	50
F-ratio	2·2819	1·7249	5·3783
Level	>·05	>·05	<·01

subjects assigned to a particular type of test item to score higher on that type of test than on the other two types, the differences overall were statistically significant only for the creative applications condition (significant at the 0·01 level). Next, the t-test was used to compare the means of subjects in each condition on the assigned type of test and the pooled means on all other subjects on that type of test. Only on the memory-type test was the t-ratio statistically significant, and this was due primarily to the outstanding performance of one of the two sections assigned this condition. The other section assigned the memory condition resisted the idea of preparing for and taking this type of test. Many expressed a feeling that there is something almost immoral about administering a memory-type test, even though the questions dealt with important and meaningful information rather than detailed and insignificant information.

An analysis of variance was also run for the amount of time spent in preparing for the chapter tests. An F-ratio 1·3435 significant at better than the 0·001 level of confidence was obtained (table 8). Students assigned to the multiple-choice-type item spent by far the

Table 8. Type of item given and mean number of minutes spent preparing each chapter

Type of item administered	Mean number of min.
Multiple-choice	281·85
Memory-recall	249·07
Creative applications	178·35
Combination	241·63

F-ratio = 7·3435; $p < ·05$

most time in preparing for the tests than did students in the other conditions. In fact, they spent about twice as much time in preparing for the tests as did students assigned to the creative applications test. Apparently the subjects in this study had been rather thoroughly conditioned to studying for and taking multiple-choice tests, had learned how to prepare for this type of test, and when assigned this type of test they devoted more time to preparation than did students who were assigned to take a type of test for which they had had little or no practice. It is interesting, however, that this greater preparation for the multiple-choice-type test did not pay off in superior scores on the multiple-choice sub-test given unannounced two days after the completion of the unit covered by the test.

In this study, the most marked contrasts were between the performances of students assigned the multiple-choice-type test items and those assigned the creative applications items. On the final test, those assigned the multiple-choice condition achieved slightly over one standard deviation higher on the multiple-choice items than did those assigned the creative applications condition ($t = 6.5476$, significant at 0·001 level). Similarly, those assigned the creative applications condition achieved about one standard deviation higher on the average on the creative applications sub-test than did those assigned the multiple-choice condition ($t = 4.1748$, significant at 0·001 level). Their total scores on the memory items were almost identical.

Conclusion

Although the results yielded by the four experiments described in this paper are somewhat complex and not altogether conclusive, there is rather consistent evidence that the type of test administered does have an influence on a student's learning. The evidence regarding the differential effects of the recognition-type, multiple-choice test and the divergent production creative applications items seems to be strongest and most consistent.

References

Bentley, J. C. (1966) 'Creativity and academic achievement.' *J.educ. Res.*, **59**, 269-72.

Garrison, K. C., Kingston, A. J. and McDonald, A. S. (1964) *Educational Psychology* (2nd edition). New York: Appleton-Century-Crofts.

Torrance, E. P. (1965) *Rewarding Creative Behavior.* Englewood Cliffs, N.J.: Prentice-Hall.

Torrance, E. P. (1967a) 'Different predictors, criteria and routes to criteria.' In Gowan, J. C., Demos, G. D. and Torrance, E. P. (eds) *Creativity: Its Educational Implications.* New York: Wiley, pp. 289-94.

Torrance, E. P. and J. P. (1967b) 'Influences on a student's learning of the type of test to be administered in eight sections of undergraduate educational psychology.' Unpublished paper, Department of Educational Psychology, University of Georgia.

Torrance, E. P. and Harmon, J. A. (1961) 'Effects of memory, evaluative and creative reading sets on test performance.' *J.educ. Psychol.,* 52, 204-14.

Torrance, E. P. and Harmon, J. A. (1962) 'A study of instructional sets for four types of test items.' Unpublished manuscript, Department of Educational Psychology, University of Minnesota.

CHANGES OF ATTITUDE TOWARDS STATISTICS AFTER OBJECTIVE TESTING

NURIA CORTADA de KOHAN

It is common knowledge that many students who take psychology as a main subject show lack of interest in the statistics courses, especially at the beginning of their studies. This seems to be quite general, and was suggested some time ago by McNemar (1957) when he said: 'One can secure practical working knowledge of statistical techniques without first becoming a mathematician, provided this deficiency in mathematics is not accompanied by an emotional reaction to symbols'. Ombredane in his introduction to *Méthodes Statistiques en Psychologie Appliquée* by Faverge (1954) emphasized the students' anxiety: 'L'étudiant en psychologie [est] traditionnellement effrayé par l'obligation d'apprendre la statistique'.*

Since 1955, when I first started teaching statistics to students of psychology and sociology, I have been deeply concerned over their antagonistic feelings towards the subject. I thought it most important to change this attitude, especially because they were only beginning to learn statistics, and because I believed if this antagonism persisted, it could be very harmful to their progress in psychology and sociology and to research.

I think I should mention that psychology and sociology were not introduced in Argentina as autonomous studies and independent university professions until 1955; before then they were considered to be courses for the degree in philosophy. Although they have now officially become separate fields of specialization, they are still located in the schools and departments of philosophy. In many cases—like anthropology, education, history, literature and classics—the student who decides to do psychology has not been given enough information on the nature of the subjects required, and is not aware of the need for the study of statistics. If, by any chance, he has had trouble with mathematics at school, this comes as an unpleasant surprise, and his feeling of antagonism is strengthened by the difficulty he experiences and is very hard indeed to uproot. This has become a serious problem when statistics has been taught by mathematical statisticians, who, although sometimes very efficient in their field, have not grasped the difficulty that students of psychology find, and have not been able to help them with their anxieties adequately.

*'The student of psychology [is] traditionally frightened by the requirement to learn statistics.'

I shall not describe here the different ways I have tried successively, during all these years, to change the emotional attitude of my students. Let me only say that my attempts have ranged from a preliminary conversation with each pupil to the publication of informative pamphlets on the different fields of psychology in which a psychologist uses statistics. I have also tried showing in class some modern psychological journals in different languages plagued with statistical symbols. I have tried to organize preliminary non-compulsory courses in elementary arithmetic and algebra to refresh the students' knowledge of basic skills. I believe that all this has helped in some measure, but I could never properly evaluate the progress made. However, there is a fact which suggests that some positive change of attitude has occurred. In 1962 I started a second course of lectures on statistical techniques. This course was not considered compulsory for the curriculum, and in the first term the course was given only to eight students (in the elementary course, which is compulsory, there are around 300 pupils). Since 1962 the number of students who have applied for the second course of statistics has increased regularly. The last term, to my surprise and bewilderment, there were eighty students!

Of course, the problem of the students' attitudes is presented here because of the recognition that learning is not determined by cognitive factors alone (Levine and Murphy 1943), and that a person enters a learning situation as a complete individual, with his own needs, desires and values, and his own frame of reference; a positive or negative attitude towards the subject therefore assumes great importance. Through his past experience an individual acquires many different expectations of a particular object, and the structure of the whole system of his expectations of this object makes up his attitude towards it. Thus we may consider an attitude to be an organization of concepts, beliefs, habits and motives associated with a particular object, and the verbal expression of an attitude is the opinion stated. The components considered by many to be at the core of an attitude are affective and conative. This is why the means which make use of intellectual reasoning and verbal information, and which appeal to the individual's cognitive side have usually little success in changing attitudes (Allyn and Festinger 1961). It is more effective to find some way of providing new experiences that enter the field of the individual and counteract the influence of his old beliefs (Katz and Lazarsfeld 1955) and prejudices. This is why I thought I could use the objective test taken in the middle of the statistics course as an indirect way of modifying the prejudices that students of psychology had against statistics. To take a different type of test (the usual type in my country

Table 1

Questions	Answers	N	%
1	Yes No	50 230	15 85
2	−IBM courses −History −Education −Psychology	10 15 10 20	
3	−Very positive −Positive −No opinion −Negative −Very negative	80 150 − 50 −	32 53 − 15 −
4	−Very positive −Positive −No opinion −Negative −Very negative	90 140 40 10 −	33 50 14 3 −
5*	−Analysis −Synthesis −Abstraction −Generalization −Other functions	200 110 50 20 3	71 39 15 7 1
6*	−Lack of theory −Lack of practice −Lack of adjust. t. and pract. −Lack of clearness of items −Other	70 80 30 100 3	25 32 10 35 1
7	Yes No	100 180	35 65
8	Yes No	115 165	42 58

*The pupils underlined more than one alternative.

Changes of attitude towards statistics

is the essay-type) is a new experience, and although its content points to specific knowledge and to the cognitive functions of the student, his expectation of success or failure arouses in him deep emotional tensions and anxieties. We thought it could be perhaps an efficient message in order to change his feeling against the subject. That impression, which I cannot state as a working hypothesis in this first paper, led me to collect the opinions of the students on the test itself and on the subject matter.

One week after the multiple-choice test of achievement in statistics had been administered, the pupils were asked to answer a short questionnaire. I waited a week so that the pupils had already had the opportunity to learn their results on the test, to talk to my assistants about the errors they had made, and to have quietened down their anxiety about the whole situation.

The main purpose of the work, to find out a change of attitude, was disguised. Most of the questions refer to the students' opinions of objective testing, which was also of interest to me and which I decided to make explicit to them. Instead I did not put any emphasis in the last question, which had to do with their attitude towards statistics. However, as I expected, this was the question that was given the most consideration by the pupils; the answers given were longer and more interesting. The results are shown in table 1.

The questionnaire was administered to all the students who had taken the test (280). There was no time limit. After a few lines which stated that anonymity was guaranteed and that the students were free to make any side comments about the questionnaire, the following questions were asked:

1. Is this the first time that a test of this type has been administered to you?
2. If your answer is *No*, when and where have you taken an objective achievement test?
3. What is your personal attitude to objective testing in general for any subject matter?
    A. Very positive
    B. Positive
    C. No opinion
    D. Negative
    E. Very negative
4. What is your personal opinion on the objective achievement testing in this specific subject (statistics)?
    A. Very positive
    B. Positive

C. No opinion yet
D. Negative
E. Very negative

5. Each type of test seems to need a special organization of your knowledge. In relation to the objective test statistics, do you think that it required ability particularly for:
    A. Analysis
    B. Synthesis
    C. Abstraction
    D. Generalization
    E. Others (state which)
    (Underline those you consider most important.)

6. It is assumed that you took the test with a certain amount of knowledge of theoretical and practical facts on the subject. Did the test show you that your failures, difficulties or errors in some items were due to:
    A. Lack of theory
    B. Lack of practice
    C. Lack of adjustment between theoretical knowledge and the concreteness of the items
    D. The questions were not clearly expressed
    E. The test was too long
    F. Other

7. Although you know that objective testing implies less subjectivity on the part of the professor than other types of examination, do you still think that an essay test better reveals the individual effort made by the student?
    Yes   No
Why?

8. Do you think that the objective achievement test has introduced any kind of change in your interest in and opinion of the subject?
    Yes   No
Why?

I am not interested here in analysing table 1, but question 8 deserves special attention. Forty-two per cent of the pupils strongly indicate a positive change of attitude, and in the open part of the question (Why?) we find statements such as the following, which are quoted verbatim:
    'My interest increased very much.'
    'The test made me see many theoretical reasons that I could not grasp during the classes.'

'The test diminished the fear that even the word "statistics" aroused in me.'
'It made me feel that the subject was not so difficult to me as I used to believe.'
'It made me understand the importance of systematic learning.'
'Now I feel much more able to cope with the course.'
'The test taught me all the tricks necessary to understand the subject.'
'It is just at the end of the course that I began to "love" statistics.'

I tried to code the results in the open part so that I could tabulate them in a 2 × 2 table. If we study the reasons given by the students who answered that their interest was not modified, we find that they show on the open question that they already had a positive attitude towards learning statistics. Table 2 shows answers 'Yes' and 'No' to the first part of question 8 related to evidence of interest in the past (+) or lack of interest (−). In this table we suppressed the answers of the students who made no reference to the original attitude (49 people).

Table 2

Original attitude towards statistics

	+	−	T
Yes	9	80	89
No	120	22	142
	129	102	231

This table makes it quite clear, without further analysis, that the change is produced mainly in those whose original feelings towards statistics were negative (80). We are not concerned with those who indicate a positive attitude from the beginning (129), since either they do not show a change (120), or else they state in the open question (9) that their originally strong interest in the subject was reinforced. Our concern is for the twenty-five students whose responses indicate that no change took place and whose attitude is now as negative as it was at the beginning of the course. But, undoubtedly, if there were no such people, we should not have such problems! They represent only the 9 per cent of the reduced group of table 2.

This is a preliminary study, and we decided to present it hoping that you would accept it as a starting-point for a wider and deeper research.

We are taking steps to follow this lead in a more controlled experiment, and have already interested the Professors of General Psychology in Buenos Aires Dr Virgina Prosdocimi and Lic. Friedrich Kaufman, who, after administering an objective achievement test in their subject, have given a similar questionnaire to their pupils. We are planning to design a joint research to gather more facts, and to be able to delimit working hypotheses and test them.

References

Allyn, J. and Festinger, L. (1961) 'The effectiveness of unanticipated persuasive communications.' *J. abnorm. soc. Psychol,* **65**, 35-40.

Faverge, J. M. (1954) *Méthodes Statistiques en Psychologie Appliquée.* Paris: Presses Universitaires de France.

Katz, E. and Lazarsfeld, P. F. (1955) *Personal Influence: The Part Played by People in the Flow of Mass Communication.* Glencoe Ill: Free Press.

Levine, J. M. and Murphy, G. (1943) 'The learning and forgetting of controversial materials.' *J.abnorm. soc. Psychol.,* **38**, 507-17.

McNemar, Q. (1957) *Psychological Statistics.* New York: Wiley.

Newcomb, T. M., Turner, R. H. and Converse, P. E. (1965) *Social Psychology: The Study of Human Interaction.* New York: Holt, Rinehart & Winston.

# TEACHERS AND TESTING TECHNIQUES

ESSAY OR OBJECTIVE TEST?

ERIC F. GARDNER

Introduction

Since we are focusing on the classroom teacher as a test maker and test user this morning, I am addressing myself to a question often raised in the United States by teachers at all levels. Should I use an essay or objective test? Although raised as a question, the query is usually accompanied by a determined and predetermined attitude. Although I am confident that to a sophisticated group such as this I will be saying nothing new, the real concern and prejudice exhibited by so many teachers makes the topic worthy of consideration.

During the past six decades educationists in the United States have witnessed the rise of educational measurement to the plane of conscious striving for objective, impartial and comparative means for portraying the absolute and relative achievements of pupils. Before the beginning of this century, teachers, although long familiar with examinations, did not view their tests and examinations as measurements in the current technical meaning of the word. Oral quizzing, Socratic or otherwise, had been from time immemorial a part of the daily classroom routine; in fact, at times it was all of teaching. Formal written examinations are probably more recent than oral testing, but these date their origins many centuries ago; certainly formal written examinations were firmly entrenched in the educational system of China 1,300 years ago, and were familiar to Greek and Roman teachers. In the United States, examinations are as old as formal education itself, although the popularity and utilization of a particular format—*oral, written essay* and *written objective test*—have varied. All are, obviously, not equally good measuring instruments, nor are they equally appropriate for a specified purpose (e.g. a mastery test would not be expected to have the same characteristics as a test designed for measurement).

Oral v. essay examinations

The oral examination which was widely used in the United States at that time was attacked as early as 1845 by Horace Mann, who formulated a clean-cut concept of the written examination and elaborated in detail on its superiority. An analysis of his report to the Boston School Committee shows the following propositions specified as desirable characteristics for an examination:

1. Uniform examination questions should be presented to all students under the same conditions.
2. Examinations, when administered to a group, are more economical of time than oral or individually administered examinations.
3. Examination questions differ greatly in difficulty, and these variations may obscure real differences in pupils' abilities and achievements when the same questions are not administered to all.
4. Since any examination is a limited sampling of a pupil's knowledge, the larger the number of questions the better the coverage of content.
5. Examinations should be long enough to reduce the marked chance element in success or failure on a short examination.
6. Examinations should be free of the inadvertent and very human tendency of teachers to assist pupils in their answering of questions.
7. Examinations should be systematic and not deflected from the aim of the examiner by unforeseen circumstances.

These arguments advanced in justification of the use of written essay examinations in what was really the first American school survey, that of the grammar and writing schools of Boston in 1845, gave impetus to the use of essay questions in important examinations rather than relying on the previously used oral questioning. (It is interesting to note that the enthusiastic advocates of the objective test have used the same arguments in support of the short-answer objective test over essay tests.) Increasingly from that time on the essay examination played a major role in classroom testing within the United States.

Criticism of the essay test and development of the objective test

At the beginning of the twentieth century two movements, which were to have great effects on testing, were initiated by psychologists: (1) the development of new type, short-answer, group-administered objective tests, and (2) empirical studies devoted to an investigation of the properties of the examinations then being administered.

Development of the objective test

Before the First World War, considerable progress had been made in the development of individually administered tests—primarily in an attempt to identify the feeble-minded. Work by the French physicians, Esquirol and Seguin, which antedated the work of Binet, initiated the efforts which later led to the development of the Stanford-Binet Intelligence Test by Lewis Terman. The mental test movement, which involved the construction of tests to measure complex mental functions, was initiated by the work of James McKeen Cattell, and the German psychologists, Kraeplin, Oehrn and Ebbinghaus, who devised tests of arithmetic computation, memory span and sentence completion.

The first large-scale group testing like the first Binet Scale was developed to meet a pressing practical need. At the time the United States entered the First World War, 1917, the American Psychological Association established a committee to consider ways in which psychology might aid in the conduct of the war. This committee recognized the need for the rapid classification of the million and a half recruits with respect to general intellectual level. To aid in such decisions as rejection, discharge from military service, assignments to different types of service, or admission to officers training camp, the first group intelligence test was developed. Two tests, known as Army Alpha and Army Beta, which drew upon all currently available test materials, were finally developed by the army psychologists. The former was designated for general routine testing; the latter was a non-language scale employed with illiterates and with foreign-born recruits, who did not have a functional command of English.

After the war, the army tests were released for civilian use. At this point the testing movement underwent a tremendous spurt of growth, and numerous intelligence tests, as well as large numbers of group-administered tests, were developed. The first achievement test battery, using the objective test item, was the Stanford Achievement Test devised by Lewis Terman and Truman L. Kelley in 1923. Numerous other tests in arithmetic, reading and other school subjects, all using short-answer types such as true-false, multiple-choice and matching, were published. These were not only widely used, but in a short time many teachers began to construct and use similar tests.

Criticism of essay tests

Simultaneously, with the development of the objective test in the early 1920s, the essay examination came under heavy attack. Studies done as early as 1912 by such pioneers in the measurement field as Starch and Eliot showed that when the same set of English essay examinations was submitted to presumably competent teachers, the grades assigned to the same paper ranged all the way from 50 per cent to 98 per cent. The grading by 115 teachers of a paper in geometry showed that they did not agree in their grading any better than did the English teachers. A replication of the studies of Starch and Eliot in the field of geometry by Ruch, studies by Wood of the reliability of the examinations of the College Entrance Examination Board, and a number of other studies on the reliability and validity of essay examinations of that time caused the essay question to be attacked on several grounds.

In addition to subjectivity of marking which was shown to lower reliability, stress was laid on the inadequate sampling of content in the usual essay test prepared by the teacher. It was pointed out that the sampling must be limited to a smaller number of broad questions in contrast with a broad sampling of a large number of issues. Arguments were made that the essay examination employed an intensive type of sampling, while the objective-type item employed an extensive type of sampling, and that the objective examination could cover far more ground in the same amount of working time because there was no need to spend time in writing a mass of words. A response of underlining, encircling or checking was so rapid that the major portion of the examination period was spent in thinking about the responses. With respect to the essay examination, a larger fraction of time was spent in writing. Hence, it was claimed that the essay examination was wasteful of the pupil's time. Some writers argued that in a sixty-minute examination a pupil spends from fifteen to thirty minutes, sometimes more, in writing his answers, whereas if no writing were necessary the examination might include at least twice as many questions. Worse still, they maintained that most of the words which are generally written convey little information about the real knowledge of the pupil. Language requires a large number of 'filler words', useful, to be sure, for grammatical reasons, but useless for examination purposes if we view the examination as a measuring instrument of content.

A third objection was that the essay examination encouraged bluffing, and that when a pupil was confronted with a broad discussion question he, in one sense, could choose the line of attack. He might be entirely ignorant of the import of the question, but at that time he would be completely in charge. He could even naively misunderstand 'the question' and write on some alien topic where his meagre store of knowledge could be turned to better advantage. He could at times go around, under or over the topic in a very skilful manner. In fact, he would have nothing to lose, and conceivably he might win in the hands of a philanthropic teacher. An objective test, on the other hand, was one in which he would be forced to respond to stimuli satisfactory to the teacher. This type of examination would force the pupil to react to a variety of questions designed to elicit specific responses, and would give the teacher the opportunity to force the student to react to those things she thought important.

In general, the conclusions accepted by a number of writers on measurement at that time could be summed up essentially in the following fashion. The element of subjectivity in the traditional essay examination was a source of marked unreliability. Such examinations had been found to be wasteful of time in the sense that the pupil was required to write an excessive number of words which conveyed no important information to the marker of the paper. Such wasted time would have allowed the answering of a much larger number of short-answer or objective questions. An objective test over the same ground covered by an essay examination would have yielded a far more extensive sampling of the pupil's knowledge. One author, whose opinion was representative of that of a large group of educationists, specified, 'The essay examination should be employed principally when the subject matter does not lend itself to complete objective measurements; even in such cases the results must be taken with a great deal of conservatism'.

Although the essay test continued to be the primary method used by classroom teachers, the inclusion of courses in test and measurement in the curricula of teacher-training institutions encouraged an increasingly large number to use the objective-type item. Let us consider in a systematic way some of the major advantages and limitations of the objective test.

Advantages and limitations of objective examinations

Advantages

Objectivity. One of the major claims for the objective examination is, as its name implies, its objectivity, which is a prime essential for reliability of measurement. Much of the educational process must be highly subjective, but measurement implies accuracy. It is desirable that an examination exclude so far as is possible personal opinions, biases, whims and temperaments of teachers; it should be a measure of the pupil's competence in a particular domain unadulterated by factors which represent the psychological reactions of the teacher at the time. Although the objective examination can be made wholly, or almost wholly, objective with respect to scoring, it is worth pointing out that it is no more objective than any other kind of examination in terms of the selection of content which has been included.

Economy of scoring. A second major advantage of the objective test is that, if planned carefully as to its mechanical features, it may be scored far more rapidly than can essay tests of comparable length. The term 'comparable' has been used advisedly to include comparison in terms of numbers of items, or questions, equal working times, or equal reliability. With the advent of newer scoring machines and high-speed computers, the advantage of scoring an objective test, which is quick, easy and consistent, becomes even more obvious. As a matter of fact, without the capacity to score thousands of tests rapidly and accurately—as is done by newer scoring machines such as the one at the University of Iowa—any of the large-scale testing programmes such as the College Entrance Examination Board examinations, state and national surveys, and large city testing programmes would be impossible.

High reliability per unit of working time. If discussional types of tests are given, in general much more time is required to obtain reliability as high as that of an objective test requiring a much shorter period of time. Reliability of the ordinary ten-question essay examination of sixty minutes very rarely averages more than 0·60 or 0·70. A well-constructed sixty-minute objective test may contain, not five or ten questions, but as many as from 100 to 200 items. A number of studies beginning with one by Ruch in the early 1920s have compared reliabilities of objective tests and essay tests. The objective test has shown a much higher reliability per unit of working time.

Sampling of content. The objective test provides an extensive sampling of course content, due to the large number of questions that can be included in a test in a limited amount of time. Studies have shown that by checking, underlining or inserting occasional words, from three-fourths to nine-tenths of the writing may be eliminated in an examination. This results in an obvious economy of effort, an increased allowance of time for thought, and an increased breadth of sampling in a given amount of examination time. The objective test is highly efficient for measuring knowledge of facts. Some types, in particular multiple-choice items, can also measure understanding, thinking skills and other complex outcomes.

Freedom from bluffing. Objective tests limit a pupil to the type of response desired by a complete structuring of the item. Thus, bluffing, which freedom to respond in one's own words encourages, is avoided. Emphasis is placed upon knowledge and understanding, uninfluenced by the pupil's ability and skill in writing.

Influence on learning. There is considerable evidence which indicates that the technique students use in the United States in studying for an objective test is different from the technique they use in studying for essay tests. The objective test usually encourages pupils to develop a comprehensive knowledge of specific facts and the ability to make fine discriminations among them. Well-constructed objective items can encourage the development of understanding, thinking skills and other complex outcomes. This type of item, however, is much more difficult to construct than is one that is related more nearly to factual material.

Limitations

Omits important objectives. The objective test has been criticized on the grounds that it is inefficient or inappropriate for measuring ability to organize, integrate and express ideas effectively. There is undoubtedly justification in this criticism. To measure such objectives, it is obvious that one should ask the student to engage in organizing, integrating and presenting ideas. This can be done most effectively in an essay.

Preparation of questions. Although considerable emphasis was placed upon the efficiency and rapidity of scoring the objective test, the time saved here needs to be balanced against the substantial amount of time required for the preparation of the questions for an objective test. A relatively large number of questions is needed for such a test, and their preparation is difficult and time consuming. One of the fallacies currently present in the United States is that it is easy to construct a test consisting of true-false items. Nothing is further from the truth. Although it is relatively easy to construct large numbers of true-false items in a short period of time, these generally turn out to be rather poor, ambiguous items.

Open to guessing and chance. One of the obvious deficiencies of an objective item, other than a completion item, is that it is open to guessing. The problem of how to handle guessing is an old one, and there is still no agreement on the best solution. Some measurement experts advocate the use of a correction factor for guessing, others recommend no correction and rely on the instructions in the directions to minimize guessing. Others recommend that the directions specify that pupils should try all questions. Research is still being done to determine the amount of guessing which is taking place and the ways in which it can be minimized.

Influence on learning. Pupils, knowing they are to be tested by an objective examination, tend to concentrate less on larger units of subject matter and are little concerned with preparing to demonstrate their ability to organize, integrate and express their ideas effectively. Less emphasis is placed upon complex, intellectual functioning and more on lower-order activities such as the learning of facts and specific knowledge.

Criticism of the objective test and renewed interest in the essay

The extensive use of tests, particularly 'intelligence' tests, in gathering and using data for making decisions far exceeded their technical improvement. When the tests failed to meet unwarranted expectations, scepticism and hostility towards all testing often resulted.

Criticism of objective tests

In the past five years there has been a flurry of articles in the United States criticizing the use of objective tests. These articles, especially those by Hoffman and recently by La Fave in a paper published in the January 1966 issue of *Psychology in the Schools,* have severely criticized the multiple-choice item. Criticisms have been made that multiple-choice items, even when the directions specify the choice of the best answer, are inappropriate in that the examinee is typically given no criteria by which he may know which correct answer is best. Hoffman makes the claim that the essential dilemma of multiple-choice tests is that, to make the items difficult enough, it is necessary to make them ambiguous—thus handicapping the brilliant student. La Fave even goes so far as to say 'the questions that are not trivial (i.e. which measure relationships between facts or analogies) are basically illogical; the questions that are not basically illogical are trivial'. La Fave then goes on to present an extensive argument in favour of the essay examination. Hence, just as in the early 1920s the essay examination came under attack, now the objective item has been subjected to a similar attack. Simultaneously, there has developed a new interest in the essay test and ways of improving essay tests to eliminate some of the deficiencies originally uncovered.

Renewed interest in essay testing

Essay test items are used extensively today as an informal method of evaluating educational achievement by classroom teachers. Although the objective-type test item reigns supreme in the realm of standardized achievement testing, there are several notable exceptions. Two such are the Writing Ability Test, which is included as part of the Sequential Tests of Educational Progress, and the General Composition Test included in the College Entrance Examination Board test. Although the College Entrance Examination Board has experimented with the essay test for a number of years, at the present time only a Writing Sample has been added to the battery of objective test items. The Writing Sample is an essay-writing exercise which provides colleges with direct evidence of a pupil's competence in written expression. This essay is not graded by the Educational Testing Service staff as are the rest of the CEEB examinations, but a copy is sent directly to each college that requires the inclusion of the Writing Sample. The college, in turn, decides how the paper shall be graded and how the results shall be used.

Construction

Part of the increased interest in the use of essay items is due to recent research, which has attempted to provide means for improving their construction and scoring. Four major considerations confronting the teacher as he constructs essay test items are the following: (1) relating the essay test item to one or more cells of his table of specifications; (2) adapting the essay test item, in terms of vocabulary and depth, to fit the academic background of the pupils to whom it is to be administered; (3) determining the amount of freedom of response to be allowed the pupil and making clear what is required; (4) establishing a suitable time allotment for the response and conveying this information to the pupil.

Since the freedom of response provided by essay questions is a matter of degree, those questions falling at the extremities of this continuum can be conveniently classified as extended response and restricted response items respectively. In the process of constructing essay questions, it is helpful to consider the appropriateness and characteristics of each type separately. The extended response essay is rather unstructured and requires the pupil to display such traits as the ability to organize, to evaluate, to write clearly and to be creative. The reliability of the scoring of such a test is customarily low and, for this reason, has tended to restrict the value of the extended-response essay test items for measurement purposes. In spite of the fact that test items of this type reflect important educational objectives, their practical utility is curtailed by the teacher's inability to score them reliably. However, they are used extensively as a teaching device.

The restricted-response type of essay item differs from the

extended-response type in that the boundary within which the pupil's response is to be formulated is more precisely defined. A specific problem is presented which requires the pupil to recall the proper information, organize it in a suitable manner, arrive at a defensible conclusion and express the entirety in his own words. Such restrictions imposed also simplify the scoring problem, hence increasing the reliability of the score.

Scoring

The second major thrust has been an attempt at improving the scoring of essay tests to insure greater reliability. Among the procedures which have been extensively used, the following four have been shown to improve the reliability of the scoring substantially. One of these is to score the pupil's response anonymously. This procedure tends to reduce the halo effect that is likely to occur because a teacher, knowing a certain pupil, expects a certain quality of response and has, in effect, prejudged the outcome. Data are available to show that identical responses written by pupils with decidedly different reputations will receive different amounts of credit.

Secondly, it has been shown to be desirable to score all responses to each item at one time rather than to score an entire paper. One method which has been shown to be effective is to rapidly read the responses of all pupils to the same item, and then go back and grade all the pupils' responses to that item before undertaking the ration of the next one. Such a procedure makes it easier to maintain a constant or near-constant set of standards. Details of the correct response can be remembered more easily, and comparisons between and among various pupil responses can be made more effectively. In addition, there is a tendency for teachers to give a larger amount of credit to a poor answer which is surrounded by a number of good answers and less credit to a good answer that is surrounded by a number of poor answers. The purpose of this approach is to minimize the effect of a pupil's previous answers on the teacher's judgment when he scores the pupil's response to the next test item.

Thirdly, if the spelling, penmanship, grammar and writing style of the responses are to be scored in, for example, a science or history test, it is desirable that they be scored independently of the content of the responses. Otherwise, it is difficult to determine what particular variable is being measured—what proportion of the score is due to knowledge of content and what proportion to some of the other variables. This is not to say that all these variables are not important, but to obtain the most useful kind of information it would be desirable to have separate scores on each function.

Finally, in situations where the results of the test are extremely important, it is desirable to have the tests scored independently by more than one person. As a substitute for this procedure, an effective device is a second scoring by the same person some time later without reference to the results of the first scoring. A number of procedures for scoring essay items have been presented in professional journals and books. However, no details will be presented here; I shall only indicate that these devices range all the way from analytical methods, which assign points to different portions of the answer, to general rating methods, where the teacher reacts to the overall response.

Studies related to two of the major criticisms levelled against the essay test, namely, its unreliability and difficulty of scoring, are currently being undertaken by a number of research workers. Efforts are being made to improve the construction of the essay item as well as to improve the reliability of its scoring. Up to the present time, the use of computers and scoring machines which have been designed to handle objective responses has resulted in such rapid and efficient scoring that large-scale testing programmes have almost, of necessity, been forced to use objective test items. Currently, research is being undertaken in the United States on the scoring of essay examinations by computer. Among the more interesting studies in progress are those of Ellis Page at the University of Connecticut.

Conclusion

In conclusion it is appropriate to say that there is a fair degree of consensus among educationists in the United States about the role of the essay and objective test. Since classroom tests are designed to provide information on the extent to which pupils are achieving the learning outcomes considered important by the teacher, a test is needed which provides a representative sample of pupils' behaviour in each of the areas representing an important objective. The tests constructed by the classroom teacher should sample these objectives as well as possible, and may be either objective or essay in form. Despite the many valid criticisms of both objective and essay tests, both forms apparently provide important information for the teacher. The objective test provides the pupil with a highly structured task, which limits the pupil's response to recall or making discriminations between given responses. The essay test permits the pupil to respond by selecting, organizing and presenting those facts he considers most relevant. Both types of tests serve useful purposes in measuring pupils' achievement. The type to use in a particular situation is best determined by the learning outcomes to be measured, and by the unique advantages and limitations of each type. It is common practice to design a test, especially one covering an extensive area of work, such as that covered by a final examination, to include both kinds of items. A group of objective items is used to sample widely (extensive sampling) the material covered. In selecting these items, special emphasis is placed upon knowledge of facts, principles and their application to problem solving. A smaller number of essay items on well-defined topics are frequently included. These questions require the student to reply in depth on a fairly narrow aspect of the content covered (intensive sampling). Both types have their place and both are needed to measure more completely the usual objectives set up by a teacher.

TEACHERS' PERCEPTIONS OF THEIR TESTS AND MEASUREMENTS NEEDS

BENJAMIN ROSNER

In the United States, the typical classroom teacher has little competence in tests and measurements and is reluctant to invest heavily in more. This is a strong statement—perhaps too strong—but I believe it is true. However, before I am completely alienated by the community of American teachers, let me add the following qualifications.

First, my indictment of the incompetence of the American teacher in tests and measurements is solely a matter of personal opinion—an opinion, however, born out of years of association with many classroom teachers, supervisors and administrators in a number of pre-service and in-service teacher-training programmes in educational measurement. But I cannot document the assertion. I have no hard data. It remains, therefore, one man's opinion.

Secondly, in decrying the incompetence of teachers in measurement, it must be clearly understood that I am not indicting their competence as teachers. I am referring here to a single dimension of the multi-dimensional character of instructional competence. Specifically, I am critical of the inability of the American teacher to design and construct relevant measures of students' attainment, to capitalize on the diagnostic utility of measurement data for instructional purposes, and to develop fair and interpretable summaries of students' achievement. It would be serious injustice to the American teacher to generalize an assertion of incompetence in testing to an assertion of incompetence in teaching. I believe that the education of teachers in the United States leaves much room for improvement; but the typical programme demands proficiency in an area of specialization, a broad background in general education, and a strong orientation to the knowledges and skills that define professional education. Unfortunately, the programme is deficient in measurement.

With little or no data, I have indicted the measurement competencies of teachers in America. Now, without even the flimsy protection of personal experience, I suggest that in the matter of educational measurement teachers in the United States share much in common with their colleagues through the world. Fortunately, this is not the only bond that ties them.

At this point let me not impugn the efforts of the many individuals and institutions who have spent considerable time and money on the training of teachers in measurement. Those we have reached we have helped—at least we have exposed them to the limitations and pitfalls of untutored measurement practice. Unfortunately, we have reached too few with too little. At the undergraduate or pre-service level, training in measurement is frequently restricted to a two- or three-week unit on testing in a course more generally concerned with educational psychology. Less fortunate students may be offered three or four lectures on measurement and evaluation in a year-long sequence designed to provide insight into the psychological foundations of education. It is the rare student who is offered an opportunity for the intensive study of tests and measurements in the undergraduate programme.

Most teachers who receive instruction in educational measurement tend to acquire their training as practising teachers. Those who are studying for advanced degrees in education usually take a course in evaluation, or in educational and psychological measurement. In addition, many teachers receive assistance in testing through programmes of in-service training. I would guess that no more than 20 per cent of the 1,700,000 teachers currently employed in the United States have received some kind of formal instruction in testing. Assuming, then, that our message has been transmitted to 300,000 practising teachers—and I must remind you that this number is no more than a half-educated guess—how much of it has been received? How much of what we preach has been implemented? In brief, how effective have we been?

Much as I would prefer to answer these questions by reference to empirical studies, I am compelled to fall back once again on personal impression. My belief is that our training programmes in educational measurement—undergraduate, graduate and in-service—have been only marginally effective. By this I mean that we have reached the teacher on an intellectual level, but that they have left our classrooms uncommitted to the development of more sophisticated measurement practice. We have argued the merits of objective testing, but they prefer the essay. We have espoused the virtues of multiple-choice items, but they rely on true-false and matching. They recognize the need to assess higher levels of cognition, but their examinations reward the accumulation of trivia. They appreciate the necessity for at least two independent readings of each essay examination, but few will attempt to make the necessary arrangements. They acknowledge the economy of an item file, but few will invest in the effort. They recognize the diagnostic utility of item analyses, but they will rarely commit themselves to the undertaking. They know that examinations should be prepared well in advance of their administration dates, but they postpone test development to the last possible moment. They do, however, avoid 'specific determiners'. They measure the lengths of item options. And they add an additional option to the choices in a matching exercise. But they will not eliminate options in an essay examination. They will continue to report test scores on a scale from zero to 100 per cent. And they will prefer pass/fail grading systems to systems requiring additional differentiation, arguing the greater reliability of fewer levels of classification. In sum, they may appreciate the elegance of our theoretical models, they may respect the rigour of our professional practice, but what they apply are the tricks of our trade.

I suspect that I exaggerate, but I believe the point is valid. Teachers appear reluctant to commit their energies to rigorous assessment procedures. Have we failed? I think not. But we are only marginally effective.

What accounts for the reluctance of teachers to invest heavily in the improvement of measurement practice? There are many answers. Let me suggest a few.

First, I believe we can agree that many teachers have absolute faith in the validity—the infallibility—of their personal impression. Regardless of how frequently we demonstrate to them the distortions inherent in human perception, teachers continue to maintain unshaken confidence in the fundamental accuracy of their subjective appraisals. Convinced of their infallibility, it is difficult to persuade them to more exacting psychometric procedures.

A second factor, and one which bears closely upon the first, is the limited range of human behaviour currently assessed by professionally prepared, fully operational psychometric devices. In general, standardized tests offer the teacher measures of academic aptitude and measures of academic achievement. Useful as these instruments may be, their measurements are restricted to a relatively small number of cognitive abilities. Teachers are compelled to rely on subjective appraisal for judgments about students' interests and assessments of social-emotional development. Required to depend upon personal impressions for the assessment of a host of instructionally relevant aspects of students' behaviour, teachers regard the precision of standardized measures of ability and achievement as a steel link in an otherwise paper chain. In their judgment, the intensive study of tests and measurements is at present unrewarding because of the limited utility of educational measures in the management of the instructional process.

Although considerations of 'infallibility' and a 'limited psychometric repertoire' may account for some of the resistance to rigorous measurement practice, these factors do not adequately account for the reluctance of the majority of teachers. In my judgment, teachers hesitate to commit their time and their energies to the development of measurement competences because they fail to associate measurement competencies with the instructional demands of their jobs. There are, in this audience, few, if any, who would not agree that measurement is an essential component of the instructional process—not an appendage, not an addendum or a postscript, but an indispensable ingredient of the process of education. Unfortunately, teachers do not share our conviction. For them testing is a peripheral component of instruction. It is an externally imposed administrative requirement of the job. This is not to imply that testing is regarded as unimportant, but, rather, that it is perceived as contributing principally to administrative decisions, not instructional decisions. Tests provide useful information about students' performance *after instruction*. Accordingly, test scores are important determinants of grades. Tests also motivate learning—but this is an incidental by-product of their significant contribution to the grading process. Test scores, moreover, assist in the organization of class groups and, on occasion, they help to identify students with learning disabilities. But tests do not establish a climate for learning. They do not select course content. They do not formulate instructional objectives. And they do not suggest appropriate instructional strategies. Tests have primarily administrative utility, not instructional utility. This is, admittedly, a myopic interpretation of the scope and function of educational measurement and an equally myopic orientation to the instructional process. But it is a point of view held by a large number of teachers. In brief, then, teachers dissociate competence in measurement from competence in teaching. There is little point, consequently, to the adoption of more stringent measurement standards or to the development of more sophisticated measurement skills. The daily challenge of the classroom simply does not demand such psychometric elegance.

Some time ago, I became interested in this matter of the contribution of measurement and evaluation to the day-to-day instructional problems and practices of the classroom teacher. Accordingly, I decided to ask a number of teachers to identify for me the specific requirements of their jobs which were based on a knowledge and understanding of the principles and procedures of educational measurement and evaluation. Although these data were gathered for another purpose, they have some small relevance to the discussion at hand.

As a member of the faculty of the Department of Education at Brooklyn College, I had access to a sample of New York City teachers who were enrolled in a seminar in educational research, a required course for all students who were candidates for the master's degree. There were at that time ninety students registered in the several sections of the course, and to these students I distributed a one-page questionnaire, inviting them to list the specific activities of teachers associated with the theory and practice of educational measurement. Sixty-five teachers responded to the question. Of these, twenty-two were teaching in elementary schools and forty-three in secondary schools. On the average, these teachers had acquired three years of teaching experience, although some were still in their first year of teaching and some had been teaching for more than twenty years. Finally, thirty-nine had completed a course in tests and measurements, and twenty-six had not. Overall, these sixty-five teachers generated 462 specific responses to the question—an average of approximately seven responses per teacher. The responses were then analysed by typical content analysis procedures.

It was immediately apparent that the vast majority of teacher behaviours could be classified under two major headings—testing and grading. It was equally apparent that each of these classes could be dichotomized into two additional sub-groups: testing into objective examinations and essay examinations, grading into assigning letters and assigning numbers. No novel insights here. Closer scrutiny, however, suggested the following classifications:

1. *Preparing examinations:* e.g. working on test committees, defining course objectives and writing test items.
2. *Administering and scoring tests:* e.g. establishing test-taking routines, administering tests, scoring tests and recording test results.
3. *Selecting tests:* e.g. identifying tests suitable for particular age or grade groups, determining the appropriateness of test content for specific classes, evaluating tests in terms of reliability and validity, and recommending tests to administrative and supervisory personnel.
4. *Employing other evaluative devices:* e.g. using check-lists and rating scales, interviewing pupils and parents, observing work habits, class discussions and interpersonal relations, administering sociometric questionnaires, and writing anecdotal reports.

5. *Computing and interpreting statistical data:* e.g. computing measures of central tendency and variability, computing percentages, reading graphs, and reading tabular reports of test results.
6. *Using test results for instruction:* e.g. pre-testing to determine instructional emphases, organizing homogeneous groups on the basis of test performance, examining test data to anticipate level of class performance, and using test scores to evaluate teaching.
7. *Evaluating pupil performance:* e.g. assigning course grades, recommending promotion, acceleration or retardation, recommending employment, and recommending higher education.

These seven classes of activity are not particularly unique. As a matter of fact, one can readily identify them with chapter headings in many introductory texts in tests and measurements. It would be an error, however, to assume that the 462 teacher behaviours were evenly distributed across the seven measurement categories. As I have already indicated, the greatest emphasis was placed on the development, administration and scoring of teacher-made tests and on the evaluation of students' performance. Activities related to standardized tests and activities suggesting systematic observational procedures were identified with less frequency. Relatively few activites were concerned with the computation and interpretation of statistical data or with the *use of test results for instructional purposes.* Incidentally, the primary difference between the 'measurement' and 'non-measurement' groups was that the measurement group seemed more aware of specific test titles and made more frequent use of such phrases as 'know the validity', and 'know the reliability', and 'remember the error of measurement'.

Admittedly, the data are weak. Sample size and sample procedure leave much to be desired. The direct question approach may encourage only the most obvious associations—although it is significant that teachers do not consciously associate instructional activity with measurement theory and practice. Moreover, there is no necessary association between the incidence of *reported* measurement activity and the incidence and duration of measurement activity itself. It is conceivable that rarely reported activity may require more teacher time than frequently reported activity. Finally, teachers may not know enough measurement to respond knowledgeably to the question. Nevertheless, the data are *not inconsistent* with the hypothesis. Teachers tend to dissociate measurement practice from instructional activity. It can explain their reluctance to invest heavily in measurement skills.

I have argued that teachers are unwilling to commit their time to the improvement of measurement practice because they regard measurement as a peripheral component of the instructional process. If this is so, how do we explain it? What factors contribute to the dissociation?

I have already suggested one possible explanation. In my judgment, the scant and fragmentary pre-service programme in tests and measurements is a major contributor to the depreciation of measurement competencies among classroom teachers. The undergraduate curriculum in teacher education is designed to prepare teachers for entry-level competence in their profession. Accordingly, the programme highlights with proportional emphasis those elements of the instructional process which educationists deem vital to successful performance on the job. If the undergraduate programme in tests and measurements is relegated to secondary status in the press for curricular space, teachers in training and teachers in practice are unlikely to regard competence in measurement as an essential element of competence in teaching.

In the United States the National Council on Measurement in Education has for many years attempted to persuade State Education Departments to include formal instruction in tests and measurements as one of the requirements for a state teaching certificate. Unfortunately, it has met with little success. Unless State Education Departments and teacher education programmes give greater recognition to the import of measurement competencies in the preparation of classroom teachers, their failures will reinforce the perceived separation between measurement and instruction.

A second explanation for the tendency of teachers to discount the relevance of testing to teaching is the possible disagreement between teachers and measurement specialists on the measurement competencies essential to effective instruction. If teachers and experts in measurement do, in fact, disagree, then the substance of training in measurement might, indeed, bear little relation to the teacher's tests and measurements needs. Fortunately, there are some data to suggest that teachers and measurement specialists are very much in accord on the competencies vital to teaching.

Several years ago, Dr Samuel T. Mayo of Loyola University in Chicago and the National Council on Measurement in Education received a grant from the U.S. Office of Education to determine what experts thought teachers should know about educational measurement.

Table 1. A check-list of measurement competencies ranked in order of teachers' ratings of importance*

Item no.	Measurement competency	Teacher	Expert
14	Knowledge of the general principles of test construction (e.g. planning the test, preparing the test and evaluating the test)	2·84	2·74
4	Understanding of the importance of adhering strictly to the directions and stated time limits of standardized tests	2·83	2·89
17	Ability to construct different types of test items	2·81	2·60
11	Knowledge of advantages and disadvantages of teacher-made tests	2·79	2·81
16	Knowledge of the techniques of administering a test	2·76	2·78
21	Knowledge of effective marking procedures	2·74	2·82
10	Knowledge of general uses of tests, such as motivating, emphasizing important teaching objectives in the minds of the pupils, providing practice in skill, and guide learning	2·71	2·86
3	Ability to interpret achievement test scores	2·64	2·89
20	Knowledge of effective procedures in reporting to parents	2·63	2·77
22	Knowledge of advantages and disadvantages of essay questions	2·62	2·71
15	Knowledge of the advantages and disadvantages of various types of objective test items	2·60	2·61
28	Knowledge of limitations of tests that require reading comprehension	2·60	2·70
19	Knowledge of the principles involved in scoring subjective and objective tests	2·57	2·59
24	Ability to interpret diagnostic test results so as to evaluate pupils' progress	2·55	2·69
35	Knowledge of limitations in interpreting I.Q. scores	2·55	2·82
70	Understanding of the fact that interpretation of achievement from norms is affected by ability level, cultural background and curricular factors	2·53	2·79
1	Knowledge of advantages and disadvantages of standardized tests	2·51	2·80
29	Understanding of the limitations of the 'percentage' system of marking	2·51	2·65

*Measurement competencies and expert ratings by Samuel T. Mayo, Loyola University, Chicago.
†A rating of 3·00 was assigned to statements regarded as 'essential'. Statements regarded as 'desirable' were rated 2·00 and rating of 1·00 denoted 'little importance'.

Table 1 (contd)

Item no.	Measurement competency	Teacher	Expert
66	Understanding of the fact that a raw score has no meaning alone, and needs some context in which it can be interpreted	2·51	2·78
13	Ability to state measurable educational objectives	2·48	2·68
34	Knowledge of the limitations of ability grouping based on only one measure of ability	2·44	2·64
12	Knowledge of the fact that test items should be constructed in terms of both content and behaviour	2·40	2·63
33	Ability to do a simple item analysis for a teacher-made test	2·39	2·38
2	Ability to compare standardized with teacher-made tests and choose appropriately in a local situation	2·30	2·52
6	Knowledge of general information about group intelligence tests	2·29	2·58
26	Familiarity with expected academic behaviour of students classified in certain I.Q. ranges	2·29	2·56
51	Knowledge of the limitations of using the normal curve in practice as the fact that in large heterogeneous groups it 'fits' most test data rather well and that it aids in the interpretation of test scores, but does not necessarily apply to small selected groups	2·28	2·50
50	Knowledge of the fact that the normal curve is an ideal distribution, an abstract model approached but never achieved fully in practice	2·23	2·53
54	Knowledge of the common application of standardized scores	2·22	2·24
7	Knowledge of general information about individual intelligence and aptitude tests	2·20	2·27
41	Understanding of the nature and uses of the mode, mean and median	2·17	2·54
42	Ability to compute the mode, median and mean for simple sets of data	2·17	2·35
30	Understanding of the limitations of applying national norms to a local situation	2·14	2·61
32	Knowledge of concepts of validity, reliability and item analysis	2·13	2·46
43	Knowledge of advantages and disadvantages of the mode, median and mean	2·12	2·39
67	Familiarity with the nature and uses of the common derived scores, viz. age scales, percentile scales, grade scales and standard score scales	2·12	2·56

Table 1 (contd)

Item no.	Measurement competency	Teacher	Expert
18	Understanding and application of correction-for-guessing formula to an objective test	2·08	1·85
25	Ability to interpret the ratio formula relating C.A., M.A. and I.Q.	2·08	2·39
27	Ability to interpret a profile of sub-test results of standardized tests	2·08	2·52
69	Ability to interpret raw scores from a given set of norms	2·08	2·47
37	Familiarity with techniques of ranking a set of scores	2·06	2·27
36	Familiarity with the nature and uses of a frequency distribution	1·95	2·34
5	Knowledge of sources of information about standardized tests	1·91	2·24
39	Understanding of the basic concept of the standard error of measurement	1·86	2·20
8	Familiarity with need for and application of personality and interest inventories	1·85	1·77
31	Ability to compare two classes on the basis of the means and standard deviations of a test	1·84	2·02
44	Understanding of the meaning of the term 'variability' and its connection with such terms as 'scatter', 'dispersion', 'deviation', 'homogeneity' and 'heterogeneity'	1·77	2·19
55	Knowledge of how to convert from one type of standard score to another	1·77	1·72
63	Understanding of the meaning of a given correlation coefficient in terms of whether it is 'high', 'low' or 'moderate'	1·75	2·18
46	Understanding of the nature and uses of the standard deviation	1·73	2·21
48	Knowledge of the approximate percentile ranks associated with standard scores along the horizontal base-line of the normal curve	1·73	1·98
38	Ability to set up class intervals for a frequency distribution	1·72	2·10
9	Familiarity with need for and application of projective techniques	1·71	1·42
58	Knowledge of the fact that any normal distribution can be completely described in terms of its mean and standard deviation	1·71	1·84
23	Familiarity with the blueprint scheme for dealing with the content and behaviour dimensions in test planning	1·69	2·12

Table 1 (contd)

Item no.	Measurement competency	Teacher	Expert
64	Familiarity with the scatter diagram and the ability to make simple interpretations from it	1·68	2·25
59	Ability to define the concept of correlation, including such terms as 'positive correlation', 'negative correlation', 'no relation' and 'perfect relation'	1·64	2·26
56	Knowledge of the fact that the mode, mean and median coincide for a symmetrical distribution	1·55	1·94
49	Knowledge of the percentage of the total number of cases included between − or + 1, 2 or 3 standard deviations from the mean in a normal distribution	1·52	1·96
65	Knowledge of what size of correlation to expect between two given variables in terms of logical reasoning, e.g. in terms of a common factor	1·51	1·80
57	Knowledge of the meaning of the terms used to designate certain common non-normal distributions such as 'positively skewed', 'negatively skewed' and 'bimodal' distributions	1·50	1·76
52	Ability to convert a given raw score into a z score from a mean and standard deviation of a set of scores	1·46	1·64
61	Knowledge of the fact that correlation coefficients do not imply causality between two measures	1·43	2·28
62	Knowledge of the fact that correlation coefficients alone do not indicate any kind of percentage	1·43	2·16
68	Understanding of certain concepts associated with scale theory such as types of scales (nominal, ordinal, cardinal and absolute); translation of scores to a common scale; units of equal size; and common reference points (zero or the mean)	1·38	1·67
40	Understanding of the nature and uses of the histogram and frequency polygon	1·36	1·79
47	Ability to compute the semi-interquartile range for simple sets of data	1·33	1·57
53	Knowledge of the means and standard deviations of common standard score scales, such as the z, T, stanine, deviation I.Q. and CEEB scales	1·32	1·78
45	Understanding of the nature and uses of the semi-interquartile range	1·30	1·68
60	Knowledge of the significance of the numerical magnitude and the sign of the Pearson product-moment correlation coefficient	1·14	1·93

Accordingly, Mayo and his colleagues assembled a list of seventy measurement competencies distributed across four content categories: (1) standardized tests, (2) construction and evaluation of classroom (teacher-made) tests, (3) uses of measurement and evaluation, and (4) statistical concepts. Table 1 presents the list of seventy measurement competencies and table 2 identifies the items by content category.

Table 2. Number of check-list statements in various content categories rated 'high', 'medium' or 'low', in terms of mean response

Content category	High	Ratings* Medium	Low	Totals	Identifying item nos
1. Standardized tests	7	1	2	10	1-10
2. Construction and evaluation of classroom tests	7	5	1	13	11-23
3. Uses of measurement and evaluation	4	9		13	24-36
4. Statistical concepts	2	18	14	34	37-70
Totals	20	33	17	70	

*Legend for ratings

Rating	Range of means
High	2·65-2·89
Medium	2·02-2·64
Low	1·42-1·98

It is interesting at this point to examine the relative emphasis placed upon each content area, for the list as a whole provides an operational definition of the substance of training of teachers in measurement. Of the seventy statements, thirty-four, or approximately 50 per cent, are concerned with statistical concepts. Thirteen statements, or fewer than 20 per cent, are concerned with the construction and evaluation of classroom tests and similarly, thirteen statements alone are concerned with the utility of measurement and evaluation. The remaining ten items, or approximately 15 per cent, are devoted to standardized testing.

At first blush, one might easily infer that measurement experts are very much out of tune with the measurements needs of teachers. Considering the relatively heavy emphasis on statistical concepts and the relatively small emphasis on the construction of classroom tests, one might conclude either that measurement specialists are totally unfamiliar with the realities of the classroom, or that they are more concerned with the preparation of students in their own image than with the training of teachers in measurement. Here, at last, one might argue, is explanation enough for the resistance of teachers—and State Education Departments—to the intensive study of educational measurement. Moreover, with less than one-fifth of the content devoted to the *utility* of measurement and evaluation, is it any wonder that teachers dissociate competence in measurement from competence in teaching? But the distribution of competencies across content categories belies the judgment of the experts.

Following the development of the check-list, Mayo distributed the items to a number of measurement specialists, requesting that they rate each item in terms of its import to teachers. The statements were rated by 185 measurement specialists using a three-point scale: 'essential', 'desirable' and 'of little importance'. (Two other response options were available: 'do not understand statement' and 'no response'.)

Table 2 summarizes the ratings of the check-list statements in the four content categories. As the table indicates, statements in category 4, statistical concepts, received the lowest mean ratings. Highest ratings were earned by competencies associated with standardized tests (category 1), while classroom tests (category 2), and measurement applications (category 3) were rated slightly lower. Overall, then, the ratings of experts are much more consistent with the incidence of reported measurement activity than the distribution of content would suggest.

It would be a mistake, however, to make much of the small differences that obtain among categories 1, 2 and 3. These differences can be principally attributed to differences in item specificity and item classification. For example, item 10, ranked third in order of importance by measurement experts, contains almost all the instructional utility of teacher-made and standardized examinations. By contrast, item 35, which is ranked fourth, is concerned with knowledge of the limitations in interpreting an I.Q. score. Moreover, item 10, concerned as it is with the general uses of tests, is classified not in category 3, uses of measurement and evaluation, but in category 1, standardized tests. Similarly, item 35, specifying the limitations of I.Q. scores, is categorized not in standardized tests, but in uses of measurement and evaluation. Because of the inequalities in item specificity and the uncertainties of item classification, it seems wiser to ignore the differences in ratings among the first three categories.

In general, the incidence of reported measurement activity and the ratings assigned to classes of measurement content suggest that discrepancies between teachers and measurement experts are likely to be small. (It might be noted here that in New York City teachers play a small part in the selection and evaluation of standardized tests. Standardized testing in New York City is largely under the control of central administration offices. For this reason there appears to be a greater difference between the impact of standardized tests as rated by experts and the incidence of teacher-reported test activity than actually obtains.)

Although the ratings of measurement experts suggest that they are sensitive to the measurement needs of the classroom, it is important to compare their ratings with similar ratings obtained from teachers. Fortunately, some such data are available. During the past few years, Mrs Miriam Bryan, my colleague at ETS, and I have conducted several workshops in measurement for classroom teachers. Shortly after an introductory session, Mrs Bryan and I would distribute the Mayo check-list and ask for ratings of the competencies on the same three-point scale used by Mayo's experts. In this manner we obtained item ratings from 183 teachers and supervisors in four school districts in New York and Pennsylvania.

Table 1 presents the check-list statements in order of mean rating by teachers. The ratings themselves appear to the right of the statement. Note that ratings that approach 3·00 are regarded as essential, whereas those near 1·00 are regarded as relatively unimportant.

Figure 1 presents the scatter-plot of the relation between the two sets of ratings. The association is obviously positive and strong. As a matter of fact, the Pearson product-moment correlation coefficient is 0·885. The data clearly contradict the assertion that measurement specialists are unaware of the measurement needs of teachers.

Although the relative ratings of experts and teachers are remarkably similar, there are several interesting differences. First, the mean rating of experts is significantly higher than the mean rating of teachers. One possible explanation is that measurement specialists are more likely to rate all measurement principles and procedures as more important than teachers. After all, measurement specialists are measurement specialists. Another equally plausible explanation, however, is that the ratings of teachers are depressed by the incidence of 'do not understand' responses. If teachers are uncertain of the meaning of a statement, they are not likely to rate the statement as important. As a point in fact, the association between ratings of import and the incidence of 'do not understand' responses is strong and negative; that is, higher ratings are associated with fewer 'do not understand' responses. The fact remains, however, that the relative ratings of teachers and experts are very similar.

Two other differences between the ratings of teachers and experts

Teachers' perceptions of their tests needs 361

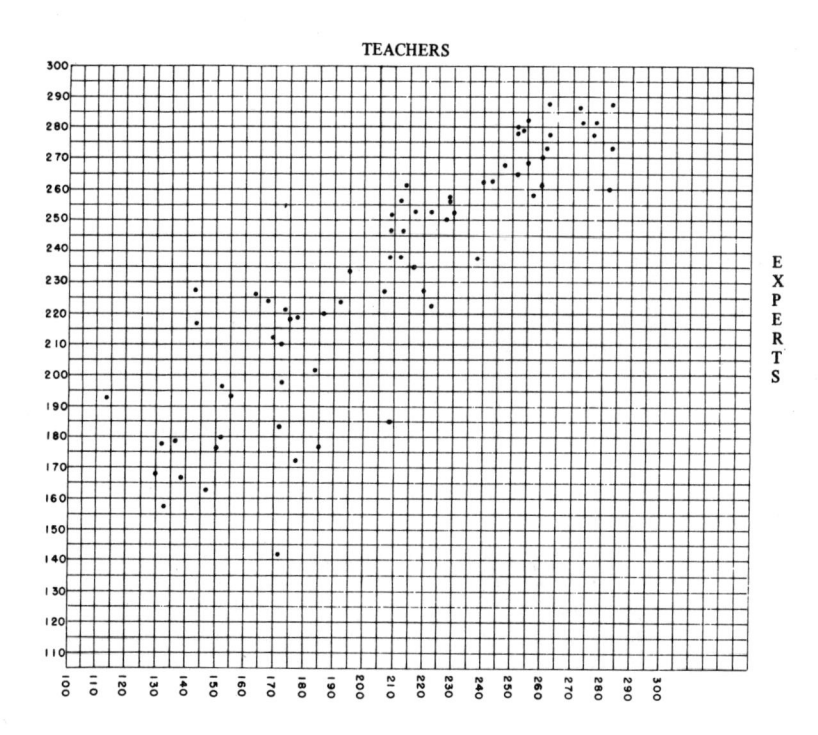

Figure 1 Scatterplot presenting relations between teachers' and experts' ratings of measurement competencies ($r = 0.885$)

are also worth noting. The first is that test construction competencies are rated higher by teachers than by experts. The second is that correlational concepts are assigned greater value by experts than by teachers. Although I cannot account for the relatively lower ratings of test construction competencies by experts, I believe that the lower ratings of correlation concepts by teachers are a function of ignorance. My suspicion is that teachers would place greater value on understanding correlational principles after a programme of instruction. Unfortunately, I do not have the data.

Beyond the small differences that obtain between teachers and experts on item-writing techniques and correlational understandings, teachers and experts agree very well on the relative import of measurement competencies. Assuming the measurement experts are likely to organize instructional programmes in measurement in terms of their perception of teachers' measurement needs, we may conclude that curricular irrelevance is not an issue in the depreciation of measurement competencies by teachers.

Before closing these remarks, we should consider one additional explanation for the tendency of teachers to dissociate tests and measurements from instructional competence. It is possible that measurement experts have not sufficiently explored the intimate association between testing and teaching. To date, we have tended to emphasize the role of tests as a motivating agent, as a reinforcer of important educational objectives, as an aid in the diagnosis of individual or group learning difficulties, and as a determinant of final assessments of students' achievement. There is a passive quality to these several functions, as far as teaching is concerned. Teachers regard instruction as activity. Students learn by doing. Measurement seems to stop the action. It is a passive intruder. It is, perhaps, a silent partner—but it is not in the mainstream of instructional activity. If measurement is to be regarded as an active ingredient in the chemistry of instruction, measurement skills need to be visible in the selection and organization of curricular experience and in the identification of instructional strategies. Fortunately, the past decade has provided measurement specialists with two focal activities for the display of such talents—curriculum evaluation and programmed instruction. As teachers begin to recognize the role of measurement competencies in the design and development of instructional materials and procedures, measurement will assume increasing import in the development of instructional proficiency. It would not be at all surprising to discover in the years ahead that measurement plays a vital role in the pre-service education of teachers.

In summary, I have asserted that teachers in the United States have little competence in educational measurement and that they are reluctant to acquire more. I have argued that the major factor contributing to this reluctance is the inability of teachers to associate competencies in measurement with competencies in teaching. To explain the perceived dissociation of measurement and instruction, I have indicted the inadequacy of undergraduate programmes in tests and measurements. But I have also demonstrated that measurement specialists are sensitive to the measurement needs of teachers, and I have discounted thereby, the curricular irrelevance of instructional programmes in tests and measurements. Somewhat obliquely, I have indicated that teachers are principally concerned with the design, development and scoring of teacher-made tests, the administration and interpretation of standardized tests, grading procedures, and the possibility of integrating measurement practice with the instructional demands of their jobs.

TEACHERS AND TESTING TECHNIQUES

SCARVIA B. ANDERSON

I heard recently of a final college examination on the novel *Moby Dick*. It consisted of two questions:
1. List and describe the ships encountered by the *Pequod* in its last voyage.
2. List and describe the various species of whales.*

As Paul Diederich, who cited this example, pointed out, 'the professor who set these questions probably congratulated himself on his ingenuity in devising an examination that only a few students could pass, that could be scored with nearly perfect reliability, and that would reveal which students had read the work with minute attention . . . . What never entered his mind was the possibility and desirability of finding out to what extent the students were able to understand and appreciate the literary qualities of a work of this stature.'

Ask any student what things he is supposed to get out of a course, and he will answer in terms of the tests his teacher sets for him. If they concentrate on minutiae, he will underline the most obscure bits of information in his textbook. If the tests focus on larger issues, relations and understandings, he will study accordingly. Before you start decrying the state of affairs in which the student studies pretty strictly for the tests and examinations, remember back to your own school days. It may be true that you worked hard on some subjects just because you loved them, but I bet that in the majority of cases you studied only what you thought you had to know for examinations.

Good classroom tests can really serve three purposes: direct and correct students' learning; evaluate and stimulate teaching efforts; and focus teachers' and pupils' attention on the objectives of the course. In our curriculum evaluation studies, we frequently find that it is only through the development of the criterion tests that we and the curriculum developers find out just what it is the curriculum is all about.

Some of you may say that I am making the wrong speech—that what I am talking about is testing, and what I really want to talk about is learning. Frankly, I am *bored* with the dichotomy. Frequent classroom tests can serve to motivate and reinforce; they can provide direct feedback without punitive effects. These are the necessary conditions

---

*Diederich, P. B. and Link, F. R. (1967) 'Cooperative evaluation in English.' In Wilhelms, F. T. (ed.), *Evaluation as Feedback and Guide*. Washington, D.C.: Association for Supervision and Curriculum Development, NEA, p. 191.

for learning. Teachers have got to be constantly aware that testing can be part of teaching. And being tested can be a major stimulus to learning. But the tests have to be good ones.

Most teachers use what they call essay tests or discussion questions. The reasons they give are that these force the pupil to think through problems in depth and express himself cogently in writing. Having looked at some of these tests, and taken a few during my own school and university days, I must confess that I think many of these teachers are just giving excuses. You can make up an essay test—maybe not a very good one, but *some* kind of test—while riding to school on the bus. You cannot make up any kind of objective test in this way. Dr Gardner has pointed out that objective tests are generally more reliable than essay tests, and can provide more adequate coverage of a topic. It has also been demonstrated that objective questions can be shaped to require critical as well as factual responses. But they do take time, energy and insight. So, by the way, does a good essay examination, and I am certainly not saying that there is no place for these in our schools. But there is not much place for those thought up on a bus on the way to school.

Those who decry a 'startling absence of creative efforts to devise evaluation instruments and procedures at the local level' must ask themselves why this is so.

One reason may be that, partly through the efforts of the test specialist himself, teachers 'have become convinced of their own amateurishness in test construction'. As one author said recently, 'The practitioner feels as though he were challenging General Motors with a machine "made at home with loving hands" '.* A second reason is, of course, that examination development must compete for time with the hundreds of other demands on teachers. Thirdly, some of the major objectives of educational programmes are, in fact, very difficult to measure—by test specialists, what's more classroom teachers. Fourthly, most teachers have had very little training (pre-service or in-service) in test construction.

It is the last reason which those of us here are in the best position to work on. Personally, I feel that in-service training with a strong emphasis on 'doing' is the most fruitful approach. Let me give you an example of one such programme.

It was developed by the Cooperative Test Division of ETS several years ago and has very limited scope. For example: (a) it focuses on multiple-choice items only—four-choice items; (b) it concentrates on

*Quotations in the last two paragraphs from Bebell, C. F. S. 'The evaluation we have.' Ibid., pp. 39-40.

the cognitive area, and introduces a very limited (and possibly misleading) classification scheme; (c) it considers only marked responses, though it does suggest the use of stimuli other than the printed word; (d) it tackles few of the complex problems of measurement, and is designed only to acquaint teachers with some of the most rudimentary techniques without scaring them.

The programme materials consist of three filmstrips with accompanying records and a teacher's work kit which summarizes and amplifies somewhat the content of the filmstrips and records. It was recommended for use in a six-session programme, extending over that many weeks.

1. In the first session, the filmstrip on planning a test would be shown. It emphasizes outlining the test, indicating the emphases which topics should receive, listing ideas for items, collecting materials on which to base them, and considering the skills to be measured. The limited skills classification scheme suggested is remembering, understanding and thinking. The idea was simply to focus teachers' attention on developing some items which required pupils to do a little more than give back what she or the textbook had said. Homework for the next session would be development of a test outline on an appropriate unit of subject matter each teacher was responsible for.

2. At the second session, outlines would be discussed and reviewed by the participants. Homework: revision of the outlines.

3. At the third session, the filmstrip on test construction would be shown and discussed. It focuses on mechanics of test making: writing stems and choices for multiple-choice items, review and revision, assembling the final test, and production of test booklets and answer sheets. Homework: development of a fifty-item test based on the outlines already prepared and revised.

4. At the fourth session, teachers would break up into teams of two or three and review each others' test items. Homework: revision of tests on the basis of reviews; actual administration of the tests to students.

5. At the fifth session, the filmstrip on analysing test results would be shown. It includes discussion of simple indices of item difficulty and discrimination, test speededness, and using such information to improve tests in the future. Homework: scoring and analyses of the tests already administered.

6. The sixth session would be devoted to discussion of the test analyses and laying plans for building tests in the future.

Let me show you the second filmstrip on mechanics of test making to give you an idea of the approach and the level of communication. (A summary of the filmstrip is given below.)

SUMMARY OF CONTENT OF FILMSTRIP SHOWN

Mechanics of item writing

Item cards

Professional item writers write each item on a separate 5 × 8 card. You may very well want to follow the same flexible procedure. At the bottom of the card, write the topic and skill categories for the item. Write the intended key (A, B, C or D) on the back of the card. If a set of items is based on a single piece of material, that material may be written out (or described) on a separate card and clipped to the item cards that go with it.

Item stems

If an item has a stem, the stem should meet these standards:
1. It should set the task. Generally, the student should know before he reads the choices just what problem he must solve. Here are examples of good and poor item stems:
   Good What is the inverse operation used to check division?
   Poor Which of the following is true?
   Poor Multiplication is . . . .
2. The stem must allow for the number of choices you have decided upon. If you are committed to four-choice items, the following stem might trick you into the absurd fourth choice shown:
   When you add two even numbers, the result is
   A. always an even number
   B. always an odd number
   C. sometimes an even number and sometimes an odd number
   D. neither an even number nor an odd number
3. The stem should be worded as briefly and clearly as possible.
4. The stem should be grammatical both within itself and in its relation to the choices. If the ordinary rules of grammar are not observed, this kind of thing can happen:
   The roots of the equation $x^2 - x - 20$ are
   A. −4, +5
   B. +4. −5
   C. 4
   D. 5

5. The stem should not include material which automatically determines the correct choice or rules out one or more incorrect choices. In the above example, 'roots' and 'are' in the stem tell the student who may not know anything about the solution of quadratic equations that the right answer cannot be C or D.

Item choices

1. Like item stems, item choices should be brief and clear.
2. They should also be grammatical.
3. Item stems should not 'give away' information. 'Give aways' may include physical characteristics, as well as wording. For example, in the following item the right answer may be chosen for quite the wrong reason—because it is shorter than any of the other choices:
    According to the stage manager, the first act of *Our Town* is called 'Daily life'; the second act, 'Love and marriage'. Which of these is the best name for the third act?
    A. 'Growing up, love, marriage and children'
    B. 'None can escape the Judgment Day'
    C. 'Life in a republican, protestant town'
    D. 'Death'
4. Item choices should be parallel in terms of grammar, as well as physical properties. The following item is faulty in almost every respect, including the lack of grammatical parallelism of choices:
    Franklin Roosevelt was
    A. the 14th President of the United States
    B. the son of Theodore Roosevelt
    C. successful in revising the complement of the Supreme Court
    D. elected to his first term by a majority of the popular vote
Note the following example of extreme lack of parallelism of choices, in terms of content.
    The first President of the United States was
    A. Christopher Columbus
    B. George Washington
    C. John F. Kennedy
    D. Kangaroo

Incorrect choices

For every correct choice you write, you will need to construct incorrect choices which have some plausibility to students with varying degrees of information or misinformation. There are three general approaches to writing such choices:

1. Administer open-ended questions to students and have them supply their own answers. Then use the most frequent wrong answers as incorrect choices when you reshape the questions into multiple-choice form—for administration to another group of students. For example, this question might be given:

    On an arithmetic test, Bill got 32 as an answer to one problem. In working this problem, Bill's only mistake was multiplying by 4 in the last step when he should have divided by 4. What is the correct answer to the problem?

    (This procedure is time consuming and may not be possible in many schools.)

2. Develop incorrect choices on the basis of your knowledge of common misconceptions students hold and errors which they make. For example, in the arithmetic question shown above, a student might divide 32 by 4 to get 8, or subtract 4 from 32 to get 28, or multiply 32 by 4 to get 128. These numbers (8, 28 and 128) are all good candidates for incorrect choices.

3. Think about reasonable confusions in terms of the stem or the correct answer. For example, in constructing a vocabulary test including the word 'ingenuous', you might use the incorrect choice 'clever'.

Do not forget the possibility of including such choices as the following, but, when you use them, make sure that they represent the correct answer in some cases:

It cannot be determined from the information given
None of these
No error
All of the above

By all means avoid trickery in constructing your items. For example, if you are testing students' knowledge about the statesmen involved in some historical event, do not include and count as wrong a slightly misspelled version of a prominent participant's name.

Preparing the test for administration

After you have written a group of items of which you are reasonably proud (it goes without saying that you have discarded several along the way), proceed through the following steps:

Step 1: Submit the items to a willing colleague or two for careful review. A fresh eye may be able to detect errors, mis-keys or ambiguities which you are too close to the items to see.

Step 2: Rewrite or replace defective items. Sometimes an item can be improved by the insertion of just a word or two. However, if the basic idea for an item is faulty, it may take so much time and trouble to correct it that writing a new item will be easier.

Step 3: Arrange the items into a test. The usual arrangement is in terms of your estimates of item difficulty—from easy to hard. Sometimes, however, you may want to arrange the items in groups according to common subject matter or common material on which the items are based. In this case, it may be a good idea to try to arrange the items from easy to hard within groups. If some of your test material is printed and some specially presented (e.g. by recording), you may want to place the items on the special material at the beginning of the test, for administrative convenience.

Step 4: Position the choices for each item, so that the correct answer appears in each position about an equal number of times. Two convenient ways to achieve satisfactory arrangement are random or alphabetical. Alphabetical arrangement involves no more than positioning choices according to the first letters in them, e.g.

The Romantic Age was characterized by
all of the following *except*

Choices as they were written
    A. religious discrimination
    B. the rise of literary magazines
    C. growing interest in the theatre
    D. humanitarian emphasis in literature

Choices arranged alphabetically
    A. growing interest in the theatre
    B. humanitarian emphasis in literature
    C. religious discrimination
    D. the rise of literary magazines

Random arrangement may be accomplished through the use of a table of random numbers or the throwing of a die.

Do not use random arrangement of choices where the choices have a natural order, e.g. numbers, dates, letters.

A movie opened in a theatre on April 6 and was shown every day through April 27. On how many days was it shown?

Confusing	Better
A. 22	A. 20
B. 20	B. 21
C. 23	C. 22
D. 21	D. 23

Step 5: Prepare directions for your test. They should be as straightforward and brief as possible, including information on how the student is to mark his answers, how much time he has, and how his score will be derived.

Sometimes you will need special instructions, in addition to the general directions, to introduce an item or set of items; e.g. 'In question 10-20 choose the name that does not belong with the other three'.

Step 6: Prepare the test booklet for the students' use. The essential ingredients are your item cards (edited and correctly ordered), the directions, a typewriter, a duplicating system, paper and a penchant for accuracy.

In typing a test page, factors to be considered include the use of one or two columns, clear punctuation, typography for emphasis words, spacing and readability of charts. Test material and the items that go with it should appear on the same page, and an item should not be broken in the middle and continued on another page.

Step 7: Prepare your answer sheets. (It may be useful to run off enough answer sheets for several tests.)

Step 8: Prepare a final key for your test by marking the correct answers in red pencil on an answer sheet. Label the sheet 'key', and indicate the test title and date of administration.

Prepare a scoring stencil. Place an 8½ × 11 sheet of stiff, clear plastic over the key, aligning the edges carefully. Take a black china marking pencil and circle (on the plastic) each correct response. Write the name of the test at the top to aid in correct positioning for scoring.

PRESENTATION OF TEST RESULTS TO TEACHERS AND THEIR INTERPRETATION BY TEACHERS

HELPING TEACHERS TO MAKE BETTER USE OF TEST RESULTS

S. S. DUNN

The formulation of the topic for this session—presentation of results and interpretation by teachers—gives the impression that we are concerned with the teacher's use of typical standardized tests which are in such common use in the United States and Canada, but not so commonly used by teachers elsewhere. While I will include this in my discussion, I intend to broaden the topic to the more important one of 'How can a teacher make use of test information, whether from his own or externally prepared tests, to improve the learning of his pupils?'

The teacher's competence to use test information will depend in part on his competence in measurement derived from pre-service and in-service training, and in part from the help he receives from test manuals. However, his willingness to exercise and improve his competence will depend upon additional factors, namely, how important he feels the use of test information is to what he is trying to achieve. What he is trying to achieve can be the improvement of his pupils' learning, or it can be to create a good impression with the head of a school (or in my country, with the inspector, on whose judgment promotion largely depends).

Now if teachers are going to make better use of tests, I think we must tackle the problem not only in terms of competence (a task largely in the cognitive domain), but also in the area of interests and attitudes (a task in the affective domain). The fact that this question has been posed for this international conference presupposes, I think, that we are not satisfied. Is this so?

The greatest efforts at training teachers in competence in educational measurement have undoubtedly been in the United States and Canada. What, then, is the position there? From conversations with leading authorities in the last few years, and from my reading of the literature of such bodies as the National Council on Measurement in Education, I am certain they are not satisfied; and I doubt if the position is very different from 1953 when Traxler, Durost and Lennon (Lennon 1966) all commented on the gap between test specialists and the classroom teacher. Some important changes in approach in the United States, which I will comment on later, may have led to significant improvements.

I have some knowledge of the position in Great Britain, Australia and New Zealand, and I doubt if they would claim any great sophistication on the part of their typical classroom teachers or even their public examination authorities, although in all three countries there have also been interesting developments in recent years. I cannot speak for other countries, but I hope you will accept the proposition that a case has been made out that we are not at present achieving our objective of having all classroom teachers reasonably competent in educational measurement.

Now if we are not achieving our objectives, it may be that our objectives are unrealistic in the circumstances, or that the learning experiences we provide are unsatisfactory.

One of the problems of discussing a topic such as this at an international conference is the vast differences in the pre-service and in-service training systems of the various countries, including differences within the same country for teachers at different levels. Perhaps in discussion we can get some indication of the amount of pre-service training in educational measurement given in various countries to the different groups of teachers. In Australia I doubt if any trainee teacher has twenty hours of formal instruction, although he may have been required to do additional private reading, and may have gained some incidental information from his work in psychology.

If the time for training is limited, it is important that our objectives be carefully thought out so that we concentrate on major ones only and do not, by attempting too much, achieve in fact very little. Each of us will have his priorities. I propose to spend a short time indicating my priorities and my reasons for these.

Lennon (1966, pp. 169-70), in his 1953 address to the Invitational Testing Conference on 'The test manual as a medium of instruction', commented thus on the poor performance of teachers in answering questions on the manual:

> 'It is impossible to suppose that the problem here is one of readability or comprehensibility of the material as presented. One must seek the explanation in the attitude, or set, or motivation, which the user, or in this case the examinee, brings to the task of reading the manual. It is hard to believe that the average teacher, if sufficiently interested, could not locate in a test manual information of the kind called for in the question just cited. Perhaps our real problem is that of discovering why they are not interested and how this interest can be stimulated—which brings us back to the principle earlier stated, that testing and test results take on meaning when the user sees them in relation to his own needs and problems.'

As you will guess from my earlier address to this conference, I feel

Lennon's statement is still true, and that our major task in pre-service training is, in a sense, to create a need for tests by showing our teachers in training that tests can help them to do a better job of teaching—which they see as their prime function.

Our objectives belong to both the cognitive and the affective domains, but what I am suggesting should be a major aim is a shift in the affective domain to the objective listed as Valuing in the *Taxonomy of Educational Objectives, Handbook II—Affective Domain* (Krathwohl et al. 1964). If we achieve this in the short period available for training, then we have some prospect that at a later stage the teacher will read our test manuals with interest, read appropriate literature in his own time, and attend in-service or summer school courses.

A change of attitude will not be achieved by preaching, but by showing that a need exists for certain information that can be obtained by testing and above all by *practising* this in our own courses. The existing attitudes of our students are almost certainly coloured by their own experiences as takers of tests. This common experience and their existing attitudes seems to me to be the logical starting-point if you accept the proposition that the development of appropriate attitudes is important.

What help, as students, have they received from tests? What help did they think their teachers obtained? Can they remember any teacher who seemed to make good use of test results? How did he do it? If they were teaching, what use could they make of tests (a) to help the pupil learn better, and (b) to help themselves teach more effectively? Effective treatment of these questions cannot be achieved in large lecture groups, but only in small group discussion. While the presence of a tutor may be helpful, I do not think it is essential. A group leader could report. It is unlikely that discussion groups will exhaust all the possible uses of tests, but through discussion amongst themselves our teachers in training will begin to see possible uses of testing that they have previously overlooked. At this point formal lectures may structure the uses that can be made of tests. A shift of attitude without the development of competence is insufficient, but attempts to achieve competence without a felt need are not likely to be any more successful.

Time is short, and what we do may be more important than what we say. I would be prepared to settle for some understanding of a few basic concepts, some elementary attempts at question writing, and a minimum of statistics. Training in statistics presents a first-class opportunity to show how a test can help in the organization of learning experiences. Our students are certain to differ widely in prerequisite skills. Therefore a suitable diagnostic test can be used and marked by the students to reveal their own weaknesses and to organize groups who need differential treatment. The possibilities will depend upon the resources available, but we should not overlook the virtues of trainee teachers giving remedial lessons to their fellow trainees.

Skill in item writing will not be achieved by formal lecturing alone, but must be practised by the student. Even if he does not become very competent, the attempt to write items with various objectives in mind will leave him with a better appreciation of the problems of developing good tests. And here I would ask that the virtues of essay questions for individual diagnosis be explored. Oral questioning of a single person is extremely valuable for understanding the peculiar difficulties of that individual and his thought processes. When this is too time consuming a well-constructed essay question may be a useful substitute. In these circumstances the teacher is not concerned with ranking pupils or with the problem of reader reliability, but only with gaining knowledge about the difficulties of individual pupils. There is a place for diagnostic objective tests too, but these often give information about product and not process.

Assuming that the course is a short one, the most basic concept is the problem of drawing inferences from a sample. We are drawing upon the student's experience when we show him how any test samples in a content dimension. It is not difficult to make him aware that one can sample in other dimensions, the most important of which is objectives. The importance of some simple classification of objectives and their relation to teaching as well as testing can readily be understood by trainee teachers. This would seem to be the place to discuss immediate and ultimate objectives, and their relation to the tests we use. The trainee could also note the possibilities of different methods of presentation (written, oral, pictorial, demonstration) and different forms of answering (oral, written, diagrammatic, behavioural), and also the effects of sampling at different times and of sampling markers if the questions are not capable of objective scoring. Repeatedly we can go back to his own experience as a taker of tests. If our trainee teacher appreciates this problem of drawing inferences from samples, he is less likely to make a fool of himself than the teacher who can compute reliability coefficients and standard errors, and still does not understand why he is doing it. Depending on the time available, one can deal more formally with the concepts of reliability and content validity, using the ideas already developed.

Item discrimination techniques are better left alone than taught badly, and to imply to a teacher that every item should discriminate in accordance with a total test score is misleading and reflects an administrator's and not a classroom teacher's approach to testing. Every subject has content that the teacher wishes every pupil to master, and he is perfectly justified in including in his tests questions to check mastery, and even feeling a little excited if these turn out to have zero difficulty and therefore no discrimination. If a discrimination index is to be computed for these questions, it should be based on a before-teaching, after-teaching difference in difficulty.

The amount of information needed on standardized tests will naturally differ from country to country, depending on the use made of such tests in each country. In any case, the use made of such tests is likely to reflect itself in the time available for educational measurement in the teacher education programme. However, if the classroom teacher is to understand the idea of norms, we can again make use of his experience of how relative performance differs when compared with different reference groups, and to the problems which arise because of difficulties in sampling adequately from the reference groups which most concern him.

It is not my purpose here to map out a course in detail, but rather to outline an approach to the organization of learning experiences in educational measurement for trainee teachers which I believe could lead to their 'valuing' educational measurement as a most important tool in their teaching armoury. Textbooks reflect the value system and needs of their country of origin. Changes have been occurring in the American texts, and more attention is being given to the problems of the classroom teacher. However, in terms of the aims I have enumerated, they are in general too concerned with measurement *per se* and with the needs of the headmaster and administrator, and too little concerned with the needs of the classroom teacher.

However, until the teacher has been in the school and face to face with the problems of constructing tests to meet his own needs, one may think of him as being motivated by anticipation rather than reality. I suspect that in the teacher's first year or so he is tremendously concerned with the task of organizing his lessons, and only when he begins to feel confident in this role will he begin to become more concerned with his measurement problems. In any case, after a short period in the classroom the conscientious teacher will be aware of deficiencies in his competence in educational measurement.

The importance of summer schools, of in-service training and of instructional material cannot therefore be overrated. ETS has made an important contribution in this field with its little booklet *Making the Classroom Test* and with its workshop materials including strip films and records, and you have heard Dr Scarvia Anderson, who had a lot to do with the workshop materials, comment to this conference on their use in the United States. I have some reservations about the content, but nothing but praise for the idea. England has recently entered the field with *Examination Bulletins* of the Secondary Schools Examination Council (1963-5) and the Schools Council (1965-7). These have been written with the practising teacher in mind, but their emphasis is more towards formal examinations than the diagnostic and teaching use I have stressed as the prime concern of the classroom teacher. I am sure anybody who has taught measurement to practising teachers cannot help but be impressed with their interest in the topic.

I do not know the position in other countries, but some of the most useful in-service training in Australia is beginning to emerge from the subject associations, and I think there have been signs of this in the United States. Measurement specialists and subject associations working together and exploiting various media such as pamphlets, strip and loop film, television, etc., can make a most significant contribution to the practising teacher's ability to develop his own tests, select agency tests more wisely, and interpret his results more intelligently.

Where the system is large enough, then in-service training and special assistance can be provided. I imagine that the work of Wayne Wrightstone and his department in the New York system has had a most significant impact on that system.

To date what I have been saying is fundamentally that the first task of those interested in educational measurement is to help the classroom teacher to help himself. Nevertheless, no matter how competent he becomes in developing good classroom tests, he can still be helped by external agencies which have greater resources and specialist competence. Testing agencies will help teachers make better use of test results when they provide them with better tests of the kind they need but cannot hope to build themselves.

What kinds of tests can agencies most usefully provide?

The most important of these for the future will be tests that are developed as an integral part of major curriculum projects. A curriculum project known all over the world is the PSSC physics course. An integral part of this project was the diagnostic tests. Along with the modified programme for use in Victoria as a two-year course, Australian Council for Educational Research developed a special variation of the diagnostic tests. Integrated with the diagnosis, which the pupil could carry out himself under the teacher's guidance, were

Helping teachers to make better use of results

learning cards which directed him, in the light of his mistakes, to appropriate learning material. We are now, through a workshop convened at Monash University, in the process of adding to these tests a pre-PSSC diagnostic test, aimed at showing whether or not pupils beginning a PSSC course have the necessary foundation concepts. Here, too, we hope to link diagnosis with appropriate remedial ideas. If we help the teacher diagnose, we must also help him to treat.

I can use another example from Australian experience to illustrate further this idea. We have developed a kit of programmed material for elementary mathematics, basically for grades 3 and 4 (ages 8 and 9), which permits individual progress but has regular tests built into it to check mastery as the pupils progress and to direct remedial learning. The idea is not novel, but I am sure we are going to see it exploited more in the future. These kinds of tests, which are an integral part of the programme, can be very useful to the classroom teacher who is using that particular programme in whole or in part. And, above all, these tests do not demand a great deal of sophistication on the part of the teacher to understand and use them effectively.

Agencies are in a better position than a teacher to develop more sophisticated diagnostic tests. Of course, we have many useful tests now, but I am sure that with changes in curriculum and, more particularly, in objectives, and with subjects placing more emphasis on the 'structure' of the subject and on the importance of the kind of learning experience of the child, we will find a need for new kinds of diagnostic tests.

A friend of mine in New Guinea has been busy using a group form of Piaget-type tests to check on pupils' understanding of concepts of conservation. In their final year at secondary school quite a few are still having difficulties.

The work of Gagne (1965) has given us new ideas for developing diagnostic tests in mathematics which will focus on the point of breakdown in any process. This has applications in other subjects and also offers a better basis for curriculum development.

Again the great virtue of diagnostic tests for use by the classroom teacher is that, in general, it is not difficult for the teacher to understand what the test developer had in mind or to interpret the results.

Test batteries to meet the needs of a particular system are not likely to be developed by individual teachers. Where a system is reasonably large, it is possible for testing agencies to develop a testing programme in co-operation with the system. The tests chosen for the battery and the presentation of results can be closely integrated with the existing competence of teachers, in-service courses, and the development of special manuals. One of the best-known examples of this approach is the Iowa Test of Basic Skills and the Iowa Test of Educational Development. No teacher could produce such a battery himself. The testing programme is supported by first-class reporting to both teachers and pupils, and normed in such a manner as to give ideas of growth. In Australia, though teachers are less test sophisticated and funds are more limited, the Australian Council for Educational Research in conjunction with the New South Wales Education Department, has attempted to do something similar. Since the NSW Basic Skills Testing Programme is a voluntary programme which has expanded since its inception, one can only assume that teachers are finding it helpful. Here an attempt had to be made to use the manual to convey concepts which in Iowa could probably be assumed to be known by teachers.

In the United States and Canada publishers of standardized achievement batteries have done a great deal to improve their manuals and their advisory services. In other English-speaking countries, special semi-official bodies such as the National Foundation for Educational Research in England and Wales, the Australian Council for Educational Research, and the New Zealand Council for Educational Research have been trying to develop improved tests and better means of communicating with teachers. One extremely difficult problem is to provide adequate and up-to-date norms of a kind that are meaningful to the teacher. Does the classroom teacher really want national norms? How does he interpret the results of batteries from two publishers whose 'national norms' are not strictly comparable? Maybe he is entitled to be confused. Think of all the confusion which arises over the interpretation of I.Q.s derived on different bases and normed on different samples. Systems which develop local norms for these achievement batteries may get a lot more value from their testing than those who rely solely on published norms. Also systematic use will pay greater dividends than casual use. In this sense the local system is converting a publisher's set of tests into a system battery without the benefits of full consultation. It may be cheaper, but in general is less satisfactory. I understand that the use of basic batteries with modifications for local systems is growing in the United States.

In summary, then, if we want teachers to make better use of test results, we must train them in such a way that they see test information as valuable to them. Unless they feel a need, they will not be interested. Both pre-service and in-service training are essential.

Improved diagnostic tests and tests integrated with curriculum projects will appeal to classroom teachers.

Batteries of achievement tests worked out in conjunction with a school system are more likely to be useful, and can be better serviced than standardized tests normed on a national basis.

References

Gagne, R. (1965) *Conditions of Learning.* New York: Holt, Rinehart and Winston.

Krathwohl, D. R., Bloom, B. S. and Masia, B. B. (1964) *Taxonomy of Educational Objectives: Handbook II, The Affective Domain.* New York and London: Longmans.

Lennon, R. T. (1966) 'The test manual as a medium of communication.' In Anastasi, A. (ed.) *Testing Problems in Perspective.* Washington, D.C.: American Council on Education.

Schools Council (1965-7) *Examination Bulletins,* nos 5-17. London: H.M. Stationery Office.

Secondary Schools Examinations Council (1963-5) *Examination Bulletins,* nos 1-4. London: H.M. Stationery Office.

THE APPLICATION OF TEST RESULTS BY TEACHERS TO IMPROVE INSTRUCTION

M. J. WANTMAN

At the start, I would like to make two points:
1. When I refer to 'tests' in this paper, I mean to include all types of tests, including essay examinations.
2. I am aware that I may be accused of 'lowering standards' by what I shall advocate here, but I would maintain that in the long run following my recommendations will result in 'raising standards'.

In order to improve their instruction and their students' learning, teachers must understand the basic principles and purposes of testing, just as they must be knowledgeable about children's development and principles of learning in addition to being competent in the subject matter field they teach. Nevertheless, it is not necessary that teachers master the statistical techniques of testing: i.e. they do not have to be able to deal with test data in the way the measurement expert does. Such things as biserial rs, sampling for norms, and standard error formulae are not necessary for a teacher's proper understanding of principles of testing.

There are a number of areas of measurement in which the teachers must be competent. The concept of reliability should be understood, in that the teacher should be aware of the sources of unreliability. Validity should be familiar to teachers so that they understand the nature of the criterion which is being used for determining whether or not the test is useful for a purpose: in order to do this, teachers should know what the different purposes of a test may be, e.g. ranking, motivation, encouragement, evaluation, guidance, etc. They should know how to use norms, how to perform an item analysis in a teacher's practical way, and how to construct informal classroom tests.

In general, one finds that teachers now in the schools do not show these competencies in testing, and I am not confident we are training teachers any better today than we trained the previous generation of teachers. Even in the elementary courses in teachers' training colleges and in universities, we have tended to discourage the prospective teacher from learning the concepts we want him to learn, because we have persisted in trying to teach him the theory and principles of testing in the ways in which we are accustomed to think about them. We use such terms as biserial r, random sampling, parameter, standard error, regression, etc., with the formulae which accompany these terms. With the resistance of the bulk of our prospective teachers to statistical concepts and operations, we often end up with their missing the very concepts of which we are trying to teach an understanding. It would be better, perhaps, to deviate from rigorous statistical procedure and interpretation, and allow teachers to use 'rule of thumb' techniques which have a chance of being functional rather than to insist on the techniques we as testing people would be expected to apply. For example, in my attempts over the years to teach at a university the concept of a standard deviation and a standard error, I have found that the use of the Σ sign, the use of the word 'standard', the use of the letter σ for standard deviation and for standard error have led to confusion, frustration and resignation. When speaking to teachers at one-day institutes and workshops, because I have not had enough time to teach the statistical formulae and the use of the mathematical terms, I seem to get better understanding when I substitute the word 'average' for 'standard'; when I use neither symbols nor formulae; and when I discuss verbally the sources of errors in testing, the possible causes of difference in performance on a test of different individuals, and the implications of such differences. Without using statistics, I have discussed with teachers other concepts which are important for them to understand, such as school norms versus individual norms, standard error of the difference between two scores as opposed to the error of an individual score, the phenomenon of regression for a given student when his total I.Q. score *for a test of intelligence is at a more extreme percentile rank than both the percentile rank for his verbal I.Q. score and the percentile rank for his quantitative I.Q. score based on the same test.

All these concepts can be taught without resorting to statistical formulae and symbols, to which teachers show an avoidance reaction. To be sure, it usually takes longer to explain these things without formulae and abbreviated symbols. The formulae for Pearson product-moment correlation and the linear regression equations are most useful when one wants to teach about regression and prediction, but is it not worth the extra time and effort, sometimes seemingly awkward, to teach these concepts without formulae so that the teacher will stay with us and attempt to understand our message?

In the time allotted to me I want to attempt to discuss four specific procedures in testing; there are many more which can be taught to

---

* The need for attaching the word 'score' to I.Q. to remind the teacher of the similarity of the limitations of the I.Q. number to those of a test score is not widely acknowledged even today, although this usage was impressed upon me over thirty years ago by Professor P. J. Rulon of Harvard University.

teachers and which do not require any use of mathematics beyond primary school arithmetic. The four are:
1. Using confidence bands when interpreting scores.
2. Combining measures for obtaining a composite or aggregate.
3. Assigning letter grades from the results of an objective-type test.
4. Using item analysis data for diagnosing pupils' learning deficiences.

1. Confidence bands

After adequate *verbal* discussion of the concepts of reliability, errors of measurement, true score and confidence bands, teachers may be permitted to use the values of the standard error of measurement for the objective tests they construct as given in the following table:*

Table 1

Number of questions in the test	Standard error of a score
< 24	2
24- 47	3
48- 89	4
90-109	5
110- 29	6
130- 50	7

Thus, if a teacher builds a test with 115 questions, he assumes from the table that the standard error of a score on his test is 6. Then if a student, Karl, earns a score of 83, the teacher can be taught to write the confidence intervals as follows:

83 ± 6 68 per cent confidence band for Karl is 77-89.
$83 \pm 2(6)$ 95 per cent confidence band for Karl is 71-95.
$83 \pm 2 \cdot 5(6)$ 99 per cent confidence band for Karl is 68-98.

Even though the teacher is allowed here to obtain the fiducial limits in such a way that he may confuse the percentages above with probability figures, nevertheless little harm will result so long as he is alerted to the

* Diederich, P. B. (1964) *Short-cut Statistics for Teacher-made Tests* (2nd edition). Evaluation and Advisory Service Series no. 5. Princeton, N. J.: Educational Testing Service, p. 16.
 This booklet, while it presents some simple statistical computations and formulae, has proved invaluable to thousands of teachers because it contains 'rule of thumb' techniques. See also Lord, F. M. (1959) 'Tests of the same length do have the same standard error of measurement.' *Educ. psychol. Measur.*, **19**, 2, 233-9.

The application of test results by teachers

limitation of the conclusion that can be drawn from a single test score. Similarly, the use of 2 σ_e instead of 1·96 σ_e, and 2·6 σ_e instead of 2·58 σ_e can be justified in the practical application which the teacher is making here if it results in his determining the confidence bands, whereas he might not have obtained them at all if he had been required to use the more exact figures.

2. Combining measures to obtain a composite or aggregate in order to rank pupils

I am confident that we would all be in agreement that the scores obtained on a single test built by a classroom teacher have errors of measurement which are much too large to allow any important educational decision to be based on them. It is for this reason that we depend more on the composites or aggregates which a teacher obtains from a number of measures which he records for a student over a period of time. Teachers must be taught that weighting the various measures to obtain the composite is necessary if the various measures are not to 'weight themselves'. Table 2 illustrates a simple worksheet for doing this. The weights for C_1 are all unity with Quentin's composite, viz. 27, already recorded as is the rank on composite 1 (C_1) for Samuel, viz. 1·5. (A method for assigning ranks to pupils who are tied also becomes apparent to the teachers from this illustration.) The teacher is then asked to use the weights for composite 2 (C_2), where all the weights are again unity except for test II, which is assigned a weight of zero, i.e. it is ignored. The composite using these weights has already been recorded for Peter, as has the rank for Quentin. A comparison by the teacher of the R_1 and the R_2 ranks should make the point to him that the scores on test II, because they have no variability, have no effect on the ranking of the pupils, irrespective of what weight is given to these scores.

The weights for C_3 are applied next, and the composites are again ranked. In order to attempt to give 'equal weight' to the four measures, the weights for C_3 were chosen inversely proportional to the values of the 'range' for each measure. The 'range' is taught here simply as the *highest integral score* minus the *lowest integral score,* disregarding the actual limits of a score, and this 'range' is taken as the measure of variability rather than requiring the teacher to go to the trouble of computing standard deviations. Also, only integral values are used for the weights, so that they are not exactly inversely proportional to the values of the range. After the teachers have obtained the ranks, R_3, which are shown on p. 389, they see at once that the weighting

Table 2. Weighting results to rank pupils on a composite

Name of pupil	Test I X_I	Test II X_{II}	Test III X_{III}	Homework X_{IV}	Rank C_1 R_1	Rank C_2 R_2	Rank C_3 R_3	Rank C_4 R_4
Peter	2	9	6	8		16		
Quentin	4	9	6	8	27	3·5		
Robert	5	9	5	8			77	72
Samuel	8	9	6	10	1·5			87
Thomas	10	9	5	9				78

C(omposite) = $W_1 X_1 + W_2 X_2 + W_3 X_3 + W_4 X_4$

C_1 = (1) X_I + (1) X_{II} + (1) X_{III} + (1) X_{IV}

C_2 = (1) X_I + (0) X_{II} + (1) X_{III} + (1) X_{IV}

C_3 = (1) X_I + (0) X_{II} + (8) X_{III} + (4) X_{IV}

C_4 = (1) X_I + (1) X_{II} + (10) X_{III} + (1) X_{IV}

	R_2	R_3
Peter	5	4
Quentin	3·5	3
Robert	3·5	5
Samuel	1·5	1
Thomas	1·5	2

procedure has resulted in shifts in the ranks.

Finally, the weights for C_4 are applied. Here a discussion of the choice of weights and the resulting ranks of the pupils may bring out a number of points of which the following are illustrative:

a) There may be morale problems with the students if test II is ignored, so that it can be included without any harm done.
b) A test such as test III may be given a greater weight than called for in C_3 because it is a more cumulative measure than the previous two tests, and thus one is justified in increasing its weight.
c) Homework may not reflect completely independent work by the pupil, so that less weight may be given to it.
d) The ranks from composite 4 (C_4) are not the same as for any of the other procedures; subjective judgment was allowed to enter into the choice of weights.

Further discussion can now take place on the relative magnitude of the composites for each of the four schemes. Thus, even though composite 4 yields numbers which resemble marks which teachers—at least in the United States—are more accustomed to assign to pupils, this does not mean the marks are necessarily the 'best'. The other composites can easily be adjusted up or down to yield any final marks the teacher prefers without upsetting the rankings of the pupils. The scale used, be it 1-20 or 40-55 as in some countries, does not limit the application of the scheme above.

3. Assigning letter grades from an objective-type test

Teachers feel comfortable about assigning letter grades to students on the basis of performance on oral examinations and essay-type tests. They are not at all sure of themselves about assigning such marks on the basis of objective-type test results. Often they will resort to using 100 questions in the test so that the number of correct answers is automatically the traditional percentage, or they will compute the percentage as $\left(\dfrac{\text{Number correct}}{\text{Number of questions}}\right)100$

or they will assign marks on the basis of the normal distribution. The inherent defects in the 'percentage scheme' need no discussion for this audience, but a word might be in order about marking on the basis of the normal curve because some textbooks in measurement urge that some such scheme be used. It should be made clear that there is no unique way to assign marks 'on the curve' There are an infinite number of ways in which the distribution of scores may be cut. There is no mathematical basis on which to justify giving, say, an equal number of *excellent* marks and *failure* marks. There is less and less justification for a fixed percentage of failures as one goes up in the educational ladder, and as one deals more and more with a select student body. The teacher's subjective judgment which is omnipresent when assigning marks in essay-type testing is still with us when assigning marks from objective test results, and the use of so many sigmas above the *mean* for an *excellent* grade and so many sigmas *below* the mean for a *failure* grade is arbitrary and may be completely unjustified in a particular situation.

Just as a teacher subjectively decides on the quality of performance on an essay-type test required for a particular letter grade, he similarly must exercise this judgment for an objective-type test. The objective-type test, on the other hand, allows the teacher to be more systematic in the exercise of this judgment if he uses the scheme I am about to describe.

Let us suppose that the teacher has constructed an objective-type test which has 105 questions in it. Ideally, these questions would be ones with which he has had some experience with his previous students. If not, he will have to judge the questions as to difficulty (the usual definition of difficulty is used here, viz. per cent correct). Because he wants to be able to rank his students reliably, the bulk of the questions will be in the 30 per cent to 70 per cent range with a large number around 50 per cent difficulty. A workable classification of questions by difficulty is as follows:

Difficulty	*Per cent right*
Very easy	90
Easy	70
Moderate	50
Difficult	30
Very difficult	10

The application of test results by teachers

We shall assume that we intend to assign letter grades to the students to be tested on a five-point scale, viz. excellent–A, credit–B, pass–C, marginal pass–D, failure–E. Once the difficulty of each of the 105 questions is known or determined by teachers' judgment for all the students similar in training and background to those who are about to be tested with this instrument, the difficulty of each question should be judged for the lowest student in each of the four groups of students who are to receive the letter grades. Thus, each question will have four estimates of difficulty in addition to the known or estimated difficulty for all students.

After each question has been judged for difficulty for the *lowest* student in each of the A, B, C, D groups, four frequency distributions can be made which can be combined into a table such as table 3.

Table 3

		Number of questions			
Estimated difficulty		*A group*	*B group*	*C group*	*D group*
Very easy	90%	70	30	8	2
Easy	70%	20	20	25	10
Moderate	50%	10	45	55	19
Difficult	30%	5	10	13	59
Very difficult	10%			4	15
	Total	105	105	105	105

We then compute a 'tentative' cut-off score for an A student, as:

$$70 \times 0.90 + 20 \times 0.70 + 10 \times 0.50 + 5 \times 0.30 = 83.5 \text{ or } 84$$

Similar computations are made for the other groups, yielding the tentative letter grade scheme shown in table 4.

Table 4. Tentative grade scheme

Scores	Grade
84 and above	A
67–83	B
57–66	C
38–56	D
37 and below	E

The teacher administers the 105-question test and obtains the results as follows, where each X designates a student.

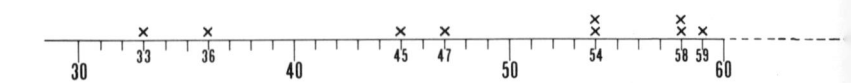

```
           x    x            x   x       x        x
                                         x        x x
────┬──┬──┬──┬──┬──┬──┬──┬──┬──┬──┬──┬──┬──┬──┬──┬──┬── ─ ─ ─ ─
    │  33 36                 45  47      54       58 59
    30          40                50              60
```

We next mark on the scale above the vertical cut-off points for the five grades as they were tentatively chosen in the scheme in table 4. We see at once that two students who received scores of 83 would be given Bs by the tentative scheme, while the student who received the score of 84 would be given an A. Because of the unreliability of the scores, it is not defensible to give different letter grades to these three students. On the other hand, the student who ranks next below the students who earned the score of 83 has a score of 80—three points fewer. Therefore, we move the cut-off point for an A grade down to 83 instead of maintaining it at 84. The lowest score for the B grade is reasonable, because there is a big gap between the students who got 65 and the ones who got 73. The tentative cut-off for the C grade is 57, but we note that two students obtained scores of 54 and the next student is as low as 47. Rather than give these three students the same grade, we move the cut-off for C down to 54. An inspection of the division point for the D and E grades reveals that there is a large gap between the students, so that we retain the original cut-off. As a

Table 5. Final grade scheme

Scores	Grade
83 and above	A
67-82	B
54-66	C
38-53	D
37 and below	E

consequence of the decisions above, the final grade scheme is as shown in table 5.

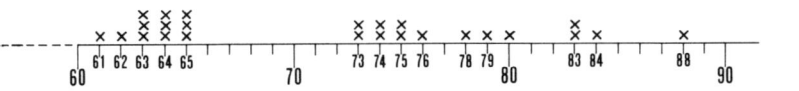

```
                  x x x                    x x x
            x x   x x x           x x x x  x x x x      x x       x
         ┼──┬─┬─┬─┬─┬──┬──┬──┬──┬──┬─┬─┬─┬──┬─┬─┬──┬──┬─┬──┬──┬──┬──┼
           61 62 63 64 65                 73 74 75 76  78 79      83 84         88
          60                    70                        80                       90
```

It should be noted that teacher-made classroom tests in general do not approach in length the 105 questions assumed here. Many 'classroom' tests have as few as ten questions in them. The need for bearing in mind the error of a score and for seeking gaps in the distribution where cut-offs may be made should therefore be impressed on teachers.

The teacher might still want to consider the scheme in table 5 as almost final. If the grade scheme in table 5 yields what he considers an unusual or abnormal distribution of letter grades on the basis of his experience with previous classes, he might compare the actual question difficulties for these thirty-five students with the known or estimated question difficulty before the test was administered. If there are great discrepancies, a re-appraisal of his judgment of the difficulties for the four letter-grade groups would be in order, and a new table of cut-off scores obtained.

The procedure above may on first examination seem unduly complicated, but I can testify that I have found it practical and straightforward in testing my university classes over the years. Other teachers who have been exposed to it have not shrunk in horror from it.

Incidentally, a similar procedure can be used for assigning letter grades to a composite where the individual measures making up the composite can be treated as if they were questions. The lowest possible score is subjectively decided on for each measure for each letter-grade group, and the weights chosen in accordance with what the teacher learned in section B above. A tentative grade scheme can thus be worked out for the composites.

4. Use of item analysis for diagnosing learning difficulties

Other speakers have already discussed the steps to be followed in test construction and the techniques of item analysis. When making the classroom test, the teacher should follow many of the same procedures, even though he cannot always use the techniques in their most refined way. If he builds his test in accordance with a table of specifications and has accumulated experience with the questions on classes in previous years, he can devise for himself a chart such as that illustrated in table 6. The classification schemes and categories used here are taken from the Social Studies test of the Sequential Tests of Educational Progress of the Cooperative Test Division, Educational Testing Service. The classification of each question is indicated by the dots appearing in its row under the different column headings. A given question may be classified under more than one column for a classification, as is the case for questions 1, 2 and 3 under Skill. The teacher determines the difficulty of each question from his class *and then looks for discrepancies between the results for this class as opposed to classes in previous years. Clusters of discrepancies under any column will lead the teacher to re-teach these skills, understandings, materials or subject matter areas. A discrepancy under a column for a single item would not necessarily be a signal for more instruction in that classification category, but a group of such discrepancies would call for action. If the test is not a secure test and there is no particular reason for not discussing the questions, the very questions can be used for instructional purposes. Similarly, the distractors in a question often serve as a basis for further instruction. Other uses which can be made of the questions on a test to improve learning are described in the *Teacher's Guide* of the Sequential Tests of Educational Progress.

Summary

1. In order to improve instruction by teachers and learning by students, teacher training in testing needs to be improved and in-service training of teachers is necessary.
2. Teachers should be taught the different values which may be derived from a testing programme.
3. We should not burden teachers with statistical and technical procedures.
4. Many of the good practices and sound principles of testing can be taught to teachers whose inclination and/or ability towards mathematical procedures and language is not favourable. These practices and principles may be taught by verbal explanation and by 'rule of thumb' techniques.

* *Teacher's Guide*, Cooperative Sequential Tests of Educational Progress (1959). Princeton, N. J.: Cooperative Test Division, Educational Testing Service.

Table 6. Evaluating pupils' success*

Question number	Correct answer	% correct in previous years	% correct in this class	Identify generalizations	Identify values	Distinguish fact, opinion	Compare data	Draw conclusions	Social change	Geographic environment	Forces of nature	Democratic society	Society behaviour	Economic wants	Interdependence	Map	Graph	Cartoon	Diagram	Text	American history	Geography	Social anthropology	Government	Economics	World history	Quest. no.
1	1	80					•	•	•												•		•					1
2	5	71		•			•	•	•												•		•					2
3	4	84		•			•	•	•												•		•					3
4	5	77		•				•	•												•		•					4
5	4	57		•				•	•				•								•		•					5
6	5	81		•				•	•												•		•					6
7	4	78		•					•			•									•				•			7
8	1	84		•								•									•				•			8
9	1	86		•								•		•							•							9
10	5	79		•							•			•			•				•		•					10
11	3	36		•			•				•						•				•		•					11
12	1	84		•			•				•						•				•		•					12
13	3	57					•	•			•						•						•					13
14	3	68		•							•						•						•					14
15	2	64		•				•			•						•						•					15

*Adapted from *Teacher's Guide*, Cooperative Sequential Tests of Educational Progress.

5. I have cited only four specific examples where this may be done:
   a) Using confidence bands when interpreting scores.
   b) Combining measures for obtaining a composite or aggregate to rank pupils.
   c) Assigning letter grades from the results of an objective-type test.
   d) Using item analysis data for diagnosing pupils' learning deficiencies.

PRESENTATION OF TEST RESULTS TO TEACHERS IN ENGLAND, AND THEIR INTERPRETATION WITH SPECIAL REFERENCE TO RANKING AND GRADING PROBLEMS IN THAT COUNTRY

DAISY M. PENFOLD

Up to the present, objective tests have been used mainly in primary schools, rarely in secondary schools in Great Britain. This has tended to have a 'back-wash' effect on the syllabus content of secondary school teacher training. The period available for initial professional training of graduates is only one year, and does not allow time to give a full course on the principles and practice of educational measurement. Nevertheless, both primary and secondary teachers have, since 1944, been obliged to accept the consequences of at least one large-scale operation involving measurement, namely the 11-plus selection procedure. Currently, the proposed adoption of scientific methods of examining in the secondary school leaving examinations underlines the necessity for the inclusion of some knowledge of the principles of these methods in the initial training course.

The majority of graduates who present themselves for training have little statistical background. It is possible that in ten years' time the inclusion of statistics in many of the new subject syllabuses—for example, Nuffield Science, School Mathematics Project—in schools, will effect a considerable change in this position. At present, however, we use the two or three hours' lecturing time available to give a summary of the terms which are necessary to understand the reported research evidence which bears on the use of tests in the educational system. Mention is made of scale types—for example, nominal, ordinal, interval and ratio scales—and the relation of percentiles and means and standard deviations to these concepts as they concern test scores is considered. Correlation coefficients and regression lines are referred to in relation to scatter charts only; no actual calculations can be undertaken. Since there is, however, considerable encouragement for follow-up work to be undertaken in the courses offered in a number of diplomas for practising teachers, the work to be reviewed in this paper will not be entirely restricted to that normally discussed in the initial course only. Once the initial statistical hurdle is overcome, there is scope for the introduction of the wealth of British evidence on the subject of testing with which we have to buttress every point in order to satisfy the inquiring, intelligent young people with whom we have to deal.

Though there are signs that what Cattell (1944) has termed

'ipsative' use of testing (i.e. testing for the purpose of comparing performances of the same individual in different test situations) may henceforward be of interest in the United Kingdom, at present a 'normative' interpretation is more common (i.e. comparing different individuals on one test). However, either usage of test results, corresponding roughly to guidance or selection, depends for its precision on the degree to which test scores are error free. Sources of error of interpretation, other than intrinsic unreliability of an examination mark, include effects of age, practice and guessing.

The classic studies of Hartog and Rhodes (1935), which highlighted the inconsistencies of examiners in marking public, essay-type examinations for sixteen-year-old pupils, were followed in the 1940s and 1950s by many investigations reported at length in the *British Journal of Educational Psychology* concerning the marking of English essays (e.g. Cast 1939, 1940, Nisbet 1955). In an effort to justify the retention of 'composition' in the 11-plus examination, analytic marking schemes have been considered. While Burt (1917) suggested consistency of marking for 'the power of logical coherent thought', little agreement was found on 'creativity' displayed in short compositions. Indeed, Finlayson (1951) showed high 'within individual' variability between topics. Correlation between marks allocated to the same set of essays by different examiners, and analysis of variance, have been used to demonstrate these facts. It has been claimed that the worst inconsistencies, namely, differing mean standards revealed by the latter method, may be corrected by statistical adjustments. Hence Wiseman (1949) advocated using total marks of teams of three examiners, justifying this by demonstrating correlations between examiners of the order of 0·8. He recommended rapid, impressionistic marking, rather than analytic. Penfold (1956), on the other hand, showed errors of impressionistic marking to be high; however, there is promising, unpublished evidence that variations between examiners in this type of marking may, by factor analysis, reveal dispositional typologies, and that marking by teams heterogeneous in examiner types might be more consistent, team for team. The case for the retention of the composition has rested on ensuring that practice in continuous writing does not disappear in primary school routine, and on some evidence—for example, Peel and Armstrong (1956)—that it has predictive validity for the secondary school course. The case against the essay-type public examination for school leavers was again argued quite recently in an excellent operational study by Lindley (1961).

Though the 11-plus examination has, to a large extent, died a natural death from other causes, it might be expected that this evidence would affect the thinking of teachers in relation to other forms of examining, in particular, the new Certificate of Secondary Education. However, it will be seen that, throughout the discussions on the standards to be adopted in this, it is assumed that teachers are not prepared to give up the essay-type examination, if it is in their view appropriate for assessing special syllabuses, even though multiple marking, moderating tests, and so on, may be required to ensure reasonable marking consistency. This may, in part, be due to their lack of comprehension of the statistical evidence against the essay-type test. Analysis of variance, factor analysis, often only begin to be understood by students for higher degrees, who are motivated to learn the methodology for research purposes and are prepared to involve themselves in the calculations. Yet it is not obvious that their purpose—namely, to study the significance of differences between means and to explain systems of intercorrelations respectively—is incomprehensible. Possibly the evidence on the other side of the coin on the effects of practice on test results, and the lack of control over the factor of guesswork, swings the balance away from a readier acceptance of objective forms of testing.

The effect of practice and coaching on 11-plus test results has been fairly thoroughly investigated. A series of experiments by Navathe, cited by Watts et al. (1952), suggested that practice in verbal reasoning tests can yield a maximum gain of about ten points of standardized score, this gain occurring in the 'border-zone' region containing the 'cut-off' selection point, but depending on the degree of sophistication of the testees. Coaching, in periods ranging from about one to four hours, resulted in gains of up to sixteen points. Practice in directions, analogies and number series yielded greater gains than were exhibited in synonyms or vocabulary, opposites and information, and, on the whole, the effects of practice were more lasting than those of coaching. Though Watts (op. cit.) criticizes these findings, especially those concerning coaching, on the grounds of the biased nature of the Navathe sample, the results of the larger experiment conducted by the National Foundation for Educational Research, which he also reports, on the whole confirm them; the NFER's results suggest, too, that optimum gains are obtained with about three hours' practice or coaching, practice showing maximum advantage, and also that coaching tended to favour boys, as compared with girls, and more able, rather than less able pupils. However, the findings of these, and other, experiments also reviewed by Watts, are not entirely consistent, though they offer some guidance to teachers and administrators who are anxious to do justice to their pupils by giving them the necessary amount of coaching and practice.

Since 11-plus tests have, in many areas, been scored by teacher markers, it has been possible to incorporate 'open-ended' items as well as multiple-choice. Thus the problem of correcting for guessing has not arisen in practice; in theory, however, the probability argument on which the formula $R-W/n-1$ is based is obviously not fully understood by teachers. Gupta and Penfold (1961) suggest that the results of seventy-five pupils, aged 16, in a true-false science test support the use of the correction $R-0.5W$ rather than $R-W$. Their argument is based on evidence that questions are wrongly answered in some cases because of wrong information, which should not be penalized. The statistical information was obtained by including in a long test certain items which were paired, being identical in content but true in one form and false in the other. This technique is recommended to teachers who are concerned about the guessing problem, though it is not claimed that the results of the particular experiment reported have generality. 'The deductions were made from frequency tables showing the incidence of consistent and inconsistent responses on the pairs of items. For example, a discussion of the 2 × 2 tables below,

Table 1
True items

		R	W	Total
False items	R	2,500	500	3,000
	W	500	1,500	2,000
	Total	3,000	2,000	5,000

Table 2
True items

		R	W	Total
False items	R	3,500	500	4,000
	W	500	500	1,000
	Total	4,000	1,000	5,000

summarizing fictitious results of 100 testees on two tests incorporating fifty pairs of items, helps to show that the symmetry of the inconsistent replies suggests that random guessing has taken place in both cases. Table 2 shows a frequency in the *WW* category equal to those in the

RW, WR categories, demonstrating that there is no wrong information, and that 3,000, or *R−W,* answers correct through right information should be scored. Table 1, if obtained in practice, would suggest that only 500 of the *WW* frequency should be adjudged to have occurred through guesswork, and that the correction formula should be 3,000 (500 + 500) on this type of item when used singly in a non-experimental test, corresponding to the formula $R-0.5W$. This also brings out the point that any correction may do injustice to individuals.

When a test is used to rank all children aged between, say, 10:6 and 11:5 on the date of the examination, the question of age advantage becomes important. As early as 1932, Thomson, the founder of the Moray House organization, pointed out that the arithmetic means of test results for monthly age groups over a year showed a reasonably consistent linear upward trend, which might be extrapolated over a second year. Whether a similar trend could also be observed at higher ability levels, say, the mean plus two or three standard deviations, however, depended on the 'headroom' offered by the particular test. After this, 'age allowances' based on the slopes of the regression lines at the various levels concerned, have been treated as an essential correction to 11-plus test scores, in the form of a bonus to the younger pupils. If, for example, a line is to be fitted to monthly means $m_0, m_1, \ldots, m_r, \ldots, m_{11}$ the formula for the slope of the regression line is

$$b = \frac{\sum_{k=0}^{k=5} (m_{11-2k} - m_{2k})(11 - 2k)}{\sum_{k=0}^{k=5} (11 - 2k)^2}$$

For purposes of ranking pupils on a basis of a single test score, or the total score of several tests, provided that the standard deviations of the composite total are equalized, this bonus method may be all that is required; it retains the discriminatory power of the raw test scores, which often have high standard deviations. Whether the slopes of the lines should be based on equivalent percentile levels rather than means and standard deviations is, of course, open to discussion.

However, Lawley (1950) prefers to regard age allowances as a norming problem. While there appears to be little justification for the perpetuation of the quotient system in the overall British system, in which the break at 11 plus results in even a fall in subjects like mechanical arithmetic performances after the age of twelve, it will be found that NFER tests are normed on a basis of converting raw score to standard score, taking age into consideration, over a narrow age range. The Lawley method, on which the NFER norms are based, assumes that for a given raw score, there will be a constant fall in standardized score for each month of age. These standardized scores are read off in the body of a table in which age and raw score are calibrated on the two main axes. The constant slope b on which the method is based is obtained by carrying out the following computational steps:

1. Distribute raw scores for each month of age.
2. Select any particular score (say, mean, median, approximately) and calculate percentage of each monthly age group below it.
3. Using this percentage, convert the score chosen into a standardized score, mean 100, standard deviation 15, for each month.
4. To these standardized scores, fit a line stand. score = const. $- b$(age).
5. Combine all distributions, and treat the result as one frequency distribution corresponding to the middle of the age range.
6. After checking b, by repeating steps 1 to 4 for another score level, standardize the ends of the intervals of the distribution of step 5, using the cumulative frequencies, to a mean 100, S.D. $\sqrt{(225 + 12b^2)}$.
7. Calculate points on lines with slope b through the standardized end-points obtained in step 6, for each month of age.
8. Interpolate lines between the lines of step 7 to complete table.

So far, regional problems have tended to result in regional, rather than national, norms. However, Peaker (1953) has drawn attention to the desirability of considering the application of scientific sampling methods to the selection of groups used for standardization purposes. Butcher (1966) considers that attempts to use good sampling procedures in educational research generally are 'as rare as a white blackbird', and Peaker's model, which stratifies on the factors known at the time to cause most variation in test performance in England, is a significant attempt to obtain norms on a reading test which are truly national. His sample is described as 'two-stage, stratified', the first stage being to draw a probability sample of local education authorities weighting 'urban v. rural' and the second stage involving stratification on 'type of school' within the areas selected on the first drawing. He quotes standard errors for the mean scores of the resulting test performances of 2,380 pupils from urban schools and 261 rural pupils, and considers that such a design has maximum efficiency for obtaining the information required, consistently with economy of sampling. Since Peaker reported these results, there are many new factors affecting mobility of the population in the United Kingdom which makes it increasingly necessary to have national standards for tests, although the factors affecting norms may have changed.

There has always been a tacit assumption that the gradings awarded by the various boards administering the General Certificate of Education both at the Ordinary level administered at the age of sixteen and the Advanced level, at the age of eighteen, are consistent from board to board. However, certain unpublished evidence (available to me) on the performances of children in different areas on the same 11-plus test suggests that regional differences are likely to be considerable. 'O' level GCE uses grades 1-9 in all boards, but syllabuses differ from board to board, rendering comparison of standards virtually impossible; the same difficulty applies to comparisons within subjects of any one board's examinations. Yet a GCE grade appears to be accepted as a standard without question of comparability as a qualification for entry to various kinds of further education, and by employers generally

With the advent of the Certificate of Secondary Education, catering for about 40 per cent of the same age group as the GCE but for the level of ability just below the top 20 per cent for which the GCE is intended, these problems have become even more acute. The CSE is administered by fourteen regional boards, in each of which there are three modes of examining, mode 1, examined entirely by the boards' examiners and prescribed syllabuses, mode 2, examined by the boards' examiners and special school syllabuses, and mode 3, examined by school examiners and special school syllabuses. Of the five passing grades awarded for the CSE, the first is regarded as a GCE pass, equivalent to a GCE grade 6 or higher. There seems to be no suggestion that the grades of the two types of examination are related to anything more than ordinal scale, although it is possible that they might be considered roughly as a twelve-point scale. In research on the subject, they have been used as though the grade numbers constitute as interval scale.

The early thinking about the problem of comparability appears to owe something to methods used by some education authorities for grading primary school pupils by their own head-teachers, in which a monitoring, general ability test was used to correct for the subjectivity of personal assessment. One method which found favour used a general ability test to establish a quota of places for each school concerned, leaving the selection of pupils to the school itself. This was described in an NFER publication (Yates and Pidgeon 1957). The first monitoring experiments concerning CSE also used a general ability test to check the general standards of all the boards concerned (Yates and

Pidgeon op. cit.). In 1965, stratified samples of nine schools representing each of seven GCE boards and twenty schools representing each of nine CSE boards were drawn at random, stratification being on sex and size, and the pupils of these schools were asked to work a special 100-item general ability test. This test was constructed and validated by the University of Manchester Department of Education, and contained roughly equal proportions of items thought to measure numeracy and more verbal items, though the two halves could not be usefully distinguished in the subsequent analysis (Schools Council 1967, pt 2). This test proved to be a little difficult for the majority of candidates (Schools Council 1966, pt 1), and this may have accounted for the somewhat low correlations between grades and reference test, reported as follows (Schools Council 1966, pt 2):

	English	Math.	Geog.	History	French	Science
CSE	0·32	0·49	0·43	0·31	0·17	0·33
GCE	0·36	0·45	0·28	0·25	0·29	0·37

these being average negative correlations over all the boards, since the better the performance, the lower the grade number. Evidence in detail is presented by means of regression of grade on reference test that, on the whole, the average grades allocated by boards are within calculated tolerance limits. However, the small correlations shown above might prompt the critic to regard this evidence as being open to rebuttal, and the experiment was continued on a smaller scale in the same year using subject reference tests in place of the general test (Schools Council 1967). Tests in mathematics and English were devised by the University of Southampton Department of Education with the object of being 'without bias in favour of candidates who have followed one type of subject course rather than another'. The English test contained sections on comprehension, and a continuous writing task, 'Write a story or description suggested by the picture'. The reliability of the objective sections was between 0·8 and 0·85, and the correlations between the complete test and the CSE or GCE scores of samples of children numbering between 600 and 200 children were:

	GCE	CSE
Board 1	0·62	0·59
Board 2	0·55	0·36

A reference test of mathematics containing general mathematics and only traditional mathematics with a Kuder-Richardson reliability of 0·94 gave correlations

	GCE	CSE
Board 1	0·47	0·75
Board 2	0·78	0·76

and both reference tests, therefore, gave rather more encouraging results than the general ability test. In the presentation of other forms of comparison, a comparison of percentile levels in the reference test corresponding to the bottom of groups of candidates awarded each grade in the CSE examination was made, and also a comparison in the form of ladders of the overlap between GCE and CSE grades was presented. Though these were considered reasonably satisfactory, the remarks of the NFER in a recent unpublished memorandum are very wise, namely, that a lot of trouble would be saved if use were made of an item bank which is now being compiled, offering pre-tested items from which those suited to the special syllabuses of boards and teachers within those boards may be selected. This project will, it is understood, be completed in 1968, but the crucial question is, will teachers use these items? First, it seems, we must effect a radical change of attitude among teachers towards scientific measurement, which means that more time must be devoted to the inclusion of the subject in their course of training. Secondly, it is desirable that more informed relations should be encouraged by responsible parties between examining boards and teachers. Thirdly, perhaps, it is desirable that every citizen should be educated to be more statistically minded.

References

Burt, C. (1917) 'The distribution and relations of educational abilities.' Report to the London County Council.
Butcher, H. J. (1966) *Sampling in Educational Research.* Manchester: Manchester University Press.
Cast, B. M. D. (1939, 1940) 'The efficiency of different methods of marking English composition.' *Br. J. educ. Psychol.,* **9**, 256-69, and **10**, 49-60.
Cattell, R. (1944) 'Psychological measurement: ipsative, normative and interactive.' *Psychol. Rev.,* **51**.
Finlayson, D. S. (1951) 'The reliability of the marking of essays.' *Br. J. educ. Psychol.,* **21**, 126-34.

Gupta, R. K. and Penfold, D. M. (1961) 'Corrections for guessing in true-false tests: an experimental approach.' *Br. J. educ. Psychol.*, **31**.

Hartog, P. and Rhodes, E. (1935) *An Examination of Examinations.* London: Macmillan.

Lawley, D. N. (1950) 'A method of standardizing group tests.' *Br. J. statist. Psychol.*, **3**, 2.

Lindley, D. (1961) 'An experiment in the marking of an examination.' *Jl R. statist. Soc.*, series A, no. 124, 3.

Nisbet, J. (1955) 'English composition in secondary school selection.' *Br. J. educ. Psychol.*, **25**, 51-4.

Peaker, G. F. (1953) 'A sampling design used by the Ministry of Education.' *Jl R. statist. Soc.*, series A, no. 116, 2.

Peel, E. and Armstrong, H. (1956) 'The predictive power of the English composition in the 11+ examination.' *Br. J. educ. Psychol.*, **26**.

Penfold, D. M. (1956) 'The use of essays in selection at 11+.' *Br. J. educ. Psychol.*, **26**.

Schools Council (1966) *The 1965 CSE Monitoring Experiment.* Working paper no. 6. London: H. M. Stationery Office.

Schools Council (1967) *Standards in CSE and GCE English and Mathematics.* Working paper no. 9. London: H. M. Stationery Office.

Thomson, G. H. (1932) 'The standardization of group tests and the scatter of intelligence quotients.' *Br. J. educ. Psychol.*, **2**, 2.

Watts, A. F., Pidgeon, D. A. and Yates, A. (1952) *Secondary School Entrance Examinations.* NFER. London: Newnes.

Wiseman, S. (1949) 'The marking of English composition in grammar school selection.' *Br. J. educ. Psychol.*, **19**, 200-9.

Yates, A. and Pidgeon, D. A. (1957) *Admission to Grammar Schools.* NFER. London: Newnes.

THE USE OF TESTS FOR THE ASSESSMENT AND IMPROVEMENT OF NEW TEACHING METHODS, PARTICULARLY IN THE FIELD OF PROGRAMMED LEARNING

TESTING, EVALUATION AND INSTRUCTIONAL RESEARCH

C. TITTLE

Overview

Educational testing has tended to reflect the main tradition from which it has developed: the psychology of individual differences and the accompanying emphasis of the psychometrician on measurement. In its applications, educational testing has been an area relatively unconcerned with problems of experimental design. Evaluation, as one of the main applications in education of testing, has generally followed the techniques arising from this tradition. Tests are intended to provide a distribution of scores for normative purposes. Instructional research has more often been aware of problems of experimental design; the development of tests used in the research (often limited to one dependent variable) has not received as much attention.

Recent work indicates a broadening of the viewpoints of both those engaged in instructional (or broad curricular) research and development and those engaged in educational testing. There is the development of an awareness of the importance of individual differences in evaluating methods of instruction—what characteristics of the learner, what characteristics of the teacher, what size group and/or other conditions are related to the achieving of defined purposes with a method of instruction?

Evaluation studies using educational tests are becoming broader in their conceptions—to include problems of experimental design, to consider alternative methods of test development, to develop various types of educational tests, to find wider uses for educational tests in instructional or curriculum 'systems', and to explore the use of techniques from other disciplines to assist in evaluation. The synthesis, or at least cross-fertilization, of the educational testing/individual differences tradition with the methodology in instructional research seems a logical step. As a result of this trend, those engaged in educational testing need to be aware of methodologies from other fields of inquiry.

Definitions of the context and purpose of any particular study are necessary to the realization of the possibilities of educational testing; the person working in educational test development is often placed in the position of helping others to define context and purpose before being able to develop assessment devices. This paper notes some of the trends in the use of tests in evaluation and instructional research. Two examples of the use of tests—in the field testing of instructional materials and in an external examination of a new curriculum—are described.

Contexts for using educational tests

The list below contains some of the types of studies in evaluation and instructional research in which tests are used. The types of studies serve to define the purpose, in a very broad sense, for which an educational test might be used. The second dimension is the possible sources of variance that may be a part of the context of a study in which tests are used.

Studies of instruction

Type of study	Potential source of variance
Evaluation, within curriculum or media	School
Comparison, between two or more curricula or media	Teacher
Development of curriculum or media	Student
Revision/improvement of curriculum or media	

The sources of variance considered in the design of the study in which educational tests may be one or more dependent variables will serve to limit or expand generalizations of the results of the study. Examples of their relevance are given below in the descriptions of the type of variables that might be relevant for each main source of variance—school, teacher and student. As with test validity, these sources of variance contribute to the assessment of the validity of the evaluation, comparison, development or revision (improvement) study. They may also affect decisions about the test to be used in the study. In most cases, it will be the consideration of all the sources of variance that lead to the 'construct' validity of the study. It may be noted that educational tests are limited in this design or context sense, since their use is no guarantee that the evaluator of any study can make the decision he needs to make unless he gives consideration to this broader design setting in which the tests are used.

The relevance of these sources of variance can be shown for studies of programmed instruction as well as for other 'methods' studies. For this purpose programmed instruction will be defined broadly and considered in the more general sense of systems of learning or instruction, where the systems may be a combination of media such as films, computers, television, printed materials, practical work and laboratory work, language laboratories or personal teaching. These various media, either alone or in combination, can be considered as a part of programmed instruction as long as the system is amenable to improvement as a result of some testing of its components (see Leith 1966).

The sources of variance are considered as relevant to the 'product' assessment of programmed instruction as to studies of the basic characteristics of programmed instruction as a general method. This important contrast between the study of the effectiveness of a product and the study of the basic characteristics of the method has been described by Lumsdaine (1963, 1965).* The sources of variance are also relevant to the development and field testing of many educational materials being published.

a) The school

An analysis of the school environment as related to pupils' achievement has received attention in a study by the U.S. Office of Education (1966). A major finding indicated that schools were remarkably similar in the way they related to the achievement of their pupils when the socio-economic background of students was taken into account. However, this analysis was carried further to look at the relation of schools to the achievement of various racial and ethnic groups. These analyses indicated that the achievement of minority pupils depends more on the schools they attend than does the achievement of majority pupils. It was found that 20 per cent of the achievement of Negro students in the South was associated with the particular schools they attended; the corresponding figure for Whites in the South was 10 per cent. (The only exception to this general relation found for all minorities was that for Oriental Americans.) This relation was interpreted as indicating that it was for the most disadvantaged children that improvement in school quality would make the most difference in achievement. Particular school characteristics that might be related to achievement were compared; for the minorities, facilities such as the

---

* Lumsdaine notes that 'Evaluation of programmed instruction as a method is a . . . difficult and elusive question to answer . . . because of the difficulty of defining the "method" of programmed instruction in general terms or of defining it—as well as alternative "methods"— . . . meaningful experiments thus must have either the purpose of determining the effects produced by specific programmes or must seek to test propositions about the effects of definable, describable properties of programmes' (1965).

existence of science laboratories showed a small but consistent relation to achievement.

The quality of the teacher, as measured by the teacher's score on verbal skills and his educational background, was related to achievement; and, more important, a pupil's achievement was consistently related to the educational backgrounds and aspirations of the other students in the school. The analysis indicated that children from a given family background, when in schools of different social composition, achieved at different levels. Again this finding was most marked for the minority pupils. If a minority pupil from a home without much educational strength was put with schoolmates with strong educational background, his achievement was likely to increase.

Findings such as these in the USOE survey are relevant to effective study of programmed instruction or other methods of instruction. The school environment is potentially a source of variance in studies in instructional methods.

b) The teacher

Thelen and Ginther (1964) have noted the importance of the teacher's viewpoint in using programmed instruction in the classroom. Although their investigation was concerned with the satisfaction or dissatisfaction with programmed materials as reported by teachers, they concluded that the 'satisfaction' resulting from use of programmed materials was dependent only partly on characteristics of the material, and that other factors can be far more important determiners of how the materials were judged. Their survey showed that teachers might decide to logically 'enrich' the programme by bringing in additional materials. If the teacher considered the method inadequate, he would 'reinforce' the programme by discussion, practice and application of the content in situations which he devised. In view of the decisions which teachers may make for using programmed instruction in their classrooms, it would seem valuable in developing or evaluating programmed materials to consider as relevant the teacher's possible decisions to enrich or reinforce the programmed materials themselves in actual classroom use.

In a study of teachers using one of the Biological Science Curriculum Study (BSCS) texts, Gallagher (1967) summarized past studies of teachers as establishing that 'Teachers differ in their style of classroom behaviour', 'Teachers from different training backgrounds show different classroom styles', 'The type of patterns used by the teacher influence the type and amount of student learning'.

He goes on to note that the 'major curriculum movements have operated on an assumption . . . that the key variable for *student outcome* was rather exclusively a function of curriculum organization'. In view of the differences in teacher training and styles of teaching, this seems an untenable assumption. A study of one major topic of the BSCS indicated that students' achievement differed on several measures. Analysis of transcripts of classroom presentation and students' discussions showed differences in the manner of presentation, content of presentation, and amount of student participation in classroom discussions for six classrooms where teachers were presenting the same BSCS concept of photosynthesis. The study was limited by the measures of students' achievement, and Gallagher felt that an analysis of performance on items measuring only the concepts discussed in the classroom presentations would have aided the evaluation of the potential influence of different teaching presentations.

c) The student

There is a need to define the student for whom a programme is appropriate. Some studies have considered the appropriateness of programmes to students of 'high, average, and below average general ability'. This would seem to be the minimum requirement in describing the student or the type of student for whom the programme is effective. Although some of the following factors would be highly related to 'general ability', they are possible variables or characteristics of students which could be used to try to define the group for whom a particular programme will be satisfactory: reading level, level of present understanding of the 'subject' or content in the materials, possible approaches to learning such as verbal manipulation, problem solving or inquiry, and possible preferred ways of working such as independent, project group, etc. (Thelen and Ginther 1964). Those doing research or evaluating programmed learning need to define the most relevant characteristics of the student which will lead to the desired outcomes of instruction.

Lumsdaine (1965) emphasized the importance of knowing the conditions of utilization of programmed instruction in the classroom. He also suggested that characteristics of the learner should be described, and in particular that specification of prior knowledge and general ability were important for two purposes: (1) as a base-line for the effectiveness of the programme; and (2) to define characteristics needed for the programme to be effective.

These characteristics might be additional skills such as reading level or general ability needed to work through the programme effectively.

With regard to establishing the base-line for the effectiveness of the programme, there may be a special problem in determining the 'latent' internal knowledge (prior knowledge which might not be recalled on a particular instructional achievement test, but which would be readily learned in the course of the programme).

The sources of student variance are important to the definition of studies of programmed or other methods of instruction in learning. The consideration of measuring students' characteristics in the outcome of instruction has led to several suggestions for uses or modifications of educational tests. The modifications have been proposed when researchers have been evaluating or comparing 'methods' of instruction. Suggestions of alternative uses of educational tests have arisen in development or improvement of instructional materials/methods for the classroom.

Modifications of educational tests

Several writers have discussed differences in test development techniques for 'norm-referenced' tests versus those which can be considered 'criterion-referenced'. The criterion-referenced test has been proposed by Bereiter (1962), Cox and Graham (1966), and Glaser (1963) as being the most relevant to the measurement of the effects of instruction. The criterion-referenced measure depends upon an absolute standard of quality and the degree to which a student's achievement resembles desired performance at any specified level is assessed (Glaser 1963).

Bereiter describes the importance of measuring those traits that are susceptible to differential change under the influence of curricular experiences, and contrasts this with the selection or prediction approach in which change becomes a troublesome source of error. In terms of the purpose of education, stability is troublesome, for it means that education is having little impact. The procedures used in test development work can function to make tests insensitive to differential change if it exists. There is a need to develop tests which will detect small but reliable differences in the effectiveness of educational practices in the hope that they will point the way towards practices which will make a large difference.*

The technique that both Bereiter and Glaser suggest to maximize

* Bereiter suggests two approaches to developing tests to detect change. The first is that of factored tests, those that will provide a number of fairly thoroughly defined factors as offering more promise of sensitivity to differential change. The second suggestion is in paying more attention to content validity so that questions which a bright student can answer without having studied will not be included.

sensitivity to change is to administer a large number of items before and after instruction, and then construct the test of items which show significant differences between pre- and post-test performance. This is a change from the conventional techniques of test development, but as Bereiter points out, although it may lead to tests that are sensitive to change, the technique will not guarantee sensitivity to differential change which might result from different educational practices. Bereiter's suggestion to obtain test sensitivity to *individual differences* in change was to score items plus 1 if answered incorrectly the first time and right the second time (on two administrations), minus 1 if the reverse was true, and zero if the item was answered right both times or wrong both times. He reports the use of this method in developing differential change scores on an attitude inventory, although the inventory was used in a correlational rather than an experimental study.

Glaser's discussion of criterion-referenced measures focuses on yielding achievement tests that discriminate among different instructional procedures by analysis of *group differences*. To maximize *group differences*, he would administer a large number of items both pre- and post-training and retain those items which were responded to correctly by all members of the post-training group, but which were answered incorrectly by students who had not yet been trained. The main problem that could arise using Glaser's technique would be that items which would appear to have face validity in terms of the desired outcomes of the instruction could be eliminated from the evaluation test if, in fact, the instruction was not successful for the initial group used for item analysis. Glaser specifically considers standards of performance for tests to measure individual achievement, but his empirical approach to selecting items to maximize *group differences* raises the problem of standards of performance in comparing methods of instruction.

A recent study by Cox and Graham was aimed at the problem of the standard of performance. They also suggest that the student's performance must be compared to an absolute standard as opposed to the normative standard of traditional achievement testing and that the student's score should reflect the degree of competence in certain behaviours (see also Ebel 1962). The purpose of their study was to develop a test (using Guttman's scalogram analysis), where the total score would indicate the response pattern of the individual. Using a very simple objective, the ability to add two-digit numerals involving carrying, they constructed a test of 15 items where there were 2-5 tasks per 'item'. The results show it is possible to develop a sequentially scaled achievement test, even though it was administered on a limited area of subject matter. They note, 'it also seems reasonable to hypothesize that by manipulating the content taught in the classroom one can dictate a series of objectives that would yield an empirically scaled test'.

This study shows a merging of test development into studies of learning of sequences of instructional objectives in order to build scaleable achievement tests. One might rephrase their hypothesis slightly to suggest that if we knew the optimum sequences of instruction from learning studies, it might be possible to develop content defined and scaled achievement tests (see also Gagne 1961).

Another suggestion for modification of the uses of traditional approach to developing educational tests has been suggested by Heath (1964). Heath points out that many of the new curriculum courses are distinctive in trying to teach the student how to acquire, evaluate and retrieve knowledge in a given field. He describes different modes of attaining the subject matter of the course, and labels these as cognitive preferences. He developed a test intended to measure students' preferences for: (a) memory of specific facts; (b) practical applications; (c) critical questioning of information; and (d) identification of fundamental principles.

In a study of the Physical Science Study Committee course, students were compared to a 'traditional' group of students. The PSSC students were lower in cognitive preferences for both memory and application, and higher on cognitive preferences for questioning and principles. This suggests an additional dimension of the evaluation of educational achievement through further exploration of elusive objectives for some of the new curricula or method studies.

Another suggestion for modification of the uses of traditional achievement tests has been made by Frederiksen (1962). He lists a number of methods for obtaining measures for use in evaluating outcomes of instruction, and suggests that the most valid is the measuring of real-life behaviour. However, the observing of behaviour in real life is rarely a good technique for evaluation because of lack of control of the test situation. The method of eliciting life-like behaviour in situations which simulate real life was recommended for first consideration as a measurement technique.

Some of these suggestions for modifications of educational tests are such that progress or achievement may in the future be defined in terms of how far or successfully a student progresses through a programmed or learning 'system'. Information from testing may yield scores which define standards of performance or pass/fail at various points yielding decisions for the next stages in instruction rather than ranking students

Testing, evaluation and instructional research

for normative comparisons. Instructional systems using a variety of media, including computers, will yield possibilities of more continuous assessment of individual students in terms of defined standards of performance.

Uses of educational tests

Several writers have suggested that particularly in relation to programmed instruction there is a need for the use of diagnostic achievement tests (Glaser 1963, Lumsdaine 1965). Lumsdaine has also suggested the use of diagnostic tests for programme revision in the sense that the effects of the programme on specific points related to instructional objectives need to be separately measured. The diagnostic test for programme revision would not focus much attention on the total score, but would instead focus on subscores or specific test questions. The use of a test in this fashion would require a large sample of items and students to achieve stability of results. In addition to aiding in programme revision, the diagnosing of subscore results might also indicate what additional instruction would be needed to achieve defined goals and would identify them for special attention in classroom instruction. In this context, the usefulness of the total score would be limited to indicating whether or not it would be worth while to use the programme at all.

Cronbach (1963) has also described the principle of defining uses for tests which are appropriate when they are used for course improvement or development, and contrasted these with the precise measures needed for decisions about individuals. He suggested the use of tests to identify aspects of a course where revision is desirable, and emphasized that the focus of the study should be designed primarily to measure the post-instructional performance of a well-described group with respect to the objectives and side effects, rather than yielding equivocal results from group comparisons. Proficiency and process measures, aptitude measures and follow-up studies of the later careers of those who took part in the course were considered valuable approaches to be used in studies for improvement of instructional methods and materials.

Item-sampling techniques as suggested by Lord (1962) may be useful, since giving all of the group the same set number of questions yields less information for development or revision than giving different sets of questions to the same set of pupils. The use of different types of tests such as essay tests and open-ended questions can be helpful by administering them to a representative sample of pupils, yielding valuable information without as much cost as if given to the total group of pupils. Cronbach also suggested that test questions should not be course-specific (in terminology), but should be course-independent so that they are comprehensible to pupils who have not taken the course. This relates to his suggestion for examining transfer of learning, and the distinction between applicational transfer and the transfer of slower-acting effects of instruction which would be recognized as gains in aptitude. Focusing on the longer-term transfer might yield measures of the increased ability in a particular field. Cronbach suggested that the techniques of programmed instruction may be adaptable to appraise this transfer of learning ability.

In a symposium on the role of evaluation in national curriculum projects, Cahen (1967) and Hollenbeck (1967) presented studies which implemented suggestions similar to those of Cronbach. A long-term study evaluating a mathematics curriculum, described by Cahen, is using Lord's item-sampling technique to establish group means on measures of performance. Hollenbeck suggested that for curriculum development it is important to look at individual items for students grouped by ability. This can help to pin-point the relative strengths and weaknesses of different parts of the curriculum or methods under study, although in item analysis it is important to ensure that the results reflect students' understanding or misunderstanding rather than ambiguity in the item. This also suggests the value of paying careful attention to the structure of item alternatives to yield interpretable information for the revision process.

An example of using tests in instructional materials

The tests accompanying the instructional materials described below serve two purposes: to make decisions regarding course improvement, and to make decisions about individuals within the 'course' (not normative comparisons, but diagnostic for the learning process).

The SRA Basic Reading Series attempts to make use of linguistic principles in a beginning reading programme. The basic materials consist of an alphabet book and six readers, with accompanying workbooks for each reader. The readers control the presentation of vocabulary by using only words which are already in the child's speaking vocabulary. There is also a control in terms of presentation of sound-spelling relations in consistent patterns and in terms of whole words.

Additional materials for the programme include an administrator's guide, a teacher's handbook, a series of master tests, and two cumulative tests provided to measure progress at important points in the programme. The tests are designed to help the teacher evaluate

Testing, evaluation and instructional research

pupils' progress in mastering the grapheme-phoneme relations.

For the purpose of field testing the reading series, the schools taking part were selected from different areas of the United States and representative of different types of communities. Information was collected on class size, background of the teacher, her use of supplementary reading materials, and the usual reading programme used in the school. In addition, standardized tests were administered to measure intelligence (Lorge-Thorndike Intelligence Test) and reading achievement (SRA Achievement series and the Stroud Hieronymus Primary Reading Profile). Information on rate of using the readers was collected by having the teacher record the date at which individual students started each reader. Classroom visitation, observations and teacher interviews were also used to help discover any problems within the reading programme.

The development of the tests was based on the idea that they should be tied closely to the skills the reading programme attempted to develop. The first four mastery tests provided tasks which would measure the child's ability to decode sound-spelling patterns in somewhat different situations from those used in the workbooks and readers.* One task was aural-grapheme recognition: the teacher presented the word and the child selected it from among three printed alternatives. The alternative words were selected to provide contrast in word beginnings and individual sound-spelling patterns. The second task presented a word visually by means of a picture, with the child asked to select the pictured word from among three printed alternatives. Again, the alternative words were selected for pattern contrasts. The third task involved decoding sentences. The child selected the picture clue of a word needed to complete the sentence. The fourth task involved decoding a series of sentences. Printed sentences were given, the child asked to comprehend the story, then to select the correct one of three alternative pictures to complete a sentence.

A cumulative test followed the completion of the readers, workbooks and mastery tests for the first four levels. The cumulative test is a survey of the sound-spelling patterns in the first four levels, but also places emphasis on trying to project the pupil's ability to decode patterns which are presented in the final two readers of the series. Again there was a control within the test so that the words used remained within the child's speaking and listening vocabulary, but they were selected to be unfamiliar to him in terms of presentation in the first four

*See SRA Basic Reading Series *Testing Guide*. Developmental edition. Chicago: Science Research Associates, Inc., 1965-6.

readers. These unfamiliar words followed patterns from the last two readers in the series. The intention in providing these unfamiliar words was to help the teacher pace the child for the next two levels. The mastery test for the last two readers were controlled for the sound-spelling pattern in the readers and consisted of two tasks:
1. Auditory presentation of a word with the pupil asked to select the presented word from two printed alternatives.
2. Presentation of stories for the pupil to read, followed by six questions testing ability to comprehend each story.

The final cumulative test covering the entire series contains words from the sound-spelling patterns presented in all readers, with an emphasis on the later readers. The test has two parts:
1. A comprehension section, consisting of a story followed by six questions.
2. An oral reading section, where the student reads sentences to the teacher, and the teacher records words which are not read correctly. This section is primarily for diagnosis and to ensure that the child has learned the sound-spelling patterns in the readers.

The pattern tested in each question is cross-referenced to the readers for each mastery and cumulative test to facilitate the teacher's use of the materials. The tests are not standardized and the questions were not pre-tested before their use in experimental versions of the tests. Since the pupil may, by chance, make an error which is, in essence, random rather than a result of not having learned the materials, the directions for using the test emphasize this point to the teacher. Although the manual suggests that the teacher look at an individual pupil's test booklet for errors on particular sound-spelling patterns, it also points out that the teacher should check that it is not a random error by going back to the reader at the appropriate point, and having a child read words and sentences containing the missed pattern words. The focus of the discussion in the manual is that the teacher records missed items as a *clue* to be followed up.

The purposes of the test, then, are to provide diagnostic information and to help the teacher quickly survey that the child has indeed mastered the instructional materials within each level in the series. They are also intended to help her pace the pupil in going through the materials in order to maintain a high level of interest for those pupils who rapidly learn to decode the words in the readers.

Although the tests were developed on an analytical or logical basis, trying to measure transfer for individual pupils, they can also serve to

Testing, evaluation and instructional research

provide information necessary for future revisions of the reading series. It was intended that the tests from the field test schools be collected for item analysis by the publisher. Through the use of field test schools and the collection of test data from a number of teachers and schools, it was hoped that the revision process would be aided by being able to eliminate alternative hypotheses when looking at the results of the item statistics. A sampling of teachers and pupils with information on the pupil's ability and reading level should help to evaluate whether item errors are due to these various sources or to a problem in the instructional materials themselves. It was hoped that the planning of the mastery and cumulative tests would permit assessment of the individual pupil's learning for the teacher and provide revision information for the authors of the series.

An example of using tests in an external examination programme

The purposes of the tests described in this section are to provide a reliable assessment of individual achievement in a situation where the test results are used to make decisions about individuals. In England external achievement examinations are set at several major points in the educational system before the end of the secondary school. At about the age of sixteen many students will sit the Ordinary level examination developed by one of the eight General Certificate of Education (GCE) examining bodies. The purpose of these examinations is to provide information relative to decisions on further education or job selection.

For one of the major new curriculum innovations in England, the Nuffield Science Teaching Project, the University of London Entrance and School Examination Council provides, on behalf of all boards, an Ordinary level examination which is taken by students who normally would sit any of the eight GCE boards. The examination as it has been developed at the University of London includes a variety of testing techniques, some of which are traditional in the English setting and one, the use of multiple-choice questions, which is not usual for the GCE boards. The combination of multiple-choice questions with the use of the more traditional forms of examination (open-response or essay) questions has yielded data which promises some comparison of examining techniques. A great deal of effort has gone into structuring the overall examination to provide, in so far as is possible, an assessment which meets the spirit and objectives of the new curriculum scheme. It has also yielded information about the reliability and correlation of the different examining techniques among themselves and with teachers' estimates of students' performance.

The instructional materials prepared for the Nuffield Science Teaching Project in chemistry are intended to encourage the development of 'lively inquiry, understanding, and an ability to interpret evidence'. The materials aimed to provide up-to-date thought and technology in chemistry which could be used to give students an understanding of science, scientists and the scientific approach, through a teaching project which emphasizes the spirit of inquiry and investigation. Although some preliminary work in evaluation was done during the field trials of the material, the main systematic work on evaluation has been done within the context of the Ordinary level GCE examination. An Advisory Committee for the examination had representatives from the Nuffield Project staff, teachers using the Nuffield materials, and examiners in chemistry from other GCE boards. Since the examination was to include a multiple-choice section, Dr Frank Fornoff of the Educational Testing Service provided consultant help, and conducted two workshops to train teachers and university staff in the writing of multiple-choice items for the Nuffield Scheme.

The 1966 examination consisted of two papers; paper I had seventy multiple-choice questions (one hour); paper II, section A (one hour) consisted of seven short-answer questions of which candidates had to answer four; section B (one hour) consisted of seven questions of which candidates had to answer two.

The multiple-choice section attempted to provide a broad survey of the topics and major concepts in the scheme. Questions were included which assessed the student's knowledge, his comprehension or understanding of what he had learned, his ability to analyse presented information and to evaluate it. The seven short-answer questions in section A were designed so that candidates had a clear idea of the scope and limitations expected of them. Questions were broken down into several parts so that each aspect of a candidate's approach to a particular problem was examined separately.

For some questions the candidate was asked to give a brief explanation or to show how he arrived at his answer. Section B allowed candidates to demonstrate more freely their knowledge and understanding of topics which they had studied in some depth. This section was marked impressionistically by the chief examiner.

The content validity of the examination was determined by the examiners defining the universe of topics to be measured, major areas of emphasis or activities in the scheme, and the abilities which the scheme was intended to develop. In preparing the test specifications, weightings were assigned to each of these three dimensions and the final examination was assembled with these weightings in mind. Teachers' assessments were obtained in terms of their estimate of each student's probable level of achievement on the Ordinary level examination. This was done in the month preceding the administration of the examination. The correlations between teachers' estimates and examination performance were:

Paper I	0·65
Paper II section A	0·64
Paper II section B	0·54

For the examination as a whole a correlation of 0·71 was obtained with teachers' estimates.

The reliability of the papers was estimated. For paper I the coefficient of reliability was 0·87. For paper II approximations of the reliability coefficients were 0·74 for section A, and 0·63 for section B. The coefficient of reliability for the total examination was estimated at 0·89. (The intercorrelations of the parts of the examination were: paper I v. section A = 0·67, paper I v. section B = 0·55; section A v. section B = 0·63.)

While no attempt has yet been made to use the examination results to help provide any assessment of the Nuffield materials, it is possible that as the number of students taking the examination increases, analysis relevant to such an assessment could be carried out. Data would be available for a variety of types of schools, which would permit a comparison of performance on individual items and on the various individual questions in paper II of the examination. As the chief examiners in chemistry have surveyed the item analysis of paper I, many of their comments would be relevant feedback to those using the Nuffield scheme. Although it is an external examination, use of the item data and error analysis of questions may be useful to teachers if presented in a form so as to minimize any direct control of the examination over the curriculum. This means that the analysis could not be for individual teachers or schools *per se,* but should only provide leads or hints to schools, in general, for further checking in their internal examining.

Summary

These suggestions and examples of the different uses of tests in curriculum development or methods studies can be useful when placed within a broader design context which helps the evaluator to rule out or define the importance of the school, the teacher and the student in the test results. As Hastings (1966) points out, the evaluator and developer of methods or materials of instruction needs to know the 'why' of the test results; furthermore, the general nature of instructional research may begin to look much more like the research on learning which is done in psychology. Combining these various uses of educational tests with attention to the design context of the study may begin to yield to relevant data systematic enough so that theories in learning and teaching could use it to start to provide the basis for the design of learning systems. Tests have an important role to play in this process.

References

Bereiter, C. (1962) 'Using tests to measure change.' *Personnel and Guidance J.,* September, 6-11.

Cahen, L. S. (1967) 'The role of long-term studies in curriculum evaluation.' Paper read at the meeting of the American Educational Research Association, New York, February.

Coleman, J. et al. (1966) *Equality of Educational Opportunity.* Washington, D.C.: U.S. Government Printing Office.

Cox, R. C. and Graham, G. T. (1966) 'The development of sequentially scaled achievement tests.' *J. educ. Measur.,* **3**, 147-50.

Cronbach, L. J. (1963) 'Evaluation for course improvement.' *Teachers College Record,* **64**.

Ebel, R. (1962) 'Content standard test scores.' *Educ. psychol. Measur.,* **22**, 15-25.

Frederiksen, N. (1962) 'Proficiency tests for training evaluation.' In Glaser, R. *Training Research and Education.* Pittsburgh: University of Pittsburgh Press, pp. 323-46.

Gagne, R. M. and Paradise, N. E. (1961) *Abilities and Learning Sets in Knowledge Acquisition. Psychological Monographs,* vol. 75, no. 14, pp. 1-23. Psychological Association, Inc.

Gallagher, J. J. (1967) 'Teacher variation in concept presentation in BSCS Curriculum Program.' *BSCS Newsletter,* **30**, January, 8-18.

Glaser, R. (1963) 'Instructional technology and the measurement of learning outcomes: some questions.' *Am. Psychol.,* **18**, 519-21.

Hastings, J. T. (1966) 'Curriculum evaluation: the whys of the outcomes.' *J. educ. Measur.,* **3**, 27-32.

Heath, R. W. (1964) 'Curriculum, cognition, and educational measurement.' *Educ. psychol. Measur.,* **24**, 239-53.

Hollenbeck, G. P. (1967) 'Using the results of evaluation.' Paper read at the meeting of the American Educational Research Association, New York, February.

Leith, G. (1966) 'Developments in programmed learning.' *Trends in Education,* no. 2, pp. 20-6. London: H.M. Stationery Office.

Lord, F. M. (1962) 'Estimating norms by item-sampling.' *Educ. psychol. Measur.*, **22**, 259-68.
Lumsdaine, A. A. (1963) 'Instruments and media of instruction.' In Gage, N. L. (ed.) *Handbook of Research on Teaching*, pp. 583-682. Chicago: Rand McNally.
Lumsdaine, A. A. (1965) 'Assessing the effectiveness of instructional programs.' In Glaser, R. (ed.) *Teaching Machines and Programmed Learning, II Data and Directions.* Washington: NEA.
Thelen, H. and Ginther, J. R. (1964) 'Experiences with programmed materials in the Chicago area.' In *Four Case Studies of Programmed Instruction*, pp. 42-62. New York: Fund for the Advancement of Education.

USING TESTS TO IMPROVE INSTRUCTION

ROBERT L. EBEL

The title of this paper makes an assumption that I, for one, am quite willing to grant. It is that tests *can* be used to improve instruction. I would go farther. With all their imperfections, with all the abuses of them, tests as ordinarily used *do* help to improve instruction. Indeed, I will commit myself to an even stronger endorsement. Systematic improvement of instruction is virtually impossible in the absence of tests. To determine whether a change in instructional practices is an improvement, we need to know what results we were getting before the change, and what results we get after it. Tests provide an efficient, unbiased means of gathering evidence about the results of instruction.

I will not at this time undertake to defend the credibility of these assumptions, even though I think I could do so—to my own satisfaction at least—if called upon. For my assignment is not to argue that tests can be used to improve instruction. It is rather to describe how they can be so used. If I do a good job with the assignment, you may be the more willing to grant the underlying assumptions.

One of the ways in which tests can be used to improve instruction is so simple to say that it sounds almost tricky. It is merely to use them to measure achievement. For when a teacher makes a test, or selects one, to measure achievement, his attention is directed more clearly than might otherwise be necessary to the results his instruction ought to attain. With purposes more clearly defined, his efforts are likely to be more efficient and effective. Knowledge that a test will measure the students' achievements is likely to have a similar effect on their efforts, and to lead them to respond in ways that improve the climate for instruction, and thus that improve the instruction itself.

I realize that not all teachers, and not all students are prepared to accept the argument just made for the usefulness of tests in improving instruction. While they may agree that purposeful efforts are more likely to be effective than random efforts, and that motivation usually contributes to learning, they may doubt that tests provide the proper direction to the teacher's instructional efforts, or the proper motivation of the student's study. They may also fear that the side effects of testing—anxiety, hostility, cramming or cheating—are actually hostile to effective learning. Let us pause to consider each of these concerns.

To ask what is the proper direction for educational efforts to take is to ask what are the proper aims and outcomes of education. Despite what is sometimes claimed in defense of intangible outcomes of

Using tests to improve instruction

education, the main thing that teachers try to accomplish in instruction, and the main thing that pupils try to accomplish in study, is to get command of useful verbal knowledge. What gets talked about in classrooms is verbal knowledge. What students read and write about outside the class is also verbal knowledge. To get command of verbal knowledge is to acquire the ability to use it to solve problems, to make decisions and to understand the world in which we live. Practically all the systematic instructional programmes of demonstrated effectiveness that the schools have to offer are concerned with giving the students command of useful verbal knowledge. The only significant exceptions are their programmes of physical education, and the courses they offer to cultivate skills in vocal and manual arts. Even in these, verbal knowledge usually plays an important part.

Few would deny that good tests require a student to demonstrate his command of verbal knowledge. A good test simply cannot be passed by a student whose knowledge is superficial. Knowledge learned by rote, or acquired at the last minute by cramming, is almost certain to be superficial. What teachers must do in instruction, and students in study, to enable them to pass a good examination is identical with what they must do to attain the chief ends of education.

What of the side effects of tests—the anxiety of students, the antagonism between students and teacher, the incentive to cheat? The first is unavoidable, but usually more helpful than harmful to efforts in study and to achievement on a test. The second is likely to be serious only if the teacher or the student has other serious problems. The third is inexcusable under any circumstances. None of them separately, nor all of them together provide any justification for failing to take advantage of what tests can do to improve instruction.

The influence of tests on the improvement of instruction that we have discussed so far is an indirect influence. It tends to improve both teaching and learning by defining goals more clearly and by providing a rather specific and rather immediate incentive for efforts to achieve, on the part of both teachers and students. It seems to me that these indirect influences are entirely appropriate, and that they represent the major contribution that tests have to make to the improvement of instruction. Believing this, I reject the claim of some educationists that only to the degree that a test has direct educational value, only to the extent that a student emerges from a test better educated than he was when he started it, can the use of tests in schools be justified.

The main job of a test is to measure, not to teach. If it measures accurately what it is supposed to measure, it is a good test, regardless of its direct contribution, or lack of contribution, to the student's learning. The physician does not scorn his thermometer because it does not cure the patient's fever. He does not abandon his manometer because it does not cure high blood pressure. No more should a teacher scorn an intelligence test that does not increase the pupil's intelligence, nor abandon a reading test that does not teach the pupil to read.

Clearly an educational test that does not contribute to learning *in any way* directly or indirectly, is as worthless as a physiological test that leaves the physician as puzzled as he was before giving it about the nature of his patient's ailment. My point here is simply that a test need not teach directly in order to be useful educationally.

But, fortunately, most educational tests do teach directly, even when no special effort is made to use them instructionally. James B. Stroud, the educational psychologist, has suggested that the time a student spends taking a good test may be as valuable a learning experience to him as an equivalent amount of time spent in any other kind of educational activity. Students do, ordinarily, emerge from a test better educated than they were when they started. The increment may not be large, but it almost always occurs.

By making special efforts, we can, however, increase the direct contributions of tests to students' learning. Let me describe in some detail two of the ways that I have found effective.

One is to re-use a previous achievement test as a pre-test. This is done early in the term. The purpose of this pre-test is not to provide a base-line for measuring educational growth. It is primarily to indicate to the students, concretely and specifically, the kind of achievement expected of them and the bases on which that achievement will be evaluated. It is secondarily to serve several other purposes.

The students are allowed to keep copies of the pre-test. They are encouraged to use the questions to check informally the development of their own understanding during the term. Later on, each of the questions in the pre-test is assigned specifically to one of the students in the class, who is charged with responsibility for writing a brief statement defending his answer to it. In a review session late in the term these statements are presented to the class and discussed as time allows.

The responses of the students to the pre-test items are analysed. Particular attention is paid to the proportion of correct responses to each item. Any item that most of the students are able to answer before taking the course is obviously not a very good item for measuring achievement in the course. Such items are either revised for future use or discarded.

The pre-test scores are also used to identify individual differences among the students in their backgrounds in the area. Rarely, but occasionally a student who enrols in the course already knows so much about the subject that he is unlikely to spend his time profitably in taking the course. Much more often students enrol whose fund of relevant information, or whose facility in the use of it is so limited that they are likely to spend their time in futility and frustration. It is a service to such students to warn them of what lies ahead.

When the students take the pre-test, they are advised to try to make the highest possible score on it, since it will be counted, but not heavily weighted, in determining their final grade in the course. This procedure helps to assure that the students will take the pre-test seriously, but the low weight given to it guards against their taking it too seriously. It contributes to the validity of the scores as measures of background knowledge. It also contributes, however slightly, to the validity of final grades, when these are intended to reflect the level of achievement reached rather than the amount of progress made. For, since all achievement builds on prior achievement, those who start the course knowing most are likely to complete it also knowing most.

One possible objection to the use of an achievement test as a pre-test in the way we have described is that it is one way to use up a lot of good achievement tests. But this is not necessarily true. It has not been true in our experience. We started with four completely different mid-term tests and four completely different final tests. All are objective in form, and comprise from 90 to 120 items. After one of these has been used to measure achievement and as a pre-test, it is extensively revised. Items low in discrimination as measures of achievement, or low in difficulty in the pre-test are rewritten or replaced. Between one-third and one-half of the items are essentially new each time the test is used to measure achievement. These changes, plus the large number of items available, have permitted the use of these tests as pre-tests and instructional exercises without jeopardizing the fairness or validity of the tests.

Another way of using an achievement test to contribute to learning is to give it twice, first as an in-class closed-book test and immediately afterwards as a take-home no-holds-barred test. It is our practice when giving a test to hand the student two answer sheets, one to be turned in at the conclusion of the test period, the other at the next class meeting. Of course, the students are allowed to keep their copies of the test. They are encouraged to record in the test booklet for future reference and reconsideration the answers they put on the in-class answer sheet.

During the hours between class meetings the students are free to use any means of improving on the answers they gave in class—except asking the instructor. Often they meet in small groups to compare their answers and, when differences are found, to discuss the justifications of alternative answers. Many of them refer back to the text, and to their class notes to check a questionable answer.

The second answer sheet is scored in the same way as the first, and the student's total score on the test is the sum of his scores on the in-class and take-home phases of it.

With an ideal test, and ideal students, everyone might get a perfect score on the take-home test. But with real tests and real students the scores are different. Few if any of them are perfect. Of course, almost all the students get substantially higher scores on the take-home test than they did on the in-class test. The greatest gains, naturally, tend to be made by the students who had the lowest scores in class, but even here there are wide differences. Some come close to perfect scores. Others improve only a little. Some have time, and choose to spend much of it in the pursuit of perfection. Others have less time, or choose to spend it in other ways.

Occasionally a student who scores high on the test in class complains that our system is unfair to him, since he does not have as much opportunity to improve his score as a classmate who did poorly. This is true. But it is also true that his take-home test score is almost certain to be higher than that of his classmate. His initial advantage persists, so that the final difference between his score and his classmate's score is almost certain to be greater than it was on the in-class test.

The original intent and still the principal justification of this procedure is to augment the instructional value of the test. But it also increases the reliability of the test, and probably the validity, too. In our situation, at least, it has seemed to work very well.

Earlier in this paper I quietly inserted the word *good* before the word *tests* in asserting their usefulness in improving instruction. Re-emphasis of that point provides a good note on which to close this paper. If you undertake to use a poor test as a pre-test or as a take-home test in the ways I have just described, you are asking for trouble. Students will detect the ambiguities and irrelevancies of your questions. They will report them with glee to you and to their classmates. They will enjoy your embarrassment. You may escape this hazard to some extent by relying only on the indirect contributions of tests to learning. But even here, if the test is a poor one, the motivation will be misdirected, and the rewards of effective study and teaching scant. It is much, much better to acquire the skill, and to take the time and the pains to make and use good tests. Then truly will their use improve instruction.

THE NATURE AND FORMAT OF CRITERION TESTS IN THE CONTEXT OF PROGRAMMED LEARNING

S. S. KULKARNI

1. Distinction between criterion-referenced and norm-referenced tests

The emphasis on training as distinct from measurement *per se,* which is highlighted in the field of programmed learning, has brought into focus the distinction between a criterion-referenced measure and a norm-referenced measure (Glaser and Klaus 1962). One can develop tests which reflect the desirable behaviour which is a goal or a criterion for a given training programme. Such tests may or may not discriminate among those who take that programme.

The old term 'mastery test' is closer to the concept of criterion-referenced measure. Ebel's (1962a) concept of the content standard test is also similar to the concept of the criterion-referenced measure. The conventional standardized tests, on the other hand, are norm-referenced measures. Their objective is to assess the capability of an individual compared with the performance of other individuals. In other words, their main function is to rank individuals.

It is pointed out by programmers that what we need in the field of programmed learning are criterion-referenced measures rather than the norm-referenced measures. The controversy is rather sharp when the problem of evaluating certain programmed material is to be faced. A programmer claims that he is aiming at a 90/90 standard, i.e. 90 per cent of the students from the population for which that programme is prepared should get 90 per cent of marks on the criterion test after working through the programme. A conventional test constructor would then say that if most students are getting such a high score on a test, the test needs improvement, because it does not discriminate.

To my mind the controversy is more superficial than fundamental. There was a time when the controversy regarding the achievement test as distinct from the aptitude test was also quite sharp. The concept of developed ability testing as reflected in the STEP tests by the Educational Testing Service can, however, provide us with a higher synthesis. One may say that the same test measuring developed ability could be used to assess past achievement or to predict future achievement, that is to say, present aptitude. Something of the kind will happen to the controversy between criterion-referenced and norm-referenced tests, if we start discussing the functions that a test (or tests) needs to perform in the context of programmed learning.

2. Functions of a test in the context of programmed learning

Evaluating the efficacy of programmed learning material. Schools which use programmed material and a programmer need a test to assess whether students learn with the help of a given programme, i.e. to say if they arrive at the criterion behaviour after going through the programme; in other words, a test is needed to evaluate the effectiveness of the programmed material for a given population. Such a test should reflect all the important elements of the criterion behaviour. An item in such a test will justify its placement in the test, not on the ground that it discriminates among students who are taking the programme, but on the ground that it reflects the criterion behaviour. In theory, it might turn out that all the students who take a programme get all the items right, or that no student gets any item right. Strictly speaking, then, the justification for any item's inclusion in these tests does not lie in its discriminatory or difficulty indices, but in its representing the criterion behaviour.

Diagnosis. A teacher using a programme and even a programmer, would need a test for another reason, too. They would like to know where the students are committing errors, and what are their weaknesses or their strong points. This knowledge would help a programmer to improve his programme. It would also enable a teacher to supplement the programme. This implies the construction of what is called a diagnostic test. Such a test reflects not only the elements of the final criterion behaviour, but also the transitional behaviour, i.e. that behaviour the learning of which leads ultimately to the criterion behaviour. If a student cannot respond to items which refer to a certain transitional behaviour, either the programmer has to change his programme or the teacher has to help the student to understand that mediating concept so that the student can reach the criterion behaviour.

Selecting students for a given programme. A teacher and a programmer may also need a test which reflects the initial behaviour or the prerequisites of a programme. A programmer has to specify what he assumes to have been previously learned by a student. If a student does not possess the knowledge or skills assumed by the programmer, then that student cannot work through the programme successfully. In order to decide whether a particular piece of programmed material should be given to a student, a teacher will need a tool which contains items on these prerequisites.

What does this add up to? We need a test to assess: (a) criterion

The nature and format of criterion tests

behaviour (function 1), (b) transitional behaviour (function 2), and (c) initial behaviour (function 3). It could be one test consisting of sub-tests, or a series of tests depending upon the number of items necessary to represent the universe of behaviour with adequate reliability and validity.

Ranking students. Now let us consider the function of ranking students performed by the standardized achievement tests or the conventional achievement tests used in examinations, etc. It is true that a programmer is not primarily interested in ranking students who have taken his programme. He would ideally like all students to achieve the criterion performance. But then the problem arises of how he knows that a given test reflects the criterion behaviour reliably? One source of evidence is, of course, the subject matter expert looking at the test and saying that the items in it reflect the criterion behaviour. But, then, the whole history of measurement suggests that the subject matter experts' opinion on the reliability and validity of an item is not adequate evidence. An item may look good, and still a person who is an acknowledged expert in a field may not be able to solve it correctly, while a novice may get it right. Here we get into the techniques of constructing items. The procedure of item analysis—computing item difficulty and discrimination indices, etc., etc.—has arisen in order that additional evidence should be obtained to see whether an item works in the right direction. The problem faced by a programmer that an item may not discriminate among students who are taught by a given programme could be solved by a slight change in the procedure of collecting the item statistics. Ebel (1962b) has suggested, in the context of constructing classroom tests, a procedure which may be helpful in this context, too. Following this procedure, a test constructor in the try-out phase may give his test to a group consisting of experts, trainees who have taken the programme and novices who have not taken the programme but who can be matched with the trainees on all the important variables except the training under consideration. No programmer should deny that an item in the test reflecting the criterion behaviour should be responded to correctly by all the experts. The novices, on the other hand, should not be able to get more than 40 per cent of the criterion items. If, however, they are getting more than 40 per cent of the items, it is clear that the programme, which aims to teach some new criterion behaviour, is not teaching something which the trainees do not already know. A group of experts, trainees and novices ranging widely in their achievement would help in collecting item statistics which will allow item analysis in the conventional sense.

(Of course, there is nothing sacred in the figure 40 per cent. Any other, preferably stricter, standard could be fixed.) In short, although ranking of students may not be the main function of a test to be used in the programmed learning context, the data regarding discrimination between the experts, trainees and novices would help in constructing a reliable and valid test without sacrificing the functions 1, 2 and 3 referred to above.

3. Nature of a learning-set test

Is it necessary, then, to construct tests separately for assessing the criterion behaviour, transitional behaviour and initial behaviour? It seems to me that constructing a test/tests which can perform all the three functions mentioned above would save a lot of time and cost if the task was taken up simultaneously. Programmed material usually, although not always, represents a certain hierarchy. A programmer takes a student from a specified initial behaviour to the criterion behaviour through certain mediating concepts or transitional behaviour. A programmer worth the name has to prepare a task analysis or flow chart, whatever the name may be, which reflects the initial behaviour, the transitional behaviour and the criterion behaviour. By the time that a programmer finishes writing a programme, he has a clear map of the whole hierarchy or sequence that he has built into the programme. In most programmed materials there are also what are called 'criterion frames'. Criterion frames may be defined as frames within a programme which are minimally cued (prompted) and the correct response to which is considered by a programmer as learning (or mastery) of a subtask or unit he was trying to teach in the sequence prior to such a criterion frame. Of course, in most programmes, especially those following the Skinnerian technique, the error rate is very low even on the criterion frames. But all the same, such a frame is more or less equivalent to a test item. The error rate or, in psychometrical terms, the difficulty value of such a criterion frame is low because care is taken to see that students learn the subtask through the learning frames which precede it.

A test constructor usually has to spend a lot of time in preparing a table of specification. On the other hand, a programmer has no escape but to prepare a task analysis. The task analysis prepared by a programmer can easily be transformed into a table of specification by a test constructor. He can then independently write items to represent all the three phases, the initial, the transitional and the criterion behaviour. Such a test may be called a learning-set test. Gagne (1962) defines a learning set as 'knowledge relevant to any given final task to be learned.

The nature and format of criterion tests

These are considered to be arranged in hierarchy such that any learning set may have one or more learning sets subordinate to it in the sense that they mediate positive transfer to the given learning set. These subordinate sets in turn have other learning sets subordinate to them and so on.'

Such a learning-set test can perform all the three functions referred to above. It is, of course, a criterion-referenced test. It is also in a sense a norm-referenced test; i.e. it can discriminate between experts and trainees on the one hand and novices on the other.

An additional advantage of a learning-set test is that it allows re-appraisal of a sequence in the programme. In most programmes, there is an assumed hierarchy of learning sets. The preconceived hierarchy goes through some modifications during the try-out of a programme. But even then, the try-out itself is somewhat biased to the sequence preconceived by a programmer, unless, of course, a programme is built completely in a learner-controlled manner, as suggested by Mager (1961). How does one know whether a sequence built in the programme is the necessary sequence? How does one know whether a concept—a sub-learning set is essential or inessential for another supposedly higher learning set? One method to test this is to administer a learning-set test to students after they have worked through a programme and also to the novices. On the basis of the scores obtained by students, one can prepare an item by individual scalogram (see the appendix). The rationale and the procedure of constructing this scalogram is basically the same as proposed by Guttman (1947). The basic assumption is that a student getting a lower score would not be getting correct items which represent higher concepts. The coefficient of reproducibility will then be an index of a perfect sequence in the programme. If, on the other hand, there are inversions—meaning that some students are getting items on the higher concepts correct without getting the items on the lower concept—it will mean that the sequence is not perfect. It may turn out that some of the learning sets which are put later in the programme are easier or can be taught earlier or may not be taught at all.

The scalogram reproduced in the appendix is based on the post-test scores obtained by students who have worked through a programme on 'earth rotation and revolution', in an experiment conducted by Sharma and Kulkarni (1967). The X axis gives items in the post-test arranged in an order representing the sequence/hierarchy in the programme. The Y axis represents students selected randomly from each score interval of 3. The range of scores obtained on the post-test was 20 to 48. The scalogram suggests that the hierarchy in parts A, B, C, D is empirically justifiable. But as regards the sequence of part D and part E, some reconsideration is necessary. In this particular programme, part D deals with the topic of latitudes and part E with the topic of longitudes. There is no logical or psychological necessity of teaching latitude before longitude. This is what is indicated by the empirical data as presented in the scalogram. Various other inversions may also be studied by a programmer/subject matter expert for more hints in revising the organization of the programme.

From a teacher's point of view also such a scalogram analysis of post-test items would be enlightening. He would be able to locate students who need help and the exact step at which they require such help. He could then provide them with remedial material or arrange for individual instruction.

4. Distinction between learning-set test and standardized achievement test

The conventional procedure of constructing achievement tests does not give enough importance to the transitional behaviour and to the initial behaviour. It focuses more on the criterion behaviour—the final product of the educational treatment. Diagnostic tests, on the other hand, take into consideration the transitional behaviour. As such the conventionally prepared standardized achievement test cannot perform the second and third function referred to above, namely, diagnosis and selecting students for a training programme. In evaluating programmed material, too, standardized achievement tests suffer from some limitations. Such a test may have certain elements which are not included as goals for a particular programme, or it may not have certain elements which a certain programmer is including as goals for the specific programme. In other words, a given standardized achievement test may not be representing fully or adequately the criterion behaviour which a given programme is aiming at.

A standardized achievement test also suffers from another limitation when it is used in a research of pre- and post-test design. Most programmers would like to know where a student stands before he takes the programme, so that the gain in his learning after he works through the programme can be measured. The conventional standardized achievement test, as stated above, may not contain items on the prerequisite knowledge and skills, and, therefore, when it is administered as a pre-test, the variations within a group at the starting-point may not come out. On the other hand, if a learning-set test is administered which has items representing the initial behaviour,

The nature and format of criterion tests

it can allow a teacher/a programmer to note the variations in the starting-point of different individuals. This will allow a teacher or a programmer to help students if and where necessary, or to allow a student to omit certain sections of a programme if he has already mastered the behaviour referred to in those sections.

Items representing the initial behaviour in a test which is to be administered as a pre-test also help in another very important way. If a test has items representing only the criterion behaviour but not the initial behaviour, the likelihood is high that students would not get any items correct and thereby would get frustrated. On the other hand, a learning-set test by having items representing the initial behaviour, allows a student to demonstrate what he does know, and thereby gives him a feeling of satisfaction and confidence.

The sequential test idea as exemplified by the Sequential Test of Educational Progress by Educational Testing Service goes a long way in this important direction. But most achievement tests commercially available are not developed on the sequential model.

5. Distinction between learning-set test and criterion frames within a programme: the problem of transfer

As noted above, most programmes have criterion or subcriterion frames spread out within them. If one separates such frames from a programme and modifies them wherever necessary, one can develop a test. Some programmers suggest that there is no need to develop separate tests because there is a test in the form of criterion frames built in a programme itself. Here the important issue is that of transfer of learning. A programme may be teaching students certain behaviour, but this behaviour may be too specific. Even when one accepts the fact that criterion frames within a programme are minimally prompted or cued, sequence itself is an important prompt. Then again, even if one separates these frames from a programme and administers them by mixing up the order, one does not really solve the limitation of specificity. Independent evidence must be obtained before one concludes that students have arrived at the criterion behaviour. The criterion frames in a programme constitute only one sample of the population of items which can be generated out of the defined criterion behaviour. Can trainees of a given programme solve items from another sample of a population of items based on the same definition of criterion behaviour? This is a relevant and important question, and unless it is answered satisfactorily by independent evidence, one cannot feel assured of the effectiveness of a programme.

It is true, however, that it is not easy to generate complete population of items for a defined criterion behaviour, and then to draw item samples randomly. Operationally, then, what it amounts to is to get items constructed by an independent competent person who works on the basis of the same definition of criterion behaviour or table of specification. In the context of programmed learning, one may arrange the operations as follows. The task analysis representing the initial, transitional and criterion behaviour of a programme should be given to a test constructor other than the programmer. This test constructor(s) should write items to represent the various specified behaviours. In other words, a learning-set test should be prepared.

Of course, the point remains of whether schools would agree with the criterion behaviour. But this is a separate question. A programmer may first ask the schools to define the criterion behaviour and then prepare a programme to arrive at that criterion behaviour. Schools can also satisfy themselves on the representativeness of a learning-set test, that is to say, whether the test reflects the desirable learning.

6. The problem of transfer

The problem of transfer from one sample of items to another is only one dimension of the concept of transfer. The transfer of learning can also be considered on various other dimensions like situations, complexity of elements, etc. To what extent a programme enables a student to transfer his learning to these various dimensions is a problem which will always be asked but which is not easy to solve. The major difficulty here is to define in operational terms the extent of transfer on these various dimensions. Programmers claim that if the degree of transfer and the specific nature (its dimension) is defined by the consumer in operational terms, they may be able to programme for it. There are now programmes which enable children to get higher scores on intelligence tests. I do not wish to enter into this field in this paper. I only want to point out here that to the extent the degree of the transfer is defined in operational terms, it can be translated into a pool of test items. Such test items should form a part of the learning-set test referred to above. One may also like to assess the criterion behaviour under different conditions—like immediate *v.* delayed retention, recognition *v.* recall, etc. In all such circumstances, learning-set tests, as defined above, could be useful.

7. Conclusion

It is not the contention of this paper that a learning-set test must be one test without parts. In fact, it would be advisable to arrange a learning-set test in parts: the first part reflecting the initial behaviour, the second part representing the transitional behaviour, and the third part representing the criterion behaviour. What is emphasized, however, is that while constructing a test, one should have a complete analysis of all these three phases and construct items to represent this total universe of behaviour. It may also be pointed out here that within a given part the items need not be presented to the students in a sequential order. They should preferably be presented in a random order. For the purposes of the scalogram referred to above, they could, however, be rearranged when necessary to represent the hierarchy in the programme.

If tests are developed on the model of a learning-set test, much of the sharpness of the controversy over criterion-referenced *and* norm-referenced would fade, and we should have a functional test which could be used for variety of purposes.

References

Ebel, R. L. (1962a) 'Content standard test scores.' *Educ. psychol. Measur.*, 22, no. 1.

Ebel, R. L. (1962b) *A Program for the Improvement of Classroom Tests.* Princeton, N.J.: Educational Testing Service.

Educational Testing Service (1959) *Sequential Tests of Educational Progress.* Technical Report. Princeton, N.J.: Educational Testing Service.

Gagne, R. M. (ed.) (1962) *Psychological Principles in System Development.* New York: Holt, Rinehart & Winston.

Gagne, R. M. and Paradise, N. E. (1961) *Abilities and Learning Sets in Knowledge Acquisition.* Psychological Monograph vol. 75, no. 14. Psychological Association, Inc.

Glaser, R. (1965) *Teaching Machines and Programmed Learning II.* Washington, D.C.: NEA.

Glaser, R. and Klaus, D. P. (1962) 'Proficiency measurement assessing human performance.' In Gagne, R. M. (ed.) *Psychological Principles in System Development.* New York: Holt, Rinehart & Winston.

Guttman, L. (1947) 'The Cornell technique for scale and intensity analysis.' *Educ. psychol. Measur.*, 7, 247-79.

Mager, R. F. (1961) *Preparing Objectives for Programmed Instruction.* Fearon Publishers.

Sharma and Kulkarni (1967) 'A study of achievement in geography through Programmed Learning Method Department of Psychological Foundations.' NCERT, Delhi. (Unpublished).

APPENDIX: ANALYSIS OF POST-TEST SCORES FOR SEQUENTIAL PROGRESSION OF THE PROGRAMME ON 'EARTH'S ROTATION AND REVOLUTION'

Sequential order of the post-test items in each part of the programme

No. of item		A							B						C						
Sl. no.	'Scores'	6	5	4	2	44	45	3	1	10	7	9	16	12	11	24	34	38	39	40	50	15	8
1	48	.	.	.	.	.	.	.	.	.	.	.	.	.	.	.	.	.	.	.	.	.	.
2	45	.	.	.	.	.	.	.	.	.	.	.	.	.	.	.	.	.	.	.	.	.	.
3	42	.	.	.	.	.	.	.	.	.	.	.	.	.	.	.	.	.	.	.	.	.	.
4	38	.	.	.	.	.	.	.	.	.	.	.	.	.	.	.	.	x	.	.	.	.	.
5	36	.	.	.	.	.	.	.	.	.	.	.	.	.	.	x	x	.	.	.	x	.	.
6	34	.	.	.	.	.	.	.	.	.	.	.	.	.	.	.	.	.	x	.	.	.	.
7	32	.	.	.	.	.	.	.	x	.	.	.	.	.	.	.	.	.	.	.	.	.	.
8	28	.	.	.	.	.	x	x	.	.	.	.	.	.	.	.	.	.	.	.	.	.	.
9	25	.	.	.	.	.	.	.	x	.	.	.	x	.	.	.	.	.	.	.	.	.	x
10	22	.	.	.	.	.	.	.	x	.	.	.	.	x	x	.	.	.	.	.	.	.	x
11	20	.	.	.	.	.	.	.	x	.	.	.	.	.	x	.	.	.	.	.	.	x	x

	No. of item	13 46 17 43 28 41 25 26 27 23 21 18 20 19 29 30 22	36 37 35 48 47 14 32 33 42 31 49
Sl. no.	'Scores'	D	E
1	48	. . . .	. . . . x x
2	45	. . . . x x	. . . . x x x
3	42	. . . . x x . . . .: .	x x . . . . . . x x x
4	38	. . . x . . . . x . . . . . x x .	x x x . . . . . x x x
5	36	. . . . . . x x . . . . . x . x x	x x . x x . . . x x x
6	34	. . . x . . . . x x x x x x	x . x . x . x x x x x
7	32	. . . . . . x x x x x x x x x x x	. . . x . x . x x x x
8	28	. . x x x x x x x x x x x x x x x	. . x . x x x x x x x
9	25	. x x x x x x x x x x x x x x x x	. . . . x x x x x x x
10	22	x x x x x x x x x x x x x x x x x	. . . . x x x x x x x
11	20	x x x x x x x x x x x x x x x x x	x x x . x x x x x x x

A = Shapes of Earth and Sun   D = Latitudes
B = Earth's movements   E = Longitudes
C = North and South Poles

Items 31 and 49 refer to the topic on international data line taught at the end of part E.

. = Correct response
x = Incorrect response

PROBLEMS IN ESTABLISHING TEST VALIDITY AND IN THE USE OF PREDICTION TABLES. ADVANTAGES AND DISADVANTAGES OF VARIOUS TYPES OF NORMS

VALIDITY STUDIES AND NORMS AS AIDS IN SCORE INTERPRETATION

W. B. SCHRADER

The fact that the interpretation of objective test scores depends to a remarkably large extent upon statistical data stands as a persistent challenge to anyone doing statistical work in testing. Statistical studies can provide information about what tests are measuring, data about the performance of students belonging to a defined group on a specific test, and predictions of performance based on test data. Along with the technical problems in analysing the data, there is the equally pressing problem of communicating the results to test users, at least some of whom find statistical concepts not only unfamiliar but even painful.

The empirical validation of test scores seems to go back to 1890, when Francis Galton, in commenting on an article about testing, made the following statement: 'One of the most important objects of measurement is . . . to obtain a general knowledge of the capacities of a man by sinking shafts, as it were, at a few critical points. To ascertain the best points for this purpose, the sets of measures should be compared with an independent estimate of a man's powers. We thus may learn which of the measures are the most instructive.' The building of tests and examinations for various purposes goes far back into history, but the specific concept of validation by empirical studies has a much more recent origin.

It is fortunate that Galton did not stop with the formulation of the concept of test validation, but proceeded, in co-operation with his colleague, Karl Pearson, to develop the appropriate tools for making the kind of studies now known as validity studies. Correlation and regression methods, including multiple correlation and regression, were developed by these pioneer workers. These methods still constitute the main analytical tools for empirical validation of tests. It is pleasant to think of Galton, having constructed a scatter diagram so that the spread of data of the two variables was approximately equal, using a stretched silk thread to estimate by eye the slope of the regression line which would best describe the data. Of course, the formulation of entirely objective methods of establishing the regression line greatly increased the utility of the concept.

During the past fifty years, innumerable studies have sought to determine correlation coefficients between test scores and subsequent performance, especially as performance is demonstrated in academic grades earned in college or other educational institutions. The popularity of the correlation coefficient among statisticians is apparent. Test users, on the other hand, often find the correlation coefficient unsatisfactory, partly because there seems to be no easy way of interpreting it as a percentage.

As long as the correlation coefficient retains its pre-eminent position as a way of expressing the degree of relation between a predictor and a criterion or between two test scores, there will be a need for understanding the meaning of a correlation coefficient in terms of more familiar concepts. If test users are to be able to understand statistical results reported in this form as a way of understanding the meaning of test scores, ways must be found to enrich the meaning of correlation coefficients. One method of accomplishing this which has proved helpful is shown in table 1. The values shown were based on the excellent tables of the bivariate normal distribution published by the National Bureau of Standards in 1959. Table 1 is based on the assumption that the distribution of scores follows a bivariate normal distribution.

In some respects, the most interesting aspect of table 1 is the comparison of results for a validity coefficient of 0·40 with the results for a validity coefficient of 0·70. Notice that of a hundred students who score in the top fifth on the predictor, seven will fall in the bottom fifth on the criterion when the validity is 0·40. A prediction in the top fifth followed by an actual performance in the bottom fifth is presumably a cause for serious concern. With a validity coefficient of 0·70, these errors are certainly not eliminated. However, only 1 in 100 of those predicted to be in the top fifth turn out to be in the bottom fifth on the criterion. Thus an improvement in the prediction represented by a gain in validity from 0·40 to 0·70 reduces very markedly the number of serious or relatively serious errors of prediction that are made. At a different level, the figures for a correlation coefficient of 0·90 are useful for the interpretation of reliability coefficients.

A second way of interpreting correlation coefficients, developed by Brogden (1946), is useful in estimating the value of a particular test when used in selection. Brogden's approach is based on the biserial correlation coefficient, and requires the assumption that the criterion measure is distributed normally in the sample. Essentially, Brogden's approach can be considered a percentage measure of the efficiency of a predictor for selection. Suppose that a predictor having a validity coefficient of 0·50 with the measure of success is used in selecting candidates for a particular school. What this approach states is that the improvement in the mean performance accomplished by selecting the

Table 1.* Relation between standing on predictor and standing on criterion for various values of the correlation coefficient

Correlation coefficient	Standing on predictor	Percentage of students standing in each criterion group		
		Bottom fifth	Middle three-fifths	Top fifth
·10	Top fifth	16	60	24
	Middle three-fifths	20	60	20
	Bottom fifth	24	60	16
·20	Top fifth	13	59	28
	Middle three-fifths	20	60	20
	Bottom fifth	28	59	13
·30	Top fifth	10	57	33
	Middle three-fifths	19	62	19
	Bottom fifth	33	57	10
·40	Top fifth	7	55	38
	Middle three-fifths	18	64	18
	Bottom fifth	38	55	7
·50	Top fifth	4	52	44
	Middle three-fifths	17	66	17
	Bottom fifth	44	52	4
·60	Top fifth	2	48	50
	Middle three-fifths	16	68	16
	Bottom fifth	50	48	2
·70	Top fifth	1	43	56
	Middle three-fifths	14	72	14
	Bottom fifth	56	43	1
·80	Top fifth	0·2	35·4	64·4
	Middle three-fifths	11·8	76·4	11·8
	Bottom fifth	64·4	35·4	0·2
·90	Top fifth	(0·002)	25·2	74·8
	Middle three-fifths	8·4	83·2	8·4
	Bottom fifth	74·8	25·2	(0·002)

*Tables 1 and 2 and figure 2 are reprinted from *J. educ. Measur.*, June 1965.

top students using the available predictor will be 50 per cent as great as the improvement which would have been obtained if a perfect predictor of the criterion had been available. An interesting feature of this approach is that it does not depend on what percentage of the applicants is selected. From an algebraic viewpoint, the development of Brogden's interpretation from the equation for the biserial correlation coefficient is quite straightforward. I think I should say, however, that this way of interpreting correlation coefficients, although it does use the concept of a percentage, is not as readily understood by test users as one might hope.

Still another way of interpreting correlation coefficients for tests used in selection is that developed by Taylor and Russell in 1939. Using tables of the bivariate normal distribution, they estimated the percentage who would be satisfactory within a selected group as a function of three variables: first, the percentage of applicants who would be successful if no selection took place, secondly, the validity of the selection instrument or instruments, and thirdly, the percentage of applicants who were selected. A particularly attractive feature of the Taylor-Russell approach is that it emphasizes the important of the quality of applicants in relation to the standards for success in the school or job in determining the quality of the selected group.

These relatively abstract methods of interpreting coefficients must be supplemented by experience with the outcome of studies in specific fields of application. Testers have learned that a reliability coefficient of 0·90 is reasonably good, while a reliability coefficient of 0·80 raises serious questions unless there is a specific reason why the reliability is low in a particular application. By contrast, a validity coefficient of a test score against college grades which turned out to be 0·80 would probably lead most test workers to do an additional check of the numerical work which led up to it. In any case, when validity coefficients are frequently calculated for a particular kind of application, a knowledge of the usual range of coefficients is a very important factor in interpreting any given coefficient.

Two considerations which complicate the interpretation of validity coefficients, but which are nevertheless essential, are sampling error and the effects of selection. Although sampling error is quite familiar to statisticians, it is by no means safe to assume that it is understood by test users. Moreover, the size of the sampling error of correlation coefficients becomes especially pertinent, since many validity studies are based on relatively small samples. To make this point somewhat more explicit, it may be noted that if the population value of a correlation coefficient is 0·50, it may be expected that 95 per cent of

Validity studies and norms as aids

observed coefficients based on samples of fifty will fall between the limits of 0·26 and 0·68. That the interpretation of a validity coefficient of 0·26 would differ radically from the interpretation of a coefficient of 0·68 need hardly be stated. Even when one-hundred-case samples are drawn, 95 per cent of the coefficients would fall between 0·34 and 0·63. Although this range is still relatively large, we have used eighty-five as the minimum number of cases to be used in a conventional validity study. Clearly, a minimum sample size of eighty-five, although convenient for student groups in small colleges and professional schools, results in a relatively large sampling error for the validity coefficient obtained. It is true, as Hotelling showed in 1940, that when validity coefficients of two highly correlated predictors are compared, using the same criterion measure and the same group, the sampling error is appreciably smaller. Nevertheless, the sampling fluctuation of correlation coefficients needs consideration whenever coefficients are interpreted.

A more interesting influence on the validity coefficient is selection. Quite frequently, validity coefficients are based on groups which have been selected in part on the basis of scores on the test being validated. As a matter of common sense, it seems reasonable that when the group has been selected on the basis of the test, the validity coefficient of the test will be somewhat reduced. Intuitively, the exclusion of the low-scoring students, by reducing the range of ability represented in the group, would be expected to reduce the validity coefficient. A more powerful approach to thinking about the effects of selection is based on the idea that the regression of the criterion measure on the predictor will continue to have the same slope and intercept, even though there is selection on the predictor. If it is recalled that the regression line fits the means of the vertical arrays, and if it is assumed that the regression is linear, it is plausible that the regression line would not be affected systematically by the elimination of some of the vertical arrays. If it is further assumed that the errors of estimate (the standard deviations of the residuals) are uniform for the various vertical arrays, it is possible to calculate the effect on the correlation coefficient of varying degrees of selection on the predictor. These results, which were originally worked out by Pearson, are well known to statisticians. Here, again, test users are much less familiar with these results. A serious complication in the application of the equations for restriction of range arises from the fact that the selection is often based on a number of abilities, and data for at least some of the measures are not readily obtained for the unselected population. Moreover, there is always some degree of scepticism with respect to adjusted coefficients.

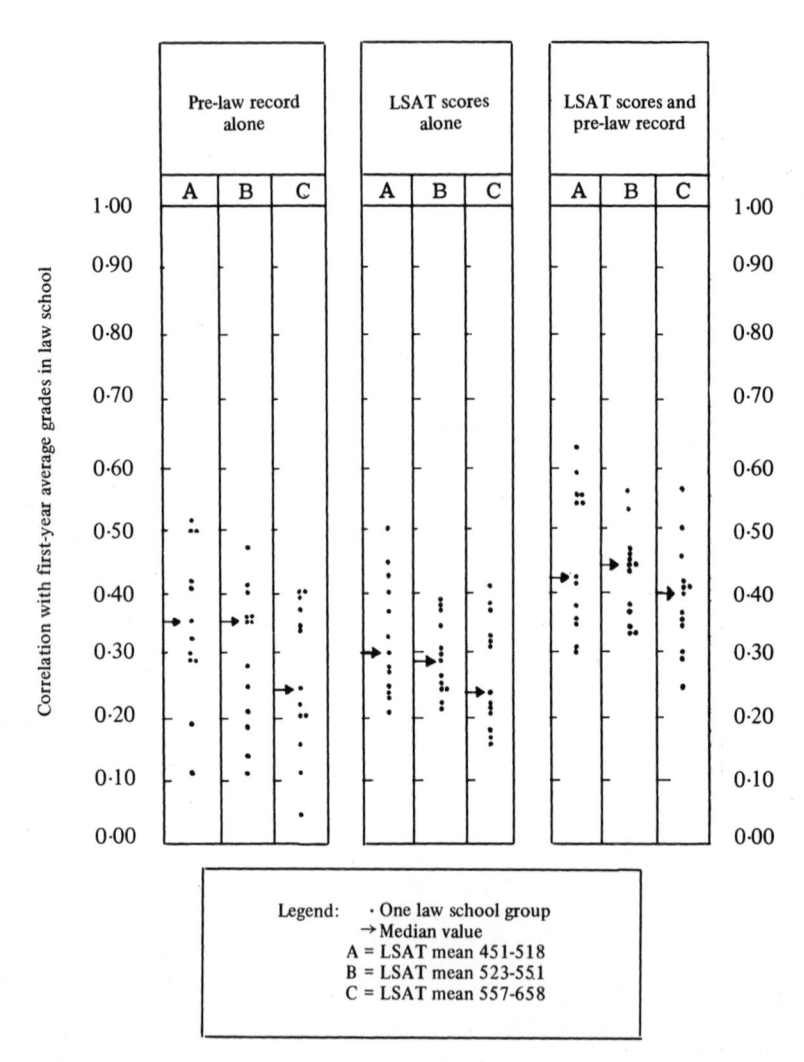

Figure 1a. Validity coefficients of pre-law record alone, LSAT scores alone, and pre-law record combined with LSAT scores. (Based on studies conducted in 1965-6 for thirty-nine law schools. Law school groups arranged according to LSAT mean.)

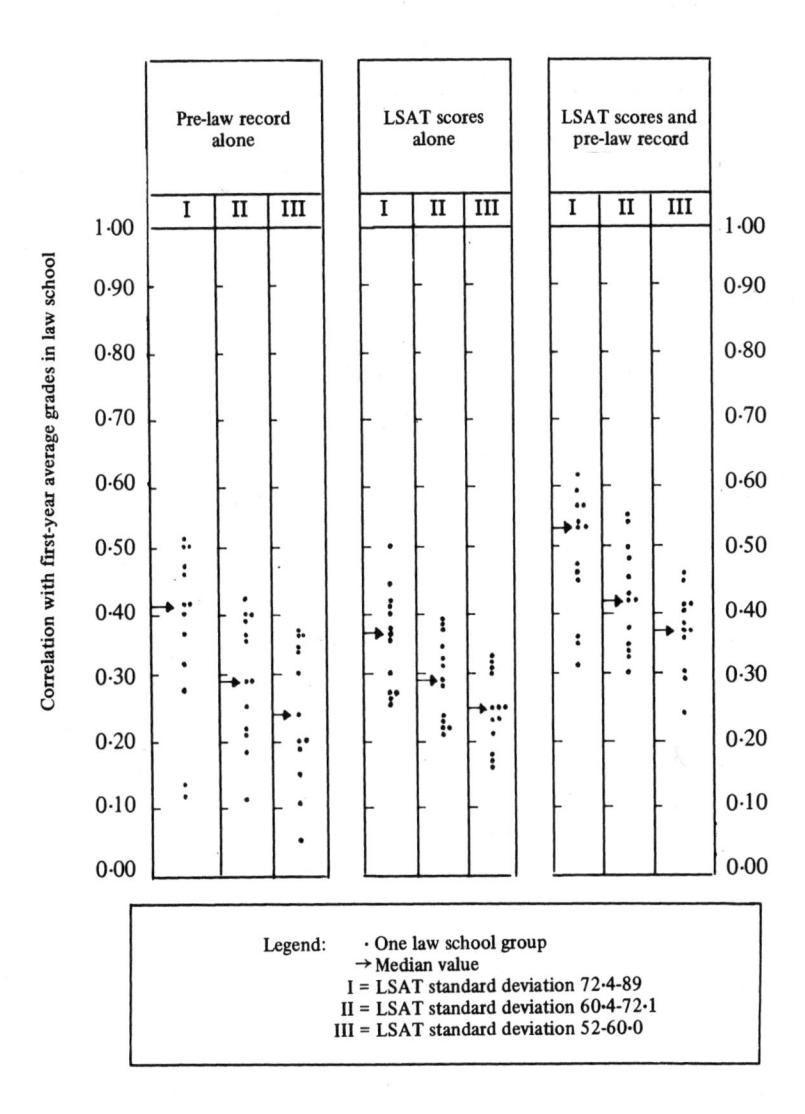

Figure 1b. Validity coefficients of pre-law record alone, LSAT scores alone, and pre-law record combined with LSAT scores. (Based on studies conducted in 1965-6 for thirty-nine law schools. Law school groups arranged according to LSAT standard deviation.)

Figures 1a and b show the results of validity studies in thirty-nine law schools completed during the academic year 1965-6. Figure 1a shows the results classified according to the mean score on the Law School Admission Test, and figure 1b shows the same results classified according to the standard deviation of the Law School Admission Test scores in each of the thirty-nine schools. Although it is true that selection should be expected to raise the mean at the same time that it reduces the standard deviation, the results shown in these two charts suggest that it is the range of talent within the group, as measured by the standard deviation, rather than the ability level of the group, as represented by the mean test score, which is most directly related to the effect of selection on validity. This is what the statistical theory with respect to selection would lead one to expect. The results shown in these two charts are in no way intended to serve as proof of the effect of selection on validity coefficients. Rather they are intended to show that this particular set of results is consistent with the view that the standard deviation of the test score is a relevant kind of datum to consider in interpreting a validity coefficient. Figure 1b shows that the schools which have a relatively large standard deviation on the Law School Admission Test tend to have relatively high validity coefficients not only for LSAT, but also for pre-law average, and for the multiple correlation based on both predictors. It is also clear from figure 1b that law schools having relatively small standard deviations of LSAT scores tend to have low validity coefficients. Although alternative hypotheses might be offered to account for the outcome found, the most probable implication would seem to be that the correlation coefficient obtained for a particular group of students should be interpreted in the light of the range of talent represented by that group.

One outcome of this discussion of the effects of selection may be regarded as most fortunate. If it is assumed that the regression line (or plane) is not affected by selection on the predictors, and if it is further assumed that the standard error of estimate is not affected by selection on the predictors, it can be argued that regression rather than correlation should be the main tool in validity studies. Indeed, it seems likely that the most valuable contribution of a conventional validity study lies not in the correlation coefficients which are produced, though they may be of some interest for comparing results from one group to another, but in the regression equation which permits the translation of relatively unfamiliar predictor data into the more readily understood form of predicted grades.

Figure 2 shows one device for facilitating the use of a regression equation by test users. Using a student's score on the Law School

Validity studies and norms as aids

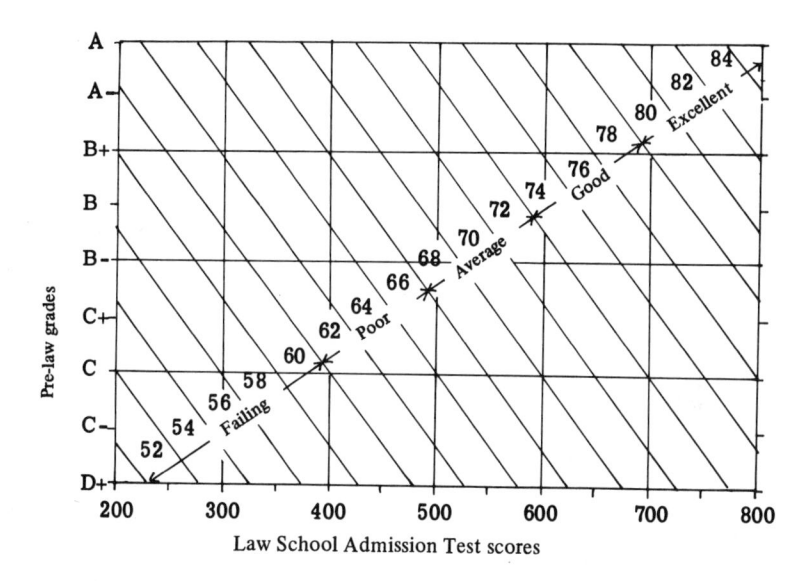

Figure 2. Sample Abac for predicting first-year grades in law school from Law School Admission Test scores and pre-law grades

Admission Test and his average grade earned in four years of undergraduate college (designated as 'Pre-law grades'), the table may be read so as to locate the band in which his predicted performance lies. Thus a student whose LSAT score was 500 and whose pre-law grades averaged B− would have a predicted grade of 68 in this particular law school. Once a prediction chart has been developed for a law school, the results can be used for estimating the probable performance of subsequent applicants.

Regression theory clearly implies that it is undesirable to stop merely with making a prediction. With correlation coefficients of the level ordinarily encountered, it is well known that the standard error of estimate will be relatively large. Table 2 was developed, using the standard error of estimate, to show the expected amount of variation above and below the regression plane. A student with a predicted grade of 68 has, of course, 50 chances in 100 of earning a grade of 68 or better. What would be less apparent without table 2, a student with a predicted grade as 68 has 87 chances in 100 of earning a grade of 62 or better, and 1 chance in 100 of earning a grade of 80 or better. In a

Table 2. Chances in 100 that students with various predicted grades (based on figure 2) will equal or excel various first-year average grades in law school

Predicted grade	52	54	56	58	60	62	64	66	68	70	72	74	76	78	80	82	84
84											99	97	94	87	78	65	50
82										99	97	94	87	78	65	50	35
80									99	97	94	87	78	65	50	35	22
78								99	97	94	87	78	65	50	35	22	13
76							99	97	94	87	78	65	50	35	22	13	6
74						99	97	94	87	78	65	50	35	22	13	6	3
72					99	97	94	87	78	65	50	35	22	13	6	3	1
70				99	97	94	87	78	65	50	35	22	13	6	3	1	
68			99	97	94	87	78	65	50	35	22	13	6	3	1		
66		99	97	94	87	78	65	50	35	22	13	6	3	1			
64	99	97	94	87	78	65	50	35	22	13	6	3	1				
62	97	94	87	78	65	50	35	22	13	6	3	1					
60	94	87	78	65	50	35	22	13	6	3	1						
58	87	78	65	50	35	22	13	6	3	1							
56	78	65	50	35	22	13	6	3	1								
54	65	50	35	22	13	6	3	1									
52	50	35	22	13	6	3	1										

Chances in 100 that a student will earn an average of at least:

sense, *figure 2* indicates what the predictors *will do,* while *table 2* provides information about the *limitations* of the predictors. Both kinds of information seem essential to a full understanding of how prediction is taking place.

Admittedly, figure 2 and table 2 create a smooth, regular picture which is likely to be markedly different from the irregular, complex details which would appear in the underlying data. The regression approach has the virtue of insuring that a student who is higher on both predictors will have as high as or higher prediction than a student with lower scores on both predictors. In the original data, it might well happen that certain combinations of relatively low predictor scores might be associated in fact with a high mean performance in a particular sample, whereas certain other combinations of high predictor scores would be associated with relatively low mean performance. Ordinarily, this may be attributed to sampling fluctuations in the particular sample at hand. It would be unfortunate, however, if the use of linear regression and a uniform standard error of estimate prevented the search for possible curvilinear relations or for possible variations in the standard error of estimate in different score ranges.

For many kinds of tests, particularly measures of subject matter achievement, *norms* rather than empirical validation constitute the primary statistical aid to score interpretation. Rather than attempt a broad treatment of this complex subject, I have chosen to limit myself to two rather special topics related to normative data. First, I would like to describe briefly a way of obtaining comparable scores when the candidate is allowed to choose within a set of *optional* tests. Secondly, I would like to mention the desirability of using the standard error of measurement along with norms in score interpretation.

When all students in a designated group take all tests in a given set, it is quite a straightforward matter to develop norms which permit the test user to assess the relative excellence of a given student on the various tests.

It is clear that a special problem arises when not all the tests are appropriate for all the students in the norms group. For example, in the College Entrance Examination Board testing programme, virtually all students take an aptitude test yielding verbal and mathematical scores during the morning session. However, each student chooses one, two or three tests out of some fourteen different tests that are offered at the afternoon session. Thus, a student who has emphasized science and mathematics in his high school programme might take a test in physics, mathematics and English composition. Another student might take French, social studies and English composition. Clearly, very many combinations of tests could be chosen to reflect differences in the programmes of studies. If, as one might expect, the ability level on the aptitude test differs appreciably for students taking different achievement tests, the question arises as to whether scores that are in some sense comparable can be derived. In practice this question is restated as a problem of estimating the performance on the achievement test which would be expected for a standard group. In the case where there are two common tests, the standard group is defined as having a fixed mean and standard deviation for both tests, and the correlation between the common tests is also fixed.

A solution to this problem can be achieved if it is assumed that the linear regression of the optional test on the two common tests determined on the self-selected groups would also describe the standard group. It is further assumed that the standard error of estimate for the group for which data are available would remain the same in the standard group as for the self-selected group. Strictly speaking, the assumptions imply that the self-selection is directly on the abilities measured by the common tests, and only upon them. To the extent that other influences are at work in the self-selection, the results obtained must be regarded as approximations. In any case, the assumptions make it possible to determine appropriate equations, using data from a group which took both the test to be scaled *and* the two aptitude tests. The predetermined descriptive statistics for the standard group can be substituted in these equations. The results yield an estimated mean and standard deviation in raw score units of the test to be scaled for the standard group. (The necessary equations are given in Angoff (1961), *Basic Equations in Scaling and Equating*.) Thus, we have estimated how well the standard group would have performed on the test which is being scaled. For convenience in making comparisons, we then report scores on a scale, so that the standard group would have a reported score mean of 500 and a reported score standard deviation of 100 for each test in the set. This procedure, then, makes it possible to take account statistically of the difference in ability level of groups choosing different optional tests. In this sense, the resulting scores on the different tests are comparable.

This application of statistics to the problem of trying to obtain some degree of comparability of scores on optional tests has been received with some scepticism—a point of view well stated by Henry Dyer thus: 'It is, indeed, a grave question whether there is any rigorous sense in which a score in Latin reading can be regarded as "comparable" to a score in, say, spatial relations, i.e. can be put upon the "same" standard scale. There are serious logical difficulties. What the Board has done is

Validity studies and norms as aids

to compromise with the logic to produce a set of standard scales for the afternoon tests such that in actual practice a student who is known to excel in all fields will tend to have scores with similar high values on all the tests, and a student who is incompetent in all fields will tend to have similar low values on all the tests.' It is fair to say that similar logical difficulties arise even when the comparable scores are obtained by giving the same tests to all members of the norms group. Moreover, it seems reasonable to use statistical methods to take account of differences in ability levels of student groups taking different optional tests.

Finally, it is appropriate to discuss briefly the use of the standard error of measurement whenever norms are used to interpret individual test scores. The standard error of measurement has a long history of acceptance by test specialists. On the other hand, there is reason to believe that at least some test users ascribe an unwarranted degree of precision to a given test score or a given percentile rank derived from a norms table. Small differences in scores or small differences in percentiles are given undue importance in comparing two students. Although information on standard error of measurement has been given in test manuals for many years, the emphasis given to this concept is greatly increased when test users are encouraged to think in terms of 'score bands' rather than specific scores. In practice, we have used the range of one standard error of measurement above and below the obtained score as the basis for defining a score band. Users are encouraged to ignore differences in scores between students or between scores on different tests for the same student if the score bands overlap for the scores being compared. Thus, if the student's score band covers the fifty-second to eightieth percentile on a verbal test and the seventy-third to eighty-fourth percentile on a quantitative test, the user would be urged not to ascribe any special significance to the difference. On the other hand, if the score bands do not overlap, the user can be reasonably confident that genuine difference in relative standings exists. It need hardly be emphasized that more elaborate and more rigorous ways could be found for testing differences between scores. The band approach may be thought of as a compromise between a complex system which would tend to sink of its own weight and the unduly simple approach of ignoring the standard error of measurement when comparing an individual's scores on different tests or when comparing scores of two students on the same test. It may well be that a more effective plan for using standard error of measurement in conjunction with norms tables will be developed. As a means of avoiding over-interpretation of small differences, however, the use of a one standard error of measurement band has, I think, much to commend it.

References

Angoff, W. H. (1961) *Basic Equations in Scaling and Equating.* Statistical report. Princeton, N. J.: Educational Testing Service.

Bingham, W. V. (1951) 'Expectancies.' *Année psychol.,* **50**, 549-55. (Reprinted in *Educ. psychol. Measur.,* 1953, **13**, 47-53.)

Brogden, H. E. (1946) 'On the interpretation of the correlation coefficient as a measure of predictive efficiency.' *J. educ. Psychol.,* **37**, 65-76.

Cooperative Test Division, Educational Testing Service (1957) *Cooperative School and College Ability Tests: Manual for Interpreting Scores.* Princeton, N. J.: Educational Testing Service.

Dyer, H. S. (Undated) *College Board Scores: Their Use and Interpretation,* no. 1, p. 70. New York: College Entrance Examination Board.

Gulliksen, H. O. (1950) *Theory of Mental Tests,* p. 486. New York: Wiley.

Hotelling, H. (1940) 'The selection of variates for use in prediction with some comments on the general problem of nuisance parameters.' *Ann. math. Statist.,* **11**, 271-83.

Hull, C. L. (1928) *Aptitude Testing,* p. 535. Yonkers-on-the-Hudson, New York: World Book Company.

National Bureau of Standards (1959) *Table of the Bivariate Normal Distribution Function and Related Functions.* National Bureau of Standards Applied Mathematics Series, no. 50. Washington, D.C.: U.S. Government Printing Office.

Schrader, W. B. (1965) 'A taxonomy of expectancy tables.' *J. educ. Measur.,* **2**, 29-35.

Taylor, H. C. and Russell, J. T. (1939) 'The relationship of validity coefficients to the practical effectiveness of tests in selection: discussion and tables.' *J. appl. Psychol.,* **23**, 565-78.

AN EMPIRICAL INVESTIGATION OF THE PROBLEM OF HOMOSCEDASTICITY

RUDOLF GRONER

Although in 'classical' test theory the assumption of homoscedasticity of residual variances around the regression line is seldom mentioned as a necessary requirement, it is nevertheless an essential condition for a considerable number of statistical operations. The assumption of homoscedasticity implies that errors of measurement are independent of the size of test values, i.e. that a test measures the characteristic which it is intended to measure with the same degree of error at all points along the scale. Closely linked with the concept of homoscedasticity is that of linearity of regression. One can easily visualize this connection if one considers that in an area of greater error variance the regression line tends to flatten out, so that the curve as a whole becomes non-linear. Nevertheless, lack of homoscedasticity does not directly imply non-linearity, nor vice versa.

The need to assume homoscedasticity becomes evident, for example, in the formation of confidence limits, where the same distribution of expected 'true' values, or criterion scores, is formed around every test value, irrespective of its size. But in general it can be stated the homoscedasticity of residual variances is assumed whenever the total measurement error of a test is contained in a single term. It would be difficult to find any formulae in classical test theory which do not contain an error term, since it is an essential aim of psychological testing to keep the error of measurement, which is often considerable, well under control.

Originally the assumption of homoscedasticity was purely axiomatic. The view then was that a psychological test should be so constructed that the residual variances are equally distributed over the whole area of measurement; if this was not the case, the test was thought to be badly constructed. Only later, as empirical evidence for heteroscedastic variations began to appear in different areas of diagnostics (Ghiselli and Brown 1948), social psychology (Adorno et al. 1950) and clinical psychology (Weinberg 1961), did interest in this problem increase.

In the course of personnel studies Ghiselli and his collaborators (Ghiselli 1963, Ghiselli and Brown 1948, Kahneman and Ghiselli 1962) obtained evidence of heteroscedastic variations, finding that the predictive power of certain tests depended on the level of the qualification required for each particular occupation. It can be argued that at the higher occupational levels the existence of positive qualities is of greater importance, and that the lack of such qualities is a decided disadvantage.

On the other hand, in occupations where poorer qualifications are acceptable, positive qualities are much less important and play only a very slight role in differentiating between individuals in regard to their occupational success. This argument is based on the idea that there are more opportunities and causes (i.e. unexplained variance components) for the absence or failure of an action than for its successful performance.

However, this line of thought does not appear to be very fruitful in view of a number of investigations which have produced contrary results. Terman and Oden (1947), for instance, found better predictive powers for school and occupational success in the lower regions of the test scale.

It would be difficult to include all the different forms of heteroscedasticity as shown in psychological tests within one integrated theory. Besides, it has still not been determined whether heteroscedasticity is a behavioural phenomenon or a methodological artifact of test construction (Fisher 1957).

We shall concern ourselves here with the justification for assuming homoscedasticity in intelligence and school tests. Since our investigation provided insufficient data on the question of the homoscedasticity of measurement error within a given test, i.e. on the aspect of reliability, this will not be discussed here. Instead, we shall concentrate on the homoscedasticity of the residual variances between two tests, i.e. on the aspect of validity.

The test material used for our investigation consisted of the six subtests of the Analytical Intelligence Test (AIT) by Meili (1966), as well as of two school attainment tests: the Frankfurt Vocabulary Test (Anger et al. 1954) and the Frankfurt Arithmetic Test (Krüger et al. 1954). These tests can be described briefly as follows:

1. *Frankfurt Vocabulary Test.* From five alternatives one word must be selected to match a given key-word.
2. *Frankfurt Arithmetic Test.* This assesses technical mathematical ability and consists of items testing knowledge of basic arithmetical operations and understanding of number.
3. *AIT Picture Order.* Four pictures representing an event as it occurs chronologically are shown in the wrong sequence; these must be numbered in the correct order.
4. *AIT Number Series.* Number series built up on a particular principle must be continued by the addition of two further numbers.
5. *AIT Sentences.* In a given time as many different, well-constructed sentences as possible must be written down, each containing three given words.

6. *AIT Incomplete Pictures.* A square printed on a picture indicates where an important detail is missing; the name of the missing part must be written down.
7. *AIT Drawing.* Four given figure components must be combined in as many ways as possible.
8. *AIT Analogies.* A pair of figures is given, and a third figure, having a particular relation to one of these, must be drawn (cf. Progressive Matrices).

The test results of 866 eleven- to twelve-year-old children (with an average age of 11:6), representing a random sample drawn from all parts of German-speaking Switzerland, were available for this investigation. These had been obtained previously in connection with another study (Meili and Steiner 1965). The tests were administered and marked by a number of testers who had been thoroughly instructed beforehand. The data processing was carried out by computer, *using programmes designed by the writer.

In preliminary computations all distributions were standardized to z-values, in order to avoid complications due to differences in means and variances. The regression equation of x on y could thus be simplified, becoming:

$$\hat{z}_y = r_{xy} z_x$$

In this way the standardized variances (from 1·00) could be divided into a component explained by the regression lines (r_{xy}^2) and a residual component ($1-r_{xy}^2$). The programme allowed separate computon for any given part of the complete battery of predictor variables.

It is possible to calculate the residual variance for each point value of the predictor variable (i.e. for each column of the bivariate distribution) separately; but experience has shown that, if this is done, the results are unstable, because the data are divided up into many small samples (cf. Levine and Lord 1959). For this reason the complete set of the predictor variables was subdivided into five segments or arrays which, according to the probability table for a normal distribution, included all measures between the percentile ranks 0 and 5, 5 and 25, 25 and 75, 75 and 95, and 95 and 100. The Bartlett Test (Bartlett 1937) was used to test the residual variances for homoscedasticity. Generalizations in the strict sense of statistical inference are naturally not intended; the

---

*This was a BULL Gamma 30 Sr, belonging to the Institute of Applied Mathematics at the University of Berne. Sincere thanks are due to the Director of the Institute, Professor W. Nef, for making this computer available.

test of significance serves to determine whether the strength of the examined effects is adequate.

The results of the Bartlett Test are shown in table 1.

Table 1. Results of the Bartlett Test

	1	2	3	4	5	6	7	8
1	–	x	o	*	*	o	o	*
2	x	–	*	o	x	*	o	**
3	o	x	–	*	o	**	*	**
4	*	x	o	–	o	**	*	x
5	o	x	o	o	–	o	*	o
6	o	x	o	*	o	–	**	o
7	o	**	o	o	**	o	–	o
8	o	x	o	*	o	*	*	–

$$\begin{aligned} \text{o} &\ldots p \geqslant 0.05 \\ * &\ldots p < 0.05 \\ ** &\ldots p < 0.01 \\ \text{x} &\ldots p < 0.001 \end{aligned}$$

Thirty of the fifty-six regressions show significant deviations from homoscedasticity, nine of these at the 0·1 per cent level. It can therefore be concluded that the tests used in our investigation do not fulfil the requirements of homoscedasticity; this applies both to the intelligence tests and to the school tests, although they vary in strength to a significant degree. They appear to be independent of the degree of correlation.

Of greater interest than the lack of homoscedasticity as such is the incidence of the deviations observed:
  a) Is the reliability of measurement generally greater in the lower parts of the scale (i.e. are the residual variances smaller below the mean), as suggested by Terman and Oden, or
  b) are the residual variances in the upper parts of the scale smaller (increasing the mutual predictability of test results at those levels) as found by Ghiselli, or perhaps

c) is the reliability of measurement better at the top and bottom of the scale and poor in the central region? This phenomenon can frequently be observed in bivariate point distributions, although the spindle-shaped narrowing at the extremes of the distribution can be attributed to smaller numbers of subjects and therefore a smaller likelihood of the occurrence of extreme scores at the ends of the scale.

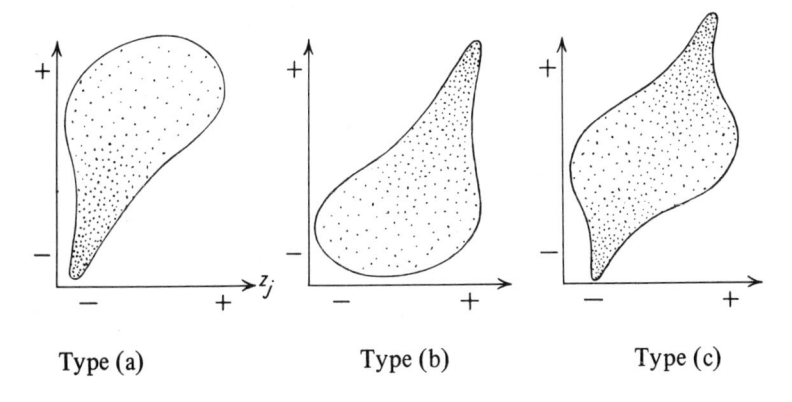

Type (a) Type (b) Type (c)

Figure 1. Bivariate distributions representing the different types of heteroscedasticity

In brief, our results showed that all three types of heteroscedastic relations, as listed in (a) to (c) above, were present in our data, the curvilinear type (c) being the most common, particularly in non-significant heteroscedastic distributions and in those with a low degree of significance.

In order to distinguish clearly between these three types of heteroscedastic residual variances, the following index was developed:

$$I_{xy} = \frac{1}{k} \sum_{j=1}^{k} z_j \frac{s^2_{x.y_j}}{1-r^2_{xy}},$$

where z_j ... are the class means of the standardized arrays (these indicate the position of the various levels of the predictor variables),

k ... is the number of the standardized arrays

$$\frac{s^2{}_{x.y_j}}{1-r^2_{xy}} \ldots$$ are the normalized residual variances within each segment j. The denominator $1-r^2_{xy}$ here eliminates the effect of the different degrees of correlation. In the case of perfect homoscedasticity this fraction would equal 1·00 in each segment.

It is only meaningful to compare indices obtained from identical, symmetrically formed arrays. In the case of heteroscedasticity of type (a) (where residual variances below the mean are smaller and those above the mean larger) the index becomes positive, since the positive z-values are multiplied by larger residual variances. In the case of type (b) (where residual variances below the mean are larger and those above the mean smaller) the index becomes negative, since the negative z-values are weighted more strongly. Finally, in type (c) (where residual variances are greater around the mean than towards the extremes), the index is close to zero, since here the negative and positive z-values are weighted to an equal extent. The apparently obvious step of weighting the normalized residual variances with the degrees of freedom was intentionally avoided, since this might have caused any possible skewed marginal distributions to have a disturbing effect on the index.

Although this index has a certain similarity with the values of a statistical test (F-values), no use is made of this fact here, nor is this point considered any further. Its use can be justified· on the basis of experimental evidence, and for the purpose of this study it is sufficient to employ it as a descriptive index of the direction of heteroscedasticity.

Table 2. Indices of the direction of heteroscedasticity 1

	1	2	3	4	5	6	7	8
1	–	−1·05	+·24	+·12	+·34	−·02	+·70	+·15
2	+·32	–	+·10	+·06	+·17	−·04	+·05	+·03
3	+·22	−·92	–	−·09	+·16	−·75	+·30	+·02
4	+·31	−1·11	+·05	–	+·08	+·08	+·32	−·37
5	+·31	−·80	+·20	−·11	–	−·19	+·27	−·03
6	+·09	−·71	+·06	−·31	+·10	–	+·32	−·11
7	+·01	−·37	+·10	−·02	+·06	+·01	–	−·01
8	+·05	−·92	+·04	−·05	−·21	−·27	+·06	–

In table 2 the matrix of the indices for all test pairs is shown, together with the frequency distribution arranged according to the significance or non-significance of the heteroscedastic residual variances.

Some representative cases of the various types of indices will now be presented. To illustrate type (a) four bivariate distributions with indices greater than +0·30 are chosen; the normal residual variances have been charted in their relation to the levels of the z-values of the predictor variable (figure 2).

For type (b), defined as $I < -0.30$, the following graph of normal residual variances was obtained (figure 3).

Finally, several examples of type (c) are shown ($-0.30 \leqslant I \leqslant +0.30$).

In order to give an impression of the strength of the heteroscedastic relations, separate coefficients were calculated for the upper and lower halves of the measurement range in the case of some coefficients. It should, however, be noted that here we are concerned not with true correlation coefficients, but rather with variance-analytical estimates of partial correlations based on the regression line of all cases.

If the residual variance of test 1 is divided by that of test 2 (the correlation between the two tests, each taken as a whole, is 0·57), one obtains a correlation of 0·32 for the lower half and one of 0·76 for the upper half. Even more marked is the heteroscedasticity of test 2 with test 4. For these two tests taken as a whole the correlation is 0·56 the lower half shows a slight negative correlation, but the correlation for the upper half is 0·79.

To illustrate type (b) the regression of test 6 on test 7 should be noted. The total correlation here is 0·29, the correlation in the lower half being 0·46, while that in the upper half is slightly negative. These figures only serve to illustrate the problem. We might be accused, not altogether without reason, of having selected only *a posteriori* cases where the sampling error was favourable to our conclusions. To clarify this matter completely would require the publication of all our data in its entirety.

The purpose of our study has been to show that in our sample of psychological tests heteroscedastic residual variances were present to an extent which could not be due to chance. It can be concluded that the accuracy of test measurement is overestimated in some parts of the scale and underestimated in others. On the whole, however, it is underestimated.

A non-linear transformation could produce homoscedasticity, but would involve two serious disadvantages:

1. This process would not increase the discrimination power of the test. The test scale would become distorted to such an extent that

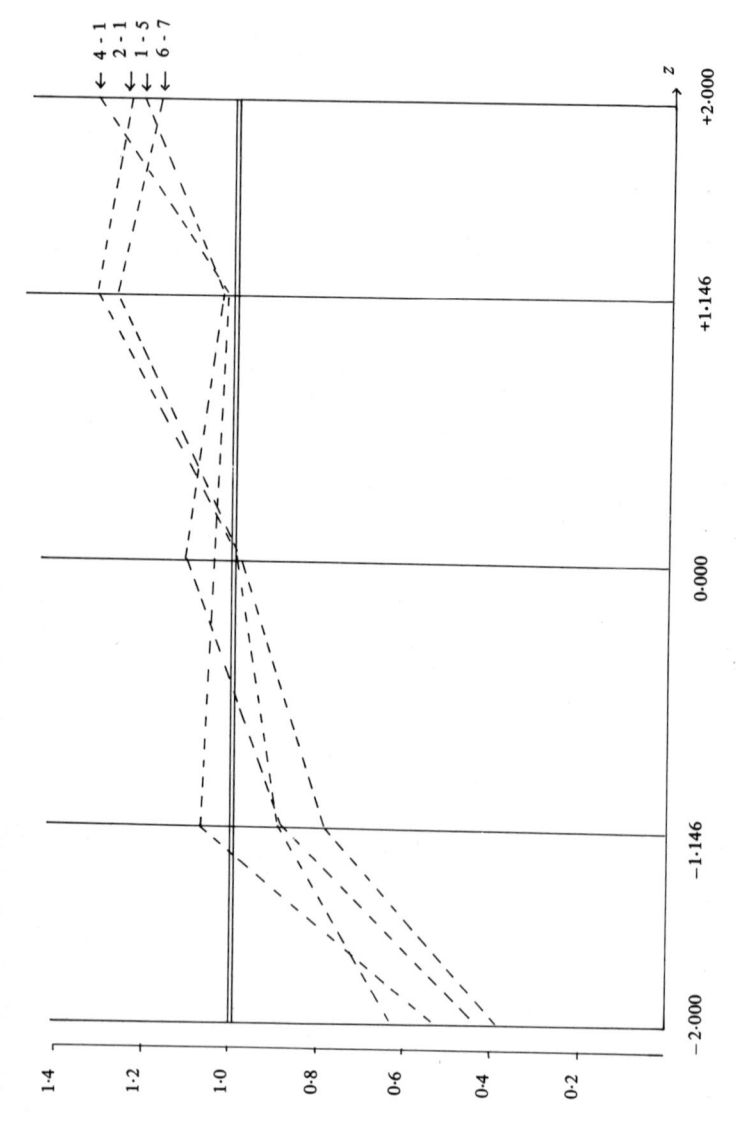

Figure 2. Normed residual variances where $I > +0.30$

Figure 3. Normed residual variances where $I < -0.30$

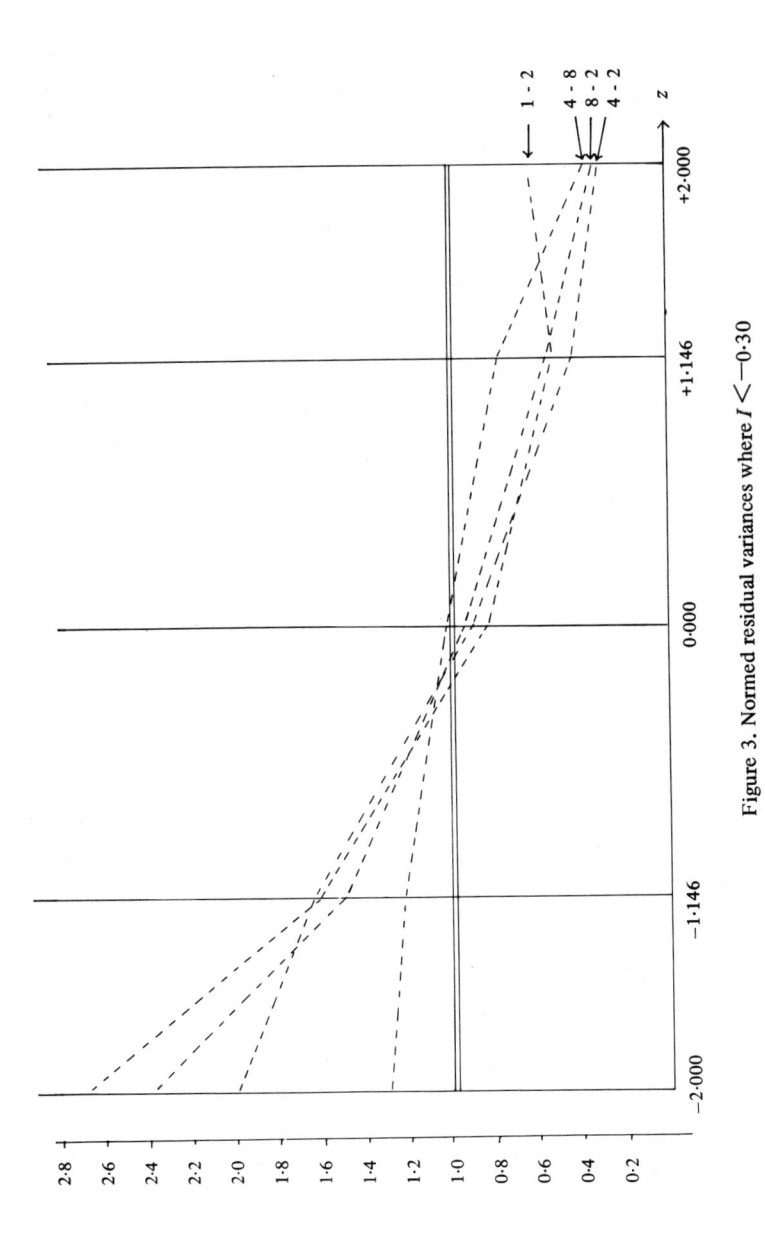

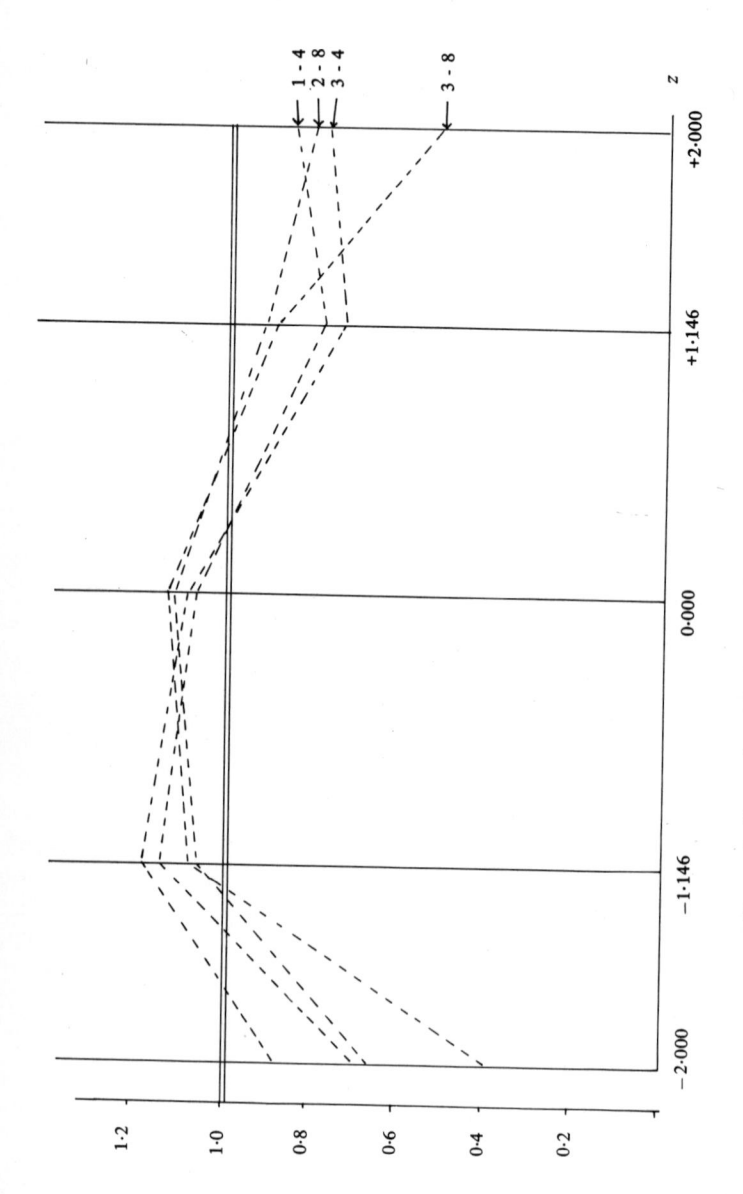

Figure 4. Normed residual variances where $-0.30 \leqslant I \leqslant +0.30$

larger units would have to be used in that part of the scale where measurement is least effective.
2. Such a transformation is effective only when it is used between two particular tests. Homoscedasticity of the residual variances with other tests, for which the transformed test could function as a predictor, would not be ensured by a single transformation. The basic reason for this remarkable phenomenon probably lies in the fact that, whereas the data obtained from psychological tests are measured on an ordinal scale, the quasi-statistical operations of test theory imply an interval scale.

This second objection is of particular importance if the transformation to mutual homoscedasticity is intended to provide the basic conditions for a multivariate process (such as multiple regression or factor analysis).

The second point also justifies the somewhat arbitrary procedure employed in this investigation, of using each test as a predictor for every other test. It certainly does not seem reasonable to do so in every case (e.g. to attempt to predict attainment in arithmetic on the basis of performance in the drawing test). But apart from the fact that heteroscedastic relations were found in certain entirely plausible combinations (e.g. AIT Number Series with Frankfurt Arithmetic Test, and Frankfurt Vocabulary Test with AIT Sentences, etc.), the multivariate procedures mentioned above assume homoscedasticity of all pairs of tests and would be sensitive to any gross deviations from this condition. The observed inconsistency of factor loadings (cf. Groner 1967 and Hürsch 1967), as well as the lack of predictive accuracy of some test batteries specifically designed for predictive purposes, might be caused, at least in part, by the violation of this assumption.

Now that the heteroscedasticity of the regression of a number of tests on each other has been demonstrated so clearly, the assumption of homoscedasticity of the measurement error within a given test (as given by test-retest or split-half reliability) appears doubtful, and should be investigated. Such an investigation should be followed by a cross-validation study; unfortunately this could not be carried out *a posteriori* on the material used for the present investigation, since the data had been obtained prior to the start of the study.

Recently attempts have been made to develop more powerful models of test theory (Lord 1965, Lord and Lees 1967) which assume neither a normal distribution nor linearity and homoscedasticity. Although these models require a considerable amount of computation and estimation of parameters, they make much more effective use of the available data and would also be more appropriate for the material of the investigation described here. Nevertheless, these expanded models, like every simple transformation, also lead into a blind alley, since they cannot go beyond the examination of the regression of only two variables on each other (e.g. in the above case, the regression of true scores on obtained scores). The extent to which these models will prove to be of practical use in multivariate procedures will only become evident at some future date.

Summary

Both classical test theory and the use of product-moment correlations in validation studies assume homoscedasticity of the residual variances around the regression line, independently of the size of the predictor variables. This assumption was investigated in an empirical study of a representative sample of 866 twelve-year-old Swiss children, on the basis of intercorrelations of six intelligence tests and two achievement tests. The marked deviations from the model of homoscedasticity which were obtained were examined to determine the direction of deviation; different types of heteroscedastic relations could be distinguished. Possible reasons for these findings, and some conclusions which can be drawn from them, were then discussed.

References

Adorno, T. W., Frenkel-Brunswick, E., Levinson, D. J. and Sandford, R. N. (1950) *The Authoritarian Personality*. New York: Harper.

Anger, H., Bargmann, R., and Hylla, E. (1954) *Frankfurter Tests: Wortschatz*. Berlin and Basel: Beltz, series: Deutsche Schultests.

Bartlett, M. S. (1937) 'Some samples of statistical methods of research in agriculture and applied biology.' *Jl R. statist. Soc. Supp.* **4**, 137-70.

Fisher, J. (1957) 'Some implications of prediction theory in standard psychological diagnostic methods.' *Proceedings of the 15th International Congress of Psychology*. Brussels.

Ghiselli, E. E. (1963) 'The validity of management traits in relation to occupational level.' *Personnel Psychol.*, **16**, 109-13.

Ghiselli, E. E. and Brown, C. W. (1948) 'The effectiveness of intelligence tests in the selection of workers.' *J. appl. Psychol.*, **32**, 575-80.

Groner, R. (1967) 'Transformationsanalytische Untersuchungen zur Überprüfung der internen Validität von Faktoren.' *Schweiz. Z. Psychol. Anwend.*, **26**, 53-60.

Hürsch, L. (1967) 'Der Einfluss nicht-kognitiver Versuchsbedingungen auf die Faktorenstruktur von Intelligenzleistungen.' *Schweiz. Z. Psychol. Anwend.*, **26**, 61-6.

Kahneman, D. and Ghiselli, E. E. (1962) 'Validity and non-linear heteroscedastic models.' *Personnel Psychol.*, **15**, 1-11.

Krüger, K., Hylla, E. and Bargmann, R. (1954) *Frankfurter Tests.* Zahlenrechen. Berlin and Basel: Beltz, series: Deutsche Schultests.

Levine, R. and Lord, F. M. (1959) 'An index of the discriminating power of a test at different parts of the score range.' *Educ. psychol. Measur.*, **19**, 497-503.

Lord, F. M. (1965) 'A strong true-score theory with applications.' *Psychometrika*, **30**, 239-70.

Lord, F. M. and Lees, D. M. (1967) 'Estimating true-score distributions for mental tests (method 16).' Educational Testing Service, RB-67-7, Princeton, N. J.

Meili, R. (1966) *Analytischer Intelligenztest (AIT).* Bern: Huber.

Meili, R. and Steiner, H. (1965) 'Eine Untersuchung zum Intelligenzniveau Elfjähriger der deutschen Schweiz.' *Schweiz. Z. Psychol. Anwend.*, **24**, 23-32.

Terman, L. M. and Oden, M. H. (1947) *The Gifted Child Grows Up.* Stanford, California: Stanford University Press.

Weinburg, A. A. (1961) *Migration and Belonging.* The Hague: Nijhoff.

THE IMPORTANCE OF EDUCATIONAL TESTING FOR CURRICULUM RESEARCH AND FOR THE EVALUATION OF EDUCATIONAL OBJECTIVES

THE PLACE OF TESTING IN CURRICULUM DEVELOPMENT AND CURRICULUM EVALUATION

S. S. DUNN

Tyler (1966a), in a paper delivered at the 1956 Invitational Testing Conference organized by Educational Testing Service, in discussing the term 'curriculum', stated: 'The term is not limited in this country [the United States], as it commonly is abroad, to refer to the outline of the content to be taught, but is used to include all of the learning of students which is planned by and directed by the school to attain its educational goals. This inclusive definition covers the formulation of educational objectives, the planning, use and organization of learning experiences, and the appraisal of student learning.'

Rugg (1936) was even more direct when he wrote, 'The curriculum is, in short, everything the young people and their teachers do'. However, I doubt if even in the United States such a wide definition would find anything like universal acceptance, and, if it did, we would need to invent new words for aspects of education not differentiated by this definition.

Tyler, in *Basic Principles of Curriculum and Instruction* (1959), seems to identify the curriculum with learning experiences, and therefore treats it separately from objectives and evaluation. He places emphasis on continuity, sequence and integration, but he also refers to 'source units' from which the teacher can select those to be used with a particular group, which seems to be a recognition of the teacher as independent of the curriculum.

If one does not make some such distinction, it seems meaningless to talk about the curriculum for the PSSC course or for the Nuffield Science Project. Every pupil would be studying a different curriculum, since no two teachers would organize identical learning experiences.

Finlay (1962), in discussing the PSSC project, states: 'Work was begun on all parts of the project: textbook, laboratory experiments, films, tests, teachers' guides, the "Study Science Series", and instructional programs for teachers'. The programme for teachers I would prefer to regard as part of a necessary teacher-training scheme for the implementation of the curriculum rather than as a part of the PSSC curriculum.

It is also true, as Tyler mentioned, that a mere outline of content is sometimes referred to as the curriculum for a specific subject; and it is not uncommon in Australia for a committee doing no more than this to be referred to as a 'Curriculum Committee'. Sometimes aims are included as part of the final document, but not always, even though some principles must have guided the selection of content.

For the purpose of this paper I intend to regard a course outline as being the minimum that any authority can offer to teachers as a curriculum, but I do not want to include more than the types of material made available by the PSSC project. I feel it is important to distinguish between objectives and learning experiences, and within learning experiences to separate the curriculum from the teacher, so that I can refer to the manner in which a particular teacher is implementing a given curriculum. Thus I will want to include in my discussion the use of tests as a part of curriculum materials (as in SRA Reading Laboratories) as well as the place of testing in comprehensive curriculum projects such as the PSSC physics course.

In the last paragraph I indicated that I intended to separate the idea of a curriculum from its implementation by teachers. This is necessary in order to discuss the influence of testing (especially of public examinations and other large-scale testing programmes such as those conducted by the College Entrance Examination Board) on the teacher's handling of the curriculum. The introduction or removal of a particular examination does not seem to me to alter the curriculum, but it may well alter the way in which a teacher organizes the learning of his pupils while using an identical curriculum.

Tyler (1966b) in his 1959 address to the Invitational Testing Conference, reports on a finding of a Regents' Inquiry and on his own experiences in the Eight-Year Study as follows: 'It was found that the achievement of the students paralleled more closely the objectives tested by the Regents' examinations than the objectives given major emphasis in the local curricula. Interviews with a sample of teachers in these communities revealed the fact that most of them were conscious of the objectives being tested in the Regents' examinations and sought to emphasize these kinds of learning in their classes rather than to follow the objectives recommended in the local curriculum guides.

'My own experience in the Eight-Year Study corroborated these findings. When new ideas regarding the secondary school curriculum were advanced, we always found teachers raising the question of the relationship of these new proposals to the achievements which were being appraised by the College Entrance Examination Board tests. Only through the arrangement worked out with colleges which permitted high school graduates to be considered for admission on the basis of scholastic aptitude tests and test data submitted by the schools in the Eight-Year Study were we able to get thoughtful consideration by the teachers of new curriculum proposals.'

There is plenty of evidence from England of the effects of 11-plus examinations on teachers' treatment of the curriculum, and in Australia it is freely acknowledged that the state-wide examination system influences the way teachers handle the curriculum and organize the learning experiences of their pupils. New teachers often begin their teaching career by consulting the public examination papers of earlier years.

I have chosen to raise this issue first because, as Tyler found, there is little point in spending vast resources on curriculum development unless our official or unofficial testing programmes emphasize the objective stressed by the curriculum. The problem becomes particularly acute where the external examination operates as a selection instrument. The influences of the CEEB and the ACT programmes in the United States are not likely to be so marked as those exercised by the examinations which are used at the end of the secondary school in Australian states, since these are used to award valuable scholarships and select students for entry to university.

If our testing programmes exercise such a strong influence on the interpretation of the curriculum by teachers, what are we going to do? Will we go ahead and develop curricula and hope for the best? Will we abandon our testing programmes? Or will we try to operate to improve both?

To spend large sums of money on curriculum development projects without due consideration of external examinations and testing programmes is likely to be a great waste of money and cannot be recommended. It is also unlikely that the public will be happy to see testing vanish where selection is involved. While we are short of university places in Australia, I feel the public will expect some form of external testing for selection, and whatever tests are used will influence the interpretation of the curriculum.

If these diagnoses are correct, we are left, as people interested in educational measurement, with the task of encouraging the use of either (a) tests which have minimum effect on teaching practices, the best examples of which are probably the Scholastic Aptitude Tests, the Iowa Tests of Educational Development, and, to be a little parochial, the Commonwealth Secondary Scholarship Tests prepared by the Australian Council for Educational Research; or (b) tests which are content-based, but are direct measures of the major objectives of the curriculum. This latter form of testing seeks to exploit the examination to give direction to the teacher's interpretation of the curriculum. For instance, the New Guinea Education Department, which has to operate its primary schools largely with indigenous teachers limited both in formal education and teacher training, is trying to use its Primary Final Examination as a guide to its teachers. For example, tests of oral English are included, despite the problems of reliability they pose, to encourage the teaching of oral English. In fact, all the questions and item types used are considered not merely for their value in the examination, but also with a view to their likely effects on the teaching practices in the schools.

Under ideal circumstances, coaching for the examination would then be directed towards the objectives of the curriculum. In practice, one never achieves the ideal, but if one is forced to use external examinations in this kind of situation, it is only sensible to exploit their virtues while trying to minimize their defects. May I humbly say that I think our ETS friends have paid too great a price in achieving objectivity and reliability in examinations for written composition, but it is pleasing to see them still working on the problem and finding it possible to move in the direction of more direct testing of the objectives of this subject.

Ebel in the paper to follow this will, I think, point out the dangers of an emphasis on process to the exclusion of content approach, and I agree with him. If we use general or special aptitude tests, we must find some way for teachers to check content mastery of specific subjects. Those engaged on curriculum development projects can help to meet this need. It is therefore appropriate now to turn to the contribution testing can make to curriculum development.

While I was engaged in the thinking and preliminary planning for this paper, Bruner's (1966) recent little book *Toward a Theory of Instruction* reached me, and I started to read it without any special thought of its relevance to this paper. However, in the final chapter I found him saying things I had in mind on the relation of evaluation to curriculum development more effectively than I am capable of doing. Certain similarities between what he has written and what I say today are not accidental, but I hope not purely derivative.

Bruner refers to evaluation as a 'form of educational intelligence'. What sort of intelligence information in the military sense do we need for curriculum development?

In the first place, we need information about children, what they already know, what they have difficulty in learning, how they go about learning, what is likely to interest them. Consider for a moment the importance of the testing work carried out by Piaget for curriculum development. In fact, a great deal of the early planning of any curriculum project will be guided by information obtained from one form of testing or another.

However, as soon as preliminary planning is over and material starts to be developed, it is essential that it be used and evaluated in normal classroom situations. Bruner states this need succinctly when he writes: 'It has been our painfully achieved conclusion that if evaluation is to be of help, it must be carried out to provide feedback at a time and in a form that can be useful in the design of materials and exercises'. It is easy to conceptualize the task as clarifying objectives and then writing material, but in reality it does not work this way. Some idea of objectives must be present to begin, but evaluation of material may lead to changes in objectives as well as modification of material. The very process of clarifying objectives is often assisted by the task of developing evaluation instruments which attempt to measure these objectives.

In developing curriculum, as Tyler has pointed out, the notion of sequence is most important. Some of the recent work of Gagne (1965) has implications here. The type of tests he is trying to develop have implications both for the development of the structure of a subject and for the diagnosis of the point of breakdown by an individual pupil.

Because the development of evaluation instruments must be derived from the same objectives as the curriculum materials, it is logical for those engaged in a curriculum project to develop test instruments as part of the project. The kind of instruments needed can take many forms, and it is wise to remind ourselves of some of the uses that can be made of tests in curriculum projects. These are:

1. As a guide to the pupils' needs before they begin a particular course. I mentioned in an earlier paper the workshop at Monash University under the direction of Mr Mackay of our staff, to develop a test on concepts* that are considered necessary for students starting on PSSC in Victoria. If this test proves valuable the plan is to develop remedial material related to the diagnoses provided by the test, and the item writers began the process of generating remedial material at the same time as they prepared their items.

2. For placement of pupils at an appropriate starting-point in the curriculum material. An excellent example of this approach is the use of the placement tests in the SRA Reading Laboratories. At the Australian Council for Educational Research we tried to make use of the same idea with a project which took the form of a kit

---

*The project drew inspiration from the work of Rathe, D., 'Certain physics generalizations desirable for students to attain before taking the PSSC High School Physics Course.' *Science Educ.*, **49,** no. 22, 127-38.

of mathematics materials published as the Individual Mathematics Programme.
3. As a part of the 'learning experience'. Tests and assignments of a 'test type' can be structured as part of the learning process. Some of the mathematics projects clearly incorporate this idea. Programmed learning is the extreme extension of the idea, and it is often difficult to distinguish a frame from a test question.
4. As a means of diagnosis after units of study. The diagnostic tests of the PSSC course are an excellent illustration of this use. As I indicated in an earlier paper, the Australian Council for Educational Research used errors made on the PSSC diagnostic tests to direct the pupil to remedial learning experiences. The same idea of trying to link diagnosis and remedial action has been incorporated into the diagnostic tests developed as part of the Individual Mathematics Programme mentioned earlier.
5. As survey tests. Teachers will want, from time to time, to make overall assessments for records and for reporting to parents. These tests need to be built to provide a profile with the full range of cognitive objectives in mind.
6. As a means of pupil feedback. Questionnaires can be developed to provide the teacher with information on the pupil's reception of the material, and so guide him in modifying it to suit local needs.

To date, this paper has been concerned with the influence of testing on curriculum interpretation, and with the more spectacular curriculum development projects. One might almost call them curriculum revolutions, but testing is also an essential element in curriculum evolution. It is often the information fed back to a teacher or to a system from testing that stimulates modifications to curricula and begets many changes.

In the mid-1940s the Australian Council for Educational Research undertook a testing survey for the six Education Departments in Australia to assess the standards of attainment of pupils aged 10 to 14 years in a variety of subjects. This Curriculum Survey, as it was called, produced evidence of differences in performance, some of which at least seemed to be related to the curriculum in operation. For many years the Curriculum Branch of each State Education Department made use of this information, and many important changes in the primary school curriculum could be traced to the study. More recently, the New South Wales Education Department, with the assistance of the Australian Council for Educational Research, initiated through its Curriculum and Research Branch, the NSW Basic Skills Testing

Programme with several purposes in mind, one of which was to provide feedback on the attainment of curriculum objectives.

In fact, no curriculum project can afford to be satisfied and not subjecting itself to constant evaluation and revision. Bruner states it this way: 'We have also learned that it is often much the better part of wisdom to design evaluation as a guide to the *preparation* of a later edition'.

Despite the advantages of a forward-looking evaluation system from the curriculum developer's viewpoint, the administrators of a system are often faced with the difficult decision of whether or not to make a curriculum change, and if so, is the cost justified. Let me illustrate with a problem not infrequently met in Australia; I will again use PSSC for illustrative purposes.

Like most authorities around the world, the Victorian authorities responsible for physics were concerned with the existing 'course of study' (These words have been chosen deliberately, as it was no more than a minimum curriculum in the sense used in this paper.) The development of the PSSC course had been widely publicized in the United States and also adopted in New Zealand, so was worth investigating. I will not detail the investigations which took a number of forms, but for various reasons, including the existence of an external public examination system, the decision to adopt a modified version was made on a state-wide basis. I have no need to inform you that such a decision was costly to implement and involved considerable retraining of teachers. Now the evaluation of the PSSC in other places is useful, but the conditions for its use in Australia are very different from those in the United States, where most of the studies have been done. In Australia it has been extended to a two-year course, following four years of secondary school science, and the pupils taking the course will all have been selected to some extent. The prior training of the teachers operating the course is another important variable. A proper evaluation before introducing the PSSC was therefore not possible. Its introduction was really an act of faith. It is now possible to begin evaluation studies to check whether or not its aims are being achieved, and to generate ideas for its modification. It is true this is backward looking, but done for the purpose of serving the future.

Members of this gathering will be under no illusions about the complexity of the task of evaluating the PSSC course as used in Victoria. The resources available to the research worker on our staff of the Faculty of Education at Monash who is attempting the project are very limited. He will tackle some major questions—teachers' reactions, achievements and attitudes of students taking and not taking the course, and studies of cognitive preferences. A major problem which could arise is an interaction between teacher and curriculum. In such circumstances, does one choose in the long run teacher education or a modification of the curriculum?

I am sure you can think of many instances when evaluation must follow the decision to make a change in curriculum, so testing has a part to play in evaluation and modification of the curriculum as well as in its development.

In summary, then, testing may affect the curriculum in three ways. It does so by giving guidance to the teacher's interpretation. It also has an essential part to play in curriculum development, both to provide intelligence information and as a part of the total project. Finally, because curriculum should not be static, testing provides constant evaluation with a view to evolutionary modification.

References

Bruner, J. S. (1966) *Toward a Theory of Instruction.* Cambridge, Mass.: The Belknap Press of Harvard University Press.

Finlay, G. C. (1962) 'The Physical Science Study Committee.' *School Rev.,* **70,** 1, 71-6.

Gagne, R. (1965) *Conditions of Learning.* New York: Holt, Rinehart & Winston.

Rugg, H. (1936) *American Life and the School Curriculum,* pp. 17-18. Boston: Ginn and Co.

Tyler, R. W. (1959) *Basic Principles of Curriculum and Instruction.* Chicago: University of Chicago Press.

Tyler, R. W. (1966a) 'The curriculum—then and now.' (1966b) 'What testing does to teachers and students' In Anastasi, A. (ed.) *Testing Problems in Perspective.* Washington, D.C.: American Council on Education.

THE RELATION OF TESTS TO EDUCATIONAL OBJECTIVES*

ROBERT L. EBEL

Any activity which takes the time of students and teachers can be justified only if it contributes to the attainment of educational goals. Indeed, most educationists would probably say that not only tests but every aspect and arrangement of the educational enterprise, such as facilities, staff, materials, organization, administration, curriculum, instruction, guidance, evaluation, and the like, should be selected and operated to contribute to attainment of the goals of education. But, since tests results are often used as one indication of the success of the school programme, as well as the success of individual pupils, the importance of relating tests directly to educational objectives deserves particular emphasis.

In the first place, a school should choose or make tests which will measure as directly as possible as many as possible of the school's educational objectives. Like many other reasonably obvious recommendations, this one is easier to state than to follow. One problem is to determine what the school's educational objectives ought to be. Another is to state these objectives clearly enough to provide unequivocal guides to test construction or selection.

Many writers have attempted to give direction to the educational enterprise by formulating a statement of its single basic purpose or general goal. For example, Spencer (1954) said, 'Education has for its object the formation of character'. Huxley (1882) elaborated the point in these words, 'Perhaps the most valuable result of all education is the ability to make yourself do the thing you have to do, when it ought to be done, whether you like it or not'. Whitehead (1949) said this: 'Education is the acquisition of the art of the utilization of knowledge', and Conant (1943) expressed the view that 'our purpose is to cultivate in the largest possible number of our future citizens an appreciation of both the responsibilities and the benefits which come to them because they are Americans and are free'.

While many educationists would challenge the views of one or another of these writers, most would applaud their intentions; that is, they would regard a valid statement of basic educational objectives as the foundation of the whole educational enterprise. Given a carefully prepared statement of objectives, they imply that one should be able to deduce the proper characteristics for all other aspects of the enterprise,

* Portions of this have been adapted from an article previously published elsewhere.

and so know how to conduct it properly. If asked where authorization can be found for such a statement of ultimate educational goals, they might reply, as Aristotle, Aquinas, Rousseau, Hutchins, Maritain and Sheen have replied, that the appropriate ends of education can all be deduced from the true nature of man.

But there are others who find this conception of the source and function of educational objectives quite unrealistic. The educational enterprise, as they view it, is far from a tight, logical, hypothetic-deductive system. They are sceptical of 'true' and complete statements of educational goals based on the 'true' nature of man. They doubt that what goes on in Mrs Everett's fourth-grade classroom at 9.30 a.m. on Tuesday, 9 January 1962 has been, or conceivably could be, deduced in all particulars from any verbal statement of single or multiple educational goals. They would argue that the educational activities in that room are determined largely by what the school, and Mrs Everett, and her pupils now are as products of their past history. They might claim that any statements of educational objectives which the school or Mrs Everett may express or endorse are more truly results than causes of the total educational process.

Grieder (1961) has recently expressed scepticism concerning the meaningfulness, validity and necessity of some recent formal statements of educational goals: 'Are not the goals of a society largely unformulated, like the unwritten British Constitution? They develop slowly and through a continuous process of interaction among various segments and levels of a society, and among societies.'

Most educational activities are clearly purposeful activities, but it does not follow that all these purposes can be explicitly stated. Nor does it follow that all of them can be derived by logical analysis from a very few statements of general goals. The foundation on which the structure of education has been erected is the nature and the needs of man and of the society in which he lives. No abstract statement of educational goals can specify or imply all the details of these natures and needs. The best they can do is to highlight certain aspects which may have been overlooked in the past or made important by contemporary developments.

Statements of educational goals serve a useful purpose if they are clear expressions of realistic choices among attractive alternatives; if they express realistic expectations instead of fond hopes; if they establish priorities which honestly recognize that, to achieve certain desired goals, other desirable goals will have to receive less attention or no attention at all. Such a statement of educational goals would be more than mere window dressing for the sake of public relations. It would provide working specifications for change—and, one would hope, improvement—in the school programme.

Unfortunately, many current statements of educational goals are designed only to be read with approval, not to serve as tools for the building of educational progress. In such statements ambiguity is more useful than explicitness, and inclusiveness more acceptable than selectivity. But even a tough-minded, realistic, directive set of educational goals is not a sufficient basis for developing the school's testing programme. It is a factor to be considered, but only one of the factors. What the school is and what it does day by day must be given full consideration, along with the statement of its goals, in planning its testing programme.

Each of the multitude of activities which occupy the hours in school of a teacher and her pupils implies an educational goal. Few of these activities could be derived by rigorous, logical deduction from any statement of ultimate educational goals. Probably all of them could be defended as plausibly relevant to one or more of such ultimate goals. But so, also, could a host of other activities which this particular class has not undertaken. In deciding whether this or that specific activity should be undertaken by a class, a teacher may find it helpful to refer to a statement of general goals of education. But seldom will a wise decision be possible on this basis alone. She must consider also her own capabilities, the unique needs of her pupils and their capabilities, the facilities of the school, the wishes of the community, and the like.

The tasks of the school—even the tasks of teaching a particular subject in a particular grade—are too numerous and diverse to be fully expressed or even implied by any manageably concise statement of goals. To build an effective school testing programme, one must consider much more about the school and its programme than can be conveyed by a verbal expression of the school's educational goals. No school should develop its testing programme solely on the basis of a formal statement of objectives or without regard for the detailed actualities of its educational programme.

A weakness of many statements of educational objectives is their abstractness, generality and ambiguity. One way of overcoming this weakness is to define the goals in terms of the overt behaviour which indicates achievement of the objective. This helps to make the statements concrete, specific and definite. The use of job analysis in developing tests of vocational competence, no doubt, suggested this approach for tests of educational achievement. Perhaps the broad appeal of behaviouristic psychology also had something to do with it. Whatever the reason, it has become the generally recommended technique, at least among specialists in educational measurement for defining educational goals in meaningful, useful terms.

Ralph W. Tyler was one of the early advocates of the definition of educational goals in behavioural terms. In a book published in 1936 (Hawkes *et al.*) he wrote: 'In order to make a list of major objectives usable in building examinations, each objective must be defined in terms which clarify the kind of behavior that the course should help to develop among the students. That is to say, a statement is needed which explains the meaning of the objective by describing the behavior we can expect of persons who have attained it.'

Many other writers, particularly those concerned with educational measurement, have expressed similar views. There have been three major efforts, culminating in the publication of three separate volumes, to define educational goals in behavioural terms at the levels of (a) the elementary school (Kearney 1953), (b) the secondary school (French *et al.* 1957), and (c) the college (Bloom 1956). At present, most specialists in educational testing recommend or approve the definition of educational goals in terms of the observable behaviour of the student.

But in spite of their virtues, behaviourally defined objectives have not proved to be entirely satisfactory. The virtue of specificity involves the burden of multiplicity. Behavioural definitions tend to be books, not paragraphs, sections or even chapters. Even in the books, the definitions cannot be completely specific, for it is obviously impossible to specify fully and exactly all the particular behaviours that are desired. The virtue of concreteness involves the burden of complexity. Appropriate behaviour in any concrete situation is always the result of awareness of all relevant factors and their interactions, and of balanced judgment concerning the weight to be accorded to each factor. Abstractions, for all their faults, do have the virtue of relative simplicity. The virtue of definiteness involves a danger of over-emphasis on conformity. For, if the goals of education are defined in terms of narrowly specific behaviour desired by the curriculum makers and the teachers, what need is there for critical judgment by the student; what freedom is there for creative innovation; what provision is there for adaptive behaviour as the cultural world changes?

The point we are concerned with here has been expressed by Jane Loevinger (1959) in these words: 'In regard to education at the nursery school and kindergarten level, no doubt specific behaviors can be used to measure the success of the educational endeavor. The aim of university education is emphatically not to inculcate such stereotyped behavior patterns, but to free the graduate from conformity to cultural and behavioral stereotypes.'

This suggests that the goals of education (at least for the upper levels of education) should be defined, not only in terms of patterns of desired behaviour—the end products of effective living—but also in terms of tested potential for inventing appropriate behaviour—that is, the means to effective living.

This view has been emphasized in a recent publication of the Educational Policies Commission (1961), in which the need for rational independence is described by its authors in these words: 'To be free, a man must be capable of basing his choices and actions on understandings which he himself achieves and on values which he examines for himself. . . . He must understand the values by which he lives, the assumptions on which they rest, and the consequences to which they lead. . . . He must be capable of analyzing the situation in which he finds himself and of developing solutions to the problems before him. . . . The free man, in short, has a rational grasp of himself, his surroundings, and the relation between them.'

The goals of education as these men would see them, and as we see them, are concerned with developing processes as well as products; with adaptability as well as with adaptations. To regard the development of specific desired behaviours as the sole goal of education is to treat the rising generation as servants of our past rather than as masters of their future.

What a student is asked to do to demonstrate his competence provides a matter of fact definition, in behavioural terms, of what the goals of instruction really are. Students recognize this and tend to study most carefully the matter on which they expect to be examined. If the tests which a school uses are poor or seriously incomplete measures of the school's educational objectives, two unfortunate results are likely to follow. Not only are the measures obtained from the test likely to be inaccurate indications of the school's real achievements, but also the efforts of the teachers and students are likely to be diverted from the goals they are supposed to be pursuing.

Tests can be valuable tools for motivating and directing students' achievement, if they are good tests, and if the students and teachers know of their general nature at the beginning of a course of instruction. Of course, this does not mean that teachers or students should seek advance knowledge of and engage in special practice for particular questions which occur in the tests. What they do need to know is the kind of abilities they are expected to develop and the tasks by which their achievement will be judged.

The intimate relation between tests and educational objectives, namely, test selection guided by educational objectives and tests helping to define the objectives, has two extremely valuable consequences. Consideration of the limitations of tests and other techniques of evaluation helps to keep our statements of objectives more realistic. Consideration of the definitions of desired achievement provided by the test helps to make teaching and learning more purposeful and effective.

Education is a complex process which results in complex, and often subtle, outcomes. It is not surprising, therefore, that writers sometimes mention the existence and importance of intangible outcomes of education. Such writers are likely to suggest that the intangible outcomes of education are difficult to measure and may be entirely unmeasurable.

An alternative view is based on two propositions. (a) A human trait is measurable, in at least an elementary sense, if the assertion that one person possesses more of it than another can be independently verified by two or more observers. This means that, if having more or less of a trait makes any observable difference, that trait is measurable. (b) In order to be important, an outcome of education must make an observable difference in the behaviour of persons who have attained different degrees of it. If attaining an alleged goal of education does not change the overt behaviour of the person who attains it in any way, on what basis can it be said to be important?

To say that all important outcomes of education are potentially measurable is not to say that all can be measured easily. But it is to say that any distinction between the tangible and the intangible outcomes of education, between the measurable and the non-measurable, is spurious.

Why is this point so often misunderstood? Two possible reasons can be suggested. The first is that we use vague, undefined, general terms in talking about the goals of education—terms like character, citizenship, open-mindedness, creativity, excellence and adjustment. Now there is nothing wrong in the use of general terms to express general ideas. On the contrary, it would be impossible to do otherwise. And statements invoking general terms do serve a useful purpose at some levels of discourse. But we err if we assume that there exist somewhere real, clearly definable, important, human characteristics corresponding to each of the many names we use in describing human behaviour. We err further if we think that our main task is that of defining what we mean when we use these traits' names. We err most grievously if we attribute difficulty in measuring these named characteristics to limitations in our techniques of testing instead of attributing it to vagueness or lack of agreement as to what the name signifies.

The relation of tests to educational objectives

Any unambiguous definition of a quantitative attribute clearly implies a method of measuring it. Conversely, any test or other means of quantifying an attribute implies a definition of it. If we know how to specify the method for determining which member of any pair of persons possesses the greater amount of the attribute in question, we know both what the attribute means and how to measure it. But if the method remains to be developed, we not only lack measurements of the attribute, but also a clear idea of what the attribute means.

A second reason why some outcomes of education are held to be unmeasurable may be that the measurement is thought to refer properly only to processes which meet all the requirements for fundamental physical measurement. Some writers, like B. O. Smith (1938), have concluded that mental testing leads to numbers which are not measurements at all. Others, like Lorge (1951) and Comrey (1951), recognize the value in quantitative processes which do not involve equality of units or an absolute zero. Bergmann and Spence (1944) have pointed out that fundamental measurement of some attributes of great interest to us is unattainable in principle. But if this were taken to mean that these attributes are unmeasurable, we should have to find some other term for our successful and useful processes of dealing with them in quantitative terms.

A third reason for denial of the measurability of some important educational outcomes may be the opportunity it provides for committed anti-scientists to re-emphasize the limitations of scientific methods. Further, the measurement of human traits opens the door to evaluations and judgments, which, since they might be unfavourable, are sometimes feared. Thus, there may be some elements of defensiveness in the opposition to probings of the human mind—some comforting shelter to be found in attributing impenetrable mysteries to the human spirit—which encourage belief in narrow limitations to the scope of educational measurements.

The practical limitations of effective educational measurement are real and many, as anyone who has laboured to improve educational measurements can testify. But they are not fixed eternally by the nature of man, nor is it useless to try to overcome them. The possibility of measuring the degree of attainment of all important outcomes of education does exist.

It may be appropriate to mention here that any paper and pencil test is essentially an intellectual task. Whatever the name of the test, whatever it purports to measure—attitudes, interests, values, character, personality, adjustment—the examinee who seeks to perform well on such a test will respond to it as thoughtfully and as wisely as he can. He will report what he knows or thinks about his attitudes, interests, values and the like, or what he believes he ought to report. Such a test is, for him, a test of self-knowledge and self-understanding. It may or may not indicate how these attributes affect his behaviour in daily life.

Reference has already been made to the intellectual component of most educational goals. While one cannot maintain physical health and vigour or develop motor skills solely by thinking about them, it does help to have and to be able to use the knowledge relevant to the attainment of such goals. This point is stressed persuasively in the publication of the Educational Policies Commission (1961) already quoted: 'The purpose which runs through and strengthens all other educational purposes—the common thread of education—is the development of the ability to think. This is the central purpose to which the school must be oriented if it is to accomplish either its traditional tasks or those newly accentuated by recent changes in the world. To say that it is central is not to say that it is the sole purpose or in all circumstances the most important purpose, but that it must be pervasive concern in the work of the school. Many agencies contribute to achieving educational objectives, but this particular objective will not be generally attained unless the school focuses on it. In this context, therefore, the development of every student's rational powers must be recognized as generally important.'

The Educational Policies Commission, in a section on 'developing rational powers', notes the importance of the 'inquiring spirit'. This is a gentler term than scepticism or critical thinking, but involves the same approach to education. Unfortunately, it is not the approach favoured by some among those who stress the non-intellectual goals of citizenship, character, attitudes, values, interests, appreciations, or personal and social adjustment. Nor is it the approach of those who would define educational goals in terms of an extensive catalogue of desired responses to particular situations.

Those who warn against over-emphasis of intellectual goals sometimes are reflecting concern, not over the neglect of other goals, but over pressure on students who find it difficult to achieve goals of any kind. Education should be enjoyable, they argue, not stressful. The child's happiness is as important as his intellectual development, perhaps more so, they say. Surely the emphasis on intellectual excellence can be overdone. To some extent such over-emphasis is self defeating and, hence, self correcting. But over-emphasis on moment to moment happiness is equally dangerous.

Modern education is remarkably effective, considering the magnitude of its problems. But it could be and needs to be much more effective. One of the ways of making it so is to abolish our double standards of talk and action. What we say about education ought to agree much more closely than it often does with what we do about education. Idealists say we must improve our performances without lowering our sights. Realists argue that we ought to do two things: (a) identify our targets a little more clearly and check to see whether they are actually within range, and (b) improve our marksmanship and gunnery. Education is a powerful tool, but there are limits to its accomplishments. Realistic, clearly perceived goals can help us maximize those accomplishments.

References

Bergmann, G. and Spence, K. W. (1944) 'The logic of psychophysical measurement.' *Psychol. Rev.*, 51, 1-24.

Bloom, B. S. (1956) *Taxonomy of Educational Objectives.* New York and London: Longmans.

Comrey, A. (1951) 'Mental testing and the logic of measurement.' *Educ. psychol. Measur.*, 11, 323-34.

Conant, J. B. (1943) *Annual Report to the Board of Overseers, Harvard University.* Cambridge, Mass.: Harvard University Press.

Educational Policies Commission of the National Education Association (1961) *The Central Purpose of American Education.* Washington, D.C.: National Education Association.

French, W. et al. (1957) *Behavioral Goals of General Education in High School.* New York: Russell Sage Foundation.

Grieder, C. (1961) 'Is it possible to word educational goals?' *Nation's Schools*, 68, 10 ff.

Hawkes, H. E., Lindquist, E. F. and Mann, C. R. (1936) *The Construction and Use of Achievement Examinations*, pp. 9-10. Boston: Houghton Mifflin.

Huxley, T. H. (1882) *Science and Culture, and Other Essays.* London: Macmillan.

Kearney, N. C. (1953) *Elementary School Objectives.* New York: Russell Sage Foundation.

Loevinger, J. (1959) 'A theory of test responses.' Proceedings of the Invitational Conference on Testing Service, 1958.

Lorge, I. (1951) 'The fundamental nature of measurement.' In Lindquist, E. F. (ed.) *Educational Measurement.* Washington, D.C.: American Council on Education.

Smith, B. O. (1938) *Logical Aspects of Educational Measurement.* New York: Columbia University Press.

Spencer, H. (1954) *Social Studies,* pt 2, chap. 17. New York: Robert Schalkenback Foundation (originally published 1851).

Whitehead, A. N. (1949) *The Aims of Education,* p. 16. New York: New American Library (Mentor Book).

EDUCATIONAL TESTING FOR EVALUATION AND IMPROVEMENT: SOME PROBLEMS OF A SOCIETY IN TRANSITION

R. WONG

The transition society

Like 'development', the word 'transition' characterizes a phenomenon associated with motion, which can be regarded either as extended or limited. Thus 'developing' is applicable to all countries in respect of the continuous process of change resulting from competitive effort, and no country would claim complacently, to have 'arrived'. At the same time, in terms of such stipulated criteria as *per capita* income, industrial strength, educational opportunity, and so on, some countries are still developing and others are developed.

'Transition' can similarly refer to a multi-stage progression from point to point in development, or limited—and in this paper specifically—to the consideration of society in which the educational process has to make good what political modernization has promised. A transition society so named in the latter sense has the outward manifestations of modern society. It has legislated to ensure enfranchisement irrespective of sex; it has planned for the development of the economy through industrialization; its philosophy with regard to equality of educational opportunity is appropriately supported by such action as provision for free universal primary education; it has modernized the structure of the school system by adding an appropriate number of years to the pupil's school span; it has added new elements to the content of the school curriculum, strongly exercised by the popular belief that the functional relation between education on the one hand and political maturity and economic growth on the other must not be ignored. It is in the qualitative sense that it is in transition because the educational process has yet to catch up with educational goals.

Characteristics of educational development in a transition society

Educational development within such a society generally bears the following characteristics:

   a) An extraordinary self-generating demand on the part of the general public for more and more educational opportunities—a

demand which results in conflict between the aspirations of the individual and the goals and resources of the state with respect to the uses of education.
b) A rapid and continuing multiplication of the physical elements of education, carefully cited in quantitative terms of more facilities, more schools, more teachers, more and more students graduating from schools.
c) An educational structure made unwieldy and complex by unprecedented demand and *ad hoc* solutions (largely pragmatic) to nagging problems of linguistic differences, multi-racialism, communalism, traditionalism, and the like; in terms of size, breadth and diversity, the educational system is far less amenable to planning and control than other sectors of development.
d) An educational system tightly interlaced with public examinations, mostly state controlled in the name of standards to be maintained in rapid expansion.

The role of educational testing

Educational testing within this context has a vital role to play, a role which should be predominantly evaluatory and change-inducing, while fulfilling the normal objectives of assessment. This, to most new societies, is also a new idea. For the public examination and the test have always had a plumb-line effect on those measured, and unfortunately the single score, or even a single mark of a total score, has been regarded as the infallible discriminator between the fit and the unfit, the able and the weak. To re-employ educational testing in the wider sense of determining whether the public examination itself can stand the test, whether the educational system or the curriculum needs reform, and whether the traditional test score would not serve its purpose better by being scrutinized together with other indicators of ability is to break new ground.

The more scientific approach to testing with its stipulated prerequisites and established statistical controls is concomitant with the advent of the technological age, which seeks closer and closer approximations to the truth and emphasizes efficiency in the end product. But the laboratory conditions which are necessary for the testing and effective use of scientific instruments are not always of the best order for the application of instruments to the measurement of human traits and achievements. The laboratory of human behaviour in a transitional society is particularly disappointing in this sense. Difficulties associated with educational testing are inherent in:

a) The nature of the transitional society itself.
b) The weight of traditional practice.
c) The time lag between practice and desire.
d) Complex configurations of social attitudes and values.
e) Lack of relevant psychological and sociological information based on research.

a) Nature of the transition society itself

The transition society takes great pains to demonstrate a break with the past. Its favourite exhortation, incessantly stressed by ministers, leaders and administrators, is the need to 'keep up with the times in order to survive'. Image building and modernization become obsessive responsibilities. Education is seen as the panacea to all the nation's ills. With eagerness, whatever educational innovation promises as a 'modern' solution to contemporary problems, is welcomed. This over-ready acceptance of the 'new' and the 'up to date' can hinder the effective role of testing for evaluation and reform.

The danger with regard to scientific testing itself lies not in possible rejection, but in too ready an acceptance of a form of things without an appreciation of the spirit. Intelligence and other tests from abroad have been known to be indiscriminately used without validation against local samples. Why construct more tests when so many are available in the world market? At the same time, conservatism with respect to the traditional belief in the unerring discriminatory power of the test remains. The testing cannot fulfil its proper role educationally.

b) Weights of historical practice

The heavy reliance of traditional examinations for a negative purpose, viz. to determine who shall *not* profit by education, carries over into new practices in testing. For example, two groups of testees entered for the same examination may prove to be significantly different with regard to educational opportunity and preparation. One group is found to achieve at a much higher level than the other. While the objective testing apparatus rightly ensures that each individual is viewed in relation to his group, the number of places is limited. Discrimination against the higher group may be allowed to enter subtly through the adoption of irrelevant scaling devices. Various considerations, political and quantitative, often induce a practice which ignores the validity of means so long as the immediate end is achieved.

There is, too, the influence of the 'payment by results' practice. The quality of a school is gauged by the percentage of passes which pupils make in a public examination. Classroom lessons tend to become nothing more than coaching efforts to increase the number of pupils who pass. While coaching does not improve individual scores significantly, teaching which is geared to the coaching practice may result in undesirable mental sets and deterioration of learning skills. The changeover to objective testing does not necessarily ensure the cessation of teaching for examinations, unless the nature of the items devised demonstrates the futility of anticipating possible responses. In fact, the introduction of objective-type examinations may even suggest abandonment of teaching which encourages coherent and expressive writing. It is most important, therefore, that the test makers are well informed enough on their subjects and sufficiently competent in their skill at item writing to be able to help minimize the desirability of coaching for examination success.

The reluctance to relinquish certain well-established methods associated with essay-type examinations also poses a problem. There is, for example, the use of an arbitrary pass mark for an examination, a mark generally accepted at 40 per cent. This mystic figure influences marking practices to the extent that in an examination most raw scores assigned to students' answers tend to hover around it as a mean, with about a third of the candidates unable to attain it. This pattern has persisted at all educational levels. It seems likely that the test scorer, assessing the essay-type answer, forms a first impression as to whether a candidate is worthy of a 'pass' or a 'fail', and then proceeds to assign a mark either above or below the accepted pass. Where the arbitrary 'pass mark' has become part and parcel of the examination procedure, those wedded to the idea of its infallibility consider the application of statistical procedures to be an attempt to tamper with examination scores. This frequently generates unmerited antagonism towards any effort to make examinations educationally sounder and fairer.

Finally, there is the problem of 'subjective-objective hybridization' This arises because of an imperfect appreciation of the uses of objective statistical analyses as applied to test scores. Subjective examination test scores are considered against the theoretical normal distribution without due attention to the underlying assumptions and prerequisite controls.

To cite an example: a certain university department was responsible for providing a course for each of three groups of students: one was from a pure science stream, two from professional streams, pursuing main courses in other faculties. No attempt was made to examine the objectives of the course for each group nor to diversify the course content for the different streams. A distribution of the end of course marks was made. It became evident that the reporting of results was a sensitive problem when students from different faculties were involved. The examiners decided that students from different faculties did indeed require knowledge of the course content in varying degrees. To be more 'objective', therefore, three different pass marks were determined on the *same* curve with the highest pass mark applicable to the pure science stream.

Thus the problems of testing multiply in an environment where the traditional attitudes to testing have not changed.

c) Time lag between practice and desire

Despite all that has been said, the desire for improvement in testing practices is genuine. However, it is generally not appreciated that much expense and time are needed for the construction and preparation of a test, particularly if it is a standardized test that is sought. A basic problem commonly encountered in this exercise is that which is associated with the establishment of test validity and reliability, namely, what reference group is exactly meant by 'representative'. The unseemly haste of pressure intrudes upon a scholarly and essential exercise, reducing the word 'standardization' to a mere shibboleth.

The time lag in acquiring or constructing appropriate tests has also given impetus to the wrong sort of local enterprise: publishers of 'courses' and 'objective' tests promise much that these authorities of good repute would find difficult to ensure.

It is easily forgotten, too, in the rush to establish more economical and reliable methods of testing that a knowledge of the proper mechanics of testing alone does not vouch for the satisfactory fulfilment of educational goals and objectives. High validation of a test against a set of ratings by school heads, say, establishes nothing more than that the test has justified the expectations of heads or that the heads have confirmed the relevance of test content to what schools have taught. What has not been established is the quality of learning which has taken place. For this, deeper probes for which time must run its course must be made.

d) Complex configurations of social attitudes and values

In most new societies, education has to provide the answers to many complex problems. Some of these stem from a wide range of racial, linguistic, tribal, religious and economic heterogeneity. To reconcile differences, various measures are introduced. The attempt is made to devise common content syllabuses for schools of different racial streams; the use of a common language is enforced to facilitate intercommunal understanding and to bring about a personal identification with national aspirations; religious schools are gradually secularized either through the giving of financial grants by the Government or compulsory retraining of staff in order that they may be brought within the ambit of modernization.

The problem of testing becomes one of constructing tests that are fair to all. Committed as emergent nations are to egalitarianism, no group wishes to be discriminated against. Where multi-lingualism in education is tolerated, should translated versions of a single test form be preferred to equivalent forms? How does one ensure that in translation meanings are not distorted? How may equivalence be determined when language developments are uneven? Is it possible to rely on solely one reference group for a standardization exercise, or are there significant differences to necessitate having multiple groups?

Again, testing of what has been taught in schools may probe only thought-level behaviour. The quality of action-level behaviour, so important to national development, may be quite another thing. Why, with all the care exercised to integrate and unify, do certain fears and tensions persist? Some groups, too, despite new vistas and opportunities of education opened to them, continue to manifest the behaviour of the disadvantaged. The educational output remains disappointing, a perceptible rebuke to the educational process. The study of attitudes and values is required to provide a backdrop for the profitable use of testing, and more urgently so in a multi-racial, multi-linguistic, and multi-religious setting so typical of many young nations in transition.

e) Lack of psychological and sociological information

As with developments in other areas, that in research on human behaviour has much leeway to make. Almost all information on child and adolescent behaviour, for example, has come from studies made in more advanced countries in Europe and in America. To help the individual so that he in turn may benefit society, it is desirable to know as much as possible about behaviour associated with the whole person.

Two difficulties attend behavioural research. First, there is a feeling that this sort of research may expose to public view failings to which a modernizing society should never admit. Thus evaluatory studies are least acceptable. One was reported as held up purely because the education officer concerned felt that the schools selected through random sampling were not 'all good enough'. To counter this, the research institution may perhaps adopt a psychological approach

Educational testing for evaluation and improvement

through sympathetic collaboration with the Government on educational problem solving in matters regarded by the latter as being of more urgent importance, and through derived studies acquire data for behavioural research. This may mean a great outlay of energy and time, but brings returns.

The second problem is that research tends to be regarded as a luxury except where its results promise to benefit industrial or economic development in the shortest possible time. One way of overcoming this is for the local research institution to enter into partnership with one in an advanced country so that joint projects may be set up with the financial support supplied by the foreign partner.

Testing for evaluation and improvement

It is obvious that within the constraints imposed, educational testing must assert its role, not so much as a cold instrument for arbitrary selection purposes, but as a dynamic method of evaluation to improve every aspect of education—its goals, its processes, its methods and its outcomes. Only when this is established can qualitative improvement be assured.

In this connection, it is useful to employ an evaluation model by way of explanation. The educational teaching-learning situation comprises three main elements—the teacher, the pupil and the material. The teacher may be a live person, or an enlivened organ, such as the programmed instructional device, or some form of the whole paraphernalia of mass media. The pupil may be the classroom charge or may be represented by the public, adult or otherwise. The material is such specified knowledge and skills as are desirable for the edification of those receiving instruction. Between these three elements, there is constant interaction in which evaluation is implicit. At the gross level, the pupil may evaluate his teacher as generally incompetent, or the latter may consider the former utterly incapable. Likewise, the teacher and pupil each has his vague ideas about the suitability or the value of the material presented.

The evaluation which is of educational concern is much more explicit than gross level judgment, viz. evaluation through educational testing. The traditional interaction-evaluation model may be represented by figure 1, p. 500. This model viewed the teacher as having the sole prerogative to assess both the pupil and the material. Neither of the others could evaluate the teacher nor reflect on his skills. If the material was found to be unsuitable, it was considered intrinsically bad. The fact that perhaps the teacher had no mastery of content

Figure 1   *Figure 2*

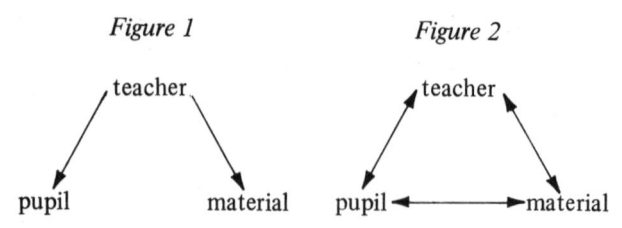

```
    teacher              teacher
   ↙     ↘              ↗     ↖
pupil    material    pupil ↔ material
```

and was ineffective in his profession, or that the pupil was being asked to respond to something for which he was not yet prepared by previous experience, was never investigated.

To make the interaction-evaluation process more wholesome, it would be preferable to promote such a situation as may be represented by figure 2. Here, interaction-evaluation is a two-way process. The following are suggestions to demonstrate how this could take place.

a) Introduction of 'personalized' testing

In a highly examination-conscious society some thought should be given to uses of the test other than as a yardstick by which individuals are shown either to have achieved or failed to have achieved their goals. Our attempts to gauge success or failure have never been 'personalized'; that is, the testee is always in the position of being scrutinized or analysed, and his learning behaviour is measured by some other person and judged in relation to a group. Much frustration and desperation are often attendant upon the testing ordeal. In some societies, the stigma of having once failed attaches to an individual for life. If improvement is the real aim of testing, the person has to come to terms with the test.

One way to do this is to put the individual in a position where he learns to assess his own efforts. Recently, in the first phase of a study of retarded children in primary schools of Malaysia, groups of exceptionally retarded subjects were put in the care of special teachers with whom the experimenter met at fixed periods to discuss and standardize procedures for teaching. One measure adopted was the preparation of a sequence of simple tests based on a carefully programmed* series of lessons. As a child masters a new concept or set of concepts, he helps himself to a test. He indicates the result and the date of the test graphically on a sheet of paper provided by the teacher and kept in a folder by the pupil. The project is still in its pilot stage, but indications are that so-called retarded children are responding quite ably and positively to this self-reporting device. The pupil soon realizes

* In planned order, not programmed in the Skinnerian sense.

that a 'creeping-up' line means he is progressing; at sight of a 'dropping' line, the pupil, quite on his own initiative, seeks the teacher's help in order to improve himself. Surprisingly, graphing has not presented difficulties to these pupils, whose ages range from eight to thirteen.

One term of remedial work has just been completed. It is intended also to adopt a new form of reporting to parents by listing briefly the skills mastered, not by comparison with other members of the class or by the award of absolute marks. It is hoped, through this use of tests and reporting of attainment, that both children and adults will grow to appreciate the intrinsic worth of knowledge for its own sake. This method of approach to testing was first adopted with normal children in a study conducted in the United States.*

b) Popularize interchange of 'tester' and 'testee' roles

At more advanced levels of study, students may be asked to set questions which they themselves will then attempt to answer. The rating of one another's questions and answers becomes an interesting class exercise. Occasionally, students may be requested to set questions on the course for the teacher to answer. Copies of the teacher's answer or answers are then circularized for critical analysis and discussion by students.

Another method is to collect common errors relating to important and difficult concepts in a course. Wrong statements and mistakes are listed with correct ones in worksheets. These are handed out from time to time for students to 'correct' and discuss at group seminars.

At the Malayan University's Faculty of Education members of staff are required to demonstrate in classrooms the principles of teaching which they have advocated to students, before the latter are sent out on teaching practice. The same rating forms used for students on teaching practice are applied to individual Faculty members, with the students in the role of raters. This annual exercise has helped lecturers to be more critical about their own methods, and indirectly promoted change in the students' attitudes as well.

Such measures as advocated above can help to promote sound study skills on the part of students, who will learn to use their own judgment to evaluate knowledge, to discriminate between necessary and non-essential details, and to develop confidence in their personal efforts to attain educational goals. Too much in the current

*Reported in 'A study of student progress through grouping associated with a program of sequenced instruction in elementary school mathematics,' by the writer. Unpublished doctoral thesis, Harvard, 1962.

teaching-learning situation savours of directed effort without meaningful action. Besides, the teacher, being no longer infallible, becomes much more human and capable of improvement.

c) Encourage effective follow-up on test or examination results

The follow-up meant here is more than the technical pursuit of statistical methods relating to validation or prediction. It refers to pedagogical measures such as identification of common misconceptions and their correction, identification of causes of error and failure, remedial work with some pupils or guidance towards better individual effort by others, and so on.

d) Devise better examinations

This will ensure that grill-drill, note-rote methods will not be perpetuated in schools. Testing sessions can be held with the practitioners of education to discuss what tests can and cannot do. Some simple principles of test construction and setting up of test objectives may be stressed.

Test technicians alone cannot meet the requirements of better examinations. Those who devise tests and analyse them without proper appreciation of psychological and educational implications of testing may produce little qualitative change in the educational system. In this connection, team work between research workers, education specialists, test technicians and teachers in the field is highly desirable. Test activities in a modernizing society, which places a premium on quick returns, tend to ignore the first two categories of workers.

Conclusion

It is possible that the problems discussed in this paper may also exist in advanced countries. The pressure for and the form of solution must differ both in degree and in kind. The acceptance of testing in correct perspective together with a knowledgeable use of tests should go a long way towards improving teaching and learning in schools as well as towards vindicating the faith placed in education.